STATISTICAL HANDBOOK ON VIOLENCE IN AMERICA

STATISTICAL HANDBOOK ON VIOLENCE IN AMERICA

Adam Dobrin
Brian Wiersema
Colin Loftin
David McDowall

ORYX PRESS
1996

The rare Arabian Oryx is believed to have inspired the myth of the unicorn. This desert antelope became virtually extinct in the early 1960s. At that time several groups of international conservationists arranged to have 9 animals sent to the Phoenix Zoo to be the nucleus of a captive breeding herd. Today the Oryx population is over 1000 and over 500 have been returned to the Middle East.

© 1996 by The Oryx Press
4041 North Central at Indian School Road
Phoenix, Arizona 85012-3397

Published simultaneously in Canada
Printed and Bound in the United States of America

∞ The paper used in this publication meets the minimum requirements of
American National Standard for Information Science—Permanence
of Paper for Printed Library Materials, ANSI Z39.48, 1984.

Library of Congress Cataloging-in-Publication Data

Statistical handbook on violence in America / Adam Dobrin . . . [et
al.]. # 33359697 2-24-97
    p. cm.
Includes bibliographical references and index.
ISBN 0-89774-945-6 (cloth)
    1. Violence—United States—Statistics. 2. Criminal statistics—
United States. 3. United States—Social conditions—1980—Statistics.
I. Dobrin, Adam.
HN90.V5S833 1995
303.6'0973'021—dc20   95-42437
                                                             CIP

cm

Table of Contents

List of Tables and Figures

CHAPTER 3 GROUPS AND SITUATIONS

CHAPTER 4 IMPACT OF VIOLENCE

CHAPTER 5   OPINIONS ABOUT VIOLENCE

reduce crime: Allow police to hold someone they suspect of committing a crime for 24 hours without bail; allow police to wiretap telephone lines of anyone they suspect; allow the police to stop and search anybody they suspect of having committed a crime; allow police to search a home without a warrant; make it illegal for anyone in the area to possess a handgun?" Percentages by Race, 1993

5.49 "In your view, should juveniles who commit violent crimes by treated the same as adults, or should they be given more lenient treatment in a juvenile court?" Percentages by Demographic Characteristics, 1993

5.50 "How do you think society should deal with juveniles (those under age 18) who commit crimes: Should society place less emphasis on punishing juvenile offenders and more on trying to rehabilitate them, or should society give juvenile offenders the same punishment as adults?" Percentages, 1994

5.51 "When a teenager commits a murder and is found guilty by a jury, do you think s/he should get the death penalty, or should s/he be spared because of her/his youth?" Percentages by Demographic Characteristics, 1993

5.52 "In your view, should the law require fines or prison sentences for the parents of juveniles convicted of major crimes, or not?" Percentages by Demographic Characteristics, 1993

5.53 "Which of the following measures do you think should be used for first-time juvenile offenders committing a major crime, but not murder—job training as an alternative to going to prison, disciplinary training in a special boot camp, or prison?" Percentages by Race, 1993

5.54 "What is the best way to keep children in your community safe from violent crime?" Percentages, 1993

5.55 "How effective do you think each of the following measures would be in reducing violence in the public schools—very effective, somewhat effective, not very effective, or not at all effective?" Percentages, 1994

5.56 "Do you think the federal government should do more to regulate violence on television and in movies, should it do less, or is it doing about the right amount?" Percentages by Age, 1994

5.57 "A judge in at least one state has ruled that public executions can be televised. Some people think that executions should be shown on television because it would be a deterrent to would-be killers. Others think executions should not be on television because such

violence shouldn't be brought into people's living rooms. How do you feel—that executions should or should not be shown on television?" Percentages, 1977, 1991, and 1993

5.58 "Do you feel that public executions should or should not be shown on television?" Percentages by Demographic Characteristics, 1993

5.59 "What do you think should be the penalty for murder—the death penalty or life imprisonment with absolutely no possibility of parole?" Percentages by Demographic Characteristics, 1993

5.60 Based on those who think the death penalty should be imposed for crimes other than murder (40 percent), "For what crimes besides murder should the death penalty be imposed?" Percentages, 1986

5.61 "Do you favor or oppose the death penalty for persons convicted of murder?" Percentages by Race and Gender, 1994

5.62 "Do you favor or oppose the death penalty for persons convicted of murder?" Percentages by Race, 1972–1994

5.63 "Do you favor or oppose the death penalty for persons convicted of murder?" Percentages by Gender, 1972–1994

5.64 "Do you favor the death penalty for people convicted of rape of an adult?" Percentages, 1991

5.65 "Please tell me whether you strongly favor, favor, oppose, or strongly oppose a mandatory death penalty for major drug traffickers?" Percentages by Demographic Characteristics, 1990

5.66 Public Support for Death Penalty for Specific Crimes, Percentages by Demographic Characteristics, 1988

5.67 "In cases where death is caused from the use of drugs, would you favor the death penalty for the drug dealer who supplied the drugs?" 1986

5.68 "Which of the following murder cases, if any, would you consider justification for the death penalty . . . ?" Percentages, 1986

5.69 "Why do you favor the death penalty for those convicted of murder?" Percentages by Race, 1991

5.70 "Why do you oppose the death penalty for those convicted of murder?" Percentages by Race, 1991

5.71 "Do you feel that the death penalty acts as a deterrent to the commitment of murder—that it lowers the murder rate, or not?" Percentages by Race, 1991

Foreword

By any measure you choose, the United States has an enormous violence problem. On an average day, over 65 people die from homicide, another 18,000 are violently victimized but survive the assault, and more than 6,000 of these victims suffer physical injuries. Homicide rates among young men in America, which more than doubled between 1985 and 1992, are vastly greater than those in other Western industrialized nations. Homicide is the second leading cause of death among 15- to 24-year-olds in the United States and the leading cause of death for young African American males and females. Moreover, the impact of family violence on women and children, while difficult to measure precisely, is no doubt very large and plays an important role in sustaining the cycle of violence in our society.

Over the last decade we have witnessed a dramatic increase in attention to the problem of interpersonal violence. Legislative strategies for addressing this problem are being hotly debated at the national, state, and local levels. Local communities are developing and implementing their own preventive approaches with unparalleled enthusiasm. The range of governmental agencies, foundations, and community-based organizations that now see preventing or controlling violence as part of their mission has rapidly expanded. Scientific attention to the causes of violence and the effectiveness of preventive programs, policies, and interventions has sharply increased. All of the participants and organizations involved in this broad range of legislative, programmatic, and research activities share a common and fundamental need—accurate and timely information on violence in America.

The *Statistical Handbook on Violence in America* provides this critical information. Moreover, it comes to print at a time when the need and demand for information about violence is at its historical apex. As the demand for information has increased so has the proliferation of inaccurate or misleading data about violence in America. This book provides accurate and reliable data on the magnitude of the violence problem, it's geographic distribution, the demographic variations in violent behavior and the risk of victimizations, the circumstances associated with violent incidents, and public opinions concerning violence and its prevention. These data have had and will continue to have a strong influence on the formulation of research hypotheses, the development of public perceptions, and the allocation of public and private resources.

The data accumulated in this handbook will be of great value to scientists who wish to ground their research in the best information available. These data, however, have value and relevance for an audience far beyond the research community. They provide a valuable resource for our political representatives as they formulate and debate legislation that will continue to come before them. These data also provide important background information for community-based organizations that may be organizing prevention programs or developing proposals for funding of programs. They provide, as well, a very useful reference for the staff of public and private funding agencies that wish to prioritize their funding in accordance with the magnitude and demographic distribution of this problem. In short, these data provide a common statistical point of departure for all of us who, in our many different capacities, seek to better understand and prevent violence.

For researchers, policy makers, service providers, students, or anyone interested in the problem of violence, the *Statistical Handbook on Violence in America* will become a cherished resource—kept close at hand for quick reference. In no small way, the dissemination and use of this handbook will hasten the day when we can effectively prevent and control violence in America.

James A. Mercy, Ph.D.
Acting Director
Division of Violence Prevention
National Center for Injury Prevention and Control
Centers for Disease Control and Prevention

Preface

Violence is one of the most important issues currently facing Americans. Its horrific results—injuries and death—diminish the quality of life for everyone. Understanding violence and formulating effective policies to deal with it require timely and accurate information about the magnitude and social distribution of the problem. Although there are many sources of statistical information on violence, they are difficult to use effectively because they are widely scattered, frequently in unpublished documents, or only available on unprocessed computer files. The purpose of *The Statistical Handbook on Violence in America* is to assemble, in one volume, the latest data on violence in a logically ordered and well-documented format.

In assembling the *Handbook,* the editors searched through both published and unpublished sources to find the most recent data characterizing patterns of interpersonal violence in the entire United States or its major divisions. Using the general definition of interpersonal violence as "behaviors that intentionally threaten, attempt, or inflict physical harm on others" (Reiss and Roth 1993:2), more than 330 tables and 40 figures were selected or created. Many came from computer files processed by the editors especially for presentation here.

The *Handbook* has five topical chapters and an appendix that describes technical features of the data sources. Chapter One describes patterns of interpersonal violence that result in death. Homicide takes the lead, not only because of its seriousness, but also because it is well documented and more accurately described than are other types of violence.

Chapter Two characterizes other types of interpersonal violence—assault, robbery, and rape. Legal categories describe the data because two of the most important data-collection systems monitor crime, not violence per se.

Chapter Three focuses on groups and situations that are vulnerable or at high risk. Risk and vulnerability reflect both higher than average occurrence of violence and the ability to protect oneself. Police officers and some other occupational groups are vulnerable because they are frequently the targets of violence and frequently intervene in violent situations. On the other hand, women and children, who have lower than average rates of violence (as victims and offenders), are vulnerable because typically they cannot effectively defend themselves from attackers.

Chapter Four describes tangible losses and measurable consequences of violence. Topics include psychological trauma, injury, economic losses, and losses in life expectancy.

Chapter Five profiles public opinion about violence. Data from many national opinion surveys address five general questions: When is violence justified? How does violence influence opinions and behavior? What precautions do people take to avoid violence? What should governments and communities do about violence? What do people believe causes violence?

The appendix provides details about the data sources used to compile this book and directs the reader to additional information. Entries are arranged alphabetically by title, and a data source number linked to the appendix appears in each table or figure. There is also a glossary defining technical terms used in the appendix.

In attempting to locate information on a specific topic, one would do well to remember that violence is complex, involving many factors. It defies easy categorization because it overlaps many of the category boundaries we might wish to draw. It follows, therefore, that no single scheme to organize data on violence would be convenient for every purpose.

The index, at the back of this volume, provides greater and more detailed access to subjects than is afforded by the book's arrangement. For example, information on "family violence" can be found in Chapter Three in sections headed Youth, Elderly, Women, and Socio-Economic Status. But, depending on one's particular focus, useful data on family violence will also be found in every other chapter of this handbook.

As is the case in using any index, users should consider checking under broader terms if narrow terms yield no listings. A case in point is the subject of "serial" murders. Despite the popular fascination with serial murders and murderers, this handbook contains no tables or figures on the topic because the event is apparently so rare (or so difficult to identify) that no national statistical data are maintained on the phenomenon. Reconceptualizing the question more broadly as an issue about repeated violent behavior will, however, reward one with a reference to tables on violent criminal arrest under "recidivism."

REFERENCE

Reiss, Albert J., Jr., and Jeffrey A. Roth (eds.). 1993. *Understanding and preventing violence*. Washington, D.C.: National Academy Press.

Acknowledgments

A work like this cannot be completed without the advice, cooperation, support, and contributions of many people. We are grateful first of all to our research assistants, Chanchalat Chanhatasilpa and Nicole Leeper, who helped us assemble, enter, and check tables and figures. We are also indebted to James A. Mercy of the Centers for Disease Control and Prevention (CDC) for both his enthusiasm for the project and his contributions of figures and data. The book also benefits from the gracious and thoughtful foreword he wrote.

Our idea for compiling a *Statistical Handbook on Violence in America*, in part, grew out of the experience and observations of members of the National Academy of Science's Panel on the Understanding and Control of Violent Behavior. Panel members were surprised and frustrated that data on violence were scattered, varied in quality, and generally difficult to access and use. We thank Jeffrey A. Roth, the panel's study director, for encouraging the publishers to undertake this project.

Over the years we have been privileged to conduct and participate in a number of projects that focused on intensive use of computer-readable data on crime and violence. In particular, our involvement with the four national workshops on the design and use of the National Crime Victimization Survey (NCVS), sponsored by the Bureau of Justice Statistics and the American Statistical Association's Committee on Law and Justice Statistics, provided us with much of the expertise to create many of the special tabulations of NCVS data that appear here. Two of us (Loftin and Wiersema) were also involved in establishing and operating, for its first five years, the National Institute of Justice's (NIJ) Data Resources Program, a program designed to acquire, review, and publicly archive NIJ-funded datasets. This gave us hands-on experience with a great variety of samples, research designs, and data structures all of which were useful in selecting data sources for this volume. More than these experiences, however, we are grateful for the continuing relationships we have had with the Centers for Disease Control, the Bureau of Justice Statistics, National Institute of Justice, and the many colleagues associated with the NCVS workshops. They have had important influences on us as we assembled this handbook.

Many other people have provided direct encouragement, advice, or made other valuable contributions. We thank our colleagues at the University of Maryland's Department of Criminology and Criminal Justice, particularly Denise Gottfredson, Cathy Gallagher, and Doris Layton MacKenzie. We are also indebted to Lloyd Potter of CDC who provided data, technical advice, and review of the life expectancy tables that appear in Chapter Four. Much of Chapter Four's structure and topic selection was influenced by the work of Mark A. Cohen and Ted R. Miller and by our many discussions with them about their research on the costs of criminal victimization. We gratefully acknowledge them as well.

We also thank Lisa Bastian, Marshall DeBerry, Michael R. Rand, and James Stephan from the Bureau of Justice Statistics; Julie Kerkhoven and Karen McCurdy of the National Committee for Prevention of Child Abuse; Toshio Tatara, director of the National Aging Resource Center on Elder Abuse; and Lynn Jenkins from the National Institute for Occupational Safety and Health, all of whom willingly provided data and useful advice. We are grateful to Stanley Presser of the Joint Program in Survey Methodology at the University of Maryland for being a friendly and important source of information on surveys and polling methods. David Finkelhor of the Family Research Laboratory, University of New Hampshire consulted with us on child victimization and other topics. We depended on Song Zhao and Bob Harper from the Office of Academic Computing Services at the University of Maryland for computer support throughout the project. The University of Maryland's Computer Science Center also generously provided computing resources on its IBM mainframe and unix workstation clusters.

Finally, we especially appreciate the support and sacrifices of our families, friends, and colleagues who have all suffered in one way or another from our preoccupation with this book.

Introduction

The estimates of the frequency and type of violent behavior reported in the *Statistical Handbook on Violence in America* are based on three general approaches to collecting data on violence. First, *administrative records* such as police reports, hospital emergency department records, or death certificates may be sampled or searched completely to identify cases of interpersonal violence that are reported to the organization. Second, samples selected from a population of interest may be asked to report their experiences as victims of violence (*victimization surveys*). Third, samples from the population may be asked to report their own violent behavior (*self-report surveys*).

Each approach has strengths and weaknesses. Most researchers accept the view that, regardless of the method used to collect data on violence, some will be missed and that different data collection techniques capture different parts of the total volume of violence. Therefore, it is useful to examine estimates derived from different data collection approaches and to treat any single estimate as a minimum estimate of the total volume. A common analogy is that violence is like an iceberg that floats with its tip above water, while most of its total volume is hidden below the surface.

In selecting data to be included in the *Handbook,* we, the editors, labored to find the very best and latest data available on each topic. However, only minimal screening of the quality of the data has been done. We rejected data that were obviously invalid, but included data that are not very precise because they were the best or only data available on an important topic. An astute reader should examine the methods described in the data description appendix and keep in mind that all statistical values are estimates that are subject to uncertainty due to the selection of a particular sample and the variable willingness of people to report their violent experiences.

No particular statistical sophistication is required on the part of the user. The majority of the tables present frequencies, percentages, or rates. Rates, as we use them here, estimate the risk that a randomly selected member of a population will experience a specified type of violence during a specified time interval. Rates are usually calculated as the number of violent events divided by the population at risk. To avoid small decimal fractions, they are expressed in terms of the number of events per 1,000 or 100,000 persons per year. For example, homicide rates are the number of homicide victims per 100,000 persons per year. In the few cases where other measures are used, they are defined in notes or in the appendix.

Each table or figure is explained in a consistent format throughout the *Handbook*. First, there is a descriptive title that tells what is being counted, the specific group or groups in the population, the geographic area (if other than the total United States), and the date to which the data refer. Next, there is a source note that names the source of data collection used and provides a complete bibliography citation for the source document (including the author, year of publication, title, and producer or publisher). Finally, there is a bracketed reference number that directs the reader to the data description appendix where the methods used to collect the data are described, technical documents are cited, and important terms are defined.

The vast majority of the *Handbook* consists of tables, although quite a few figures are also included. In general, tables are presented when individual statistics are of interest. In some instances, tabular data are also presented visually in a figure. In others, data could be conveniently summarized only in graphical form (i.e., no corresponding table is presented). When graphical information is presented in a figure, we believe the reader is most rewarded by focusing on its general patterns, trends, or other overall features, rather than using it to identify and compare individual data values as one would use a table. Nevertheless, many of the figures in the *Handbook* are detailed enough to permit even this level of scrutiny.

Chapter 1
Fatal Violence in America

Fatal violence is placed in a prominent and separate position in *The Statistical Handbook on Violence in America* because of the serious and final nature of the event. It is the ultimate violent act, culminating in the ending of a human life.

The frequency of homicide also makes it an important issue. According to the Federal Bureau of Investigation, 24,526 people were murdered in the United States in 1993 (Federal Bureau of Investigation, 1994, p. 13). At current rates, an average of 1 out of every 154 children born in the U.S. in 1992 will die of homicide (Table 4.34). Compared to other Western industrial nations, the United States has one of the highest homicide rates (World Health Organization, 1994, Table D-1).

DEFINITIONS

Clear understanding of the statistics in this chapter requires the understanding of a few key concepts. The term *homicide* is synonymous with fatal interpersonal violence. It is the killing of one person by another, regardless of intent or legal justification. It includes both *criminal homicide* and *noncriminal homicide*. Criminal homicides are those that are committed without legal justification. They include both murder and manslaughter. Murder is the more serious form of criminal homicide. Manslaughter, because of mitigating circumstances or diminished responsibility, is less serious, but it is nevertheless a criminal homicide.

Noncriminal homicides are killings that are legally justified. Examples include legal executions, the killing of a felon by a police officer, and self-defense to avoid death or great bodily harm.

This chapter (as well others in the book) includes data on different types and classifications of homicide. There are tables and figures including all homicides, murders and nonnegligent manslaughters, legal executions, and others. Each table and figure clearly identifies the type of homicide, but the reader should pay special attention to table titles and notes to avoid confusion.

The reader should also keep in mind that data may refer to offenders or victims or both. The chapter includes statistics, for example, on the race and gender of victims, on the race and gender of offenders, and also a table that shows the relationship between the race and gender of victims and offenders. Tables and figures clearly indicate whether the focus is on the victim or the offender or some other aspect of the incident. The reader will avoid confusion, however, if this feature of tables and figures is carefully noted.

DATA SOURCES

National data about homicide are obtained from two major sources: death certificates and police records. Death certificates are required in all states and contain information about the age, race, and gender of the victim, the date, time, location, and the cause and manner of death. This information is collected by state health departments and forwarded to the National Center for Health Statistics (NCHS) as part of a cooperative program. The Division of Vital Statistics at NCHS compiles the data and disseminates the results (U.S. Department of Health and Human Services, 1994).

Several features of the death certificate data are especially important. First, there is no information about homicide offenders on the death certificate, only information about victims. Second, all causes of death, including homicide, are classified according to the International Classification of Diseases (ICD) (U.S. Department of Health and Human Services, 1989). In this *Handbook*, we focus on two ICD cause of death groups: homicide and legal intervention. Together, these two groups correspond to what is referred to above as homicide (both criminal and noncriminal). The detailed ICD definitions of homicide and legal intervention are provided in the Appendix.

Police records are compiled by the Federal Bureau of Investigation from reports submitted by local law enforcement agencies as part of its Uniform Crime Reporting (UCR) program. The UCR data are somewhat more complicated than the death certificate data because they are recorded on two separate forms. The first form, "Return A", is a monthly tally of the number of murders and non-negligent manslaughters occurring within a reporting jurisdiction. Murders and non-negligent manslaughters are essentially criminal homicides, as defined above. The second form is the "Supplementary Homicide Report" (SHR). It is especially important because it contains information about victims, offenders, and circumstances of the homicide. It also includes noncriminal homicides such as justifiable homicides by police and citizens. For more information comparing UCR data with death certificate data on homicide, see Rokaw, Mercy, and Smith (1990).

CHAPTER ORGANIZATION

The chapter is divided into two major parts: patterns and trends. The patterns section places the the United States in an international context and presents tables and figures characterizing victims, offenders, victim-offender relationships, circumstances, and weapons. This is followed by patterns of homicide in U.S. regions and cities. The trends section describes patterns over time for homicide by victim age, race, gender, and weapon used. There are also tables and figures on trends across regions and cities. In each section, we include data on persons executed. Executions are included with homicides not only because they fit the technical definition of homicide, but also because they are linked to criminal homicides as a legal response to murder.

REFERENCES

Federal Bureau of Investigation. 1994. *Crime in the United States 1993*. Washington, D.C.: U.S. Government Printing Office.

Rokaw, William M., James A. Mercy, and Jack C. Smith. 1990. Comparing death certificate data with FBI crime reporting statistics on U.S. homicides. *Public Health Reports* 105, no. 5:447–455.

U.S. Department of Health and Human Services. 1989. *International classification of diseases, ninth revision, clinical modification*. Washington, D.C.: U.S. Government Printing Office.

U.S. Department of Health and Human Services. 1994. *Vital statistics of the United States*. Hyattsville, Md.: Public Health Service.

World Health Organization. 1994. *World health statistics annual*. Geneva, Switzerland.

CURRENT PATTERNS: INTERNATIONAL

1.1   Homicides and Homicide Rates, Selected Countries, Most Recent Available Year

Country (Year)	Homicides		Rate	
	Male	Female	Male	Female
Region of the Americas				
Argentina (1990)	1,368	252	8.5	1.5
Canada (1991)	394	228	2.9	1.6
Costa Rica (1991)	104	24	6.6	1.6
Mexico (1991)	13,554	1,534	31.5	3.5
Trinidad and Tobago (1991)	75	20	12.1	3.2
United States (1990)	19,298	5,316	15.9	4.2
European Region				
Armenia (1990)	177	26	10.8	1.5
Austria (1992)	66	52	1.7	1.3
Bulgaria (1992)	316	88	7.5	2.0
Czech Republic (1992)	116	85	2.3	1.6
Denmark (1992)	35	34	1.4	1.3
Finland (1992)	112	61	4.6	2.4
France (1991)	413	212	1.5	0.7
Germany (1991)	537	379	1.4	0.9
Greece (1991)	103	45	2.0	0.9
Hungary (1992)	259	155	5.2	2.9
Iceland (1992)	2	1	1.5	0.8
Ireland (1991)	14	7	0.8	0.4
Israel (1990)	58	22	2.5	0.9
Italy (1990)	1,351	176	4.8	0.6
Latvia (1990)	181	64	14.6	4.5
Lithuania (1990)	196	85	11.2	4.4
Luxembourg (1992)	3	5	1.6	2.5
Malta (1992)	4	2	2.2	1.1
The Netherlands (1991)	118	59	1.6	0.8
Norway (1991)	46	20	2.2	0.9
Poland (1992)	841	285	4.5	1.4
Portugal (1992)	113	39	2.4	0.8
Romania (1992)	839	287	7.5	2.5
Russian Federation (1991)	17,311	5,310	24.9	6.7
Spain (1990)	275	106	1.4	0.5
Sweden (1990)	70	38	1.7	0.9
Switzerland (1992)	55	46	1.6	1.3
United Kingdom (1992)	336	167	1.2	0.6
Western Pacific Region				
Australia (1992)	169	110	1.9	1.3
China: Rural areas (1990)	477	185	2.2	0.9
China: Urban areas (1990)	914	452	3.1	1.6
Japan (1992)	442	306	0.7	0.5
New Zealand (1991)	40	26	2.4	1.5
Singapore (1991)	39	12	2.8	0.9

Source: World Health Organization. 1994. *World health statistics annual, 1993*. Geneva, Switzerland: World Health Organization, Table D-1. Used with permission. [See appendix entry 59]

Note: Table includes deaths classified according to the International Classification of Diseases, Ninth Revision (ICD-9) codes E960–E969. Rates are per 100,000 residents.

1.2   Homicide Rates for Men Age 15–24 Around the World, 1988–1991

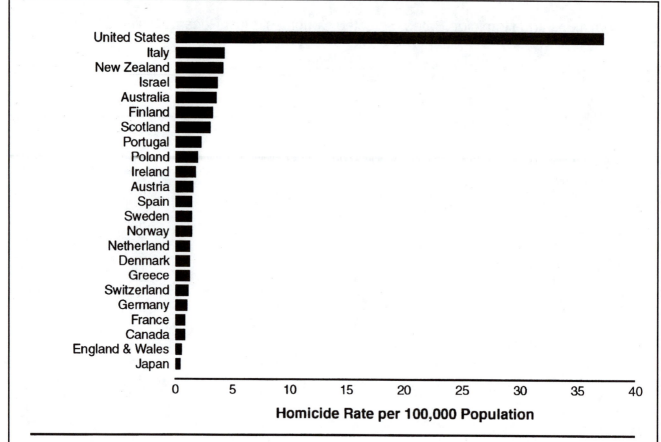

Source: Mercy, James A., Mark L. Rosenberg, Kenneth E. Powell, Claire V. Broome, and William L. Roper.
1993. Public health policy for preventing violence. *Health Affairs* 12:4 (Winter):10, Exhibit 1. Used
with permission. [See appendix entry 34 and 59]

Note: Rates are per 100,000 residents.

CURRENT PATTERNS: UNITED STATES

Characteristics of the Victims

1.3   Homicides and Homicide Rates, by Race and Gender of Victim, 1992

Race and Gender	Homicides	Rate
All races		
Both sexes	25,488	10.0
Male	20,115	16.2
Female	5,373	4.1
White		
Both sexes	12,468	5.9
Male	9,456	9.1
Female	3,012	2.8
Black		
Both sexes	12,318	38.9
Male	10,131	67.5
Female	2,187	13.1

Source: Kochanek, Kenneth D. and Bettie L. Hudson. 1994. Advance report of final mortality statistics, 1992. *Monthly Vital Statistics Report* 43, no. 6, supp. Hyattsville, Md.: National Center for Health Statistics, pp. 42, 45, Tables 9 and 10. [See appendix entry 34]

Note: Includes homicides and legal interventions (E960–E978). Rates are per 100,000 residents. Races other than white and black are included in the "All races" category.

1.4 Homicide Rates, by Age, Race, and Gender of Victim, 1991

| | White | | Black | | |
Age	Male	Female	Male	Female	All
Under 1 year	7.6	5.7	22.4	24.6	9.5
1-4	2.1	1.6	7.9	7.3	2.8
5-14	1.2	0.7	5.4	2.8	1.4
15-24	16.9	4.4	158.9	21.6	22.4
25-34	15.5	4.4	125.0	26.4	18.2
35-44	11.2	3.5	77.6	15.7	11.6
45-54	8.7	3.0	50.6	9.5	8.2
55-64	6.1	2.1	33.9	6.7	5.5
65-74	4.0	2.0	31.2	6.5	4.0
75-84	3.8	2.6	29.8	12.5	4.2
85 and over	4.4	2.9	20.3*	11.7*	4.1
All ages (crude)†	9.3	3.0	72.0	14.2	10.5
All ages (age-adjusted)†	9.4	3.0	72.5	13.9	10.9

Source: National Center for Health Statistics. 1994. *Health, United States, 1993.* Hyattsville, Md.: Public Health
      Service, pp. 130–131, Table 51. [See appendix entry 34]

Note: Includes homicides and legal interventions (ICD-9 codes E960–E978). Rates are per 100,000 residents.
  * Based on fewer than 20 deaths.
  † "Age-adjusted" rates eliminate differences in crude rates that result from differences in age distributions
    between groups. "Crude" rates are unadjusted rates. Age-adjusted rates in this table were calculated by
    the direct method using the enumerated population of the U.S. in 1940 as the standard.

1.5 Homicides, by Age, Race, and Gender of Victim, 1991

| | White | | Black | | |
Age	Male	Female	Male	Female	All
Under 1 year	121	86	77	82	380
1-4	131	95	97	87	428
5-14	178	100	150	76	520
15-24	2,569	627	4,209	578	8,194
25-34	2,791	776	3,260	770	7,832
35-44	1,856	574	1,626	380	4,591
45-54	959	337	610	138	2,120
55-64	537	203	300	77	1,161
65-74	292	183	197	59	741
75-84	135	152	84	63	438
85 and over	35	61	14	19	130
All ages	9,604	3,194	10,624	2,329	26,535

Source: National Center for Health Statistics. 1993. *Public-use data tape and documentation: Mortality detail,*
      1991 data. [Computer file]. Hyattsville, Md.: Public Health Service. [See appendix entry 34]

Note: Includes homicides and legal interventions (E960–E978). Age and/or race was unknown for 81 victims
    (of which 56 were male and 25 female).

1.6 Number of Victims in Incidents of Murder, 1992

Number of Victims	Number of Incidents	Percent of Murders
1	21,618	96.3
2	713	3.2
3	90	0.4
4	27	0.1
5	9	0.0
6	3	0.0
Total	22,460	100.0

Source: Supplementary Homicide Reports, 1992, from: Federal Bureau of Investigation. 1994. *Supplementary homicide report, 1992.* [Computer file]. Ann Arbor, Mich.: Inter-university Consortium for Political and Social Research. [See appendix entry 45]

Note: Table counts murder incidents. "Murder" includes non-negligent manslaughter. Data for Maine were not included in the 1992 data distributed by the FBI.

1.7 Murders, by Age, Race, and Gender of Victim, 1992

Age	Male			Female		
	White	Black	Other	White	Black	Other
0-14	258	251	25	173	169	13
15-19	900	1502	52	220	182	8
20-24	1,314	2,170	76	312	300	21
25-29	1,169	1,535	51	332	369	18
30-34	1,106	1,220	56	328	316	20
35-44	1,495	1,396	76	520	375	22
45-54	748	551	37	297	116	19
55-64	430	220	16	138	50	8
65 and over	445	269	15	414	152	8
All ages	7,865	9,114	404	2,734	2,029	137

Source: Supplementary Homicide Reports, 1992, from: Federal Bureau of Investigation. 1994. *Supplementary homicide report, 1992.* [Computer file]. Ann Arbor, Mich.: Inter-university Consortium for Political and Social Research. [See appendix entry 45]

Note: Table counts victims. "Murder" includes non-negligent manslaughter. The table does not include 313 cases in which age of victim was unknown, 117 cases in which race was unknown, and 3 cases in which both the gender and the race were unknown. Data for Maine were not included in the 1992 data distributed by the FBI.

Characteristics of the Offenders

1.8   Number of Offenders in Incidents of Murder, 1992

Number of Offenders	Number of Incidents	Percent of Murders
1*	19,874	88.5
2	1,738	7.7
3	573	2.6
4	214	1.0
5	44	0.2
6	10	0.0
7	6	0.0
9	1	0.0
Total	22,460	100.0

Source: Federal Bureau of Investigation. 1994. *Supplementary homicide report, 1992.* [Computer file]. Ann Arbor, Mich.: Inter-university Consortium for Political and Social Research. [See appendix entry 45]

Note: Table counts murder incidents. There were no incidents reported in 1992 involving 8 offenders. "Murder" includes non-negligent manslaughter. Data for Maine were not included in the 1992 data distributed by the FBI.

* Row includes murder incidents in which the number of offenders was assumed to be one, but was actually unknown.

1.9   Murders, by Age, Race, and Gender of Offender, 1992

	Male			Female		
Age	White	Black	Other	White	Black	Other
0-14	98	125	7	20	11	3
15-19	1,421	2,536	93	77	125	7
20-24	1,373	2,183	76	131	179	7
25-29	1,017	1,250	62	120	155	4
30-34	786	715	32	106	165	5
35-44	971	768	47	127	183	11
45-54	452	282	18	80	55	3
55-64	186	126	4	24	23	1
65 and over	148	86	1	18	15	0
All ages	6,452	8,071	340	703	911	41

Source: Federal Bureau of Investigation. 1994. *Supplementary homicide report, 1992.* [Computer file]. Ann Arbor, Mich.: Inter-university Consortium for Political and Social Research. [See appendix entry 45]

Note: Table counts offenders. "Murder" includes non-negligent manslaughter. Data for Maine were not included in the 1992 data distributed by the FBI. Offenders were unknown in 8,739 murders in 1992. These cases are not included in the table. Of the cases in which some offender information was known, the table also excludes 104 cases where race of the offender was not known and 21 cases in which both the gender and the race were not known. Overall, Supplementary Homicide Report (SHR) data were submitted for 25,382 known and unknown offenders in 1992.

Victim-Offender Relationship

1.10 Murders, by Victim-Offender Relationship and Gender, 1992

Relationship	Male	Female	Total	% of total
Family	1,364	1,334	2,698	11.9
Spouse	296	693	989	
Common-law partner	92	126	218	
Parent	125	125	250	
Child	301	227	528	
Sibling	169	42	211	
In-law	102	18	120	
Stepparent	42	0	42	
Stepchild	34	29	63	
Other family member	203	74	277	
Others Known to Victim	6,388	1,668	8,056	35.5
Neighbor	159	60	219	
Acquaintance	3,836	628	4,464	
Boy/girlfriend	258	509	767	
Ex-spouse	19	58	77	
Employee	11	0	11	
Employer	14	7	21	
Friend	712	140	852	
Homosexual relationship	25	5	30	
Other - known to victim	1,354	261	1,615	
Stranger	2,641	431	3,072	13.5
Relationship not known	7,307	1,555	8,862	39.0
Total	17,700	4,988	22,688	

Source: Federal Bureau of Investigation. 1994. *Supplementary homicide report, 1992.* [Computer file]. Ann Arbor, Mich.: Inter-university Consortium for Political and Social Research. [See appendix entry45]

Note: Table counts victims. "Murder" includes non-negligent manslaughters. Data for Maine were not included in 1992 data distributed by the FBI. The table excludes 28 cases in which the gender of the victim was unknown. Percentages in rightmost column are based on a total of 22,716 victims for which Supplementary Homicide Report (SHR) data were submitted in 1992.

1.11   Murders, by Race and Gender of Victim and Offender Where Known, 1992

Victim Gender and Race	Male Offender				Female Offender			
	White	Black	Other	All	White	Black	Other	All
Male								
White	3,766	913	55	4,790	450	32	7	496
Black	313	4,650	10	5,021	14	617	3	638
Other	73	44	145	268	3	1	14	18
All	4,166	5,620	211	10,129	467	651	25	1,157
Female								
White	1,626	253	13	1,910	122	17	5	146
Black	60	1168	2	1,242	5	165	0	171
Other	22	8	66	97	1	0	8	9
All	1,710	1,430	81	3,263	128	182	13	326

Source: Federal Bureau of Investigation. 1994. *Supplementary homicide report, 1992.* [Computer file]. Ann Arbor, Mich.: Inter-university Consortium for Political and Social Research. [See appendix entry 45]

Note: Table counts victims. "Murder" includes non-negligent manslaughters. Data for Maine were not included in 1992 data distributed by the FBI. The "All" categories include cases in which gender was known, but not race. The table excludes 7,829 cases in which information about the offender, including both race and gender, were unknown, 28 cases in which race and gender of the victim were unknown, and 4 cases in which the race of the offender was known, but gender was unknown.

Circumstances of Homicide

1.12   Murders, by Circumstances and Gender of Victim, 1993

Circumstances	Male	Female	Total	% of Total
Felony	3,699	894	4,595	19.7
Rape	10	106	116	
Robbery	1,950	351	2,301	
Burglary	119	60	179	
Larceny-theft	23	9	32	
Motor vehicle theft	50	11	61	
Arson	83	68	151	
Prostitution and commercialized vice	2	15	17	
Other sex offenses	13	12	25	
Narcotic drug laws	1,180	105	1,287	
Gambling	10	0	10	
Other-not specified	170	102	272	
Suspected felony	89	55	144	
Other than felony	9,191	3,032	12,235	52.6
Romantic triangle	257	182	439	
Child killed by babysitter	17	16	33	
Brawl due to influence of alcohol	339	42	381	
Brawl due to influence of narcotics	221	40	262	
Argument over money or property	378	67	445	
Other arguments	4,698	1,590	6,292	
Gangland killings	136	11	147	
Juvenile gang killings	1,055	92	1,147	
Institutional killings	14	1	15	
Sniper attack	5	2	7	
Other-not specified	2,071	989	3,067	
Unknown	5,059	1,352	6,441	27.7
Total	17,949	5,278	23,271	100.0

Source: Supplementary Homicide Reports, 1993, adapted from: Federal Bureau of Investigation. 1994. *Crime in the United States 1993*. Washington, D.C.: U.S. Government Printing Office, p. 21, Table 2.15. [See appendix entry 45]

Note: Includes non-negligent manslaughters. "Total" includes 44 murder victims for whom gender was unknown.

1.13   Homicides, by Day of the Week, 1991

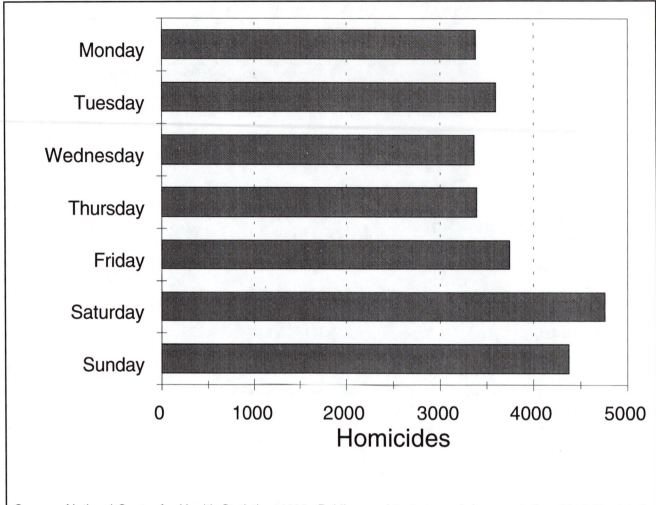

Source: National Center for Health Statistics. 1993. *Public-use data tape and documentation: Mortality detail,*
          1991 data. [Computer file]. Hyattsville, Md.: Public Health Service. [See appendix entry 34]
Note: Homicides and legal interventions (ICD-9 codes E960–E978). Days begin and end at midnight.

Weapon or Means of Death

1.14 Homicides, by Weapon, Total, and by Gender of Victim, 1991

Cause	Total	Male	Female
Fight, brawl, rape (E960)	84	74	10
Assault by corrosive or caustic substance, except poisoning (E961)	0	0	0
Assault by poisoning (E962)	55	27	28
Assault by hanging and strangulation (E963)	1,026	317	709
Assault by submersion (E964)	74	45	29
Assault by firearms and explosives (E965)	17,827	14,990	2,837
Assault by cutting and piercing intstrument (E966)	4,053	3,007	1,046
Child battering and other maltreatment (E967)	300	162	138
Assault by other and unspecified means (E968)	2,857	1,909	948
Late effects of injury purposely inflicted by other person (E969)	79	68	11

Source: National Center for Health Statistics. 1993. *Public-use data tape and documentation: Mortality detail, 1991 data.* [Computer file]. Hyattsville, Md.: Public Health Service. [See appendix entry 34]

Note: Codes in parentheses are International Classification of Diseases, Ninth Revision (ICD-9) cause of death classification categories.

1.15 Homicides, by Weapon, Race, and Gender of Victim, 1991

Cause	White		Nonwhite	
	Male	Female	Male	Female
Fight, brawl, rape (E960)	51	5	23	5
Assault by corrosive or caustic substance, except poisoning (E961)	0	0	0	0
Assault by poisoning (E962)	22	24	5	4
Assault by hanging and strangulation (E963)	203	429	114	280
Assault by submersion (E964)	24	18	21	11
Assault by firearms and explosives (E965)	6,395	1,609	8,595	1,228
Assault by cutting and piercing instrument (E966)	1,504	494	1,503	552
Child battering or other maltreatment (E967)	94	65	68	73
Assault by other and unspecified means (E968)	1,171	558	738	390
Late effects of injury purposely inflicted by other person (E969)	34	6	34	5

Source: National Center for Health Statistics. 1993. *Public-use data tape and documentation: Mortality detail, 1991 data.* [Computer file]. Hyattsville, Md.: Public Health Service. [See appendix entry 34]

Note: Codes in parentheses are International Classification of Diseases, Ninth Revision (ICD-9) cause of death classification categories.

1.16   Murders, by Weapon, 1989–1993

Weapon	1989	1990	1991	1992	1993
All Firearms	11,832	13,035	14,373	15,489	16,189
Handguns	9,013	10,099	11,497	12,580	13,252
Rifles	865	746	745	706	754
Shotguns	1,173	1,245	1,124	1,111	1,059
Other guns	34	25	30	42	38
Firearms, not specified	747	920	977	1,050	1,086
Knives or cutting instruments	3,458	3,526	3,430	3,296	2,957
Blunt objects	1,128	1,085	1,099	1,040	1,024
Hands, feet, pushed, etc.	1,050	1,119	1,202	1,131	1,164
Poison	11	11	12	13	9
Explosives	16	13	16	19	26
Fire	234	288	195	203	217
Narcotics	17	29	22	24	22
Drowning	60	36	40	29	23
Strangulation	366	312	327	314	329
Asphyxiation	101	96	113	115	113
Other weapons not specified	681	723	847	1,043	1,198
Total	18,954	20,273	21,676	22,716	23,271

Source: Supplementary Homicide Reports, 1989–1992, from: Federal Bureau of Investigation. 1994. *Crime in the United States 1993*. Washington, D.C.: U.S. Government Printing Office, p. 18, Table 2.10. [See appendix entry 45]

Note: Includes non-negligent manslaughters.

1.17 Murders, by Weapon and Age of Victim, 1993

Age in Years	Total	Firearm	Knives or Cutting Instrument	Blunt Objects	Hands, Feet, Pushed, etc.	Poison	Explo-sives	Fire	Narcotics	Strang-ulation	Asphyx-iation	Other Weapon*
Under 1	272	15	5	17	147	0	0	5	4	3	19	57
1-4	459	57	13	38	223	1	0	28	1	7	19	72
5-9	173	74	27	6	20	0	2	12	0	6	6	20
10-14	387	278	38	17	13	0	1	7	1	7	4	21
15-19	3,084	2,650	227	53	28	0	3	4	1	24	5	89
20-24	4,355	3,594	388	79	70	1	4	12	2	40	5	160
25-29	3,466	2,609	476	96	67	0	1	14	2	52	7	142
30-34	3,083	2,136	472	113	118	1	3	29	3	50	8	150
35-39	2,318	1,549	370	121	93	0	2	13	2	49	6	113
40-44	1,620	1,060	271	95	94	0	3	10	3	18	3	63
45-49	1,077	704	154	81	45	0	1	20	0	12	3	57
50-54	717	423	107	67	41	2	3	9	0	12	3	50
55-59	465	263	73	44	30	0	0	4	1	7	4	39
60-64	393	203	83	38	24	2	0	11	0	5	3	24
65-69	319	152	59	37	24	2	0	10	0	6	3	26
70-74	292	114	64	35	31	0	1	4	0	13	1	29
75 +	467	129	95	65	77	0	2	17	2	14	13	53
Unknown	324	179	35	22	19	0	0	8	0	4	1	56

Source: Supplementary Homicide Reports, 1993, from: Federal Bureau of Investigation. 1994. *Crime in the United States 1993.* Washington, D.C.: U.S. Government Printing Office, p. 18, Table 2.11. [See appendix entry 45]

Note: Includes non-negligent manslaughters.
   *   Includes drownings.

1.18   Murders, by Weapon and State, 1993

State	Total Firearms	Handgun	Rifle	Shotgun	Unknown firearm	Knives or cutting instrument	Other weapon	Hands, feet, pushed, etc.
Alabama	284	234	14	35	1	66	105	18
Alaska	27	20	5	1	1	11	14	2
Arizona	230	168	15	15	32	45	33	22
Arkansas	175	125	17	20	13	26	31	12
California	3,007	2,609	154	167	77	473	476	138
Colorado	132	111	5	6	10	32	30	12
Connecticut	139	117	5	2	15	28	30	9
Delaware	12	10	1	1	0	4	2	2
Dist. of Columbia	350	350	0	0	0	32	35	0
Florida	753	486	24	36	207	143	270	57
Georgia	506	435	24	32	15	114	94	36
Hawaii	16	12	2	2	0	12	5	10
Idaho	17	14	3	0	0	7	4	3
Indiana	260	225	14	17	4	35	46	16
Iowa	18	10	1	3	4	13	9	5
Kentucky	161	115	10	24	12	17	48	10
Louisiana	586	520	39	21	6	52	55	28
Maine	5	4	0	0	1	0	2	0
Maryland	458	427	2	22	7	80	65	29
Massachusetts	110	60	3	2	45	57	33	10
Michigan	681	379	49	70	183	90	112	39
Minnesota	69	51	8	10	0	29	17	16
Mississippi	161	141	8	8	4	32	14	11
Missouri	410	324	26	28	32	57	56	23
Nebraska	13	7	1	5	0	3	8	4
Nevada	84	79	2	3	0	17	10	18
New Hampshire	10	5	0	2	3	7	2	1
New Jersey	213	182	9	15	7	93	68	44
New Mexico	49	39	5	5	0	26	9	11
New York	1,739	1,604	16	50	69	310	262	104
North Carolina	493	368	49	71	5	107	126	45
North Dakota	5	3	0	1	1	2	3	1
Ohio	431	375	12	28	16	62	58	48
Oklahoma	170	131	22	16	1	39	48	15
Oregon	76	57	7	8	4	31	26	10
Pennsylvania	573	486	14	35	38	93	82	56
Rhode Island	21	16	2	1	2	7	9	2
South Carolina	264	213	18	24	9	53	37	21
South Dakota	10	8	2	0	0	0	4	4
Tennessee	322	271	13	32	6	58	49	21
Texas	1,535	1,107	77	133	218	281	234	92
Utah	23	17	3	1	2	13	6	16
Vermont	8	5	2	1	0	1	3	0
Virginia	394	325	17	41	11	71	48	26
Washington	155	127	15	10	3	45	49	15
West Virginia	85	53	12	17	3	12	18	10
Wisconsin	117	88	7	12	10	29	51	25
Wyoming	10	6	4	0	0	2	1	3

Source: Supplementary Homicide Reports, 1993 from: Federal Bureau of Investigation. 1994. *Crime in the United States 1993*. Washington, D.C.: U.S. Government Printing Office, p. 202, Table 20. [See appendix entry 45]

Note: Includes non-negligent manslaughter. Data for 1993 were not available for Illinois, Kansas, or Montana.

CURRENT PATTERNS: CITIES AND REGIONS

1.19 Murders and Murder Rates, by Size and Type of Place, 1993

Place Type and Size of Population	Murders	Rate
Cities		
1,000,000 or More	5,094	27.7
500,000-999,999	2,407	21.6
250,000-499,999	3,229	23.6
100,000-249,999	2,541	13.2
50,000-99,999	1,692	7.5
25,000-49,999	1,081	5.2
10,000-24,999	902	4.2
Under 10,000	710	3.9
Suburban counties	2,949	6.0
Rural counties	1,333	5.5

Source: Monthly Return of Offenses Known to Police (Return A) from: Federal Bureau of Investigation. 1994. *Crime in the United States, 1993*. Washington, D.C.: U.S. Government Printing Office, pp. 196–197, Table 16. [See appendix entry 26]

Note: Includes non-negligent manslaughters. Rates are per 100,000 residents.

1.20 Murder Rates, by Region, 1993

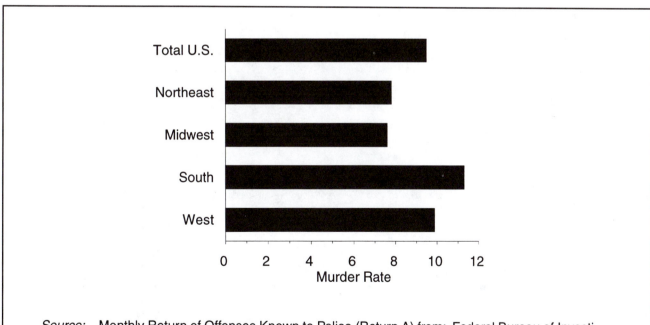

Source: Monthly Return of Offenses Known to Police (Return A) from: Federal Bureau of Investigation. 1994. *Crime in the United States 1993*. Washington, D.C.: U.S. Government Printing Office, pp. 60–67, Table 4. [See appendix entry 26]

Note: Includes non-negligent manslaughter. Rates are per 100,000 residents.

1.21 Murders and Murder Rates, by State, 1993

State	Murders	Rate	State	Murders	Rate	State	Murders	Rate
Alabama	484	11.6	Kentucky	249	6.6	North Dakota	11	1.7
Alaska	54	9.0	Louisiana	874	20.3	Ohio	667	6.0
Arizona	339	8.6	Maine	20	1.6	Oklahoma	273	8.4
Arkansas	247	10.2	Maryland	632	12.7	Oregon	140	4.6
California	4,096	13.1	Massachusetts	233	3.9	Pennsylvania	823	6.8
Colorado	206	5.8	Michigan	933	9.8	Rhode Island	39	3.9
Connecticut	206	6.3	Minnesota	155	3.4	South Carolina	377	10.3
Delaware	35	5.0	Mississippi	357	13.5	South Dakota	24	3.4
Dist. of Columbia	454	78.5	Missouri	590	11.3	Tennessee	521	10.2
Florida	1,224	8.9	Montana	25	3.0	Texas	2,147	11.9
Georgia	789	11.4	Nebraska	63	3.9	Utah	58	3.1
Hawaii	45	3.8	Nevada	144	10.4	Vermont	21	3.6
Idaho	32	2.9	New Hampshire	23	2.0	Virginia	539	8.3
Illinois	1,332	11.4	New Jersey	418	5.3	Washington	271	5.2
Indiana	430	7.5	New Mexico	130	8.0	West Virginia	126	6.9
Iowa	66	2.3	New York	2,420	13.3	Wisconsin	222	4.4
Kansas	161	6.4	North Carolina	785	11.3	Wyoming	16	3.4

Source: Monthly Return of Offenses Known to Police (Return A) from: Federal Bureau of Investigation. 1994. *Crime in the United States 1993.* Washington, D.C.: U.S. Government Printing Office, pp. 60–67, Table 4. [See appendix entry 26]

Note: Includes non-negligent manslaughters. Rates are per 100,000 residents.

1.22 Murder Rates, by State, 1993

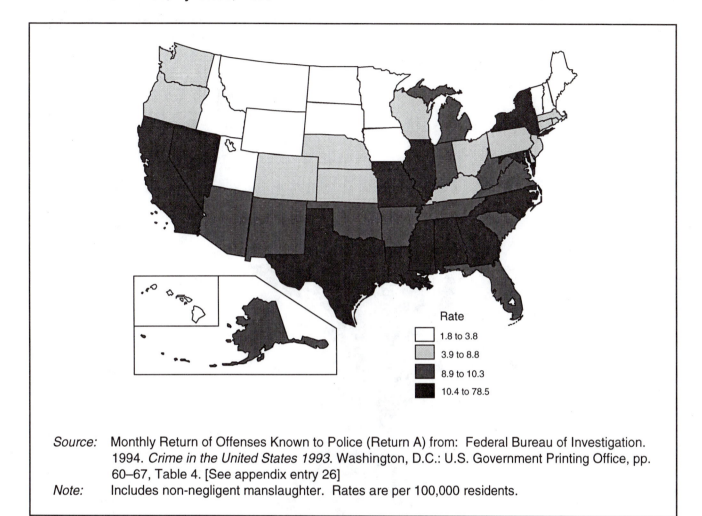

Rate

☐	1.8 to 3.8
▨	3.9 to 8.8
▨	8.9 to 10.3
■	10.4 to 78.5

Source: Monthly Return of Offenses Known to Police (Return A) from: Federal Bureau of Investigation. 1994. *Crime in the United States 1993*. Washington, D.C.: U.S. Government Printing Office, pp. 60–67, Table 4. [See appendix entry 26]

Note: Includes non-negligent manslaughter. Rates are per 100,000 residents.

1.23 Homicide Rates, by County, 1979–1987

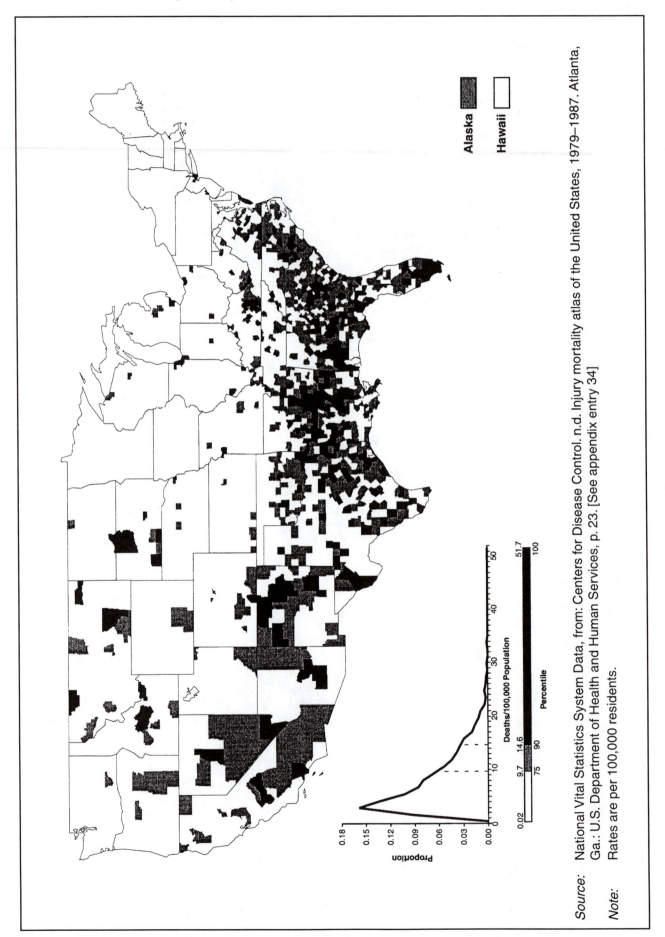

Source: National Vital Statistics System Data, from: Centers for Disease Control. n.d. Injury mortality atlas of the United States, 1979–1987. Atlanta, Ga.: U.S. Department of Health and Human Services, p. 23. [See appendix entry 34]

Note: Rates are per 100,000 residents.

TRENDS: UNITED STATES

Homicide

1.24   Homicide Rates, 1933–1991

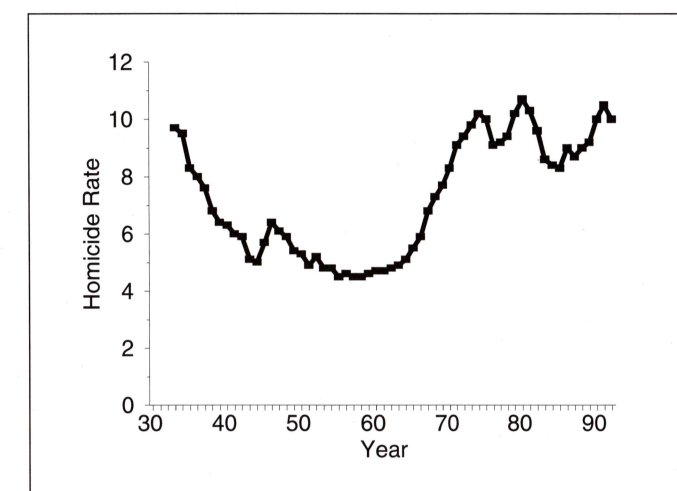

Source: U.S. Bureau of the Census. 1975. *Historical statistics of the United States, colonial times to 1970*. Washington, D.C.: U.S. Government Printing Office, p. 414, Series H 972; U.S. Department of Health and Human Services. 1970-1989 (Annual). *Vital statistics of the United States*. Volume II--Mortality, Part A. Hyattsville, Md.: Public Health Service, Various Tables (1971-1988); National Center for Health Statistics. 1994. *Health, United States, 1993*. Hyattsville, Md.: Public Health Service, p. 130 (1990, 1991). [See appendix entry 34]

Note: Prior to 1933 the vital statistics registration system was subject to underreporting in rural areas. Rates are not adjusted for changes in the population's age structure. Homicides include legal interventions. Rates are per 100,000 residents.

1.25   Age-Adjusted Homicide Rates, by Race and Gender, 1940–1992

Year	White Male	White Female	Nonwhite Male	Nonwhite Female	Overall	Year	White Male	White Female	Nonwhite Male	Nonwhite Female	Overall
1940	5.0	1.3	57.1	12.6	6.3	1967	5.9	2.0	62.7	14.0	7.7
1941	4.5	1.3	56.6	12.2	6.0	1968	6.5	2.0	68.9	13.6	8.2
1942	4.4	1.2	55.2	11.8	5.9	1969	6.6	2.1	72.4	13.8	8.6
1943	4.1	1.2	44.3	9.7	5.1	1970	7.3	2.2	72.8	13.7	9.1
1944	4.1	1.1	47.4	9.5	5.1	1971	7.9	2.3	81.6	16.0	10.0
1945	5.1	1.3	52.7	10.6	5.8	1972	8.2	2.4	83.1	14.8	10.3
1946	4.9	1.5	56.4	12.4	6.4	1973	8.7	2.8	77.1	16.0	10.5
1947	4.7	1.4	53.9	12.1	6.1	1974	9.3	2.9	77.9	15.5	10.8
1948	4.5	1.5	53.9	11.9	6.0	1975	9.4	2.9	71.6	14.7	10.5
1949	4.1	1.4	48.9	11.7	5.5	1976	8.6	2.7	63.3	13.2	9.5
1950	3.9	1.4	49.1	11.5	5.4	1977	8.8	2.9	60.1	12.5	9.6
1951	3.6	1.4	45.3	11.1	5.0	1978	9.2	2.9	58.1	12.1	9.6
1952	3.8	1.3	50.4	11.3	5.4	1979	10.1	3.0	62.9	12.8	10.4
1953	3.6	1.3	46.5	10.2	5.1	1980	10.9	3.2	61.3	12.2	10.8
1954	3.6	1.4	46.2	10.3	5.1	1981	10.3	3.1	58.5	11.4	10.4
1955	3.5	1.3	42.6	10.3	4.8	1982	9.5	3.1	52.2	10.5	9.7
1956	3.5	1.3	43.2	11.3	5.0	1983	8.4	2.8	45.2	9.8	8.6
1957	3.5	1.4	43.1	10.3	4.9	1984	8.2	2.9	42.2	9.6	8.4
1958	3.6	1.4	41.6	10.5	4.9	1985	8.1	2.9	41.4	9.3	8.3
1959	3.8	1.5	42.3	10.7	5.1	1986	8.4	2.9	46.1	10.2	9.0
1960	3.9	1.5	41.9	11.2	5.2	1987	7.7	2.9	44.0	10.5	8.6
1961	3.9	1.6	41.5	10.1	5.2	1988	7.7	2.8	47.4	10.8	9.0
1962	4.1	1.7	44.4	10.3	5.4	1989	8.1	2.8	49.8	10.7	9.4
1963	4.2	1.6	44.8	10.5	5.5	1990	8.9	2.8	53.9	10.7	10.2
1964	4.3	1.7	47.1	10.6	5.7	1991	9.4	3.0	56.7	11.5	10.9
1965	4.8	1.7	50.7	11.7	6.2	1992	9.3	2.8	53.0	10.5	10.5
1966	4.9	1.9	54.8	12.4	6.7						

Source: For 1940–1960: Grove, Robert D., and Alice M. Hetzel. 1968. *Vital statistics rates in the United States, 1940–1960.* Washington, D.C.: National Center for Health Statistics, p. 373, Table 62; [See appendix entry 34]

For 1961–1969: Klebba, A. Joan, Jeffrey D. Maurer, and Evelyn J. Glass. 1974. *Mortality trends for leading causes of death, United States-1950–69.* Series 20, Number 16. Washington, D.C.: National Center for Health Statistics, p. 49, Table U; [See appendix entry 34]

For 1970–1990: National Center for Health Statistics. 1974–1994 (Annual). *Vital statistics of the United States.* Volume II-- Mortality, Part A. Hyattsville, Md.: Public Health Service, Table 1–6 (1970–1978), Table 1–7 (1979–1987), Table 1–8 (1988, 1989, 1990); [See appendix entry 34]

For 1991: Hoyert, Donna L., and Bettie L. Hudson. 1993. Advance report of final mortality statistics, 1991. *Monthly Vital Statistics Report* 42, no. 2, supp. Hyattsville, Md.: National Center for Health Statistics, p. 41, Table 11; [See appendix entry 34]

For 1992: Kochanek, Kenneth D., and Bettie L. Hudson. 1994. Advance report of final mortality statistics, 1992. *Monthly Vital Statistics Report* 43, no. 6, supp. Hyattsville, Md.: National Center for Health Statistics, p. 48, Table 11. [See appendix entry 34]

Note: Age-adjusted rates eliminate differences over time due to changes in the relative sizes of age groups. Age-adjusted rates in this table were calculated by the direct method using the enumerated population of the U.S. in 1940 as the standard (see Grove and Hetzel, 1968, p. 35). Rates are based on deaths designated as "homicides and legal interventions" in accordance with International Classification of Diseases (ICD) and are per 100,000 residents. ICD codes employed for 1940–1948: 165–168, 198 of Fifth Revision; for 1949–1967: E964, E980–E985 of Sixth and Seventh Revisions; for 1968–1992: E960–E978 of the Eighth and Ninth Revisions.

1.26 Homicide Rates, by Age, Race, and Gender, 1985–1991

All Races	1985	1986	1987	1988	1989	1990	1991
Age under 1 year	5.4	7.5	7.4	8.4	8.7	8.4	9.5
1-4	2.5	2.7	2.3	2.6	2.7	2.6	2.8
5-14	1.2	1.1	1.2	1.3	1.5	1.5	1.4
15-24	11.9	14.0	13.8	15.1	16.5	19.9	22.4
25-34	14.8	16.3	15.3	16.2	16.5	17.7	18.2
35-44	11.3	11.5	10.9	10.9	11.0	11.8	11.6
45-54	8.1	8.4	7.8	7.2	7.7	7.6	8.2
55-64	5.7	5.4	5.5	5.3	5.1	5.0	5.5
65-74	4.3	4.4	4.4	4.3	4.1	3.8	4.0
75-84	4.3	4.6	4.8	4.5	4.2	4.3	4.2
85 and over	4.2	4.7	5.2	4.8	4.4	4.6	4.1
White male	1985	1986	1987	1988	1989	1990	1991
Age under 1 year	3.8	5.5	6.1	5.8	5.8	6.4	7.6
1-4	1.9	1.9	1.8	2.2	1.9	1.8	2.1
5-14	1.1	0.9	0.8	1.0	1.0	1.1	1.2
15-24	11.0	12.2	11.0	11.2	12.3	15.4	16.9
25-34	14.0	14.8	13.4	13.5	14.0	15.1	15.5
35-44	11.5	11.7	10.3	10.5	10.6	11.4	11.2
45-54	8.6	8.7	8.4	7.7	8.6	8.3	8.7
55-64	6.3	6.0	6.4	6.1	5.7	5.5	6.1
65-74	4.5	4.4	4.3	4.2	4.0	4.1	4.0
75-84	4.5	4.6	4.9	4.3	3.9	3.9	3.8
85 and over	3.9	4.4	5.4	5.2	5.2	4.9	4.4
Black male	1985	1986	1987	1988	1989	1990	1991
Age under 1 year	16.7	23.2	19.5	19.5	21.9	21.4	22.4
1-4	6.6	9.5	4.9	7.6	8.0	7.6	7.9
5-14	3.3	3.3	4.5	4.3	5.1	5.1	5.4
15-24	65.9	78.9	85.3	101.4	114.2	138.3	158.9
25-34	95.6	109.6	100.6	110.9	114.9	125.4	125.0
35-44	74.9	77.7	76.3	76.9	75.9	82.3	77.6
45-54	51.4	56.8	46.5	45.8	46.7	47.7	50.6
55-64	40.0	37.9	35.5	31.9	33.4	34.0	33.9
65-74	29.2	32.1	30.4	28.7	29.2	24.3	31.2
75-84	21.4	27.9	29.6	30.6	28.7	29.2	29.8
85 and over	17.7*	27.0*	31.3	33.8	37.9	27.2*	20.3*

See notes at end of table.

1.26   Homicide Rates, by Age, Race, and Gender, 1985–1991 *(continued)*

White female	1985	1986	1987	1988	1989	1990	1991
Age under 1 year	4.3	5.2	4.3	6.2	5.8	5.1	5.7
1-4	1.7	1.4	1.6	1.6	1.5	1.4	1.6
5-14	0.8	0.8	0.8	0.8	0.9	0.8	0.7
15-24	3.6	4.3	3.8	3.9	3.8	4.0	4.4
25-34	4.4	4.4	4.7	4.5	4.2	4.3	4.4
35-44	3.6	3.5	3.6	3.3	3.3	3.2	3.5
45-54	2.9	2.8	2.7	2.5	2.6	2.6	3.0
55-64	2.3	2.0	1.9	2.0	1.7	1.8	2.1
65-74	2.2	2.2	2.4	2.3	2.1	1.8	2.0
75-84	3.1	3.0	3.1	2.9	2.6	2.8	2.6
85 and over	3.2	3.3	3.8	3.0	2.0	2.5	2.9
Black female	1985	1986	1987	1988	1989	1990	1991
Age under 1 year	10.7	17.5	18.9	23.7	23.6	22.8	24.6
1-4	6.3	6.8	7.3	6.3	7.3	7.2	7.3
5-14	2.0	2.4	2.0	3.2	3.0	3.6	2.8
15-24	14.2	16.3	17.8	17.5	17.4	18.9	21.6
25-34	20.0	22.1	22.7	25.8	23.5	25.3	26.4
35-44	14.7	14.7	14.3	14.4	14.6	15.6	15.7
45-54	9.2	8.8	10.9	8.0	8.7	7.3	9.5
55-64	6.5	6.9	7.9	7.1	8.4	5.6	6.7
65-74	7.3	8.9	7.0	9.3	8.4	6.8	6.5
75-84	7.4	8.3	10.0	9.5	9.5	11.3	12.5
85 and over	12.0*	13.8*	11.1*	13.4	16.3	19.2	11.7*

Source: For 1985–1986: National Center for Health Statistics. 1993. *Health, United States, 1992.* Hyattsville, Md.: Public Health Service, pp. 76–77, Table 43; For 1987–1991: National Center for Health Statistics. 1994. *Health, United States, 1993.* Hyattsville, Md.: Public Health Service, pp. 130–131. [See appendix entry 34]

Note: Includes homicide and legal interventions (ICD-9 code E960-E978). Rates are per 100,000 residents.

   *   These cases are based on fewer than 20 deaths.

1.27 Homicide Rates, Males Age 15–24, by Race, 1985–1991

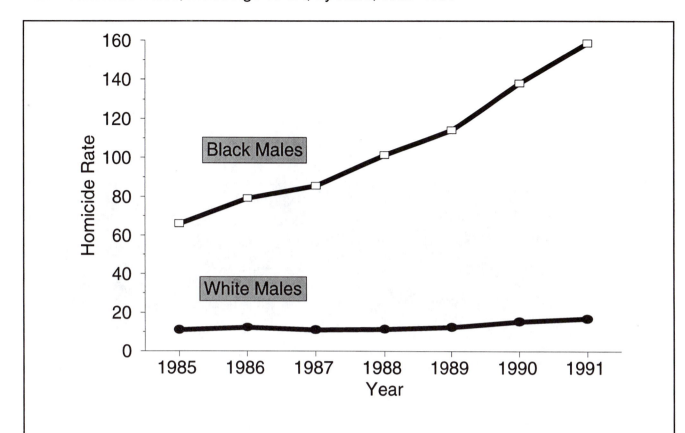

Source: National Center for Health Statistics. 1993. *Health, United States, 1992*. Hyattsville, Md.: Public Health Service, pp. 76–77, Table 43 (1985–1986); National Center for Health Statistics. 1994. *Health, United States, 1993*. Hyattsville, Md.: Public Health Service, pp. 130-131 (1987–1991). [See appendix entry 34]

Note: Includes homicide and legal interventions (ICD-9 code E960–E978). Rates are per 100,000 residents.

1.28   Number of Homicides Each Day, January 1, 1972–December 31, 1987

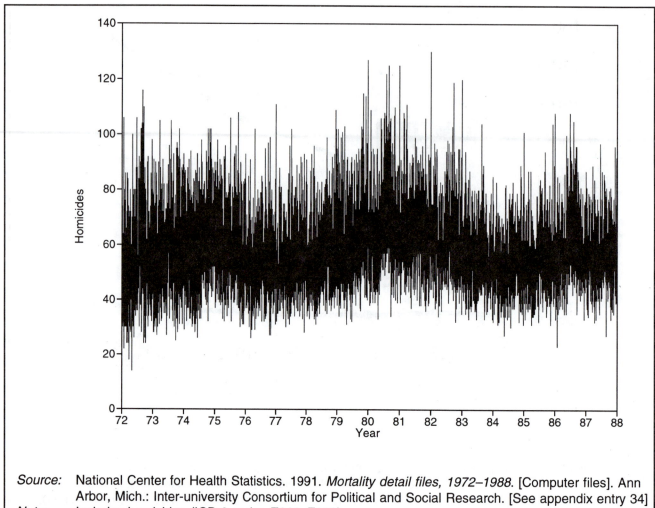

Source: National Center for Health Statistics. 1991. *Mortality detail files, 1972–1988*. [Computer files]. Ann Arbor, Mich.: Inter-university Consortium for Political and Social Research. [See appendix entry 34]

Note: Includes homicides (ICD-9 codes E960–E969).

1.29   Number of Homicides Each Month, January 1962–December 1991

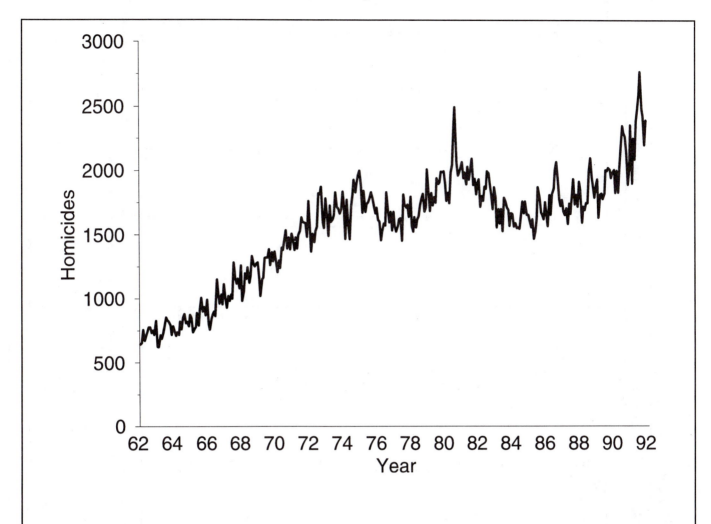

Source: National Center for Health Statistics. 1991. *Public-use data and documentation: Mortality detail, 1962-1991 data.* [Computer files]. Hyattsville, Md.: U.S. Public Health Service. [See appendix entry 34]

Note: Includes homicides (ICD-9 codes E960-E969).

1.30   Homicide Rates, by Weapon, Race, and Gender of Victim, 1960–1991

Year	Firearms and Explosives[a]				Cutting or Piercing Instrument[b]				Other Means[c]			
	Male		Female		Male		Female		Male		Female	
	White	Nonwhite	White	Nonwhite	White	Nonwhite	White	Nonwhite	White	Nonwhite	White	Nonwhite
1960	2.0	18.3	0.8	4.7	0.5	10.6	0.2	2.6	0.8	3.9	0.4	2.6
1961	2.1	18.1	0.9	4.4	0.5	10.2	0.2	2.0	0.8	4.0	0.5	2.4
1962	2.3	19.6	0.8	4.2	0.5	10.7	0.2	2.3	0.8	4.0	0.6	2.2
1963	2.3	19.9	0.8	4.6	0.5	10.8	0.2	2.2	0.8	3.7	0.5	2.3
1964	2.3	21.2	0.9	4.5	0.6	10.8	0.2	2.2	0.9	4.0	0.5	2.5
1965	2.6	23.7	0.9	4.9	0.7	11.5	0.2	2.4	0.9	3.7	0.5	2.6
1966	2.8	26.8	0.9	5.7	0.6	11.3	0.3	2.3	0.9	4.0	0.6	2.5
1967	3.3	32.0	1.0	7.0	0.7	11.6	0.3	2.3	1.0	4.3	0.6	2.6
1968	3.9	36.4	1.1	7.0	0.8	12.3	0.2	2.1	1.1	4.4	0.6	2.5
1969	4.0	40.6	1.0	7.1	0.9	11.8	0.3	2.2	0.9	4.1	0.7	2.4
1970	4.5	43.5	1.2	7.2	0.9	11.7	0.3	2.4	1.2	4.2	0.6	2.7
1971	4.8	47.5	1.2	8.3	1.1	13.0	0.3	2.7	1.2	4.9	0.8	2.9
1972	5.2	51.9	1.2	8.2	1.1	12.5	0.3	2.3	1.2	4.4	0.8	2.9
1973	5.6	48.2	1.4	8.8	1.2	11.1	0.4	2.6	1.3	5.1	0.9	3.2
1974	6.3	49.3	1.5	8.7	1.2	11.7	0.4	2.7	1.2	4.8	0.9	3.1
1975	6.2	45.8	1.5	7.9	1.3	10.8	0.4	2.4	1.4	4.8	1.0	3.4
1976	5.6	39.6	1.5	7.1	1.3	10.2	0.4	2.3	1.3	5.0	0.8	3.1
1977	5.8	37.7	1.5	6.3	1.4	10.4	0.5	2.3	1.3	4.7	0.9	3.4
1978	6.2	37.8	1.4	6.5	1.5	9.6	0.5	2.2	1.3	4.4	1.0	3.1
1979	6.7	40.5	1.5	6.5	1.8	10.7	0.5	2.5	1.4	5.1	1.0	3.5
1980	7.1	40.8	1.5	6.5	1.9	11.0	0.5	2.1	1.7	5.2	1.2	3.5
1981	6.8	38.7	1.5	5.9	1.8	10.9	0.4	2.3	1.6	5.1	1.2	3.2
1982	6.2	33.9	1.5	4.9	1.7	10.5	0.6	2.4	1.5	5.1	1.0	3.2
1983	5.3	28.5	1.3	4.5	1.7	10.0	0.5	2.3	1.4	4.5	1.0	3.1
1984	5.2	26.7	1.3	4.4	1.6	9.0	0.5	2.3	1.3	4.6	1.1	3.1
1985	5.1	26.4	1.4	4.3	1.5	9.0	0.5	2.1	1.4	4.5	1.0	3.1
1986	5.3	30.5	1.4	4.8	1.6	9.6	0.6	2.3	1.5	5.0	1.0	3.4
1987	4.9	29.5	1.4	5.0	1.6	9.0	0.5	2.4	1.5	4.8	1.1	3.3
1988	5.0	33.4	1.4	5.2	1.4	8.6	0.5	2.4	1.3	5.1	1.0	3.6
1989	5.2	35.7	1.3	5.1	1.4	8.5	0.5	2.3	1.4	5.1	1.0	3.6
1990	5.8	40.5	1.4	5.3	1.5	8.6	0.4	2.3	1.5	5.1	1.0	3.5
1991	6.2	43.6	1.5	5.7	1.5	7.6	0.5	2.6	1.5	5.1	1.0	3.6

Source: For 1960–1990:   U.S. Department of Health and Human Services. 1963–1993 (Annual). *Vital statistics of the United States.* Volume II–Mortality, Part A. Hyattsville, Md.: Public Health Service, Table 5–6 (1960, 1961), Table 1–20 (1962, 1963), Table 1–22 (1964, 1966–1968, 1979–1986), Table 1–23 (1965, 1969–1978, 1987–1990); [See appendix entry 34]

For 1991:   National Center for Health Statistics. 1993. *Public-use data tape and documentation: Mortality detail, 1991 data.* [Computer file]. Hyattsville, Md.: Public Health Service (homicides); Bureau of the Census. 1993. *Statistical abstract of the United States.* Washington, DC, p. 21, Table 22. [See appendix entry 34]

Note:
Rates are per 100,000 residents.

a   For 1960–67, homicide by firearms and explosives is defined by International Classification of Diseases (ICD), 8th revision code E981; For 1968–91, the category is defined by ICD 9th revision code E965.

b   For 1960–67, homicide by cutting or piercing instrument is defined by ICD 8th revision code E982; For 1968–91, the category is defined by ICD 9th revision code E966.

c   For 1960–67, homicide by other means includes ICD 8th revision codes E964, E980, and E983; For 1968–91 the category includes ICD 9th revision codes E960 through E964 and E967 through E969.

1.31 Homicides, by Weapon, and by Race and Gender of Victim, 1960–1991

Year	Firearms and Explosives[a]				Cutting or Piercing Instrument[b]				Other Means[c]			
	Male		Female		Male		Female		Male		Female	
	White	Nonwhite	White	Nonwhite	White	Nonwhite	White	Nonwhite	White	Nonwhite	White	Nonwhite
1960	1,637	1,823	671	496	385	1,057	123	271	665	404	359	272
1961	1,681	1,853	740	479	422	1,049	128	220	648	417	401	262
1962	1,760	2,003	668	460	419	1,097	155	252	644	421	466	247
1963	1,828	2,076	645	504	417	1,125	147	239	692	392	447	258
1964	1,887	2,325	744	518	502	1,186	165	255	733	445	461	300
1965	2,152	2,655	772	579	555	1,292	154	291	793	423	453	315
1966	2,327	3,049	794	685	533	1,286	230	281	774	465	572	311
1967	2,835	3,702	932	863	616	1,345	225	281	849	505	552	331
1968	3,328	4,270	943	884	720	1,441	196	269	895	525	560	305
1969	3,478	4,856	921	919	754	1,409	279	284	823	496	599	305
1970	3,910	5,299	1,050	954	808	1,421	234	317	993	519	652	358
1971	4,257	5,925	1,128	1,113	964	1,626	288	359	1,023	610	686	396
1972	4,610	6,540	1,112	1,120	1,004	1,576	304	312	1,070	546	740	404
1973	5,001	6,167	1,352	1,232	1,087	1,423	382	362	1,137	656	839	451
1974	5,636	6,417	1,443	1,241	1,085	1,525	370	386	1,087	628	839	433
1975	5,637	6,092	1,410	1,156	1,162	1,436	414	350	1,247	650	922	498
1976	5,079	5,373	1,262	1,052	1,199	1,384	373	348	1,142	676	909	463
1977	5,314	5,206	1,394	960	1,308	1,439	439	356	1,170	651	954	508
1978	5,669	5,328	1,385	1,004	1,379	1,350	441	342	1,239	615	939	475
1979	6,209	5,814	1,458	1,021	1,663	1,533	484	397	1,338	731	997	557
1980	6,740	6,153	1,545	1,084	1,797	1,664	538	355	1,648	777	1,092	574
1981	6,540	6,024	1,527	1,016	1,770	1,699	452	391	1,469	786	1,146	541
1982	5,960	5,448	1,566	867	1,689	1,691	564	421	1,448	799	1,045	575
1983	5,196	4,670	1,375	803	1,637	1,641	485	410	1,365	744	1,017	579
1984	5,131	4,487	1,391	811	1,586	1,504	496	429	1,283	768	1,065	559
1985	5,012	4,527	1,491	818	1,516	1,552	529	397	1,435	764	1,020	567
1986	5,303	5,362	1,450	930	1,626	1,682	583	451	1,480	879	1,086	630
1987	4,912	5,295	1,469	989	1,455	1,606	561	477	1,437	866	1,116	629
1988	5,027	6,126	1,463	1,050	1,370	1,576	520	473	1,440	933	1,082	724
1989	5,324	6,704	1,408	1,044	1,412	1,599	494	475	1,391	936	1,063	728
1990	5,903	7,738	1,484	1,109	1,517	1,641	467	476	1,534	965	1,048	732
1991	6,395	8,595	1,609	1,228	1,504	1,503	494	552	1,599	1,003	1,105	768

Source: For 1960–1990: U.S. Department of Health and Human Services. 1963–1993 (Annual). *Vital statistics of the United States.* Volume II—Mortality, Part A. Hyattsville, Md.: Public Health Service, Table 5–6 (1960, 1961), Table 1–20 (1962, 1963), Table 1–22 (1964, 1966–1968, 1979–1986), Table 1–23 (1965, 1969–1978, 1987–1990); [See appendix entry 34]

For 1991: National Center for Health Statistics. 1993. *Public-use data tape and documentation: Mortality detail, 1991 data.* [Computer file]. Hyattsville, Md.: Public Health Service. [See appendix entry 34]

[a] For 1960–67, homicide by firearms and explosives is defined by International Classification of Diseases (ICD), 8th revision code E981; For 1968–91, the category is defined by ICD 9th revision code E965.

[b] For 1960–67, homicide by cutting or piercing instrument is defined by ICD 8th revision code E982; For 1968–91, the category is defined by ICD 9th revision code E966.

[c] For 1960–67, homicide by other means includes ICD 8th revision codes E964, E980, and E983; For 1968–91, the category includes ICD 9th revision codes E960 through E964 and E967 through E969.

Legal Execution

1.32   Persons Executed, by State, 1930–1993

Jurisdiction	Since 1930	Since 1977	Jurisdiction	Since 1930	Since 1977
U.S. Total	4,085	226	District of Columbia	40	0
Georgia	383	17	West Virginia	40	0
Texas	368	71	Nevada	34	5
New York	329	0	Federal system	33	0
California	294	2	Massachusetts	27	0
North Carolina	268	5	Connecticut	21	0
Florida	202	32	Oregon	19	0
Ohio	172	0	Iowa	18	0
South Carolina	166	4	Utah	17	4
Military authorities	160	*	Kansas	15	0
Mississippi	158	4	Delaware	15	3
Louisiana	154	21	New Mexico	8	0
Pennsylvania	152	0	Wyoming	8	1
Alabama	145	10	Montana	6	0
Arkansas	122	4	Vermont	4	0
Virginia	114	22	Nebraska	4	0
Kentucky	103	0	Idaho	3	0
Tennessee	93	0	South Dakota	1	0
Illinois	91	1	New Hampshire	1	0
New Jersey	74	0	Wisconsin	0	0
Missouri	73	11	Rhode Island	0	0
Maryland	68	0	North Dakota	0	0
Oklahoma	63	3	Minnesota	0	0
Washington	48	1	Michigan	0	0
Colorado	47	0	Maine	0	0
Indiana	43	2	Hawaii	0	0
Arizona	41	3	Alaska	0	0

Source: Stephan, James J., and Peter Brien. 1994. *Capital punishment 1993*. Washington, D.C.: Bureau of Justice Statistics, p. 11, Table 10. [See appendix entry 21]

   *   This information not provided.

1.33 Persons Executed, by Race, 1930–1993

Year	All Races	White	Black	Other Races	Year	All Races	White	Black	Other Races
1930	155	90	65	0	1962	47	28	19	0
1931	153	77	72	4	1963	21	13	8	0
1932	140	62	75	3	1964	15	8	7	0
1933	160	77	81	2	1965	7	6	1	0
1934	168	65	102	1	1966	1	1	0	0
1935	199	119	77	3	1967	2	1	1	0
1936	195	92	101	2	1968	0	0	0	0
1937	147	69	74	4	1969	0	0	0	0
1938	190	96	92	2	1970	0	0	0	0
1939	160	80	77	3	1971	0	0	0	0
1940	124	49	75	0	1972	0	0	0	0
1941	123	59	63	1	1973	0	0	0	0
1942	147	67	80	0	1974	0	0	0	0
1943	131	54	74	3	1975	0	0	0	0
1944	120	47	70	3	1976	0	0	0	0
1945	117	41	75	1	1977	1	1	0	0
1946	131	46	84	1	1978	0	0	0	0
1947	153	42	111	0	1979	2	2	0	0
1948	119	35	82	2	1980	0	0	0	0
1949	119	50	67	2	1981	1	1	0	0
1950	82	40	42	0	1982	2	1	1	0
1951	105	57	47	1	1983	5	4	1	0
1952	83	36	47	0	1984	21	13	8	0
1953	62	30	31	1	1985	18	11	7	0
1954	81	38	42	1	1986	18	11	7	0
1955	76	44	32	0	1987	25	13	12	0
1956	65	21	43	1	1988	11	6	5	0
1957	65	34	31	0	1989	16	8	8	0
1958	49	20	28	1	1990	23	16	7	0
1959	49	16	33	0	1991	14	7	7	0
1960	56	21	35	0	1992	31	15	10	6
1961	42	20	22	0	1993	38	18	13	7

Source: For 1930–1991: Snell, Tracy L. 1993. *Correctional populations in the United States, 1991.* Washington, D.C.: Bureau of Justice Statistics, p. 134, Table 7.26;

For 1992: Greenfeld, Lawrence A., and James J. Stephan. 1993. *Capital punishment 1992.* Washington, D.C.: Bureau of Justice Statistics, p. 2, from text;

For 1993: Stephan, James J., and Peter Brien. 1994. *Capital punishment 1993.* Washington, D.C.: Bureau of Justice Statistics, p. 1. [See appendix entry 21]

1.34   Persons Executed, by Race, 1930–1993

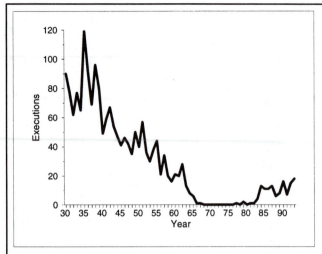

a) White

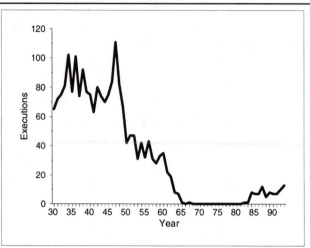

b) Black

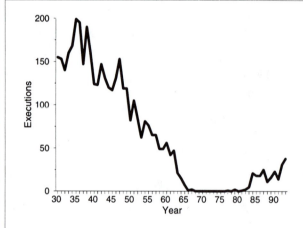

c) All races

Source: For 1930–1991: Snell, Tracy L. 1993. Correctional populations in the United States, 1991 Washington, D.C.: Bureau of Justice Statistics, p. 134, Table 7.26 [See appendix entry 21]; For 1992: Greenfeld, Lawrence A., and James J. Stephan. 1993. *Capital punishment 1992.* Washington, D.C.: Bureau of Justice Statistics, p. 2, from text [See appendix entry 21]; For 1993: Stephan, James J., and Peter Brien. 1994. *Capital punishment* 1993. Washington, D.C.: Bureau of Justice Statistics, p. 1. [See appendix entry 21]

1.35   Persons Executed, by State, and by Race, 1989–1993

	1989	1990	1991	1992	1993
State					
Texas	4	4	5	12	17
Virginia	1	3	2	4	5
Missouri	1	4	1	1	4
Florida	2	4	2	2	3
Arizona	0	0	0	1	2
Delaware	0	0	0	1	2
Georgia	1	0	1	0	2
California	0	0	0	1	1
Louisiana	0	1	1	0	1
Washington	0	0	0	0	1
Alabama	4	1	0	2	0
Nevada	2	1	0	0	0
Mississippi	1	0	0	0	0
Arkansas	0	2	0	2	0
Illinois	0	1	0	0	0
Oklahoma	0	1	0	2	0
South Carolina	0	1	1	0	0
North Carolina	0	0	1	1	0
Utah	0	0	0	1	0
Wyoming	0	0	0	1	0
Race					
White (non-Hispanic)	8	16	6	15	18
Black (non-Hispanic)	8	7	7	10	13
Hispanic	0	0	1	2	4
Native American	0	0	0	1	1
Unk. Hispanic origin	0	0	0	3	2

Source: For 1989–1991:   Greenfeld, Lawrence A. 1990–1992 (Annual). *Capital punishment.* Washington, D.C., Bureau of Justice Statistics, p. 2 [See appendix entry 21]

For 1992:   Greenfeld, Lawrence A., and James J. Stephan. 1993. *Capital punishment 1992.* Washington, D.C., Bureau of Justice Statistics, p. 2 [See appendix entry 21]

For 1993:   Stephan, James J., and Peter Brien. 1994. *Capital punishment 1993.* Washington, D.C., Bureau of Justice Statistics, p. 1. [See appendix entry 21]

1.36   Persons Executed, by Race and Method of Execution, 1977–1992

Means of Execution	White	Black	Hispanic	American Indian	Asian
Total	102	73	12	1	0
Lethal injection	47	23	11	1	0
Electrocution	50	47	1	0	0
Lethal gas	4	3	0	0	0
Firing squad	1	0	0	0	0

Source: Greenfeld, Lawrence A., and James J. Stephan. 1994. *Capital punishment 1992*. Washington, D.C.: Bureau of Justice Statistics, p. 10. [See appendix entry 21]

TRENDS: CITIES AND REGIONS

1.37 Homicide Rates, by Region, 1960–1991

Year	New England	Middle Atlantic	East North Central	West North Central	South Atlantic	East South Central	West South Central	Mountain	Pacific
1960	1.5	3.0	3.6	2.5	8.4	8.1	7.5	4.5	4.1
1961	1.4	3.2	3.8	2.6	7.9	8.5	7.2	4.3	3.8
1962	1.4	3.4	3.7	2.7	8.5	8.4	7.1	4.7	4.1
1963	1.9	3.4	3.7	3.0	8.4	8.8	7.2	4.5	3.9
1964	1.7	4.0	3.2	3.0	9.1	9.1	8.0	4.5	4.1
1965	2.2	4.0	4.2	3.4	9.3	9.5	7.7	4.4	4.9
1966	2.1	4.3	5.1	3.3	9.9	9.0	8.8	4.8	4.7
1967	2.7	5.0	6.0	4.1	11.1	9.9	10.2	5.3	5.5
1968	2.8	5.7	6.8	4.2	11.6	10.3	10.7	5.5	6.1
1969	2.8	5.9	7.1	4.5	11.8	11.1	11.0	5.4	6.8
1970	3.2	6.8	7.8	5.0	12.9	11.9	11.6	6.6	6.5
1971	3.4	8.3	8.7	4.6	13.7	12.8	12.6	6.5	7.4
1972	3.6	8.8	8.5	4.6	14.5	13.0	12.5	7.2	8.1
1973	3.9	9.0	8.6	5.0	15.1	13.0	13.3	7.7	8.2
1974	4.0	8.7	9.6	5.5	15.1	13.4	14.1	8.0	8.9
1975	3.9	8.8	9.2	5.8	14.1	13.9	13.3	8.1	9.4
1976	3.3	8.1	8.9	4.9	11.8	12.1	12.2	7.6	1.8
1977	3.4	8.0	8.7	5.4	11.1	12.1	13.1	8.1	10.1
1978	3.7	8.1	8.3	5.3	11.6	11.3	14.2	8.2	10.4
1979	3.6	9.2	9.1	5.8	12.5	12.1	16.1	8.3	11.3
1980	4.5	9.7	9.3	6.4	12.7	12.7	15.7	8.7	12.4
1981	4.1	9.6	8.9	5.9	12.5	11.7	15.5	8.5	11.3
1982	4.0	9.0	8.0	5.3	11.8	11.6	15.4	7.3	10.1
1983	3.5	8.2	7.6	4.5	10.1	9.5	13.5	6.6	9.3
1984	3.5	7.5	7.4	4.2	10.2	9.3	12.4	6.6	9.4
1985	3.5	7.3	7.6	4.4	10.0	9.6	12.1	6.6	9.4
1986	3.7	8.0	7.9	5.0	10.6	10.4	13.0	8.1	10.2
1987	3.7	8.1	7.8	4.9	10.9	9.9	11.2	6.7	9.6
1988	4.2	9.0	7.8	4.6	11.5	9.8	11.9	6.9	9.4
1989	4.3	9.3	7.9	4.7	12.1	9.8	12.2	6.7	9.7
1990	4.2	10.4	8.7	4.8	12.4	11.4	14.0	6.5	10.7
1991	4.4	10.1	9.2	5.7	12.3	11.9	15.2	7.2	11.3

Source: For 1960–1990: U.S. Department of Health and Human Services. 1963–1993 (Annual). *Vital statistics of the United States.* Volume II—Mortality, Part A. Hyattsville, Md.: Public Health Service, Table 1–W (1960), Table 1–P (1961), Table 1–13 (1962, 1963, 1966, 1979–1986), Table 1–14 (1964, 1967–1978, 1987–1989), Table 1–15 (1965) [See appendix entry 34]; For 1991: National Center for Health Statistics. 1993. *Public-use data tape and documentation: Mortality detail, 1991 data.* [Computer file]. Hyattsville, Md.: Public Health Service (homicides); U.S. Bureau of the Census. 1993. *Statistical abstract of the United States.* Washington, D.C.: p. 28, Table 31 (population). [See appendix entry 34]

Note: Includes homicides and legal interventions (ICD-9 codes E960–E978). Rates are per 100,000 residents. New England includes Maine, New Hampshire, Vermont, Massachusetts, Rhode Island, and Connecticut. Middle Atlantic includes New York, New Jersey, and Pennsylvania. East North Central includes Ohio, Indiana, Illinois, Michigan, and Wisconsin. West North Central includes Minnesota, Iowa, Missouri, North Dakota, South Dakota, Nebraska, and Kansas. South Atlantic includes Delaware, Maryland, District of Columbia, Virginia, West Virginia, North Carolina, South Carolina, Georgia, and Florida. East South Central includes Kentucky, Tennessee, Alabama, and Mississippi. West South Central includes Arkansas, Louisiana, Oklahoma, and Texas. Mountain includes Montana, Idaho, Wyoming, Colorado, New Mexico, Arizona, Utah, and Nevada. Pacific includes Washington, Oregon, California, Alaska, and Hawaii.

1.38   Homicides, by Region, 1960–1991

Year	New England	Middle Atlantic	East North Central	West North Central	South Atlantic	East South Central	West South Central	Mountain	Pacific
1960	153	1,016	1,296	391	2,186	974	1,263	310	875
1961	149	1,109	1,398	398	2,107	1,036	1,238	303	840
1962	153	1,188	1,367	416	2,313	1,040	1,261	352	923
1963	202	1,195	1,367	470	2,333	1,094	1,308	342	914
1964	192	1,441	1,191	480	2,566	1,158	1,470	347	969
1965	248	1,455	1,589	537	2,681	1,222	1,435	341	1,204
1966	241	1,593	1,981	530	2,900	1,156	1,660	373	1,172
1967	307	1,848	2,337	659	3,262	1,279	1,934	415	1,384
1968	323	2,120	2,706	670	3,482	1,349	2,052	432	1,552
1969	325	2,189	2,838	735	3,588	1,451	2,143	434	1,774
1970	374	2,540	3,145	821	3,946	1,523	2,236	546	1,717
1971	413	3,100	3,531	754	4,293	1,666	2,474	554	2,002
1972	432	3,322	3,448	764	4,616	1,708	2,504	640	2,204
1973	477	3,362	3,534	828	4,897	1,734	2,685	702	2,246
1974	483	3,232	3,908	917	5,013	1,796	2,900	749	2,467
1975	476	3,266	3,775	962	4,751	1,881	2,782	777	2,640
1976	407	3,038	3,652	818	4,011	1,656	2,581	745	2,646
1977	421	2,962	3,571	907	3,820	1,669	2,850	814	2,954
1978	451	2,989	3,403	908	4,015	1,582	3,128	854	3,102
1979	434	3,327	3,675	978	4,307	1,684	3,552	863	3,382
1980	546	3,542	3,805	1,077	4,628	1,852	3,652	962	3,903
1981	495	3,509	3,649	1,009	4,658	1,710	3,726	969	3,636
1982	486	3,262	3,270	903	4,470	1,704	3,836	856	3,286
1983	425	3,004	3,116	776	3,874	1,398	3,437	797	3,095
1984	437	2,762	3,036	732	3,978	1,375	3,203	805	3,182
1985	433	2,697	3,114	763	3,973	1,434	3,173	828	3,213
1986	464	2,938	3,254	880	4,293	1,577	3,449	1,022	3,585
1987	465	3,016	3,246	848	4,505	1,497	2,965	845	3,425
1988	535	3,366	3,232	810	4,843	1,499	3,155	895	3,449
1989	560	3,487	3,316	817	5,162	1,486	3,251	868	3,631
1990	551	3,884	3,606	840	5,335	1,726	3,709	852	4,111
1991	576	3,819	3,893	1,009	5,483	1,827	4,124	1,007	4,516

Source: U.S. Department of Health and Human Services. 1963–1993 (Annual). *Vital statistics of the United States.* Volume II–Mortality, Part A. Hyattsville, Md.: Public Health Service. Table 1-W (1960), Table 1-W (1960), Table 1-P (1961), Table 1-13 (1962, 1963, 1966, 1979–1986), Table 1-14 (1964, 1967–1978, 1987–1990), Table 1-15 (1965) [See appendix entry34]; National Center for Health Statistics. 1993. *Public-use data tape and documentation: Mortality detail, 1991 data.* [Computer file]. Hyattsville, Md.: Public Health Service. [See appendix entry 34]

Note: Includes homicides and legal interventions (ICD-9 codes E960–E978). New England includes Maine, New Hampshire, Vermont, Massachusetts, Rhode Island, and Connecticut. Middle Atlantic includes New York, New Jersey, and Pennsylvania. East North Central includes Ohio, Indiana, Illinois, Michigan, and Wisconsin. West North Central includes Minnesota, Iowa, Missouri, North Dakota, South Dakota, Nebraska, and Kansas. South Atlantic includes Delaware, Maryland, District of Columbia, Virginia, West Virginia, North Carolina, South Carolina, Georgia, and Florida. East South Central includes Kentucky, Tennessee, Alabama, and Mississippi. West South Central includes Arkansas, Louisiana, Oklahoma, and Texas. Mountain includes Montana, Idaho, Wyoming, Colorado, New Mexico, Arizona, Utah, and Nevada. Pacific includes Washington, Oregon, California, Alaska, and Hawaii.

1.39   Murder Rates, by City, 1960–1993: New York, Los Angeles, Chicago, Houston, Philadelphia

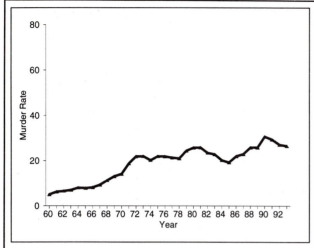

a) New York, New York

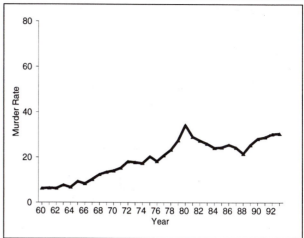

b) Los Angeles, California

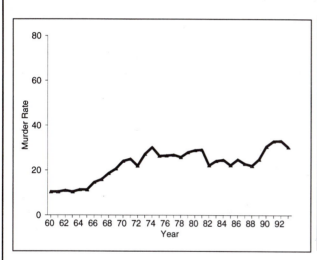

c) Chicago, Illinois

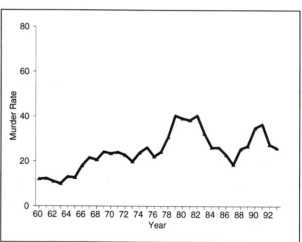

d) Houston, Texas

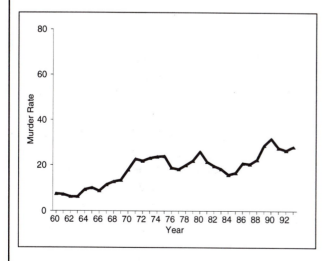

e) Philadelphia, Pennsylvania

Source: Monthly Return of Offenses Known to Police (Return A) from: Federal Bureau of Investigation. (Annual). *Crime in the United States.* Washington, D.C.: U.S. Government Printing Office. [See appendix entry 26]

Note: Rates are per 100,000 population. Murder includes non-negligent manslaughter. The five largest cities in the U.S. in 1990 were New York, Los Angeles, Chicago, Houston, and Philadelphia.

1.40   Murder Rates, by City, 1960–1993: San Diego, Detroit, Dallas, Phoenix, San Antonio

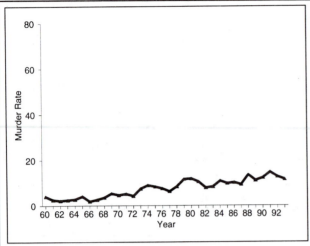

a) San Diego, California

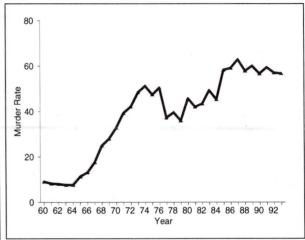

b) Detroit, Michigan

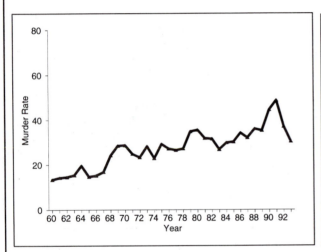

c) Dallas, Texas

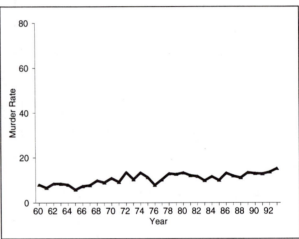

d) Phoenix, Arizona

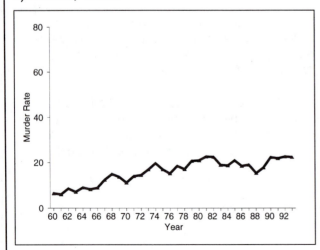

e) San Antonio, Texas

Source: Monthly Return of Offenses Known to Police (Return A) from: Federal Bureau of Investigation. (Annual). *Crime in the United States.* Washington, D.C.: U.S. Government Printing Office. [See appendix entry 26]
Note: Rates are per 100,000 population. Murder includes non-negligent manslaughter. The 6th through 10th largest cities in the U.S. in 1990 were San Diego, Detroit, Dallas, Phoenix, and San Antonio.

1.41   Murder Rates, by City, 1960–1993: San Jose, Indianapolis, Baltimore, San Francisco, Jacksonville

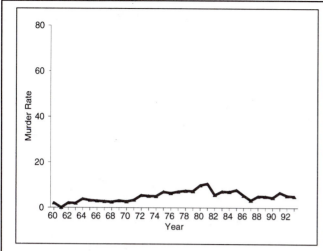

a) San Jose, California

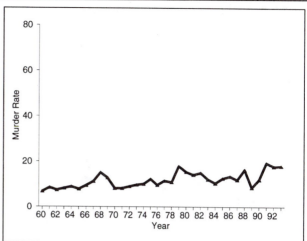

b) Indianapolis, Indiana

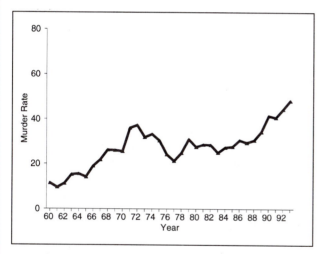

c) Baltimore, Maryland

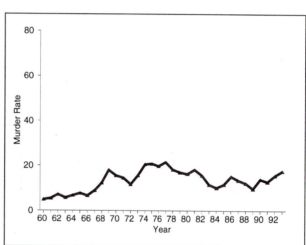

d) San Francisco, California

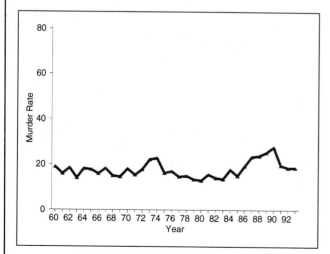

e) Jacksonville, Florida

Source: Monthly Return of Offenses Known to Police (Return A) from: Federal Bureau of Investigation. (Annual). *Crime in the United States.* Washington, D.c.: U.S. Government Printing Office. [See appendix entry 26]

Note: Rates are per 100,000 population. Murder includes non-negligent manslaughter. The 11th through 15th largest cities in the U.S. in 1990 were San Jose, Indianapolis, Baltimore, San Francisco, and Jacksonville.

1.42   Murder Rates, by City, 1960–1993: Columbus, Milwaukee, Memphis, Washington (D.C.), Boston

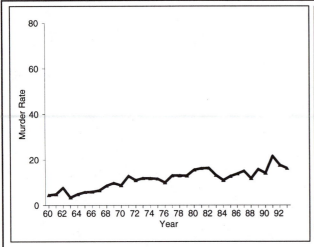

a) Columbus, Ohio

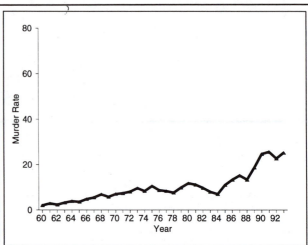

b) Milwaukee, Wisconsin

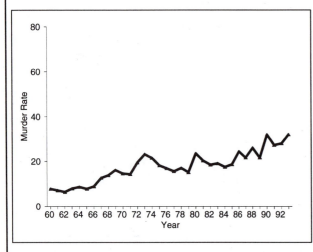

c) Memphis, Tennessee

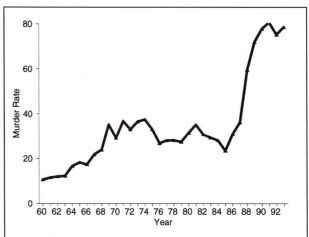

d) Washington, D.C.

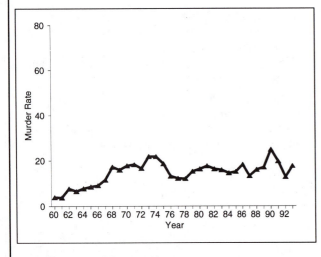

e) Boston, Massachusetts

Source: Monthly Return of Offenses Known to Police (Return A) from: Federal Bureau of Investigation. (Annual). *Crime in the United States.* Washington, D.C.: U.S. Government Printing Office. [See appendix entry 26]

Note: Rates are per 100,000 population. Murder includes non-negligent manslaughter. The 16th through 20th largest cities in the U.S. in 1990 were Columbus, Milwaukee, Memphis, Washington, and Boston.

1.43 Murder Rates, by City, 1960–1993: Seattle, El Paso, Nashville-Davidson, Cleveland, New Orleans

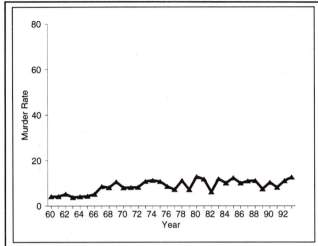

a) Seattle, Washington

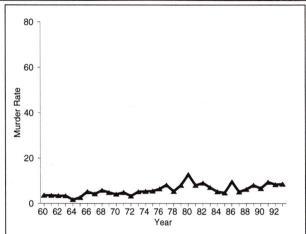

b) El Paso, Texas

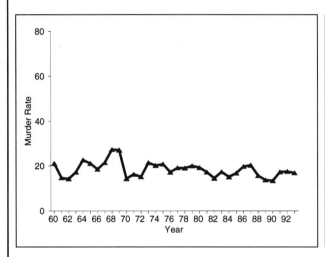

c) Nashville-Davidson, Tennessee

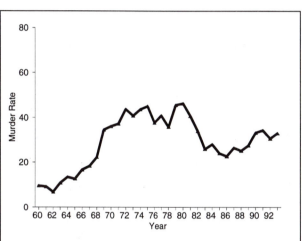

d) Cleveland, Ohio

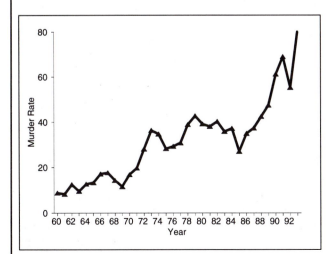

e) New Orleans, Louisiana

Source: Monthly Return of Offenses Known to Police (Return A) from: Federal Bureau of Investigation. (Annual). *Crime in the United States.* Washington, D.C.: U.S. Government Printing Office. [See appendix entry 26]

Note: Rates are per 100,000 population. Murder includes non-negligent manslaughter. The 21st through 25th largest cities in the U.S. in 1990 were Seattle, El Paso, Nashville-Davidson, Cleveland, and New Orleans.

Chapter 2
Other Interpersonal Violence in America

For every homicide there are at least 75 or more acts of violence that do not result in death. Homicides are like the tip of an iceberg. They are especially visible and widely publicized. Beneath them, however, is a much larger number of rapes, robberies, and assaults, many of which could have resulted in death had circumstances been slightly different. This chapter characterizes trends and patterns in the nonfatal rapes, robberies, and assaults.

DATA SOURCES

The data sources for this chapter are drawn from two independent, yet roughly parallel data sources: police records and victimization surveys.

The first source, police records, is compiled from reports of local law enforcement agencies submitted to the Federal Bureau of Investigation's Uniform Crime Reporting (UCR) program. Nonfatal violence is recorded on several UCR forms. The main form is called *Return A*, a monthly tally of the number of serious crimes occurring within a reporting jurisdiction. The FBI classifies nonfatal violent crimes as rapes, robberies, and aggravated assaults (see appendix, data source 26, for detailed definitions). In addition to Return A, police agencies are asked to submit a form entitled *Age, Sex, Race, and Ethnic Origin of Persons Arrested* (ASREO). The ASREO form counts the number of persons arrested by type of crime and by age/sex and age/race groups. It is the only UCR data available on rape, robbery, and assault offenders; even then it is limited to just these characteristics of arrested persons. The essential feature of all UCR forms on nonfatal violence, however, is that they contain monthly summaries of crime incidents reported to, or discovered by, police.

The second major data source are victimization surveys, principally the National Crime Victimization Survey (NCVS). Victimization surveys were developed, in part, to assess the incidence of crimes that may not have become known to police and to provide detailed characteristics that are not captured in the summary forms of the UCR. The NCVS (formerly the National Crime Survey, and before that, National Crime Panel) is conducted by the U.S. Bureau of the Census for the U.S. Bureau of Justice Statistics. In operation since 1973, the NCVS is a large, continuous survey of non-institutionalized persons at least 12 years old who are occupants of U.S. residential housing units. Violent victimizations are categorized as rapes, robberies, and assaults. As part of an extensive redesign process, NCVS data for 1993 provide better estimates of violence, especially rape and other sexual assaults. Because of the changes, 1993 data are not directly comparable with previous NCVS data (see appendix, data source 28, for details and definitions).

COMPARING UCR AND NCVS DATA

The UCR and the NCVS may provide substantially different pictures of the distributions of violence in the United States. For example, the trend in rape rates since 1973 in Figures 2.3 and 2.13 are very different. The reasons for the differences are complex (see Biderman and Lynch, 1991, for a discussion), but basically the systems produce different results because they are measuring different things. The Uniform Crime Report measures crimes that are recorded by law enforcement agencies, while the National Crime Victimization Survey measures crimes as reported by residents of households. They present complementary information that together provide a more comprehensive picture of the distribution of crime in the United States.

CHAPTER ORGANIZATION

The structure of the chapter is organized according to the crime definitions of the two data sources. There are three major sections, one each for rape, robbery, and assault. Within each section, there is a subsection presenting tables and figures by data source; estimates based on the Uniform Crime Reports appear first, followed by those based on the National Crime Victimization Survey. Although some tables in the UCR and NCVS subsections will present similar information, differences in the data sources allow different types of information to be presented. In particular, patterns and trends for states and geographic areas and data on persons arrested are presented in the UCR subsections. Patterns and trends from the NCVS provide information on detailed victim and incident characteristics not available in the UCR.

Regardless of the source, the consistent format of the chapter provides a comprehensive picture of nonfatal interpersonal violence in the general U.S. population.

REFERENCE

Biderman, Albert D., and James P. Lynch. 1991. *Understanding crime incidence statistics: Why the UCR diverges from the NCS.* New York: Springer-Verlag.

RAPE: UNIFORM CRIME REPORTS

Incidents

2.1 Forcible Rape, 1960–1993

Year	Rapes	Year	Rapes	Year	Rapes
1960	15,555	1972	46,431	1984	84,233
1961	16,012	1973	51,002	1985	87,340
1962	16,313	1974	55,209	1986	90,434
1963	16,404	1975	56,093	1987	91,111
1964	20,551	1976	56,730	1988	92,486
1965	22,467	1977	63,022	1989	94,504
1966	25,332	1978	67,131	1990	102,555
1967	27,096	1979	75,989	1991	106,593
1968	31,057	1980	82,088	1992	109,062
1969	36,470	1981	81,536	1993	104,806
1970	37,273	1982	77,763		
1971	41,888	1983	78,918		

Source: Monthly Return of Offenses Known to Police (Return A) from: Federal Bureau of Investigation. 1961–1994 (Annual). *Crime in the United States.* Washington, D.C.: U.S. Government Printing Office, Table 2 (1960–1965), Table 3 (1966–1983), Table 4 (1984–1993). [See appendix entry 26]

Note: By UCR definition, only women can be victims of forcible rape.

2.2 Forcible Rape Rates, 1960–1993

Year	Rate	Year	Rate	Year	Rate
1960	8.7	1972	22.3	1984	35.7
1961	8.8	1973	24.3	1985	36.6
1962	8.8	1974	26.1	1986	37.5
1963	8.7	1975	26.3	1987	37.4
1964	10.7	1976	26.4	1988	37.6
1965	11.6	1977	29.1	1989	38.1
1966	12.9	1978	30.8	1990	41.2
1967	13.7	1979	34.5	1991	42.3
1968	15.5	1980	36.4	1992	42.8
1969	18.1	1981	35.6	1993	40.6
1970	18.3	1982	33.6		
1971	20.3	1983	33.7		

Source: Monthly Return of Offenses Known to Police (Return A) from: Federal Bureau of Investigation. 1961–1994 (Annual). *Crime in the United States.* Washington, D.C.: U.S. Government Printing Office, Table 2 (1960–1965), Table 3 (1966–1983), Table 4 (1984–1993). [See appendix entry 26]

Note: By UCR definition, only women can be victims of forcible rape. Rates are per 100,000 residents.

2.3   Forcible Rape Rates, 1960–1993

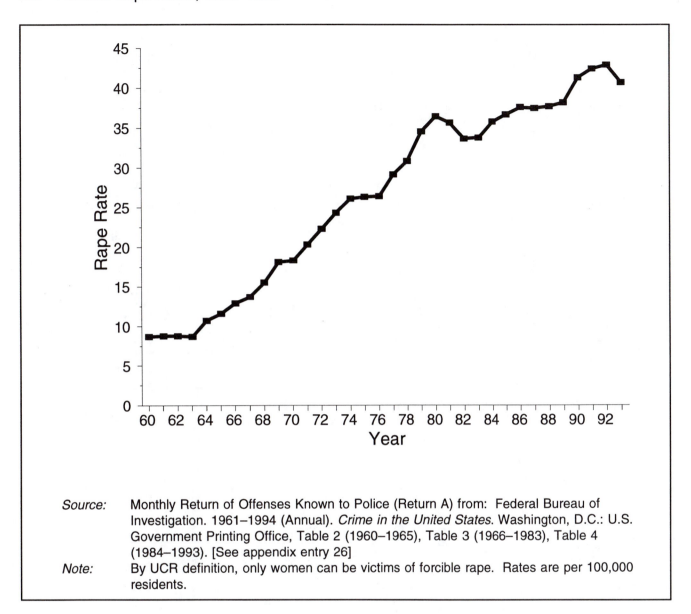

Source: Monthly Return of Offenses Known to Police (Return A) from: Federal Bureau of Investigation. 1961–1994 (Annual). *Crime in the United States.* Washington, D.C.: U.S. Government Printing Office, Table 2 (1960–1965), Table 3 (1966–1983), Table 4 (1984–1993). [See appendix entry 26]

Note: By UCR definition, only women can be victims of forcible rape. Rates are per 100,000 residents.

2.4 Forcible Rape, by Region, 1960–1993

Year	Northeast	Midwest	South	West	Year	Northeast	Midwest	South	West
1960	3,030	4,025	4,419	4,081	1977	11,182	14,326	20,554	16,960
1961	2,742	4,566	4,554	4,150	1978	11,307	14,849	22,711	18,264
1962	3,008	4,809	4,273	4,223	1979	12,681	17,213	25,881	20,214
1963	3,005	4,619	4,405	4,375	1980	13,231	17,767	28,810	22,280
1964	3,745	5,598	6,061	5,147	1981	13,421	16,924	29,074	22,117
1965	4,052	6,387	6,469	5,559	1982	12,584	15,744	28,748	20,687
1966	4,903	6,930	7,289	6,210	1983	12,887	18,253	27,356	20,422
1967	5,105	7,419	7,931	6,641	1984	13,862	19,451	30,379	20,541
1968	5,328	8,517	9,058	8,154	1985	14,227	19,885	32,401	20,827
1969	6,133	9,660	10,749	9,928	1986	14,143	21,024	33,670	21,597
1970	6,238	9,633	11,331	10,071	1987	14,725	22,106	32,958	21,322
1971	7,117	10,708	13,187	10,876	1988	14,727	22,957	33,847	20,955
1972	8,498	11,633	14,010	12,290	1989	14,380	23,468	34,807	21,849
1973	9,503	12,826	15,716	12,957	1990	14,713	25,393	38,776	23,673
1974	10,235	13,918	17,534	13,522	1991	14,748	27,373	39,364	25,108
1975	10,393	13,924	17,549	14,227	1992	15,089	27,639	40,631	25,703
1976	10,084	13,519	18,133	14,994	1993	14,567	25,831	40,387	24,021

Source: Monthly Return of Offenses Known to Police (Return A) from: Federal Bureau of Investigation. 1961–1994 (Annual). *Crime in the United States.* Washington, D.C.: U.S. Government Printing Office, Table 2 (1960–1965), Table 3 (1966–1983), Table 4 (1984–1993). [See appendix entry 26]

Note: By UCR definition, only women can be victims of forcible rape. From 1964–1983, the Midwest region was referred to as the North Central Region. For 1960–1963, the Northeast region was composed of the East North Central and West North Central regions; the Midwest region was composed of the New England and Middle Atlantic regions; the South region was composed of the South Atlantic, East South Central, and West South Central regions; and the West region was composed of the Mountain and Pacific regions.

2.5 Forcible Rape Rates, by Region, 1960–1993

Year	Northeast	Midwest	South	West
1960	6.8	7.8	8.0	14.5
1961	6.0	8.7	8.1	14.3
1962	6.6	9.1	7.5	13.9
1963	6.5	8.7	7.6	14.1
1964	7.9	10.5	10.2	16.3
1965	8.5	11.8	10.8	17.2
1966	10.2	12.8	12.0	19.0
1967	10.6	13.5	12.9	20.1
1968	11.0	15.3	14.5	24.3
1969	12.6	17.2	17.0	29.2
1970	12.7	17.0	18.0	28.9
1971	14.4	18.7	20.6	30.7
1972	17.1	20.2	21.6	34.1
1973	19.1	22.3	23.8	35.4
1974	20.7	24.2	26.1	36.3
1975	21.0	24.1	25.8	37.6
1976	20.4	23.4	26.3	38.9
1977	22.7	24.7	29.4	43.2
1978	23.0	25.5	32.2	45.5
1979	25.9	29.5	36.2	49.1
1980	27.0	30.3	38.5	51.9
1981	27.2	28.8	37.8	50.2
1982	25.4	26.7	36.8	46.0
1983	26.0	31.0	34.4	44.4
1984	27.9	32.9	37.7	43.9
1985	28.5	33.6	39.6	43.5
1986	28.3	35.4	40.6	44.3
1987	29.3	37.1	39.3	42.9
1988	29.1	38.3	39.9	41.6
1989	28.3	39.0	40.7	42.2
1990	29.0	42.6	45.4	44.8
1991	28.9	45.5	45.3	46.4
1992	29.5	45.5	46.1	46.6
1993	28.4	42.3	45.2	42.9

Source: Monthly Return of Offenses Known to Police (Return A) from: Federal Bureau of Investigation. 1961–1994 (Annual). *Crime in the United States.* Washington, D.C.: U.S. Government Printing Office, Table 2 (1960–1965), Table 3 (1966–1983), Table 4 (1984–1993). [See appendix entry 26]

Note: By UCR definition, only women can be victims of forcible rape. Rates are per 100,000 residents. From 1964–1983, the Midwest region was referred to as the North Central Region. For 1960–1963, the Northeast region was composed of the New England and Middle Atlantic regions; the Midwest region was composed of the East North Central and West North Central regions; the South region was broken down into the South Atlantic, East South Central, and West South Central regions; and the West region was divided into the Mountain and Pacific regions.

Arrest Trends

2.6   Forcible Rape Arrest Rates, by Age and Gender of Arrestee, Selected Years: 1965, 1970, 1975, 1980, 1985, 1990, 1992

Age Group	1965			1970		
	Total	Male	Female	Total	Male	Female
12 and under	0.3	0.7	*	0.3	0.6	*
13-14	7.8	15.4	*	9.0	17.7	*
15	18.9	37.1	*	23.2	45.4	*
16	27.3	53.7	*	30.8	60.5	*
17	31.3	61.8	*	38.9	76.5	*
18	37.7	75.1	*	44.3	88.1	*
19	44.6	90.2	*	44.2	89.4	*
20	37.7	76.5	*	41.5	85.9	*
21	40.2	82.3	*	40.7	85.1	*
22	32.3	66.0	*	38.0	78.2	*
23	31.4	64.4	*	34.4	70.2	*
24	26.6	54.4	*	34.5	70.5	*
25-29	20.3	41.5	*	24.9	50.6	*
30-34	13.0	26.4	*	15.8	32.3	*
35-39	7.7	15.8	*	10.0	20.4	*
40-44	4.9	10.0	*	5.4	11.1	*
45-49	2.5	5.2	*	3.2	6.6	*
50-54	1.8	3.6	*	1.9	4.0	*
55-59	0.9	1.8	*	1.0	2.1	*
60-64	0.6	1.3	*	0.7	1.4	*
65 and over	0.2	0.6	*	0.3	0.7	*

See notes at end of table.

2.6 Forcible Rape Arrest Rates, by Age and Gender of Arrestee, Selected Years: 1965, 1970, 1975, 1980, 1985, 1990, 1992 *(continued)*

Age Group	1975			1980		
	Total	Male	Female	Total	Male	Female
12 and under	0.5	1.0	*	0.5	0.9	*
13-14	10.0	19.2	*	12.7	24.4	*
15	21.8	42.1	*	22.6	43.1	*
16	28.4	55.0	*	29.4	56.5	*
17	35.6	69.1	*	38.8	75.3	*
18	42.3	82.8	*	43.8	85.7	*
19	41.2	81.2	*	42.1	83.3	*
20	42.8	85.0	*	43.9	86.9	*
21	41.0	81.3	*	46.0	90.9	*
22	38.8	77.2	*	41.9	82.3	*
23	36.0	71.7	*	42.2	84.2	*
24	36.2	72.1	*	42.1	83.6	*
25-29	29.7	59.3	*	31.2	62.3	*
30-34	19.2	38.6	*	22.1	44.5	*
35-39	14.1	28.7	*	16.4	33.3	*
40-44	8.1	16.4	*	11.3	23.0	*
45-49	4.7	9.5	*	6.5	13.3	*
50-54	2.6	5.5	*	3.6	7.4	*
55-59	1.4	2.9	*	2.3	4.9	*
60-64	0.9	1.9	*	1.2	2.5	*
65 and over	0.3	0.6	*	0.5	1.2	*

See notes at end of table.

2.6 Forcible Rape Arrest Rates, by Age and Gender of Arrestee, Selected Years: 1965, 1970, 1975, 1980, 1985, 1990, 1992 *(continued)*

Age Group	1985			1990		
	Total	Male	Female	Total	Male	Female
12 and under	1.3	2.3	*	1.2	2.3	*
13-14	21.2	40.4	*	23.3	44.3	*
15	30.6	58.8	*	34.0	65.1	*
16	32.4	62.4	*	39.9	76.7	*
17	39.4	76.2	*	43.2	82.9	*
18	42.6	83.3	*	50.6	98.4	*
19	39.9	78.9	*	43.2	83.9	*
20	41.9	82.6	*	42.1	81.6	*
21	42.2	83.5	*	44.0	85.2	*
22	40.5	80.4	*	43.8	85.2	*
23	39.0	77.6	*	42.1	82.3	*
24	38.7	76.5	*	39.4	77.2	*
25-29	34.2	67.7	*	35.1	69.2	*
30-34	25.5	50.7	*	28.3	56.0	*
35-39	19.2	38.5	*	18.9	37.7	*
40-44	14.1	28.5	*	12.4	24.9	*
45-49	9.5	19.4	*	8.7	17.6	*
50-54	6.1	12.4	*	6.2	12.8	*
55-59	3.8	8.0	*	3.9	8.1	*
60-64	2.4	5.1	*	2.5	5.4	*
65 and over	0.9	2.3	*	1.0	2.4	*

See notes at end of table.

2.6 Forcible Rape Arrest Rates, by Age and Gender of Arrestee, Selected Years: 1965, 1970, 1975, 1980, 1985, 1990, 1992 *(continued)*

Age Group	1992 Total	Male	Female
12 and under	1.5	2.8	*
13-14	23.2	44.0	*
15	32.0	60.9	*
16	39.2	75.5	*
17	40.9	78.2	*
18	50.2	97.1	*
19	42.6	82.4	*
20	41.1	79.9	*
21	40.4	78.2	*
22	39.5	76.6	*
23	35.1	68.2	*
24	36.0	70.4	*
25-29	31.5	62.0	*
30-34	26.1	51.6	*
35-39	18.9	37.6	*
40-44	12.5	25.1	*
45-49	8.3	16.8	*
50-54	5.7	11.7	*
55-59	4.0	8.2	*
60-64	2.5	5.3	*
65 and over	1.1	2.6	*

Source: Age, Sex, Race, and Ethnic Origin of Persons Arrested, 1965–1992, from: Federal Bureau of Investigation. 1993. *Age-specific arrest rates and race-specific arrest rates for selected offenses 1965–1992.* Washington, D.C.: U.S. Government Printing Office, pp. 29–33. [See appendix entry 1]

Note: Rates are per 100,000 persons.
   *   Rates are less than 0.05.

2.7   Juvenile and Adult Arrest Rates for Forcible Rape, Total and by Gender, 1965–1992

Year	Under 18			18 and Over		
	Total	Male	Female	Total	Male	Female
1965	4.9	9.7	0.0	10.5	21.9	0.0
1966	4.9	9.6	0.0	11.3	23.6	0.0
1967	5.2	10.2	0.0	11.5	24.1	0.0
1968	5.4	10.7	0.0	11.6	24.5	0.0
1969	6.3	12.3	0.0	13.0	27.4	0.0
1970	6.5	12.8	0.0	12.9	27.2	0.0
1971	6.9	13.6	0.0	13.4	28.3	0.0
1972	7.2	14.2	0.0	14.7	30.9	0.0
1973	7.9	15.4	0.0	15.4	32.3	0.0
1974	8.4	16.2	0.3	15.9	33.2	0.2
1975	7.1	13.6	0.2	15.2	31.7	0.3
1976	7.5	14.4	0.3	15.8	32.9	0.2
1977	7.7	14.8	0.3	16.4	34.2	0.2
1978	7.8	15.0	0.3	16.7	34.8	0.2
1979	8.4	16.2	0.2	17.6	36.7	0.2
1980	7.7	14.8	0.3	17.3	36.2	0.2
1981	7.8	14.9	0.3	16.9	35.3	0.2
1982	8.2	15.8	0.3	17.7	36.8	0.3
1983	8.2	15.8	0.2	17.5	36.4	0.3
1984	9.1	17.6	0.2	18.4	38.2	0.3
1985	9.3	17.9	0.4	18.4	38.1	0.3
1986	9.5	18.3	0.4	18.3	37.9	0.3
1987	9.3	17.7	0.4	17.6	36.5	0.3
1988	8.6	16.4	0.3	17.7	36.6	0.4
1989	9.1	17.4	0.4	17.4	36.0	0.3
1990	9.4	18.1	0.3	18.5	38.2	0.4
1991	9.7	18.6	0.4	16.0	37.5	0.4
1992	9.3	17.8	0.4	16.9	34.9	0.4

Source: Age, Sex, Race, and Ethnic Origin of Persons Arrested, 1965–1992, from: Federal Bureau of Investigation. 1993. *Age-specific arrest rates and race-specific arrest rates for selected offenses 1965–1992*. Washington, D.C.: U.S. Government Printing Office, p. 158. [See appendix entry 1]

Note: Rates are per 100,000 persons.

2.8   Average Age of Forcible Rape Arrestees, 1965–1992

Year	Age	Year	Age
1965	24.74	1979	26.18
1966	24.82	1980	26.49
1967	24.77	1981	26.78
1968	24.63	1982	26.78
1969	24.54	1983	27.31
1970	24.57	1984	27.84
1971	24.52	1985	27.98
1972	24.76	1986	27.88
1973	25.06	1987	27.94
1974	25.01	1988	28.27
1975	25.52	1989	28.34
1976	25.71	1990	28.25
1977	26.02	1991	28.17
1978	26.43	1992	28.57

Source: Age, Sex, Race, and Ethnic Origin of Persons Arrested, 1965–1992, from: Federal Bureau of Investigation. 1993. *Age-specific arrest rates and race-specific arrest rates for selected offenses 1965–1992*. Washington, D.C.: U.S. Government Printing Office, p. 169. [See appendix entry 1]

Note: Because arrestee's age is reported by age group and not by specific age, the FBI computes "average age" as a weighted sum over all age intervals (p. 208).

2.9 Forcible Rape Arrest Rates, by Race, 1965–1992

Year	All Races	White	Nonwhite
1965	8.0	4.4	34.7
1966	8.5	4.9	35.0
1967	8.9	5.1	36.5
1968	9.3	5.5	36.9
1969	10.7	5.8	45.2
1970	10.8	6.2	43.6
1971	11.1	6.1	46.3
1972	10.1	5.9	39.0
1973	12.5	7.2	48.3
1974	12.8	7.4	49.1
1975	12.0	7.6	41.0
1976	12.9	7.5	47.6
1977	13.9	8.0	51.8
1978	14.1	7.8	54.1
1979	14.9	8.6	54.7
1980	14.6	8.6	51.5
1981	14.4	8.5	50.1
1982	15.1	8.6	53.3
1983	15.0	8.8	51.3
1984	15.9	9.5	52.5
1985	15.9	9.6	51.4
1986	15.9	9.5	51.5
1987	15.5	9.2	50.0
1988	15.2	9.3	46.7
1989	15.3	9.4	46.6
1990	16.1	10.5	45.1
1991	16.0	10.4	44.1
1992	15.6	10.3	42.2

Source: Age, Sex, Race, and Ethnic Origin of Persons Arrested, 1965–1992, from: Federal Bureau of Investigation. 1993. *Age-specific arrest rates and race-specific arrest rates for selected offenses 1965–1992*. Washington, D.C.: U.S. Government Printing Office, p. 173. [See appendix entry 1]

Note: Rates are per 100,000 persons.

2.10   Juvenile and Adult Arrest Rates for Forcible Rape, Total and by Race, 1965–1992

Year	Under 18			18 and Over		
	Total	White	Nonwhite	Total	White	Nonwhite
1965	4.6	1.8	21.2	9.9	5.7	45.2
1966	4.5	2.0	19.3	10.8	6.5	47.0
1967	4.9	2.3	20.0	11.1	6.6	48.9
1968	5.4	2.6	21.5	11.4	6.9	48.4
1969	6.2	2.8	25.8	13.0	7.3	59.4
1970	6.6	3.0	26.8	13.0	7.7	55.6
1971	6.5	3.0	25.6	13.5	7.6	60.8
1972	5.7	2.6	22.9	12.2	7.4	49.9
1973	7.3	3.7	27.0	14.9	8.8	62.4
1974	7.8	4.2	26.6	15.2	8.8	63.6
1975	6.5	3.9	19.9	14.5	9.2	54.1
1976	7.2	3.8	24.2	15.4	9.1	61.8
1977	7.8	4.1	26.1	16.5	9.6	66.8
1978	7.8	3.9	26.9	16.7	9.3	69.5
1979	8.4	4.3	28.2	17.5	10.2	69.3
1980	7.7	4.0	25.2	17.3	10.3	65.6
1981	7.8	3.9	25.3	17.0	10.1	63.2
1982	8.2	4.2	26.1	17.7	10.2	67.4
1983	8.2	4.1	25.9	17.6	10.4	64.2
1984	9.1	4.9	27.5	18.4	11.1	65.0
1985	9.2	5.3	26.0	18.2	11.0	63.8
1986	9.4	5.1	27.7	18.2	11.0	63.1
1987	9.3	4.9	27.8	17.7	10.6	60.7
1988	8.4	5.0	22.5	17.5	10.7	58.4
1989	9.1	5.6	23.3	17.4	10.6	57.7
1990	9.5	6.1	23.0	18.4	12.0	55.5
1991	9.8	6.8	21.5	18.1	11.7	54.7
1992	9.6	6.3	22.7	17.6	11.6	51.3

Source: Age, Sex, Race, and Ethnic Origin of Persons Arrested, 1965–1992, from: Federal Bureau of Investigation. 1993. *Age-specific arrest rates and race-specific arrest rates for selected offenses 1965–1992.* Washington, D.C.: U.S. Government Printing Office, p. 182. [See appendix entry 1]

Note: Rates are per 100,000 persons.

RAPE: NATIONAL CRIME VICTIMIZATION SURVEY

Incidents

2.11   Rapes, 1973–1992

Year	Female	Total	Year	Female	Total
1973	151,700	155,730	1983	137,900	154,170
1974	159,400	163,010	1984	164,480	179,890
1975	146,400	153,740	1985	130,850	138,490
1976	129,300	145,190	1986	122,200	129,940
1977	141,900	154,240	1987	134,300	148,450
1978	153,000	171,050	1988	119,780	127,370
1979	171,200	191,740	1989	122,740	135,410
1980	151,400	173,770	1990	106,660	130,260
1981	169,700	177,540	1991	153,120	174,010
1982	140,500	152,570	1992	83,080*	140,930

Source: National Crime Victimization Survey, 1973–1992, from: Bureau of Justice Statistics. 1994. *Criminal victimization in the United States:1973–1992 Trends.* Washington, D.C., p. 19, Table 6. [See appendix entry 28]

Note: Total includes rapes of males and females aged 12 years and over. Series crimes are excluded. Series crime and other crime types are defined in the appendix.

* Expressed as a rate, the number of 1992 female rapes is not statistically different from any annual rape rate measured in the preceding 10 years (Bureau of Justice Statistics. 1994. *Criminal victimization in the United States, 1992.* Washington, D.C., p. 5).

2.12   Rape Rates, 1973–1992

Year	Female	Total	Year	Female	Total
1973	1.8	0.9	1983	1.4	0.8
1974	1.8	1.0	1984	1.6	0.9
1975	1.7	0.9	1985	1.3	0.7
1976	1.4	0.8	1986	1.2	0.7
1977	1.6	0.9	1987	1.3	0.8
1978	1.7	1.0	1988	1.2	0.6
1979	1.8	1.1	1989	1.2	0.7
1980	1.6	0.9	1990	1.0	0.6
1981	1.8	1.0	1991	1.4	0.9
1982	1.4	0.8	1992	0.8*	0.7

Source: National Crime Victimization Survey, 1973–1992, from: Bureau of Justice Statistics. 1994. *Criminal victimization in the United States:1973–1992 Trends.* Washington, D.C., p. 19, Table 6. [See appendix entry 28]

Note: Female rates are per 1,000 females aged 12 or more; total rates are per 1,000 males and females aged 12 years or more.

* The 1992 female rape rate is not statistically different from any annual rape rate measured in the preceding 10 years (Bureau of Justice Statistics. 1994. *Criminal victimization in the United States, 1992.* Washington, D.C., p. 5).

2.13   Female Rape Rates, 1973–1992

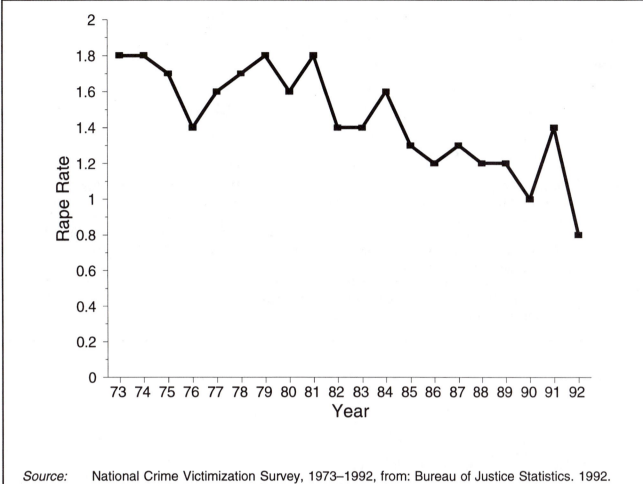

Source: National Crime Victimization Survey, 1973–1992, from: Bureau of Justice Statistics. 1992. *Criminal victimization in the United States:1973–1992 Trends.* Washington, D.C., p. 19, Table 6. [See appendix entry 28]

Note: Rates are per 1,000 persons aged 12 years or more. Series crimes are excluded. Series crime and other crime types are defined in the appendix. The 1992 female rape rate is not statistically different from any annual rape rate measured in the preceding 10 years (Bureau of Justice Statistics. 1994. *Criminal victimization in the United States, 1992.* Washington, D.C., p. 5).

2.14 Rape Rates, by Region, 1987–1992

	All Regions	Northeast	Midwest	South	West
1987	0.8	0.7	0.8	0.8	0.7
1988	0.6	0.6	0.8	0.5	0.7
1989	0.7	0.5	1.0	0.6	0.7
1990	0.6	0.3*	0.5	0.7	0.9
1991	0.9	0.9	0.6*	0.9	0.9
1992	0.7	0.6*	0.9	0.4*	1.0*

Source: National Crime Victimization Survey, 1987–1992, from: Bureau of Justice Statistics. 1989–1994 (Annual). *Criminal victimization in the United States.* Washington, D.C.: Table 19 (1988), Table 20 (1989), Table 21 (1990, 1992). Data published in this source for 1987 and 1991 were found by the Bureau of Justice Statistics (BJS) to contain minor errors. The editors have replaced them with unpublished data provided by Lisa Bastian, BJS statistician. [See appendix entry 28]

Note: Rates are per 1,000 persons aged 12 years or more. Series crimes are excluded. Series crime and other crime types are defined in the appendix.

* Estimate is based on 10 or fewer sample cases.

Characteristics of the Victim

2.15 Rapes of Females, by Age of Victim, 1993

	12-15	16-19	20-24	25-34	35-49	50 & Over	All Ages
Rape completed	9,380*	33,250	43,020	51,560	30,520	6,190*	173,910
Rape attempted	26,950*	21,280*	19,510*	7,820*	25,670	3,920*	105,150
Other sexual assault†	33,890	28,570	33,500	20,260*	19,280*	2,030*	137,530
Unwanted sexual assault without force‡	25,620*	30,560	51,010	33,650	25,560	10,100*	176,500
Verbal threat of rape or sexual assault	4,440*	8,040*	3,770*	8,770*	20,140*	1,930*	47,090
Total	100,280	121,690	150,800	122,060	121,170	24,160*	640,170

Source: National Crime Victimization Survey, 1993 preliminary data from: Bureau of the Census. 1995. *National crime victimization survey, 1992–1993.* [Computer files]. Suitland, Md. [See appendix entry 28]

Note: Data for 1993 are not comparable to previous years due to changes in the survey. Table includes series crimes. Series crime and other crime types are defined in the appendix. Detail may not add to total due to rounding.

* Estimate is based on 10 or fewer sample cases.

† Sexual attacks other than rape involving injury or force.

‡ No force, injury, or weapons involved.

2.16 Female Rape Rates, by Age of Victim, 1993

	12-15	16-19	20-24	25-34	35-49	50 & Over	All Ages
Rape completed	1.3*	4.8	4.6	2.4	1.1	0.2*	1.6
Rape attempted	3.7*	3.1*	2.1*	0.4*	0.9	0.1*	1.0
Other sexual assault†	4.6	4.2	3.6	1.0*	0.7*	0.1*	1.3
Unwanted sexual assault without force‡	3.5*	4.5	5.4	1.6	0.9	0.3*	1.6
Verbal threat of rape or sexual assault	0.6*	1.2*	0.4*	0.4*	0.7*	0.1*	0.4
Total	13.7	17.7	16.1	5.8	4.2	0.7*	5.9

Source: National Crime Victimization Survey, 1993 preliminary data from: Bureau of the Census. 1995. *National crime victimization survey, 1992–1993.* [Computer files]. Suitland, Md. [See appendix entry 28]

Note: Rates are per 1,000 females aged 12 years or more. Table includes series crimes. Series crime and other crime types are defined in the appendix. Data for 1993 are not comparable to previous years due to changes in the survey. Detail may not add up to total due to rounding.

* Estimate is based on 10 or fewer sample cases.

† Sexual attacks other than rape involving injury or force.

‡ No force, injury, or weapons involved.

2.17 Rapes of Females, by Race and Age of Victim, 1993

	12-15	16-19	20-24	25-34	35-49	50 & Over	All Ages
White							
All rapes/sexual assaults	73,160	104,100	121,580	114,010	100,640	24,160*	537,660
Rape completed	9,380*	26,550*	28,370	43,510	18,270*	6,190*	132,280
Rape attempted	11,860*	18,250*	19,510*	7,820*	21,510*	3,920*	82,860
Other sexual attacks†	26,490	28,570	30,340	20,260*	19,280*	2,030*	126,960
Unwanted sexual assault without force‡	21,000*	25,490*	39,590*	33,650	23,490*	10,100*	153,320
Verbal threat of rape or sexual assault	4,440*	5,230*	3,770*	8,770*	18,090*	1,930*	42,230
Black							
All rapes/sexual assaults	20,550*	12,510*	26,940*	4,610*	16,410*	0*	81,020
Rape completed	0*	6,690*	12,370*	4,610*	12,240*	0*	35,920
Rape attempted	15,090*	3,030*	0*	0*	4,170*	0*	22,290*
Other sexual attacks†	3,050*	0*	3,160*	0*	0*	0*	6,210*
Unwanted sexual assault without force‡	2,410*	2,790*	11,410*	0*	0*	0*	16,610*
Verbal threat of rape or sexual assault	0*	0*	0*	0*	0*	0*	0*

Source: National Crime Victimization Survey, 1993 preliminary data from: Bureau of the Census. 1995. *National crime victimization survey, 1992–1993.* [Computer files]. Suitland, Md. [See appendix entry 28]

Note: Table includes series crimes. Series crime and other crime types are defined in the appendix. Data for 1993 are not comparable to previous years due to changes in the survey.

* Estimate is based on 10 or fewer sample cases.
† Sexual attacks other than rape involving injury or force.
‡ No force, injury, or weapons involved.

2.18   Female Rape Rates, by Race and Age of Victim, 1993

	12-15	16-19	20-24	25-34	35-49	50 & Over	All Ages
White							
All rapes/sexual assaults	12.6	18.9	16.1	6.6	4.1	0.8*	5.9
Rape completed	1.6*	4.8*	3.8	2.5	0.8*	0.2*	1.4
Rape attempted	2.0*	3.3*	2.6*	0.5*	0.9*	0.1*	0.9
Other sexual attacks†	4.6	5.2	4.0	1.2*	0.8*	0.1*	1.4
Unwanted sexual assault without force‡	3.6*	4.6*	5.2*	1.9	1.0*	0.3*	1.7
Verbal threat of rape or sexual assault	0.8*	1.0*	0.5*	0.5*	0.7*	0.1*	0.5
Black							
All rapes/sexual assaults	16.6*	11.7*	19.1*	1.5*	4.5*	0.0*	0.9
Rape completed	0.0*	6.2*	8.8*	1.5*	3.4*	0.0*	0.4
Rape attempted	12.2*	2.8*	0.0*	0.0*	1.2*	0.0*	0.2*
Other sexual attacks†	2.5*	0.0*	2.2*	0.0*	0.0*	0.0*	0.1*
Unwanted sexual assault without force‡	2.0*	2.6*	8.1*	0.0*	0.0*	0.0*	0.2*
Verbal threat of rape or sexual assault	0.0*	0.0*	0.0*	0.0*	0.0*	0.0*	0.0*

Source: National Crime Victimization Survey, 1993 preliminary data from: Bureau of the Census. 1995. *National crime victimization survey, 1992-1993*. [Computer files]. Suitland, Md. [See appendix entry 28]

Note: Rates are per 1,000 persons aged 12 years or more. Table includes series crimes. Series crime and other crime types are defined in the appendix. Data for 1993 are not comparable to previous years due to changes in the survey. Detail may not add up to total due to rounding.

*   Estimate is based on 10 or fewer sample cases.

†   Sexual attacks other than rape involving injury or force.

‡   No force, injury, or weapons involved.

2.19 Rapes, by Race and Gender of Victim, 1993

	Male			Female			Total		
	White	Black	Total‡	White	Black	Total‡	White	Black	Total‡
Rapes and sexual attacks	35,940	3,900*	41,930	342,110	64,420	416,590	378,040	68,320	458,520
Rape completed	5,950*	0*	8,050*	132,280	35,920	173,910	138,230	35,920	181,960
Rape attempted	7,980*	940*	8,920*	82,860	22,290*	105,150	90,840	23,230*	114,070
Other sexual attacks†	22,010*	2,960*	24,960*	126,970	6,210*	137,530	148,970	9,170*	162,490
Unwanted sexual assault without force§	9,920*	0*	9,920*	153,320	16,610*	176,500	163,240	16,610*	186,420
Verbal threat of rape or sexual assault	4,440*	0*	4,440*	42,230	0*	47,090	46,680	0*	51,530

Source: National Crime Victimization Survey, 1993 preliminary data from: Bureau of the Census. 1995. *National crime victimization survey, 1992–1993.* [Computer files]. Suitland, Md. [See appendix entry 28]

Note: Table includes series crimes. Series crime and other crime types are defined in the appendix. Data for 1993 are not comparable to previous years due to changes in the survey. Detail may not add up to total due to rounding.

    * Estimate is based on 10 or fewer sample cases.

    † Sexual attacks other than rape involving injury or force.

    ‡ Total includes races other than black and white.

    § No force, injury, or weapons involved.

2.20 Rape Rates, by Race and Gender of Victim, 1993

	Male			Female			Total		
	White	Black	Total‡	White	Black	Total‡	White	Black	Total‡
Rapes and sexual attacks	0.5	0.3*	0.4	3.7	4.7	3.9	2.1	2.7	2.2
Rape completed	0.1*	0.0*	0.1*	1.4	2.6	1.6	0.8	1.4	0.9
Rape attempted	0.1*	0.1*	0.1*	0.9	1.6*	1.0	0.5	0.9*	0.5
Other sexual attacks†	0.3*	0.3*	0.2*	1.4	0.5*	1.3	0.8	0.4*	0.6
Unwanted sexual assault without force§	0.1*	0.0*	0.1*	1.7	1.2*	1.6	0.9	0.7*	0.9
Verbal threat of rape or sexual assault	0.1*	0.0*	0.0*	0.5	0.0*	0.4	0.3	0.0*	0.3

Source: National Crime Victimization Survey, 1993 preliminary data from: Bureau of the Census. 1995. *National crime victimization survey, 1992–1993.* [Computer files]. Suitland, Md. [See appendix entry 28]

Note: Rates are per 1,000 persons aged 12 years or more. Table includes series crimes. Series crime and other crime types are defined in the appendix. Data for 1993 are not comparable to previous years due to changes in the survey. Detail may not add up to total due to rounding.

  * Estimate is based on 10 or fewer sample cases.
  † Sexual attacks other than rape involving injury or force.
  ‡ Total includes races other than black and white.
  § No force, injury, or weapons involved.

Victim-Offender Relationship

2.21   Percentage of Rapes, by Strangers and Nonstrangers, 1993

Type of Violence	Total Number of Victimizations	% Involving Strangers	% Involving Nonstrangers
Completed rape	181,960	17.3*	81.3
Attempted rape	114,070	20.6	79.4
Other sexual attacks with injury	62,710	27.0*	73.0
Other sexual attacks without injury	99,780	17.7*	80.1
Unwanted sexual contact without force	186,420	34.2	61.4
Verbal threat of rape or sexual assault	51,530	38.2*	61.8

Source: National Crime Victimization Survey, 1993 preliminary data from: Bureau of the Census. 1995. *National crime victimization survey, 1992–1993*. [Computer files]. Suitland, Md. [See appendix entry 28]

Note: Victimizations in which the relationship between victim and offender was unknown are excluded. Table includes series crimes. Series crime and other crime types are defined in the appendix. Data for 1993 are not comparable to previous years due to changes in the survey. Detail in tables may not add up to total due to rounding.

*   Estimate based on 10 or fewer sample cases.

2.22   Percentage of Rapes Involving Strangers, by Gender and Race of Victim, 1993

	Male				Female			
	Total	White	Black	Other	Total	White	Black	Other
Rape total	36.1*	36.8*	100.0*	0.0*	18.8	15.3	36.8*	0.0*
Completed rape	40.4*	54.7*	0.0*	0.0*	16.2	8.7*	46.6*	0.0*
Attempted rape	45.3*	38.9*	100.0*	0.0*	18.5*	17.8*	20.9*	0.0*
Other sexual attack with injury	23.1*	23.1*	0.0*	0.0*	27.7*	27.7*	0.0*	0.0*
Other sexual attack without injury	35.8*	43.9*	0.0*	0.0*	14.3*	16.3*	0.0*	0.0*
Unwanted sexual contact without force	75.3*	75.3*	0.0*	0.0*	31.9	29.8	51.4*	31.5*
Verbal threat of rape or sexual assault	48.8*	48.8*	0.0*	0.0*	37.2*	36.6*	0.0*	42.2*

Source: National Crime Victimization Survey, 1993 preliminary data from: Bureau of the Census. 1995. *National crime victimization survey, 1992–1993*. [Computer files]. Suitland, Md. [See appendix entry 28]

Note: Table includes series crimes. Series crime and other crime types are defined in the appendix. Data for 1993 are not comparable to previous years due to changes in the survey.

*   Estimate based on 10 or fewer sample cases.

2.23 Percentage of Single-Offender Rapes, by Victim-Offender Relationship, 1993

Relationship of Offender to Victim in Single-Offender Victimizations	Completed Rape	Attempted Rape	Other Sexual Attack With Injury	Other Sexual Attack Without Injury	Verbal Threat of Rape or Sexual Assault
Related					
Spouse	13.7	0.0*	14.2*	0.0*	4.9*
Ex-spouse	5.1*	19.6*	0.0*	2.1*	0.0*
Parent	0.0*	1.8*	9.1*	0.0*	0.0*
Own child	0.0*	0.0*	0.0*	0.0*	0.0*
Sibling	0.0*	0.0*	0.0*	0.0*	0.0*
Other relative	2.6*	4.7*	0.0*	0.0*	0.0*
Well known, not related†	39.5	32.4	42.8*	43.5	44.9*
Casual acquaintance	28.5	19.6*	15.0*	37.9	10.2*
Stranger	10.6	21.9	18.9	16.5	40.0

Source: National Crime Victimization Survey, 1993 preliminary data from: Bureau of the Census. 1995. *National crime victimization survey, 1992–1993.* [Computer files]. Suitland, Md. [See appendix entry 28]

Note: Table includes series crimes. Series crime and other crime types are defined in the appendix. Data for 1993 are not comparable to previous years due to changes in the survey.

* Estimate is based on 10 or fewer sample cases.

† Includes data on offenders well known to the victim whose relationship could not be ascertained.

2.24 Percentage of Multiple-Offender Rapes, by Victim-Offender Relationship, 1993

	Total	Completed Rape	Attempted Rape	Other Sexual Assault with Injury	Other Sexual Assault Without Injury	Verbal Threat of Rape or Sexual Assault
Related	0.0*	0.0*	0.0*	0.0*	0.0*	0.0*
Well known, not related†	0.0*	0.0*	0.0*	0.0*	0.0*	0.0*
Casual acquaintance	20.2*	0.0*	65.7*	28.1*	0.0*	29.7*
Strangers	72.4	84.3*	34.3*	71.9*	67.3*	70.3*
Number of offenders unknown or not specified	7.4*	15.7*	0.0*	0.0*	32.7*	0.0*

Source: National Crime Victimization Survey, 1993 preliminary data from: Bureau of the Census. 1995. *National crime victimization survey, 1992–1993.* [Computer files]. Suitland, Md. [See appendix entry 28]

Note: Table includes series crimes. Series crime and other crime types are defined in the appendix. Data for 1993 are not comparable to previous years due to changes in the survey.

* Estimate is based on 10 or fewer sample cases.

† Includes offenders well known to the victim whose relationship could not be ascertained.

Weapons

2.25 Percentage of Rapes and Sexual Assaults in Which Offenders Used Weapons, Total, and by Stranger/Nonstranger Classification, 1993

| | Total Number of Victimizations | Number of Weapon Victimizations | Weapon Victimizations | | | |
| | | | Involving Strangers | | Involving Nonstrangers | |
			Number	Percentage	Number	Percentage
Completed rape	181,960	20,760*	10,140*	48.9*	10,620*	51.1*
Attempted rape	114,070	11,420*	7,010*	61.4*	4,410*	38.6*
Other sexual attacks	162,490	10,130*	3,180*	31.3*	6,960*	68.7*

Source: National Crime Victimization Survey, 1993 preliminary data from: Bureau of the Census. 1995. *National crime victimization survey, 1992–1993*. [Computer files]. Suitland, Md. [See appendix entry 28]

Note: Table includes series crimes. Series crime and other crime types are defined in the appendix. Data for 1993 are not comparable to previous years due to changes in the survey.

* Estimate is based on 10 or fewer sample cases.

2.26 Rapes and Percentages of Rapes, by Strangers and Nonstrangers, and by Specific Weapon Used, 1993

| | Completed Rape | Attempted Rape | Other Sexual Attack With Injury | All Rape and Sexual Attacks | |
				Involving Strangers	Involving Nonstrangers
Total victimizations	181,960	114,070	62,710	71,890	284,280
Weapon victimizations	20,760*	11,420*	10,130*	20,330*	21,980*
%	11.4*	10.0*	16.2*	28.3*	7.7*
Handguns	14,810*	6,100*	3,740*	10,640*	14,020*
%	80.3*	50.1*	36.9*	56.7*	63.8*
Other guns	0*	0*	0*	0*	0*
%	0.0*	0.0*	0.0*	0.0*	0.0*
Knives	3,630*	0*	2,110*	0*	5,740*
%	19.7*	0.0*	20.8*	0.0*	26.1*
Other sharp objects	0*	2,210*	0*	2,210*	0*
%	0.0*	18.2*	0.0*	11.8*	0.0*
Blunt objects	0*	3,850*	0*	3,850*	0*
%	0.0*	31.7*	0.0*	20.5*	0.0*
Other weapons	0*	0*	4,280*	2,060*	2,230*
%	0.0*	0.0*	42.3*	11.0*	10.1*
Gun type unknown	0*	0*	0*	0*	0*
%	0.0*	0.0*	0.0*	0.0*	0.0*
Number of weapons†	18,450*	12,170*	10,130*	18,760*	21,980*

Source: National Crime Victimization Survey, 1993 preliminary data from: Bureau of the Census. 1995. *National crime victimization survey, 1992–1993*. [Computer files]. Suitland, Md. [See appendix entry 28]

Note: Percentages computed within columns. Table includes series crimes. Series crime and other crime types are defined in the appendix. Data for 1993 are not comparable to previous years due to changes in the survey. Detail may not add up to total due to rounding.

* Estimate is based on 10 or fewer sample cases.

Urban-Rural Location

2.27 Rapes, by Victim's Location of Residence, 1993

| | Metropolitan Areas | | | | | | | | Non-metro Areas |
| | Outside of Central Cities | | | Central Cities | | | | | |
	Not a Place	Under 50,000	50,000-249,000	Under 50,000	50,000-249,999	250,000-499,999	500,000-999,999	1,000,000 or More	Non-metro Areas
Completed rape	23,160*	25,540	6,770*	2,030*	42,820	16,140*	4,410*	6,020*	55,070
Attempted rape	7,100*	10,020*	9,120*	12,060*	22,530	19,030*	6,210*	750*	27,250
Other sexual attack with injury	6,970*	13,740*	2,240*	2,340*	20,540*	6,690*	4,870*	1,100*	4,220*
Other sexual attack without injury	20,030*	22,700	7,210*	0*	18,300*	4,160*	9,770*	0*	17,620*
Unwanted sexual contact without force	22,780*	55,760	13,350*	4,130*	37,430	6,680*	7,110*	10,070*	29,120
Verbal threat of rape or sexual assault	12,760*	14,420*	2,080*	2,600*	3,360*	4,250*	2,200*	0*	9,860*

Source: National Crime Victimization Survey, 1993 preliminary data from: Bureau of the Census. 1995. *National crime victimization survey, 1992–1993.* [Computer files]. Suitland, Md. [See appendix entry 28]

Note: Table includes series crimes. Series crime and other crime types are defined in the appendix. Data for 1993 are not comparable to previous years due to changes in the survey. Detail may not add up to total due to rounding. "Not a Place" refers to areas that are neither incorporated (e.g., cities, towns, villages) nor otherwise defined as Census Designated Places (i.e., areas of discrete and/or concentrated settlement identifiable by name, but not legally incorporated).

* Estimate is based on 10 or fewer sample cases.

2.28 Rape Rates, by Victim's Location of Residence, 1993

| | Metropolitan Areas | | | | | | | | Non-metro Areas |
| | Outside Central Cities | | | Central Cities | | | | | |
	Not a Place	Under 50,000	50,000-249,000	Under 50,000	50,000-249,999	250,000-499,999	500,000-999,999	1,000,000 or More	
Completed rape	0.5*	0.5	0.6*	0.3*	1.8	1.5*	0.5*	0.5*	1.1
Attempted rape	0.1*	0.2*	0.8*	1.9*	1.0	1.8*	0.7*	0.1*	0.6
Other sexual assault with injury	0.1*	0.3*	0.2*	0.4*	0.9*	0.6*	0.5*	0.1*	0.1*
Other sexual assault without injury	0.4*	0.5	0.6*	0.0*	0.8*	0.4*	1.1*	0.0*	0.4*
Unwanted sexual contact without force	0.5*	1.2	1.1*	0.7	1.6	0.6*	0.8*	0.8*	0.6
Verbal threat of rape or sexual assault	0.3*	0.3*	0.2*	0.4*	0.1*	0.4*	0.2*	0.0*	0.2*

Source: National Crime Victimization Survey, 1993 preliminary data from: Bureau of the Census. 1995. *National crime victimization survey, 1992–1993.* [Computer files]. Suitland, Md. [See appendix entry 28]

Note: Rates are per 1,000 residents aged 12 years or more. Table includes series crimes. Series crime and other crime types are defined in the appendix. Data for 1993 are not comparable to previous years due to changes in the survey. "Not a Place" refers to areas that are neither incorporated (e.g., cities, towns, villages) nor otherwise defined as Census Designated Places (i.e., areas of discrete and/or concentrated settlement identifiable by name, but not legally incorporated).

* Estimate is based on 10 or fewer sample cases.

ROBBERY: UNIFORM CRIME REPORTS

Incidents

2.29 Robberies, 1960–1993

Year	Frequency	Year	Frequency	Year	Frequency
1960	88,970	1972	374,555	1984	485,008
1961	91,659	1973	382,683	1985	497,874
1962	95,260	1974	441,290	1986	542,775
1963	100,156	1975	464,973	1987	517,704
1964	111,753	1976	420,214	1988	542,968
1965	118,916	1977	404,847	1989	578,326
1966	153,423	1978	417,038	1990	639,271
1967	202,053	1979	466,881	1991	687,732
1968	261,728	1980	548,809	1992	672,478
1969	297,584	1981	574,134	1993	659,757
1970	348,380	1982	536,888		
1971	385,908	1983	500,221		

Source: Monthly Return of Offenses Known to Police (Return A) from: Federal Bureau of Investigation. 1961–1994 (Annual). *Crime in the United States.* Washington, D.C.: U.S. Government Printing Office, Table 2 (1960–1964), Table 3 (1965–1983), Table 4 (1984–1993). [See appendix entry 26]

2.30 Robbery Rates, 1960–1993

Year	Rate	Year	Rate	Year	Rate
1960	49.6	1972	179.9	1984	205.4
1961	50.1	1973	182.4	1985	208.5
1962	51.3	1974	208.8	1986	225.1
1963	53.1	1975	218.2	1987	212.7
1964	58.4	1976	195.8	1988	220.9
1965	61.4	1977	187.1	1989	233.0
1966	78.3	1978	191.3	1990	257.0
1967	102.1	1979	212.1	1991	272.7
1968	131.0	1980	243.5	1992	263.6
1969	147.4	1981	250.6	1993	255.8
1970	171.5	1982	231.9		
1971	187.1	1983	213.8		

Source: Monthly Return of Offenses Known to Police (Return A) from: Federal Bureau of Investigation. 1961–1994 (Annual). *Crime in the United States.* Washington, D.C.: U.S. Government Printing Office, Table 2 (1960–1965), Table 3 (1966–1983), Table 4 (1984–1993). [See appendix entry 26]

Note: Rates are per 100,000 residents.

2.31   Robbery Rates, 1960–1993

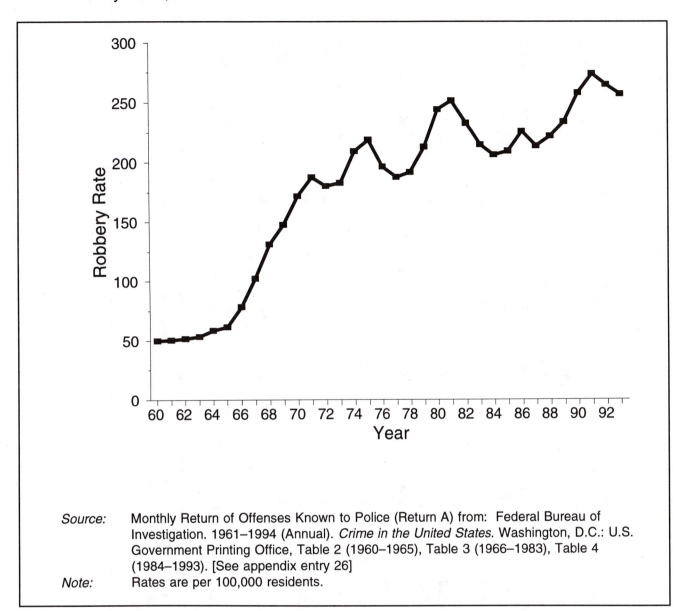

Source: Monthly Return of Offenses Known to Police (Return A) from: Federal Bureau of
          Investigation. 1961–1994 (Annual). *Crime in the United States*. Washington, D.C.: U.S.
          Government Printing Office, Table 2 (1960–1965), Table 3 (1966–1983), Table 4
          (1984–1993). [See appendix entry 26]
Note: Rates are per 100,000 residents.

2.32 Robberies, by Region, 1960–1993

Year	Northeast	Midwest	South	West	Year	Northeast	Midwest	South	West
1960	15,841	33,259	19,466	20,404	1977	128,705	94,287	97,965	83,890
1961	14,830	37,741	18,976	20,112	1978	130,282	88,826	106,323	91,607
1962	16,677	37,975	19,516	21,092	1979	149,166	92,649	124,203	100,863
1963	18,215	38,655	21,644	21,642	1980	177,905	102,993	148,465	119,446
1964	20,971	40,675	26,045	24,062	1981	192,686	103,879	154,027	123,542
1965	23,712	41,397	27,406	26,401	1982	172,347	95,396	148,966	120,179
1966	39,536	51,671	34,191	28,025	1983	155,455	98,007	136,193	110,566
1967	56,486	63,716	45,869	35,982	1984	143,650	100,778	131,580	109,000
1968	83,974	71,537	58,975	47,242	1985	145,207	97,492	141,739	113,436
1969	91,984	83,253	70,764	51,583	1986	149,133	105,910	165,547	122,185
1970	114,071	97,693	81,793	54,823	1987	142,661	103,128	160,979	110,936
1971	141,336	98,716	83,503	62,353	1988	151,177	101,312	177,004	113,475
1972	131,134	95,091	84,267	64,063	1989	163,864	106,505	185,704	122,253
1973	126,045	96,053	93,485	67,100	1990	179,258	118,450	202,626	138,937
1974	137,612	116,175	113,244	74,259	1991	179,276	134,431	218,628	155,397
1975	148,604	119,564	114,813	81,992	1992	171,704	125,878	212,328	162,568
1976	142,615	101,481	96,356	79,762	1993	165,648	124,558	210,872	158,679

Source: Monthly Return of Offenses Known to Police (Return A) from: Federal Bureau of Investigation. 1961–1994 (Annual). *Crime in the United States.* Washington, D.C.: U.S. Government Printing Office, Table 2 (1960–1965), Table 3 (1966–1983), Table 4 (1984–1993). [See appendix entry 26]

Note: Prior to 1984, the Midwest region was referred to as the North Central region. For 1960–1963, the Northeast region was composed of the New England and Middle Atlantic regions; the Midwest region was composed of the East North Central and West North Central regions; the South region included the South Atlantic, East South Central, and West South Central regions; and the West region included the Mountain and Pacific regions.

2.33 Robbery Rates, by Region, 1960–1993

Year	Northeast	Midwest	South	West	Year	Northeast	Midwest	South	West
1960	35.5	64.4	35.4	72.7	1977	261.2	162.7	140.3	213.7
1961	32.6	72.0	33.9	69.2	1978	265.4	152.5	150.5	228.4
1962	36.5	72.1	34.1	69.6	1979	304.4	158.6	173.6	245.2
1963	39.3	73.1	37.2	69.7	1980	363.1	175.7	198.6	278.0
1964	44.5	76.2	44.0	76.2	1981	390.9	176.5	200.3	280.2
1965	49.9	76.6	45.6	81.9	1982	348.5	161.9	190.6	267.0
1966	82.4	95.1	56.1	85.8	1983	313.9	166.2	171.2	240.5
1967	117.0	115.7	74.7	108.9	1984	288.9	170.5	163.3	233.2
1968	173.8	128.6	94.5	141.0	1985	291.2	164.7	173.2	237.2
1969	188.6	148.5	112.2	151.8	1986	298.2	178.6	199.5	250.6
1970	232.8	172.7	130.2	157.5	1987	283.7	173.2	191.9	223.2
1971	285.0	172.4	130.6	175.7	1988	298.7	169.2	208.5	225.0
1972	263.5	165.2	129.9	177.6	1989	322.7	177.1	217.1	236.0
1973	253.7	166.8	141.6	183.5	1990	352.8	198.5	237.1	263.2
1974	278.4	201.9	168.6	199.4	1991	351.7	223.2	251.5	287.5
1975	300.4	207.3	168.6	216.5	1992	335.9	207.3	240.9	295.0
1976	288.1	175.8	139.9	206.8	1993	322.6	204.0	235.8	283.1

Source: Monthly Return of Offenses Known to Police (Return A) from: Federal Bureau of Investigation. 1961–1994 (Annual). *Crime in the United States.* Washington, D.C.: U.S. Government Printing Office, Table 2 (1960–1965), Table 3 (1966–1983), Table 4 (1984–1993). [See appendix entry 26]

Note: Rates are per 100,000 residents. Prior to 1984, the Midwest region was referred to as the North Central region. For 1960–1963, the Northeast region was composed of the New England and Middle Atlantic regions; the Midwest region was composed of the East North Central and West North Central regions; the South region included the South Atlantic, East South Central, and West South Central regions; and the West region included the Mountain and Pacific regions.

Arrest Trends

2.34   Robbery Arrest Rates, by Age and Gender of Arrestee, Selected Years: 1965, 1970, 1975, 1980, 1985, 1990, 1992

Age Group	1965			1970		
	Total	Male	Female	Total	Male	Female
12 and under	5.6	10.3	0.7	8.0	14.6	1.2
13-14	70.4	129.5	9.4	117.0	206.1	24.7
15	112.4	211.2	9.9	195.7	354.1	31.0
16	132.2	252.3	8.1	240.9	446.5	28.0
17	130.1	248.9	8.2	266.5	501.2	23.7
18	143.6	274.0	12.3	279.9	528.0	29.2
19	158.9	306.4	14.5	267.9	512.4	28.4
20	142.0	274.0	13.8	242.9	475.2	25.5
21	146.9	285.9	14.8	231.6	454.2	28.5
22	128.7	245.9	16.6	205.4	399.8	22.3
23	123.8	236.5	17.0	162.1	310.9	19.8
24	113.0	215.0	15.6	170.1	325.3	21.2
25-29	82.4	157.9	9.9	106.0	203.4	11.8
30-34	48.1	92.7	4.8	56.9	109.9	6.0
35-39	29.9	57.5	3.5	31.0	59.7	3.7
40-44	15.7	30.9	1.3	16.4	31.7	1.9
45-49	8.2	16.0	0.9	8.9	17.3	1.0
50-54	4.4	8.6	0.5	4.5	8.9	0.4
55-59	2.3	4.5	0.3	3.3	6.8	0.1
60-64	1.4	2.8	*	1.3	2.6	0.1
65 and over	0.5	1.0	0.1	0.6	1.4	*

See notes at end of table.

2.34 Robbery Arrest Rates, by Age and Gender of Arrestee, Selected Years: 1965, 1970, 1975, 1980, 1985, 1990, 1992 *(continued)*

Age Group	1975			1980		
	Total	Male	Female	Total	Male	Female
12 and under	8.5	15.1	1.7	5.9	10.8	0.7
13-14	133.7	235.0	28.3	133.1	238.2	23.8
15	257.8	463.2	43.9	267.4	483.7	42.3
16	318.8	588.3	40.2	326.7	600.0	41.2
17	332.7	617.9	37.5	354.3	650.4	44.3
18	332.5	620.2	38.6	337.3	625.5	40.7
19	281.7	527.4	33.8	292.7	546.0	36.1
20	259.4	482.8	34.4	250.6	465.0	34.9
21	228.1	422.7	33.0	230.0	427.0	32.3
22	211.7	395.5	29.5	194.2	356.5	31.0
23	190.1	352.4	29.8	180.0	331.0	29.0
24	174.2	321.1	28.9	163.6	300.0	27.5
25-29	115.8	216.7	16.5	115.2	213.8	17.6
30-34	58.1	109.8	7.9	65.2	122.0	9.6
35-39	33.3	62.9	5.1	35.1	66.2	4.9
40-44	19.2	36.5	2.7	20.4	39.0	2.6
45-49	9.5	18.4	1.2	11.9	22.7	1.7
50-54	5.1	10.2	0.5	6.4	12.5	0.7
55-59	2.5	5.1	0.2	3.5	7.1	0.2
60-64	1.4	2.8	0.2	2.1	4.1	0.3
65 and over	1.0	2.2	0.1	0.7	1.7	0.1

See notes at end of table.

2.34   Robbery Arrest Rates, by Age and Gender of Arrestee, Selected Years: 1965, 1970, 1975, 1980, 1985, 1990, 1992 *(continued)*

Age Group	1985 Total	Male	Female	1990 Total	Male	Female
12 and under	4.9	9.0	0.6	5.2	9.2	1.1
13-14	102.9	183.6	18.2	135.9	231.0	36.1
15	198.4	358.3	30.7	251.9	446.2	46.8
16	253.6	466.3	31.6	330.8	594.7	51.1
17	286.7	528.9	32.3	344.9	633.1	38.4
18	278.1	516.2	32.9	353.2	656.3	34.8
19	250.7	467.4	30.8	294.0	544.6	32.9
20	213.8	397.6	28.7	249.2	458.0	31.0
21	200.0	370.2	28.3	234.2	428.2	31.4
22	183.7	339.1	28.7	218.0	393.5	35.1
23	163.9	299.3	28.8	206.6	374.6	33.1
24	151.5	275.2	27.5	191.4	343.7	35.2
25-29	112.0	203.7	20.0	147.3	265.2	28.6
30-34	65.4	120.1	11.1	92.6	167.1	18.7
35-39	37.1	68.8	6.1	51.1	93.1	9.8
40-44	19.4	36.5	2.9	24.0	44.4	4.2
45-49	10.3	19.0	1.9	12.0	22.2	2.1
50-54	6.0	11.7	0.6	6.3	11.7	1.2
55-59	3.3	6.5	0.4	3.2	6.0	0.6
60-64	2.1	4.0	0.4	1.4	2.7	0.3
65 and over	0.8	1.9	0.1	0.4	1.0	0.1

See notes at end of table.

2.34 Robbery Arrest Rates, by Age and Gender of Arrestee, Selected Years: 1965, 1970, 1975, 1980, 1985, 1990, 1992 *(continued)*

Age Group	1992 Total	Male	Female
12 and under	6.0	10.6	1.1
13-14	150.5	258.1	37.5
15	280.4	491.8	57.6
16	345.8	626.4	48.3
17	352.0	642.8	42.0
18	371.9	686.7	41.0
19	297.6	552.3	32.6
20	247.0	454.4	31.1
21	222.1	406.6	29.8
22	199.3	363.5	28.0
23	185.4	337.5	27.7
24	178.3	319.3	33.1
25-29	141.0	253.5	27.5
30-34	90.9	162.4	19.8
35-39	51.5	92.0	11.6
40-44	25.3	46.6	4.6
45-49	11.5	21.3	2.1
50-54	6.3	12.1	0.7
55-59	3.0	5.8	0.5
60-64	1.4	2.7	0.3
65 and over	0.7	1.6	0.1

Source: Age, Sex, Race, and Ethnic Origin of Persons Arrested, 1965–1992 from: Federal Bureau of Investigation. 1993. *Age-specific arrest rates and race-specific arrest rates for selected offenses 1965–1992.* Washington, D.C.: U.S. Government Printing Office, pp. 37–41. [See appendix entry 1]

Note: Rates are per 100,000 persons.

* Rates are less than 0.05.

2.35 Juvenile and Adult Arrest Rates for Robbery, Total, and by Gender of Arrestee, 1965–1992

Year	Under 18			18 and Over		
	Total	Male	Female	Total	Male	Female
1965	30.3	56.9	2.8	39.7	78.2	4.2
1966	32.5	61.0	3.0	40.2	79.5	4.1
1967	39.2	73.2	4.0	46.4	92.2	4.7
1968	48.2	89.5	5.3	52.5	104.2	5.7
1969	55.1	100.8	7.7	58.0	114.9	6.6
1970	59.2	108.1	8.4	61.5	122.1	6.6
1971	65.4	119.0	9.7	70.2	139.0	7.9
1972	66.4	120.3	10.4	70.5	139.3	8.0
1973	74.1	135.3	10.3	69.3	136.1	8.7
1974	84.6	153.9	12.3	78.9	154.5	10.1
1975	80.6	145.9	12.5	69.9	136.7	9.2
1976	72.3	131.3	10.9	69.3	134.9	9.6
1977	72.1	131.0	10.7	65.2	126.5	9.5
1978	84.8	155.2	11.3	66.9	130.3	9.2
1979	76.7	139.9	10.7	65.0	126.2	9.4
1980	81.1	147.7	11.5	70.6	137.7	9.6
1981	77.8	141.5	11.2	72.1	140.5	9.9
1982	71.9	131.2	9.8	74.4	144.4	10.7
1983	65.6	119.9	8.8	67.2	130.2	9.8
1984	60.7	111.0	8.0	64.0	124.4	8.9
1985	58.5	106.6	8.0	61.2	118.2	9.2
1986	57.0	103.6	8.0	67.4	129.7	10.3
1987	52.4	95.3	7.4	64.0	122.5	10.3
1988	51.0	92.0	7.9	64.2	122.6	10.7
1989	59.7	106.7	10.3	69.5	132.6	11.4
1990	66.4	118.6	11.6	73.4	140.7	11.5
1991	72.6	129.4	13.0	73.5	140.4	12.0
1992	70.5	125.9	12.3	68.7	131.2	11.1

Source: Age, Sex, Race, and Ethnic Origin of Persons Arrested, 1965–1992 from: Federal Bureau of Investigation. 1993. *Age-specific arrest rates and race-specific arrest rates for selected offenses 1965–1992*. Washington, D.C.: U.S. Government Printing Office, p. 159. [See appendix entry 1]

Note: Rates are per 100,000 persons.

2.36 Average Age of Robbery Arrestees, 1965–1992

Year	Age	Year	Age
1965	23.18	1979	22.20
1966	22.70	1980	22.36
1967	22.44	1981	22.69
1968	21.99	1982	23.05
1969	21.84	1983	23.24
1970	21.80	1984	23.44
1971	21.90	1985	23.57
1972	22.04	1986	24.09
1973	21.85	1987	24.30
1974	21.74	1988	24.52
1975	21.69	1989	24.33
1976	22.05	1990	24.13
1977	22.18	1991	24.04
1978	21.90	1992	24.09

Source: Age, Sex, Race, and Ethnic Origin of Persons Arrested, 1965–1992 from: Federal Bureau of Investigation. 1993. *Age-specific arrest rates and race-specific arrest rates for selected offenses 1965–1992*. Washington, D.C.: U.S. Government Printing Office, p. 169. [See appendix entry 1]

Note: Because arrestee's age is reported by age group and not by specific age, the FBI computes "average age" as a weighted sum over all age intervals (p. 208).

2.37 Robbery Arrest Rates, by Race of Arrestee, 1965–1992

Year	All Races	White	Nonwhite
1965	34.0	16.1	166.7
1966	35.1	15.7	178.0
1967	40.9	17.5	210.6
1968	47.0	19.5	245.3
1969	52.4	19.3	288.2
1970	55.2	21.4	294.5
1971	60.3	21.8	329.1
1972	60.5	21.9	326.6
1973	63.5	24.6	328.9
1974	71.7	29.8	354.0
1975	63.8	31.1	280.7
1976	61.2	28.0	278.5
1977	67.6	31.8	298.8
1978	72.0	31.0	333.5
1979	68.3	32.6	293.0
1980	73.6	34.8	309.9
1981	73.9	33.3	316.8
1982	73.8	32.9	313.7
1983	66.9	28.5	289.3
1984	63.2	26.9	270.9
1985	60.4	26.1	253.8
1986	64.6	27.3	271.9
1987	61.1	25.7	254.5
1988	60.7	25.4	250.9
1989	67.0	27.1	279.7
1990	71.6	31.3	280.7
1991	73.0	32.8	278.1
1992	74.0	32.8	281.5

Source: Age, Sex, Race, and Ethnic Origin of Persons Arrested, 1965–1992 from: Federal Bureau of Investigation. 1993. *Age-specific arrest rates and race-specific arrest rates for selected offenses 1965–1992.* Washington, D.C.: U.S. Government Printing Office, p. 174. [See appendix entry 1]

Note: Rates are per 100,000 persons.

2.38 Juvenile and Adult Arrest Rates for Robbery, by Race of Arrestee, 1965–1992

Year	Under 18		18 and Over	
	White	Nonwhite	White	Nonwhite
1965	9.1	134.3	19.9	191.6
1966	9.6	142.9	18.9	204.8
1967	10.7	173.5	21.1	238.6
1968	13.8	204.9	22.5	275.4
1969	13.8	247.0	22.1	318.3
1970	15.7	254.6	24.2	322.8
1971	16.0	259.2	24.7	377.9
1972	16.6	273.6	24.4	362.7
1973	21.7	290.3	25.9	354.4
1974	27.2	307.4	30.9	384.0
1975	30.1	254.0	31.6	297.3
1976	26.2	222.1	28.8	312.5
1977	31.2	280.1	32.0	309.7
1978	30.4	353.5	31.2	322.2
1979	32.3	292.0	32.7	293.5
1980	32.1	311.1	35.8	309.3
1981	29.4	300.6	34.7	326.1
1982	27.4	271.5	34.9	336.3
1983	23.7	251.5	30.1	309.3
1984	21.7	232.1	28.7	290.6
1985	22.5	213.2	27.3	273.7
1986	22.2	204.4	29.0	304.8
1987	20.0	188.5	27.6	286.5
1988	20.7	175.2	27.0	287.3
1989	24.4	202.8	27.9	316.5
1990	29.0	216.0	32.1	311.0
1991	34.2	221.5	32.4	304.8
1992	35.2	232.3	32.0	304.7

Source: Age, Sex, Race, and Ethnic Origin of Persons Arrested, 1965–1992 from: Federal Bureau of Investigation. 1993. *Age-specific arrest rates and race-specific arrest rates for selected offenses 1965–1992.* Washington, D.C.: U.S. Government Printing Office, p. 183. [See appendix entry 1]

Note: Rates are per 100,000 persons.

Weapons

2.39   Percentage of Robberies Committed, by Specified Weapon and Region, 1993

	Firearms	Knives or Cutting Instruments	Other Weapons (Clubs, Blunt Objects, Etc.)	Personal
Total	42.4	10.0	9.5	38.2
Northeast	36.7	13.5	8.9	41.0
Midwest	46.9	6.9	9.8	36.3
South	47.1	8.1	8.3	36.6
West	40.3	10.1	11.3	38.2

Source: Monthly Return of Offenses Known to Police (Return A) from: Federal Bureau of Investigation. 1994. *Crime in the United States, 1993*. Washington, D.C.: U.S. Government Printing Office, p. 29, Table 2.22. [See appendix entry 26]

Note: Percent distribution by region. Because of rounding, percentages may not add up to 100. "Personal" weapons are hands, feet, fists, etc.

ROBBERY: NATIONAL CRIME VICTIMIZATION SURVEY

Incidents

2.40   Robberies, 1973–1992

Year	Frequency	Year	Frequency
1973	1,107,800	1983	1,149,170
1974	1,198,700	1984	1,116,680
1975	1,147,100	1985	984,810
1976	1,110,600	1986	1,009,160
1977	1,083,100	1987	1,045,960
1978	1,038,500	1988	1,048,000
1979	1,115,900	1989	1,091,830
1980	1,209,100	1990	1,149,710
1981	1,380,800	1991	1,203,020
1982	1,333,700	1992	1,225,510

Source: National Crime Victimization Survey, 1973–1992, from: Bureau of Justice Statistics. 1994. *Criminal victimization in the United States: 1973–1992 trends.* Washington, D.C., p. 25, Table 10. [See appendix entry 28]

Note: Table excludes series crimes. Series crime and other crime types are defined in the appendix.

2.41   Robbery Rates, 1973–1992

Year	Rate	Year	Rate
1973	6.7	1983	6.0
1974	7.2	1984	5.8
1975	6.8	1985	5.1
1976	6.5	1986	5.1
1977	6.2	1987	5.3
1978	5.9	1988	5.3
1979	6.3	1989	5.4
1980	6.6	1990	5.7
1981	7.4	1991	5.9
1982	7.1	1992	5.9

Source: National Crime Victimization Survey, 1973–1992, from: Bureau of Justice Statistics. 1994. *Criminal victimization in the United States: 1973–1992 trends.* Washington, D.C., p. 25, Table 10. [See appendix entry 28]

Note: Rates are per 1,000 persons aged 12 years or more. Table excludes series crimes. Series crime and other crime types are defined in the appendix.

2.42 Robbery Rates, 1973–1992

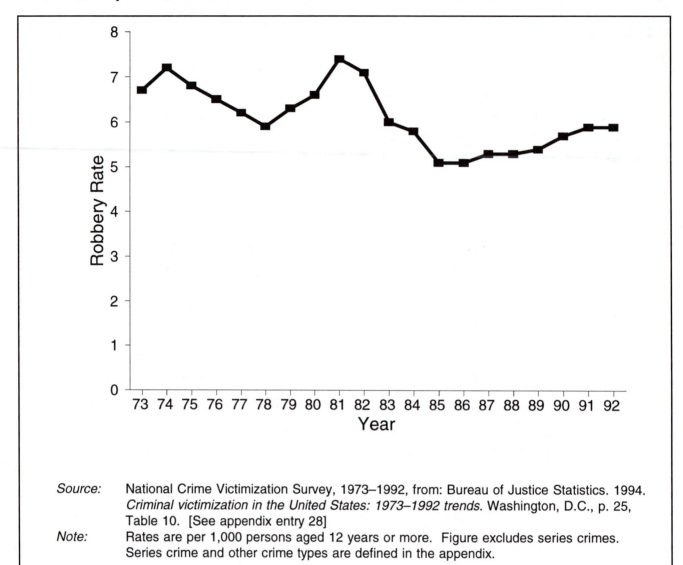

Source: National Crime Victimization Survey, 1973–1992, from: Bureau of Justice Statistics. 1994. *Criminal victimization in the United States: 1973–1992 trends*. Washington, D.C., p. 25, Table 10. [See appendix entry 28]

Note: Rates are per 1,000 persons aged 12 years or more. Figure excludes series crimes. Series crime and other crime types are defined in the appendix.

2.43 Robbery Rates by Region, 1987–1992

	All Regions	Northeast	Midwest	South	West
1987	5.3	6.5	4.6	4.6	6.1
1988	5.3	5.7	4.0	4.8	7.2
1989	5.4	6.7	3.8	5.7	5.5
1990	5.7	7.3	4.5	5.3	5.8
1991	5.9	7.1	4.6	5.4	6.9
1992	5.9	6.1	3.8	6.1	7.9

Source: National Crime Victimization Survey, 1987–1992, from: Bureau of Justice Statistics. 1989–1994 (Annual). *Criminal victimization in the United States.* Washington, D.C., Table 19 (1988), Table 21 (1989, 1990, 1992). Data published in this source for 1987 and 1991 were found by the Bureau of Justice Statistics (BJS) to contain minor errors. The editors have replaced them with unpublished data provided by Lisa Bastian, BJS statistician. [See appendix entry 28]

Note: Rates are per 1,000 persons aged 12 years or more. Table excludes series crimes. Series crime and other crime types are defined in the appendix.

Characteristics of the Victim

2.44 Robberies, by Gender, Age, Completion, and Injury, 1993

	12-15	16-19	20-24	25-34	35-49	50-64	65 & Over
Male							
Total robberies	151,900	104,890	107,860	196,280	163,090	73,390	23,960
Robbery completed with injury	28,010	19,540*	26,770*	50,950	30,660	18,170*	0*
Robbery completed without injury	48,310	31,250	48,760	56,240	79,000	28,950*	14,910*
Robbery attempted with injury	17,250*	5,470*	9,170*	14,840*	4,570*	9,540*	2,120*
Robbery attempted without injury	58,330	48,630	23,160*	74,260	48,850	16,730*	6,930*
Female							
Total robberies	56,080	39,062	69,160	107,830	104,020	22,570	17,160
Robbery completed with injury	9,620*	10,430*	13,620*	35,260	18,750*	6,940*	0*
Robbery completed without injury	16,680*	13,820*	46,080	43,590	52,590	4,300*	10,420*
Robbery attempted with injury	4,030*	410*	5,610*	13,430*	12,120*	1,740*	0*
Robbery attempted without injury	25,740*	14,400*	3,840*	15,550*	20,560*	9,590*	6,740*

Source: National Crime Victimization Survey, 1993 preliminary data from: Bureau of the Census. 1995. *National crime victimization survey, 1992–1993.* [Computer files]. Suitland, Md. [See appendix entry 28]

Note: Table includes series crimes. Series crime and other crime types are defined in the appendix. Data for 1993 are not comparable to earlier years due to changes in the survey.

*   Estimate is based on 10 or fewer sample cases.

2.45   Robbery Rates, by Gender, Age, Completion, and Injury, 1993

	12-15	16-19	20-24	25-34	35-49	50-64	65 & Over
Male							
Total robberies	19.9	14.7	11.6	9.3	5.7	5.7	1.9
Robbery completed with injury	3.7	2.7*	2.9*	2.4	1.1	1.4*	0.0*
Robbery completed without injury	6.3	4.4	5.2	2.7	2.8	2.3*	1.2*
Robbery attempted with injury	2.3*	0.8*	1.0*	0.7*	0.2*	0.7*	0.2*
Robbery attempted without injury	7.6	6.8	2.5*	3.5	1.7	1.3*	0.5*
Female							
Total robberies	7.7	5.7	7.4	5.1	3.6	1.3	1.0
Robbery completed with injury	1.3*	1.5*	1.5*	1.7	0.6*	0.4*	0.0*
Robbery completed without injury	2.3*	2.0*	4.9	2.1	1.8	0.2*	0.6*
Robbery attempted with injury	0.6*	0.1*	0.6*	0.6*	0.4*	0.1*	0.0*
Robbery attempted without injury	3.5*	2.1*	0.4*	0.7*	0.7*	0.5*	0.4*

Source: National Crime Victimization Survey, 1993 preliminary data from: Bureau of the Census. 1995. *National crime victimization survey, 1992–1993.* [Computer files]. Suitland, Md. [See appendix entry 28]

Note: Table includes series crimes. Series crime and other crime types are defined in the appendix. Data for 1993 are not comparable to earlier years due to changes in the survey.

*   Estimate is based on 10 or fewer sample cases.

2.46 Robberies, by Race, Age, Completion, and Injury, 1993

	12-15	16-19	20-24	25-34	35-49	50-64	65 & Over	All Ages
White								
Robbery completed with injury	26,500	23,620*	29,100	55,600	34,950	25,110	0*	194,870
Robbery completed without injury	46,230	26,480*	45,560	59,990	95,160	17,670*	14,880*	305,980
Robbery attempted with injury	13,080*	2,930*	13,740*	22,330*	14,760*	8,350*	2,120*	77,300
Robbery attempted without injury	61,920	46,500	27,000*	67,690	57,460	23,310*	12,750*	296,630
Black								
Robbery completed with injury	6,220*	960*	6,110*	25,950*	11,050*	0*	0*	50,300
Robbery completed without injury	17,660*	18,590*	43,920	32,360	31,040	15,580*	10,460*	169,610
Robbery attempted with injury	5,980*	2,950*	1,040*	5,950*	1,930*	2,930*	0*	20,780
Robbery attempted without injury	20,840*	16,540*	0*	17,810*	9,410*	3,010*	920*	68,530
Total†								
Robbery completed with injury	37,640	29,970	40,400	86,210	49,410	25,110	0*	268,730
Robbery completed without injury	65,000	45,070	94,840	99,830	131,600	33,250	25,340*	494,910
Robbery attempted with injury	21,280*	5,880*	14,780*	28,280	16,690*	11,280*	2,120*	100,300
Robbery attempted without injury	84,060	63,030	27,000*	89,810	69,410	26,320*	13,670*	373,310

Source: National Crime Victimization Survey, 1993 preliminary data from: Bureau of the Census. 1995. *National crime victimization survey, 1992–1993.* [Computer files]. Suitland, Md. [See appendix entry 28]

Note: Table includes series crimes. Series crime and other crime types are defined in the appendix. Data for 1993 are not comparable to earlier years due to changes in the survey.   Detail may not add up to total due to rounding.

* Estimate is based on 10 or fewer sample cases.

† Total includes races other than black and white.

2.47 Robbery Rates, by Race, Age, Completion, and Injury, 1993

	12-15	16-19	20-24	25-34	35-49	50-64	65 & Over	All Ages
White								
Robbery completed with injury	2.2	2.1*	1.9	1.6	0.7	0.9	0.0*	1.1
Robbery completed without injury	3.9	2.4*	3.0	1.7	2.0	0.6*	0.5*	1.7
Robbery attempted with injury	1.1*	0.3*	0.9*	0.6*	0.3*	0.3*	0.1*	0.4
Robbery attempted without injury	5.2	4.1	1.8*	1.9	1.2	0.8*	0.5*	1.7
Black								
Robbery completed with injury	2.5*	0.4*	2.4*	4.7*	1.7*	0.0*	0.0*	2.0
Robbery completed without injury	7.1*	8.7*	17.3	5.8	4.6	4.7*	4.1*	6.7
Robbery attempted with injury	2.4*	1.4*	0.4*	1.1*	0.3*	0.9*	0.0*	0.8*
Robbery attempted without injury	8.4*	7.7*	0.0*	3.2*	1.4*	0.9*	0.4*	2.7
Total†								
Robbery completed with injury	2.5	2.1	2.2	2.0	0.9	0.8	0.0*	1.3
Robbery completed without injury	4.3	3.2	5.1	2.4	2.3	1.0	0.8*	2.3
Robbery attempted with injury	1.4*	0.4*	0.8*	0.7	0.3*	0.3*	0.1*	0.5
Robbery attempted without injury	5.6	4.5	1.4*	2.1	1.2	0.8*	0.4*	1.8

Source: National Crime Victimization Survey, 1993 preliminary data from: Bureau of the Census. 1995. *National crime victimization survey, 1992–1993.* [Computer files]. Suitland, Md. [See appendix entry 28]

Note: Rates are per 1,000 persons aged 12 years or more. Table includes series crimes. Series crime and other crime types are defined in the appendix. Data for 1993 are not comparable with earlier years due to changes in the survey.

* Estimate is based on 10 or fewer sample cases.

† Total includes races other than black and white.

2.48 Robberies, by Race and Gender of Victim, and by Completion and Injury, 1993

	Male			Female			Total		
	White	Black	Total†	White	Black	Total†	White	Black	Total†
Robbery completed with injury	122,860	27,690*	174,100	72,020	22,610*	94,620	194,870	50,300	268,730
Robbery completed without injury	202,860	92,650	307,420	103,120	76,960	187,490	305,970	169,610	494,910
Robbery attempted with injury	47,030	13,700*	62,950	30,270	7,080*	37,350	77,300	20,780*	100,300
Robbery attempted without injury	208,860	61,810	276,890	87,770	6,720*	96,420	296,630	68,530	373,310

Source: National Crime Victimization Survey, 1993 preliminary data from: Bureau of the Census. 1995. *National crime victimization survey, 1992–1993*. [Computer files]. Suitland, Md. [See appendix entry 28]

Note: Table includes series crime. Series crime and other crime types are defined in the appendix. Data for 1993 are not comparable with earlier years due to changes in the survey. Detail may not add up to total due to rounding.

* Estimate is based on 10 or fewer sample cases.
† Total includes races other than black and white.

2.49 Robbery Rates, by Race and Gender of Victim, and by Completion and Injury, 1993

	Male			Female			Total		
	White	Black	Total†	White	Black	Total†	White	Black	Total†
Robbery completed with injury	1.4	2.4*	1.6	0.8	1.6*	0.9	1.1	2.0	1.3
Robbery completed without injury	2.3	8.0	2.8	1.1	5.6	1.8	1.7	6.7	2.3
Robbery attempted with injury	0.5	1.2*	0.6	0.3	0.5*	0.4	0.4	0.8*	0.5
Robbery attempted without injury	2.4	5.4	2.5	1.0	0.5*	0.9	1.7	2.7	1.8

Source: National Crime Victimization Survey, 1993 preliminary data from: Bureau of the Census. 1995. *National crime victimization survey, 1992–1993.* [Computer files]. Suitland, Md. [See appendix entry 28]

Note: Rates are per 1,000 persons aged 12 years or more. Table includes series crimes. Series crime and other crime types are defined in the appendix. Data for 1993 are not comparable with earlier years due to changes in the survey.

* Estimate is based on 10 or fewer sample cases.

† Total includes races other than black and white.

Victim-Offender Relationship

2.50 Percentage of Robberies, by Strangers and Nonstrangers, and by Completion and Injury, 1993

Robbery	Number of Victimizations	% Involving Strangers	% Involving Nonstrangers
Completed with injury	268,730	54.3	43.8
Completed without injury	494,910	75.6	22.0
Attempted with injury	100,300	52.6	45.2
Attempted without injury	373,310	74.8	21.2

Source: National Crime Victimization Survey, 1993 preliminary data from: Bureau of the Census. 1995. *National crime victimization survey, 1992–1993.* [Computer files]. Suitland, Md. [See appendix entry 28]

Note: Victimizations in which the relationship between victim and offender was unknown are excluded. Table includes series crimes. Series crime and other crime types are defined in the appendix. Data for 1993 are not comparable with earlier years due to changes in the survey.

2.51 Percentage of Completed and Attempted Robberies Involving Strangers, by Gender and Race of Victim, and by Injury, 1993

Robbery	Male				Female			
	Total	White	Black	Other	Total	White	Black	Other
Total	75.2	73.7	76.2	90.1	56.4	50.4	70.3	77.8*
Completed								
With injury	63.1	64.2	34.6*	91.1*	38.0	27.0*	73.0*	0.0*
Without injury	79.8	77.9	81.4	100.0*	68.7	64.9	73.4	72.0*
Attempted								
With injury	60.1	57.6	78.5*	0.0*	40.0*	49.4*	0.0*	0.0*
Without injury	81.0	78.8	86.6	100.0*	57.1	52.8	100.0*	100.0*

Source: National Crime Victimization Survey, 1993 preliminary data from: Bureau of the Census. 1995. *National crime victimization survey, 1992–1993.* [Computer files]. Suitland, Md. [See appendix entry 28]

Note: Table includes series crimes. Series crime and other crime types are defined in the appendix. Data for 1993 are not comparable with earlier years due to changes in the survey.

* Estimate based on 10 or fewer sample cases.

2.52 Percentage of Single-Offender Robberies, by Victim-Offender Relationship, and by Completion and Injury, 1993

	Completed Robbery		Attempted Robbery	
	With Injury	Without Injury	With Injury	Without Injury
Related				
Spouse	3.5*	1.0*	12.3*	0.0*
Ex-spouse	9.2*	1.7*	3.4*	1.9*
Parent	0.0*	1.6*	0.0*	0.0*
Own child	1.6*	0.8*	0.0*	0.0*
Sibling	0.0*	1.0*	3.0*	2.1*
Other relative	1.8*	2.0*	0.0*	0.7*
Well known, not related†	28.3	12.5	10.2*	3.4*
Casual acquaintance	6.1*	5.4*	23.4*	13.3*
Stranger	49.5	74.0	47.7	78.6

Source: National Crime Victimization Survey, 1993 preliminary data from: Bureau of the Census. 1995. *National crime victimization survey, 1992–1993.* [Computer files]. Suitland, Md. [See appendix entry 28]

Note: Table includes series crimes. Series crime and other crime types are defined in the appendix. Data for 1993 are not comparable with earlier years due to changes in the survey.

* Estimate is based on 10 or fewer sample cases.

† Includes data on offenders well known to the victim whose relationship could not be ascertained.

2.53 Percentage of Multiple-Offender Robberies, by Victim-Offender Relationship, and by Completion and Injury, 1993

	Total Robberies	Completed Robbery		Attempted Robbery	
		With Injury	Without Injury	With Injury	Without Injury
Related	0.5*	0.0*	1.2*	0.0*	0.0*
Well known, not related†	4.7	3.8*	5.6*	8.3*	3.1*
Casual acquaintance	7.2	13.9*	4.9*	0.0*	6.2*
Strangers	81.2	80.2	81.6	85.4	80.7
Number of offenders unknown or not specified	6.4	2.1*	6.7*	6.3*	10.0*

Source: National Crime Victimization Survey, 1993 preliminary data from: Bureau of the Census. 1995. *National crime victimization survey, 1992–1993.* [Computer files]. Suitland, Md. [See appendix entry 28]

Note: Table includes series crimes. Series crime and other crime types are defined in the appendix. Data for 1993 are not comparable with earlier years due to changes in the survey.

* Estimate is based on 10 or fewer sample cases.

† Includes data on offenders well known to the victim whose relationship could not be ascertained.

Weapons

2.54 Percentage of Completed and Attempted Robberies in Which Offenders Used Weapons, by Stranger/Nonstranger Classification, and by Injury, 1993

Type of Robbery	Total Victimizations	Weapon Victimizations	Weapon Victimizations			
			Involving Strangers		Involving Nonstrangers	
			Number	%	Number	%
Completed with injury	268,730	113,780	66,300	58.3	47,480	41.7
Completed without injury	494,910	328,170	273,450	83.3	54,720	16.7
Attempted with injury	100,300	43,090	30,490	70.8	12,600*	29.2*
Attempted without injury	373,310	126,390	115,090	91.1	11,300*	8.9*

Source: National Crime Victimization Survey, 1993 preliminary data from: Bureau of the Census. 1995. *National crime victimization survey, 1992–1993.* [Computer files]. Suitland, Md. [See appendix entry 28]

Note: Table includes series crimes. Series crime and other crime types are defined in the appendix. Data for 1993 are not comparable with earlier years due to changes in the survey. Detail may not add up to total due to rounding.

* Estimate is based on 10 or fewer sample cases.

2.55 Percentage of Robberies, by Specific Weapon Used, 1993

	Completed With Injury	Completed Without Injury	Attempted With Injury	Attempted Without Injury	Involving Strangers	Involving Nonstrangers
Total victimizations	263,620	482,990	98,080	358,450	852,010	351,130
Weapon victimizations	113,780	328,170	43,090	126,390	485,330	126,110
%	43.2	67.9	43.9	35.3	57.0	35.9
Number of weapons†	120,160	335,210	45,490	122,140	491,370	131,630
Handguns	25,100	200,890	9,890*	44,530	242,030	38,380
%	20.9	59.9	21.7*	36.5	49.3	29.2
Other guns	0*	14,780*	0*	0*	14,780*	0*
%	0.0*	4.4*	0.0*	0.0*	3.0*	0.0*
Knives	25,430*	82,510	16,980*	48,660	143,950	29,620
%	21.2*	24.6	37.3*	39.8	29.3	22.5
Other sharp objects	10,760*	7,910*	0*	2,420*	10,760*	10,330*
%	9.0*	2.4*	0.0*	2.0*	2.2*	7.9*
Blunt objects	27,160	18,370*	13,210*	11,080*	49,230	20,590*
%	22.6	5.5*	29.0*	9.1*	10.0	15.6*
Other weapons	31,710	10,760*	5,410*	15,460*	30,630	32,700
%	26.4	3.2*	11.9*	12.7*	6.2	24.8
Gun type unknown	0*	0*	0*	0*	0*	0*
%	0.0*	0.0*	0.0*	0.0*	0.0*	0.0*

Source: National Crime Victimization Survey, 1993 preliminary data from: Bureau of the Census. 1995. *National crime victimization survey, 1992–1993.* [Computer files]. Suitland, Md. [See appendix entry 28]

Note: Table includes series crimes. Series crime and other crime types are defined in the appendix. Data for 1993 are not comparable with earlier years due to changes in the survey. Detail may not add up to total due to rounding.

* Estimate is based on 10 or fewer sample cases.

† Number of weapons may exceed number of weapon victimizations because respondents were instructed to report all weapons used in the incident.

Urban-Rural Location

2.56 Robberies, by Victim's Location of Residence, and by Completion and Presence of Injury, 1993

Robbery	Outside Central Cities			Metropolitan Areas Central Cities					Non-metro Areas
	Not a Place	Under 50,000	50,000-249,000	Under 50,000	50,000-249,999	250,000-499,999	500,000-999,999	1,000,000 or More	
Completed									
With injury	30,850	49,270	12,570*	4,350*	22,750	42,080	33,040	43,220	30,580
Without injury	59,990	74,280	36,590	16,160*	63,330	48,770	47,870	103,970	43,970
Attempted									
With injury	10,510*	21,520*	5,830*	4,060*	12,530*	14,870*	5,500*	10,650*	14,830*
Without injury	54,630	93,350	27,830	6,140*	27,240	28,880*	24,910*	62,320	48,010

Source: National Crime Victimization Survey, 1993 preliminary data from: Bureau of the Census. 1995. *National crime victimization survey, 1992-1993*. [Computer files]. Suitland, Md. [See appendix entry 28]

Note: Table includes series crimes. Series crime and other crime types are defined in the appendix. "Not a Place" refers to areas that are neither incorporated (e.g., cities, towns, villages) nor otherwise defined as Census Designated Places (i.e., areas of discrete and/or concentrated settlement identifiable by name, but not legally incorporated). Data for 1993 are not comparable with earlier years due to changes in the survey.

* Estimate is based on 10 or fewer sample cases.

2.57 Robbery Rates, by Victim's Location of Residence, and by Completion and Presence of Injury, 1993

	Outside of Central Cities			Metropolitan Areas Central Cities					Non-metro Areas
Robbery	Not a Place	Under 50,000	50,000-249,000	Under 50,000	50,000-249,999	250,000-499,999	500,000-999,999	1,000,000 or More	
Completed									
With injury	0.6	1.0	1.1*	0.7*	1.0	4.0	3.6	3.5	0.6
Without injury	1.2	1.6	3.1	2.6*	2.7	4.6	5.2	8.3	0.9
Attempted									
With injury	0.2*	0.5*	0.5*	0.7*	0.5*	1.4*	0.6*	0.9*	0.3*
Without injury	1.1	2.0	2.4	1.0*	1.2	2.7*	2.7	5.0	1.0

Source: National Crime Victimization Survey, 1993 preliminary data from: Bureau of the Census. 1995. *National crime victimization survey, 1992–1993.* [Computer files]. Suitland, Md. [See appendix entry 28]

Note: Rates are per 1,000 persons aged 12 years or more. Table includes series crimes. Series crime and other crime types are defined in the appendix. Data for 1993 are not comparable with earlier years due to changes in the survey. "Not a Place" refers to areas that are neither incorporated (e.g., cities, towns, villages) nor otherwise defined as Census Designated Places (i.e., areas of discrete and/or concentrated settlement identifiable by name, but not legally incorporated).

* Estimate is based on 10 or fewer sample cases.

Carjacking

2.58   Carjacking, by Weapon, 1987–1992

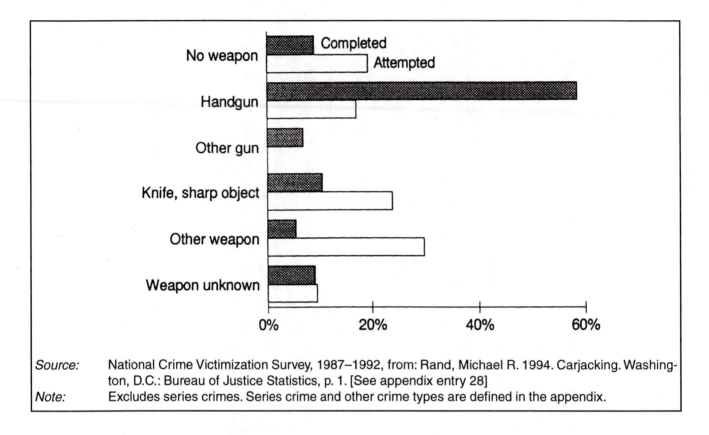

Source: National Crime Victimization Survey, 1987–1992, from: Rand, Michael R. 1994. Carjacking. Washington, D.C.: Bureau of Justice Statistics, p. 1. [See appendix entry 28]

Note: Excludes series crimes. Series crime and other crime types are defined in the appendix.

2.59   Carjacking Rates, by Race and Gender of Victim, and by Location of Residential Area, 1987–1992

		Rate
Area		
	Urban	0.31
	Suburban	0.17
	Rural	0.03
Race		
	All	0.20
	White	0.20
	Black	0.40
Gender		
	Male	0.30
	Female	0.10

Source: National Crime Victimization Survey, 1987–1992, from: Rand, Michael R. 1994. *Carjacking*. Washington, D.C.: Bureau of Justice Statistics, p. 1–2. [See appendix entry 28]

Note: Rates are per 1,000 persons aged 12 years or more. Table excludes series crimes. Series crime and other crime types are defined in the appendix.

2.60   Average Annual Total, Attempted, and Completed Carjackings, 1987–1992

	Average Annual Carjackings
Total	35,500
Completed	18,600
Attempted	16,900

Source: National Crime Victimization Survey, 1987–1992, from: Rand, Michael R. 1994. *Carjacking*. Washington, D.C.: Bureau of Justice Statistics, p. 1. [See appendix entry 28]

Note: Table excludes series crimes. Series crime and other crime types are defined in the appendix.

2.61   Percentage of Carjackings, by Perceived Race and Gender of Offender, and by Value of Automobile Stolen, 1987–1992

Characteristic	Percent of Carjackings
Race	
White	32
Black	49
Asian or American Indian	6
Multiple offenders, more than one race	5
Victim could not identify	8
Gender	
Male	87
Males and females together	6
Female	1
Victim could not identify	6
Number of offenders	
2 or more	54
One	41
Not known	5
Value	
$5,000 and over	46
$2,500-$4,999	13
Less than $2,500	41

Source: National Crime Victimization Survey, 1987–1992, from: Rand, Michael R. 1994. *Carjacking*. Washington, D.C.: Bureau of Justice Statistics, p. 2. [See appendix entry 28]

Note: Table excludes series crimes. Series crime and other crime types are defined in the appendix.

2.62 Percentage of Completed and Attempted Carjackings, by Perceived Age of Offender, 1987–1992

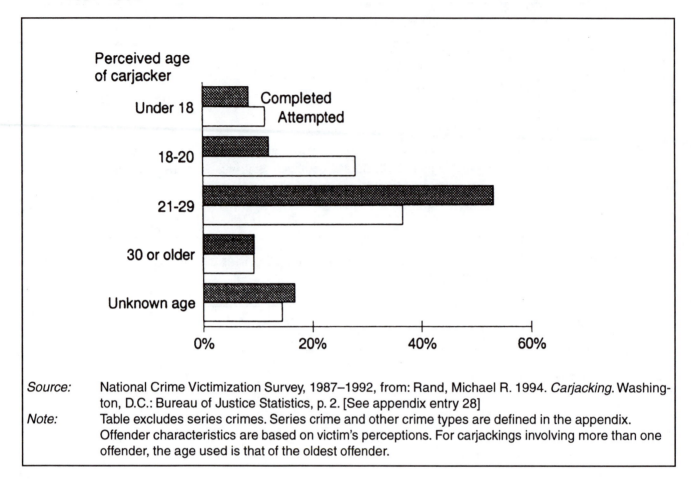

Source: National Crime Victimization Survey, 1987–1992, from: Rand, Michael R. 1994. *Carjacking.* Washington, D.C.: Bureau of Justice Statistics, p. 2. [See appendix entry 28]

Note: Table excludes series crimes. Series crime and other crime types are defined in the appendix. Offender characteristics are based on victim's perceptions. For carjackings involving more than one offender, the age used is that of the oldest offender.

ASSAULT: UNIFORM CRIME REPORTS

Incidents

2.63   Aggravated Assaults, 1960–1993

Year	Assaults	Year	Assaults	Year	Assaults
1960	130,230	1972	388,650	1984	685,349
1961	133,020	1973	416,271	1985	723,246
1962	139,625	1974	452,724	1986	834,322
1963	147,757	1975	484,713	1987	855,088
1964	184,908	1976	490,850	1988	910,092
1965	206,661	1977	522,509	1989	951,707
1966	231,824	1978	558,102	1990	1,054,863
1967	253,321	1979	614,213	1991	1,092,739
1968	282,404	1980	654,957	1992	1,126,974
1969	306,420	1981	643,720	1993	1,135,099
1970	329,937	1982	650,042		
1971	364,595	1983	639,532		

Source: Monthly Return of Offenses Known to Police (Return A) from: Federal Bureau of Investigation. 1961–1994 (Annual). *Crime in the United States.* Washington, D.C.: U.S. Government Printing Office, Table 2 (1960–1964), Table 3 (1965–1983), Table 4 (1984–1993). [See appendix entry 26]

Note: Aggravated assaults are nonfatal attacks involving serious injury and/or the use of a weapon or other means capable of causing death or great bodily harm.

2.64 Aggravated Assault Rates, 1960–1993

Year	Rate	Year	Rate	Year	Rate
1960	72.6	1972	186.6	1984	290.2
1961	72.7	1973	198.4	1985	302.9
1962	75.1	1974	214.2	1986	346.1
1963	78.4	1975	227.4	1987	351.3
1964	96.6	1976	228.7	1988	370.2
1965	106.6	1977	241.5	1989	383.4
1966	118.4	1978	255.9	1990	424.1
1967	128.0	1979	279.1	1991	433.3
1968	141.3	1980	290.6	1992	441.8
1969	151.8	1981	280.9	1993	440.1
1970	162.4	1982	280.8		
1971	176.8	1983	273.3		

Source: Monthly Return of Offenses Known to Police (Return A) from: Federal Bureau of Investigation. 1961–1994 (Annual). *Crime in the United States*. Washington, D.C.: U.S. Government Printing Office, Table 2 (1960–1964), Table 3 (1965–1983), Table 4 (1984–1993). [See appendix entry 26]

Note: Rate is per 100,000 residents. Aggravated assaults are nonfatal attacks involving serious injury and/or the use of a weapon or other means capable of causing death or great bodily harm.

2.65   Aggravated Assault Rates, 1960–1993

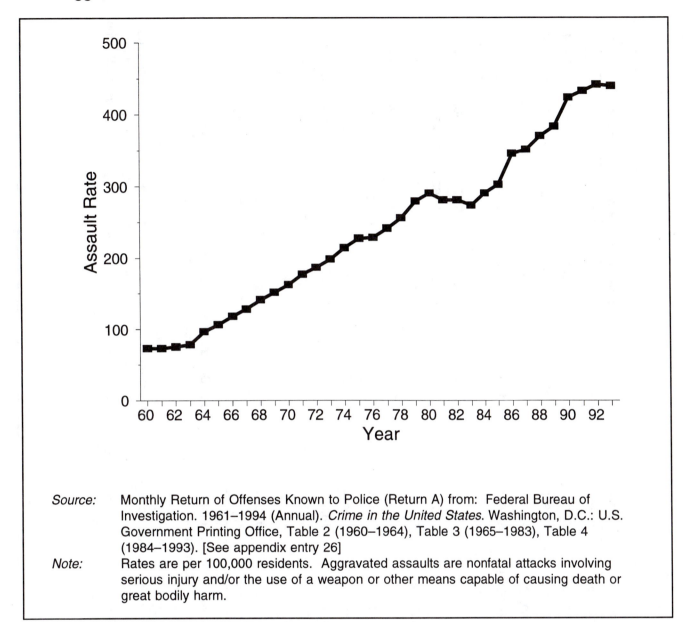

Source: Monthly Return of Offenses Known to Police (Return A) from: Federal Bureau of
            Investigation. 1961–1994 (Annual). *Crime in the United States.* Washington, D.C.: U.S.
            Government Printing Office, Table 2 (1960–1964), Table 3 (1965–1983), Table 4
            (1984–1993). [See appendix entry 26]

Note: Rates are per 100,000 residents. Aggravated assaults are nonfatal attacks involving
            serious injury and/or the use of a weapon or other means capable of causing death or
            great bodily harm.

2.66   Aggravated Assaults, by Region, 1960–1993

Year	Northeast	Midwest	South	West	Year	Northeast	Midwest	South	West
1960	24,010	27,449	54,826	23,945	1977	108,181	103,614	189,135	121,579
1961	24,248	30,544	54,258	23,970	1978	114,494	112,549	200,825	130,234
1962	26,023	34,469	53,315	25,818	1979	123,614	124,830	219,231	146,538
1963	28,169	31,857	59,725	28,006	1980	128,293	128,770	238,342	159,552
1964	34,777	41,409	74,686	34,036	1981	127,668	120,646	240,912	154,494
1965	40,239	45,425	84,408	36,589	1982	127,362	121,408	252,231	149,041
1966	47,200	49,851	93,433	41,340	1983	124,021	125,333	241,567	148,611
1967	50,861	56,291	100,462	45,707	1984	129,237	147,068	254,780	154,264
1968	57,178	60,723	112,206	52,297	1985	134,871	150,661	274,706	163,008
1969	60,550	68,146	117,676	60,048	1986	148,065	172,114	308,028	206,115
1970	65,651	71,843	127,261	65,182	1987	158,646	171,025	306,903	218,514
1971	73,801	75,642	142,779	72,373	1988	174,601	177,989	328,488	229,014
1972	80,534	81,911	147,355	78,850	1989	178,077	183,794	347,588	242,248
1973	86,122	90,266	154,084	85,799	1990	186,167	206,384	403,269	259,043
1974	93,477	100,655	160,583	98,009	1991	185,114	213,538	425,106	268,981
1975	102,071	102,197	172,854	107,591	1992	183,113	210,516	450,845	282,500
1976	103,029	101,127	173,294	113,400	1993	181,744	212,341	455,895	285,119

Source: Monthly Return of Offenses Known to Police (Return A) from: Federal Bureau of Investigation. 1961–1994 (Annual). *Crime in the United States.* Washington, D.C.: U.S. Government Printing Office, Table 2 (1960–1965), Table 3 (1966–1983), Table 4 (1984–1993). [See appendix entry 26]

Note: From 1963–1983, the Midwest region was referred to as the North Central region. For 1960–1963, the Northeast region was composed of the New England and Middle Atlantic regions; the Midwest region was composed of the East North Central and West North Central regions; the South region included the South Atlantic, East South Central, and West South Central regions; and the West region included the Mountain and Pacific regions. Aggravated assaults are nonfatal attacks involving serious injury and/or the use of a weapon or other means capable of causing death or great bodily harm.

2.67 Aggravated Assault Rates, by Region, 1960–1993

Year	Northeast	Midwest	South	West	Year	Northeast	Midwest	South	West
1960	53.7	53.2	99.7	85.4	1977	219.5	178.8	270.8	309.7
1961	53.3	58.3	96.9	82.5	1978	233.3	193.2	284.3	324.8
1962	57.0	65.4	93.3	85.2	1979	252.3	213.7	306.4	356.2
1963	60.7	60.2	102.6	90.2	1980	261.8	219.7	318.8	371.4
1964	73.8	77.6	126.0	107.8	1981	259.0	205.0	313.3	350.4
1965	84.7	84.1	140.6	113.5	1982	257.5	206.0	322.8	331.1
1966	98.4	91.7	153.4	126.6	1983	250.5	212.6	303.7	323.3
1967	105.3	102.2	163.5	138.3	1984	259.9	248.8	316.2	330.1
1968	118.3	109.2	179.7	156.1	1985	270.5	254.5	335.6	340.8
1969	124.1	121.5	186.5	176.7	1986	296.0	290.2	371.2	422.7
1970	134.0	127.0	202.7	187.3	1987	315.5	287.3	365.9	439.7
1971	148.8	132.1	223.4	204.0	1988	345.0	297.2	387.0	454.2
1972	161.9	142.3	227.2	218.6	1989	350.7	305.6	406.4	467.7
1973	173.4	156.7	233.4	234.6	1990	366.4	345.9	472.0	490.7
1974	189.1	174.9	239.0	263.2	1991	363.1	354.6	489.1	497.6
1975	206.4	177.2	253.8	284.0	1992	358.2	346.7	511.5	512.6
1976	208.1	175.1	251.7	294.1	1993	353.9	347.7	509.7	508.7

Source: Monthly Return of Offenses Known to Police (Return A) from: Federal Bureau of Investigation. 1961–1994 (Annual). *Crime in the United States*. Washington, D.C.: U.S. Government Printing Office, Table 2 (1960–1965), Table 3 (1966–1983), Table 4 (1984–1993). [See appendix entry 26]

Note: From 1963–1983, the Midwest region was referred to as the North Central region. For 1960–1963, the Northeast region was composed of the New England and Middle Atlantic regions; the Midwest region was composed of the East North Central and West North Central regions; the South region included the South Atlantic, East South Central, and West South Central regions; and the West region included the Mountain and Pacific regions. Rates are per 100,000 residents. Aggravated assaults are nonfatal attacks involving serious injury and/or the use of a weapon or other means capable of causing death or great bodily harm.

Arrest Trends

2.68 Aggravated Assault Arrest Rates, by Gender and Age of Arrestee, Selected Years: 1965, 1970, 1975, 1980, 1990, 1992

Age Group	1965			1970		
	Total	Male	Female	Total	Male	Female
12 and under	4.5	7.4	1.5	6.3	10.2	2.3
13-14	58.5	93.2	22.7	78.1	122.6	31.8
15	108.8	185.3	29.5	135.9	227.4	40.7
16	136.6	242.8	26.8	173.3	303.9	37.9
17	133.1	243.9	19.4	195.4	346.2	39.5
18	145.6	267.8	22.8	221.0	402.2	37.8
19	170.5	316.7	27.3	217.0	399.7	38.1
20	166.8	304.9	32.6	219.1	408.5	41.9
21	183.0	335.6	37.1	233.0	439.4	44.7
22	167.8	303.6	38.0	230.8	429.0	44.1
23	183.9	332.2	43.2	206.2	376.8	42.9
24	188.2	337.8	45.3	242.9	438.1	55.6
25-29	164.8	287.5	47.1	195.8	346.9	49.6
30-34	139.8	237.4	45.3	165.2	288.5	46.8
35-39	112.7	190.5	38.7	139.3	242.5	41.3
40-44	85.4	146.4	27.7	104.5	181.7	31.5
45-49	61.6	107.4	18.2	73.4	130.5	20.0
50-54	46.9	83.6	12.0	50.7	92.5	12.0
55-59	29.3	54.9	5.5	34.5	64.8	6.7
60-64	19.8	37.8	3.7	22.8	45.0	3.5
65 and over	8.5	18.3	1.0	9.8	21.0	1.7

See notes at end of table.

2.68 Aggravated Assault Arrest Rates, by Gender and Age of Arrestee, Selected Years: 1965, 1970, 1975, 1980, 1990, 1992 *(continued)*

Age Group	1975 Total	1975 Male	1975 Female	1980 Total	1980 Male	1980 Female
12 and under	8.7	14.1	3.0	7.8	13.2	2.1
13-14	103.9	162.2	43.3	113.2	178.8	44.9
15	194.4	311.3	72.8	207.0	336.4	72.4
16	255.1	434.0	70.2	268.4	448.6	80.1
17	277.5	485.1	62.6	325.2	558.0	81.7
18	314.0	554.8	68.0	339.9	593.9	78.3
19	301.5	535.4	65.5	341.4	603.3	76.0
20	296.3	525.8	65.1	345.4	613.3	75.9
21	304.3	537.5	70.3	357.9	628.8	86.0
22	292.7	517.5	69.8	340.5	597.8	81.8
23	289.2	515.4	65.6	327.3	577.2	77.5
24	294.1	523.0	67.9	318.4	563.0	74.3
25-29	235.9	418.4	56.1	264.0	468.0	61.9
30-34	190.4	336.2	49.0	198.2	351.0	48.7
35-39	168.1	294.4	47.7	162.6	287.7	41.6
40-44	128.7	222.9	38.2	128.8	228.8	33.0
45-49	89.9	160.1	24.0	93.6	167.1	24.1
50-54	63.4	115.8	15.2	64.9	118.5	15.3
55-59	40.4	75.3	8.9	41.3	76.9	9.5
60-64	28.6	55.0	5.6	26.6	51.4	5.2
65 and over	11.8	26.4	1.7	10.9	24.3	1.8

See notes at end of table.

2.68 Aggravated Assault Arrest Rates, by Gender and Age of Arrestee, Selected Years: 1965, 1970, 1975, 1980, 1990, 1992 *(continued)*

Age Group	1985			1990		
	Total	Male	Female	Total	Male	Female
12 and under	9.3	16.0	2.3	12.6	21.0	3.7
13-14	125.4	196.1	51.1	204.5	318.2	85.1
15	210.4	340.2	74.2	367.4	595.1	127.0
16	269.5	448.3	82.9	477.4	797.3	138.2
17	316.5	540.2	81.4	558.7	956.3	135.8
18	316.7	551.6	74.7	571.4	997.4	124.0
19	323.9	565.4	78.8	518.9	908.9	112.4
20	328.3	571.2	83.8	511.9	879.6	127.6
21	334.7	577.9	89.4	523.4	896.1	133.6
22	330.6	571.8	88.4	519.8	889.3	134.8
23	320.7	558.8	83.3	508.3	867.9	137.1
24	318.3	546.6	89.4	489.4	831.3	138.9
25-29	270.5	465.6	75.0	435.4	743.9	124.6
30-34	204.1	353.2	56.1	338.7	582.4	97.2
35-39	152.9	269.9	38.9	240.3	418.9	64.9
40-44	119.2	211.6	30.3	159.1	281.2	40.2
45-49	87.5	158.4	20.0	111.4	199.3	26.8
50-54	59.6	107.6	14.8	78.7	144.9	16.3
55-59	39.8	74.1	8.9	50.0	93.1	10.6
60-64	25.2	48.3	5.1	32.1	62.7	5.5
65 and over	9.9	22.2	1.6	11.6	26.0	1.8

See notes at end of table.

2.68 Aggravated Assault Arrest Rates, by Gender and Age of Arrestee, Selected Years: 1965, 1970, 1975, 1980, 1990, 1992 *(continued)*

Age Group	1992 Total	Male	Female
12 and under	14.7	24.4	4.5
13-14	241.1	370.5	105.1
15	397.2	629.2	152.7
16	524.7	863.6	165.4
17	567.2	959.7	148.6
18	617.8	1063.2	149.7
19	570.0	979.2	144.4
20	525.7	895.0	141.2
21	526.9	889.6	149.0
22	527.7	888.9	150.8
23	508.8	849.3	155.6
24	495.8	831.0	150.8
25-29	434.1	726.2	139.5
30-34	345.7	578.6	114.1
35-39	255.0	432.0	80.3
40-44	167.7	293.6	44.9
45-49	113.6	201.0	29.3
50-54	79.3	143.0	19.2
55-59	51.1	94.7	10.9
60-64	31.5	61.1	5.5
65 and over	12.6	27.8	2.3

Source: Age, Sex, Race, and Ethnic Origin of Persons Arrested, 1965–1992 from: Federal Bureau of Investigation. 1993. *Age-specific arrest rates and race-specific arrest rates for selected offenses 1965–1992.* Washington, D.C.: U.S. Government Printing Office, pp. 45–49. [See appendix entry 1]

Note: Rates are per 100,000 persons.

2.69   Juvenile and Adult Aggravated Assault Arrest Rates, Total, and by Gender of Arrestee, 1965–1992

Year	Under 18			18 and Over		
	Total	Male	Female	Total	Male	Female
1965	28.5	48.9	7.3	88.5	159.2	23.4
1966	35.6	60.7	9.6	99.0	179.5	25.3
1967	38.1	65.2	10.0	100.5	183.8	24.7
1968	37.4	64.8	9.0	102.2	188.0	24.5
1969	40.0	68.9	10.2	108.2	199.3	26.0
1970	42.2	71.1	12.1	111.1	205.1	26.1
1971	49.3	82.0	15.3	118.0	216.3	28.8
1972	51.6	85.4	16.4	121.0	221.9	29.3
1973	55.7	92.6	17.3	126.4	231.5	30.9
1974	64.1	105.7	20.7	145.1	266.2	35.0
1975	65.3	108.2	20.6	143.0	263.4	33.6
1976	67.1	111.4	21.0	136.6	250.9	32.7
1977	66.5	111.0	20.2	137.5	252.7	32.8
1978	70.9	118.8	21.0	152.4	280.4	36.1
1979	72.2	120.7	21.5	156.2	288.4	36.0
1980	70.6	117.2	21.9	156.2	288.6	35.8
1981	67.6	111.9	21.4	154.0	283.9	35.9
1982	67.3	110.6	22.0	164.6	302.3	39.1
1983	62.8	103.0	20.8	154.9	282.2	38.8
1984	65.0	105.9	22.2	156.6	285.4	39.2
1985	67.6	111.5	21.5	149.9	272.6	37.7
1986	72.5	119.6	23.1	174.2	317.5	43.1
1987	73.2	120.7	23.3	176.0	320.2	43.8
1988	79.5	131.5	24.9	190.9	346.3	48.3
1989	91.1	151.5	27.6	207.5	376.3	52.4
1990	103.9	171.9	32.4	226.2	410.2	57.1
1991	107.3	177.7	33.3	224.2	405.2	57.7
1992	112.8	183.6	38.3	227.1	403.7	64.4

Source: Age, Sex, Race, and Ethnic Origin of Persons Arrested, 1965–1992 from: Federal Bureau of Investigation. 1993. *Age-specific arrest rates and race-specific arrest rates for selected offenses 1965–1992*. Washington, D.C.: U.S. Government Printing Office, p. 159. [See appendix entry 1]

Note: Rates are per 100,000 persons. Aggravated assaults are nonfatal attacks involving serious injury and/or the use of a weapon or other means capable of causing death or great bodily harm.

2.70 Average Age of Aggravated Assault Arrestees, 1965–1992

Year	Age	Year	Age
1965	30.42	1979	28.08
1966	29.92	1980	28.20
1967	29.72	1981	28.48
1968	29.47	1982	28.64
1969	29.18	1983	28.75
1970	29.27	1984	28.83
1971	28.96	1985	28.69
1972	28.99	1986	28.90
1973	28.76	1987	29.01
1974	28.52	1988	29.03
1975	28.39	1989	28.86
1976	28.32	1990	28.65
1977	28.27	1991	28.60
1978	28.30	1992	28.80

Source: Age, Sex, Race, and Ethnic Origin of Persons Arrested, 1965–1992 from: Federal Bureau of Investigation. 1993. *Age-specific arrest rates and race-specific arrest rates for selected offenses 1965–1992*. Washington, D.C.: U.S. Government Printing Office, p. 169. [See appendix entry 1]

Note: Because arrestee's age is reported by age group and not by specific age, the FBI computes "average age" as a weighted sum over all age intervals (p. 208). Aggravated assaults are nonfatal attacks involving serious injury and/or the use of a weapon or other means capable of causing death or great bodily harm.

2.71   Aggravated Assault Arrest Rates, by Race of Arrestee, 1965–1992

Year	All Races	White	Nonwhite
1965	60.1	31.6	271.0
1966	63.6	34.7	275.0
1967	68.1	38.2	285.2
1968	75.4	42.0	315.7
1969	80.7	45.0	336.0
1970	86.5	51.6	333.4
1971	91.0	53.1	355.9
1972	93.1	56.1	349.0
1973	98.5	60.9	354.7
1974	111.7	72.3	376.6
1975	110.9	76.9	336.1
1976	109.6	73.9	343.4
1977	116.9	79.9	356.2
1978	128.5	84.8	407.3
1979	132.1	93.0	377.3
1980	132.2	95.6	355.2
1981	130.5	93.9	349.2
1982	138.1	96.7	381.9
1983	130.3	90.3	361.5
1984	132.5	91.4	367.2
1985	128.2	87.4	358.2
1986	147.7	101.2	406.2
1987	149.1	102.2	405.7
1988	161.7	109.4	444.0
1989	177.5	121.2	476.7
1990	193.8	137.1	488.4
1991	195.2	140.1	476.7
1992	208.4	145.5	524.7

Source: Age, Sex, Race, and Ethnic Origin of Persons Arrested, 1965–1992 from: Federal Bureau of Investigation. 1993. *Age-specific arrest rates and race-specific arrest rates for selected offenses 1965–1992.* Washington, D.C.: U.S. Government Printing Office, p. 174. [See appendix entry 1]

Note: Rates are per 100,000 persons. Aggravated assaults are nonfatal attacks involving serious injury and/or the use of a weapon or other means capable of causing death or great bodily harm.

2.72 Juvenile and Adult Arrest Rates for Aggravated Assault, Total, and by Race of Arrestee, 1965–1992

Year	Under 18			18 and Over		
	Total	White	Nonwhite	Total	White	Nonwhite
1965	25.1	12.9	98.1	79.7	41.7	403.9
1966	27.3	15.1	99.0	83.7	45.2	409.6
1967	31.1	17.5	110.2	88.4	49.1	417.2
1968	33.5	18.3	120.6	98.0	54.2	460.8
1969	37.1	20.3	132.8	103.8	57.4	484.1
1970	40.1	22.1	141.2	110.7	66.3	470.1
1971	44.0	24.4	152.7	115.0	67.0	497.7
1972	48.6	28.3	159.3	115.2	69.2	478.1
1973	53.1	32.2	165.8	120.4	74.1	479.8
1974	60.2	40.0	167.0	135.8	86.7	511.1
1975	60.3	43.4	148.2	133.8	91.3	453.0
1976	63.1	45.1	154.7	130.0	85.8	457.0
1977	66.9	49.4	154.4	138.2	92.1	473.9
1978	70.9	51.2	168.5	152.2	97.9	452.4
1979	72.0	55.4	153.0	156.0	107.3	500.8
1980	70.6	54.2	147.8	156.1	110.8	466.7
1981	67.7	50.9	144.6	154.3	109.2	457.4
1982	67.0	49.3	146.4	164.6	113.2	504.1
1983	62.8	45.7	138.8	155.0	105.7	475.1
1984	65.1	46.1	148.4	156.8	106.8	476.5
1985	67.7	47.8	153.2	149.9	100.8	459.1
1986	72.6	49.8	169.2	174.5	118.4	521.8
1987	73.0	48.5	175.1	176.0	120.0	517.4
1988	79.1	51.5	192.5	190.7	128.5	565.1
1989	91.1	59.8	217.8	207.5	141.2	600.6
1990	103.1	70.4	233.8	225.2	158.7	607.7
1991	107.7	77.0	228.0	225.7	160.7	593.9
1992	119.0	82.0	263.0	239.8	166.5	647.6

Source: Age, Sex, Race, and Ethnic Origin of Persons Arrested, 1965–1992 from: Federal Bureau of Investigation. 1993. *Age-specific arrest rates and race-specific arrest rates for selected offenses 1965–1992.* Washington, D.C.: U.S. Government Printing Office, p. 183. [See appendix entry 1]

Note: Rates are per 100,000 persons. Aggravated assaults are nonfatal attacks involving serious injury and/or the use of a weapon or other means capable of causing death or great bodily harm.

Weapons

2.73 Percentage of Aggravated Assaults, by Specified Weapon and Region, 1993

Region	Firearm	Knives or Cutting Instrument	Other Weapon	Personal Weapon
Total	25.1	17.6	31.0	26.3
Northeast	17.2	21.1	32.3	29.4
Midwest	28.2	16.8	31.7	23.3
South	26.8	18.5	31.2	23.5
West	24.7	13.6	27.9	33.8

Source: Monthly Return of Offenses Known to Police (Return A) from: Federal Bureau of Investigation. 1994. *Crime in the United States, 1993.* Washington, D.C.: U.S. Government Printing Office, p. 32, Table 2.24. [See appendix entry 26]

Note: Percentage by region. Because of rounding, percentages may not add up to 100. "Other Weapon" includes clubs, sticks, blunt objects, and other implements besides firearms, knives, or other cutting/piercing instruments. "Personal Weapon" denotes hands, feet, fists, etc. and involves no other instrument. Aggravated assaults are nonfatal attacks involving serious injury and/or the use of a weapon or other means capable of causing death or great bodily harm.

ASSAULT: NATIONAL CRIME VICTIMIZATION SURVEY

Incidents

2.74 Assaults, by Type of Assault, 1973–1992

Year	Total	Aggravated Assault	Simple Assault
1973	4,087,100	1,654,800	2,432,300
1974	4,148,400	1,735,500	2,412,700
1975	4,271,900	1,631,300	2,640,600
1976	4,343,400	1,695,200	2,648,200
1977	4,664,000	1,737,900	2,926,300
1978	4,731,700	1,707,800	3,023,700
1979	4,851,300	1,768,500	3,082,400
1980	4,747,300	1,706,900	3,040,500
1981	5,023,900	1,795,800	3,228,200
1982	4,972,800	1,754,300	3,218,600
1983	4,600,090	1,517,310	3,082,770
1984	4,744,480	1,727,300	3,017,180
1985	4,699,340	1,605,170	3,094,170
1986	4,376,350	1,542,870	2,833,480
1987	4,601,650	1,587,460	3,014,190
1988	4,374,190	1,741,380	2,992,800
1989	4,633,800	1,664,710	2,969,080
1990	4,728,810	1,600,670	3,128,130
1991	5,209,820	1,634,390	3,575,420
1992	5,254,690	1,848,530	3,406,160

Source: National Crime Victimization Survey, 1973–1992 from: Bureau of Justice Statistics. 1994. *Criminal victimization in the United States: 1973–1992 trends.* Washington, D.C., p. 39, Table 17. [See appendix entry 28]

Note: Aggravated assaults include all attacks (and attempted attacks) with weapons or, if no weapon was involved, those resulting in serious injury. Simple assaults are attacks (and attempted attacks) without weapons resulting in minor or undetermined injuries requiring less than two days of hospitalization. Table excludes series crimes. Series crime and other crime types are defined in the appendix.

2.75 Assault Rates, by Type of Assault, 1973–1992

Year	Total	Aggravated Assault	Simple Assault
1973	24.9	10.1	14.8
1974	24.8	10.4	14.4
1975	25.2	9.6	15.6
1976	25.3	9.9	15.4
1977	26.8	10.0	16.8
1978	26.9	9.7	17.2
1979	27.2	9.9	17.3
1980	25.8	9.3	16.5
1981	27.0	9.6	17.3
1982	26.4	9.3	17.1
1983	24.1	8.0	16.2
1984	24.7	9.0	15.7
1985	24.2	8.3	15.9
1986	22.3	7.9	14.4
1987	23.3	8.0	15.2
1988	23.7	8.7	15.0
1989	23.5	8.5	15.1
1990	24.9	8.4	16.5
1991	25.5	8.0	17.5
1992	25.5	9.0	16.5

Source: National Crime Victimization Survey, 1973–1992 from: Bureau of Justice Statistics. 1994. *Criminal victimization in the United States: 1973–1992 trends.* Washington, D.C., p. 39, Table 17. [See appendix entry 28]

Note: Rates are per 1,000 persons aged 12 years or more. Aggravated assaults include all attacks (and attempted attacks) with weapons or, if no weapon was involved, those resulting in serious injury. Simple assaults are attacks (and attempted attacks) without weapons resulting in minor or undetermined injuries requiring less than two days of hospitalization. Table excludes series crimes. Series crime and other crime types are defined in the appendix.

2.76   Simple and Aggravated Assault Rates, 1973–1992

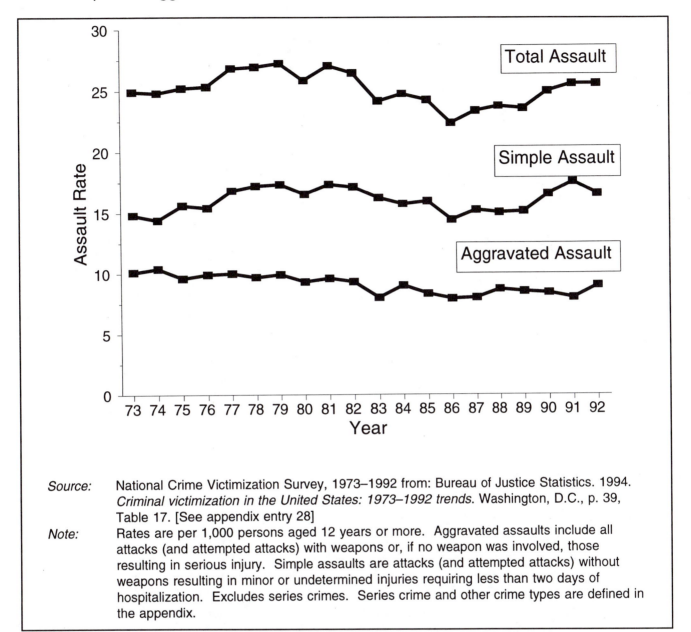

Source: National Crime Victimization Survey, 1973–1992 from: Bureau of Justice Statistics. 1994.
             Criminal victimization in the United States: 1973–1992 trends. Washington, D.C., p. 39,
             Table 17. [See appendix entry 28]

Note: Rates are per 1,000 persons aged 12 years or more. Aggravated assaults include all
             attacks (and attempted attacks) with weapons or, if no weapon was involved, those
             resulting in serious injury. Simple assaults are attacks (and attempted attacks) without
             weapons resulting in minor or undetermined injuries requiring less than two days of
             hospitalization. Excludes series crimes. Series crime and other crime types are defined in
             the appendix.

2.77 Assault Rates, by Region and Type of Assault, 1987–1992

	Assaults	All Regions	Northeast	Midwest	South	West
1987	Total	23.3	16.5	25.9	21.7	29.9
	Simple	15.2	11.0	18.0	13.8	18.7
	Aggravated	8.0	5.5	7.9	7.9	11.2
1988	Total	23.7	15.1	23.9	23.7	32.8
	Simple	15.0	10.4	15.1	13.9	21.8
	Aggravated	8.7	4.7	8.9	9.8	11.1
1989	Total	23.0	15.9	21.8	24.0	30.2
	Simple	14.7	11.0	14.7	14.6	19.1
	Aggravated	8.3	4.9	7.1	9.4	11.1
1990	Total	23.3	14.1	25.5	25.0	27.5
	Simple	15.4	10.2	17.1	15.7	18.5
	Aggravated	7.9	3.9	8.3	9.4	9.0
1991	Total	25.5	18.5	26.3	25.1	32.9
	Simple	17.5	13.4	19.5	16.1	22.3
	Aggravated	8.0	5.2	6.8	9.0	10.6
1992	Total	25.5	16.6	26.0	25.1	35.4
	Simple	16.5	11.5	17.8	15.4	22.7
	Aggravated	9.0	5.2	8.2	9.7	12.7

Source: National Crime Victimization Survey, 1987–1992 from: Bureau of Justice Statistics. 1989–1994 (Annual). *Criminal victimization in the United States.* Washington, D.C., Table 19 (1988), Table 20 (1989), Table 21 (1990, 1992). Data published in this source for 1987 and 1991 were found by the Bureau of Justice Statistics (BJS) to contain minor errors. The editors have replaced them with unpublished data provided by Lisa Bastian, BJS statistician. [See appendix entry 28]

Note: Rates are per 1,000 persons aged 12 years or more. Aggravated assaults include all attacks (and attempted attacks) with weapons or, if no weapon was involved, those resulting in serious injury. Simple assaults are attacks (and attempted attacks) without weapons resulting in minor or undetermined injuries requiring less than two days of hospitalization. Table excludes series crimes. Series crime and other crime types are defined in the appendix.

Characteristics of the Victim

2.78   Assaults, by Gender and Age of Victim, and by Type of Assault, 1993

	12-15	16-19	20-24	25-34	35-49	50-64	65 & Over	All Ages
Male								
Total assault	963,300	758,520	718,920	1,202,290	1,154,300	290,060	55,670	5,143,050
Aggravated assault With injury	70,420	46,300	85,700	80,760	79,970	11,730*	2,090*	376,970
Without injury	132,580	206,660	181,230	289,640	237,450	70,010	11,190*	1,128,750
Simple assault With injury	200,530	104,970	77,120	127,530	75,790	15,430*	4,370*	605,720
Without injury	357,360	248,880	189,010	338,250	280,970	60,750	22,880	1,498,090
Verbal threat of assault	202,400	151,720	185,860	366,130	480,120	132,150	15,140*	1,533,520
Female								
Total assault	592,730	510,780	578,430	827,110	959,010	188,780	97,440	3,754,270
Aggravated assault With injury	63,610	54,360	45,980	72,860	33,390	7,960*	4,760*	282,920
Without injury	55,080	57,820	121,580	131,780	117,250	36,930	29,860	550,290
Simple assault With injury	133,680	98,600	116,200	162,780	213,000	30,950	15,710*	770,910
Without injury	189,940	141,830	137,370	209,560	302,680	44,270	14,900*	1,040,530
Verbal threat of assault	150,430	158,170	157,300	250,140	292,680	68,680	32,220	1,109,630

Source: National Crime Victimization Survey, 1993 preliminary data from: Bureau of the Census. 1995. *National crime victimization survey, 1992–1993.* [Computer files]. Suitland, Md. [See appendix entry 28]

Note: Table includes series crimes. Series crime and other crime types are defined in the appendix. Aggravated assaults include all attacks (and attempted attacks) with weapons or, if no weapon was involved, those that result in serious injury. Simple assaults are attacks (and attempted attacks) without weapons resulting in minor or undetermined injuries requiring less than two days of hospitalization. Data for 1993 are not comparable with earlier years due to changes in the survey. Detail may not add up to total due to rounding.

*   Estimate is based on 10 or fewer sample cases.

2.79   Assault Rates, by Gender and Age of Victim, and by Type of Assault, 1993

	12-15	16-19	20-24	25-34	35-49	50-64	65 & Over	All Ages
Male								
Total assault	126.0	106.4	77.2	57.1	40.7	22.7	4.4	50.3
Aggravated assault								
With injury	9.2	6.5	9.2	3.8	2.8	0.9*	0.2*	3.7
Without injury	17.3	29.0	19.5	13.8	8.4	5.5	0.9*	11.0
Simple assault								
With injury	26.2	14.7	8.3	6.1	2.7	1.2*	0.3*	5.9
Without injury	46.8	34.9	20.3	16.1	9.9	4.8	1.8	14.6
Verbal threat of assault	26.5	21.3	19.9	17.4	16.9	10.3	1.2*	15.0
Female								
Total assault	81.0	74.5	61.6	39.0	33.0	10.5	5.4	34.4
Aggravated assault								
With injury	8.7	7.9	4.9	3.4	1.1	0.4*	0.3*	2.6
Without injury	7.5	8.4	13.0	6.2	4.0	2.0	1.7	5.0
Simple assault								
With injury	18.3	14.4	12.4	7.7	7.3	1.7	0.9*	7.1
Without injury	25.9	20.7	14.6	9.9	10.4	2.5	0.8*	9.5
Verbal threat of assault	20.6	23.1	16.8	11.8	10.1	3.8	1.8	10.2

Source: National Crime Victimization Survey, 1993 preliminary data from: Bureau of the Census. 1995. *National crime victimization survey, 1992–1993.* [Computer files]. Suitland, Md. [See appendix entry 28]

Note: Rates are per 1,000 persons aged 12 years or more. Table includes series crimes. Series crime and other crime types are defined in the appendix. Aggravated assaults include all attacks (and attempted attacks) with weapons or, if no weapon was involved, those that result in serious injury. Simple assaults are attacks (and attempted attacks) without weapons resulting in minor or undetermined injuries requiring less than two days of hospitalization. Data for 1993 are not comparable with earlier years due to changes in the survey. Detail may not add up to total due to rounding.

*   Estimate is based on 10 or fewer sample cases.

2.80   Assaults, by Race and Age of Victim, and by Type of Assault, 1993

	12-15	16-19	20-24	25-34	35-49	50-64	65 & Over
White							
Aggravated assault							
With injury	95,910	60,310	91,440	123,530	83,640	12,460*	4,260*
Without injury	152,830	205,420	237,220	382,240	282,990	88,720	35,530
Simple assault							
With injury	285,840	167,520	139,450	252,510	237,620	39,790	12,390*
Without injury	453,030	337,330	275,610	478,320	493,570	98,040	30,630
Verbal threat of assault	316,540	266,730	301,130	505,920	636,670	190,690	45,050
Black							
Aggravated assault							
With injury	38,120	33,850*	34,870	22,800*	22,510*	7,230*	2,590*
Without injury	32,940	55,640	60,030	36,370	60,100	13,410*	3,570*
Simple assault							
With injury	46,430	30,330*	50,970	25,810*	44,930	6,590*	7,680*
Without injury	81,170	44,650	29,540*	49,650	79,450	4,650*	7,150*
Verbal threat of assault	28,340	27,730*	36,850	104,740	118,700	5,780*	2,310*
Total†							
Aggravated assault							
With injury	134,040	100,660	131,680	153,610	113,360	19,690*	6,850*
Without injury	187,660	264,480	302,810	421,410	354,700	106,940	41,050
Simple assault							
With injury	334,200	203,570	193,320	290,310	288,790	46,370	20,070*
Without injury	547,300	390,700	326,370	547,810	583,650	105,010	37,780
Verbal threat of assault	352,830	309,890	343,160	616,270	772,810	200,830	47,360

Source: National Crime Victimization Survey, 1993 preliminary data from: Bureau of the Census. 1995. *National crime victimization survey, 1992–1993.* [Computer files]. Suitland, Md. [See appendix entry 28]

Note: Table includes series crimes. Series crime and other crime types are defined in the appendix. Aggravated assaults include all attacks (and attempted attacks) with weapons or, if no weapon was involved, those that result in serious injury. Simple assaults are attacks (and attempted attacks) without weapons resulting in minor or undetermined injuries requiring less than two days of hospitalization. Data for 1993 are not comparable with earlier years due to changes in the survey.

*   Estimate is based on 10 or fewer sample cases.

†   Total includes races other than black and white.

2.81 Assault Rates, by Race and Age of Victim, and by Type of Assault, 1993

	12-15	16-19	20-24	25-34	35-49	50-64	65 & Over
White							
Aggravated assault							
With injury	8.1	5.4	6.0	3.5	1.7	0.4*	0.2*
Without injury	12.8	18.2	15.5	10.9	5.8	3.1	1.3
Simple assault							
With injury	24.0	14.9	9.1	7.2	4.9	1.4	0.4*
Without injury	38.1	29.9	18.0	13.7	10.2	3.4	1.1
Verbal threat of assault	26.6	23.7	19.7	14.5	13.1	6.6	1.6
Black							
Aggravated assault							
With injury	15.4	15.8*	13.7	4.1*	3.4*	2.2*	1.0*
Without injury	13.3	25.9	23.6	6.5	9.0	4.0*	1.4*
Simple assault							
With injury	18.7	14.1*	20.0	4.6*	6.7	2.0*	3.0*
Without injury	32.8	20.8	11.6*	8.9	11.9	1.4*	2.8*
Verbal threat of assault	11.4	12.9*	14.5	18.9	17.8	1.7*	0.9*
Total†							
Aggravated assault							
With injury	9.0	7.2	7.0	3.6	2.0	0.6*	0.2*
Without injury	12.5	18.9	16.2	10.0	6.2	3.2	1.3
Simple assault							
With injury	22.3	14.6	10.3	6.9	5.0	1.4	0.7*
Without injury	36.6	27.9	17.5	13.0	10.2	3.1	1.2
Verbal threat of assault	23.6	22.2	18.3	14.6	13.5	6.0	1.5

Source: National Crime Victimization Survey, 1993 preliminary data from: Bureau of the Census. 1995. *National crime victimization survey, 1992–1993.* [Computer files]. Suitland, Md. [See appendix entry 28]

Note: Rates are per 1,000 persons aged 12 years or more. Table includes series crimes. Series crime and other crime types are defined in the appendix. Aggravated assaults include all attacks (and attempted attacks) with weapons or, if no weapon was involved, those that result in serious injury. Simple assaults are attacks (and attempted attacks) without weapons resulting in minor or undetermined injuries requiring less than two days of hospitalization. Data for 1993 are not comparable with earlier years due to changes in the survey.

* Estimate is based on 10 or fewer sample cases.
† Total includes races other than black and white.

2.82 Assaults, by Race and Gender of Victim, and by Type of Assault, 1993

	Male			Female			Total		
	White	Black	Total*	White	Black	Total*	White	Black	Total*
Aggravated assault									
With injury	298,160	69,430	376,970	173,390	92,530	282,920	471,550	161,960	659,890
Without injury	969,480	138,610	1,128,750	415,450	123,440	550,290	1,384,940	262,050	1,679,040
Simple assault									
With injury	513,420	73,590	605,720	621,690	139,150	770,910	1,135,110	212,740	1,376,640
Without injury	1,304,680	150,490	1,498,090	861,850	145,780*	1,040,530	2,166,530	296,270	2,538,620
Verbal threat of assault	1,275,830	217,220	1,533,520	986,900	107,240	1,109,630	2,262,740	324,450	2,643,150

Source: National Crime Victimization Survey, 1993 preliminary data from: Bureau of the Census. 1995. *National crime victimization survey, 1992–1993.* [Computer files]. Suitland, Md. [See appendix entry 28]

Note: Table includes series crimes. Series crime and other crime types are defined in the appendix. Aggravated assaults include all attacks (and attempted attacks) with weapons or, if no weapon was involved, those that result in serious injury. Simple assaults are attacks (and attempted attacks) without weapons resulting in minor or undetermined injuries requiring less than two days of hospitalization. Data for 1993 are not comparable with earlier years due to changes in the survey. Detail may not add up to total due to rounding.

* Total includes races other than black and white.

2.83 Assault Rates, by Race and Gender of Victim, and by Type of Assault, 1993

	Male			Female			Total		
	White	Black	Total*	White	Black	Total*	White	Black	Total*
Aggravated assault									
With injury	3.4	6.0	3.5	1.9	6.7	2.8	2.6	6.4	3.1
Without injury	11.1	12.0	10.3	4.5	9.0	5.4	7.7	10.4	7.9
Simple assault									
With injury	5.9	6.4	5.5	6.8	10.1	7.5	6.3	8.4	6.5
Without injury	15.0	13.1	13.7	9.4	10.6	10.2	12.1	11.7	12.0
Verbal threat of assault	14.6	18.9	14.0	10.8	7.8	10.8	12.6	12.9	12.5

Source: National Crime Victimization Survey, 1993 preliminary data from: Bureau of the Census. 1995. *National crime victimization survey, 1992–1993.* [Computer files]. Suitland, Md. [See appendix entry 28]

Note: Rates are per 1,000 persons aged 12 years or more. Table includes series crimes. Series crime and other crime types are defined in the appendix. Aggravated assaults include all attacks (and attempted attacks) with weapons or, if no weapon was involved, those that result in serious injury. Simple assaults are attacks (and attempted attacks) without weapons resulting in minor or undetermined injuries requiring less than two days of hospitalization. Data for 1993 are not comparable with earlier years due to changes in the survey.

* Total includes races other than black and white.

Victim-Offender Relationship

2.84   Percentage of Assaults, by Strangers and Nonstrangers, and by Type of Assault, 1993

Type of Violence	Total Number of Victimizations	% Involving Strangers	% Involving Nonstrangers
Aggravated assault with injury	659,890	34.6	58.1
Aggravated assault without injury	1,679,040	55.0	41.1
Simple assault with injury	1,376,630	24.4	73.8
Simple assault without injury	2,538,620	41.4	56.1
Verbal threat of assault	2,643,150	46.3	52.3

Source: National Crime Victimization Survey, 1993 preliminary data from: Bureau of the Census. 1995. *National crime victimization survey, 1992–1993.* [Computer files]. Suitland, Md. [See appendix entry 28]

Note: Victimizations in which the relationship between victim and offender was unknown are excluded. Table includes series crimes. Series crime and other crime types are defined in the appendix. Data for 1993 are not comparable with earlier years due to changes in the survey. Aggravated assaults include all attacks (and attempted attacks) with weapons or, if no weapon was involved, those that result in serious injury. Simple assaults are attacks (and attempted attacks) without weapons resulting in minor or undetermined injuries requiring less than two days of hospitalization.

2.85   Percentage of Assaults Involving Strangers, by Gender and Race of Victim, and by Type of Assault, 1993

	Male				Female			
	Total	White	Black	Other	Total	White	Black	Other
Aggravated assault	54.8	57.0	43.0	42.8*	39.3	42.1	31.9	38.3*
With injury	43.9	46.7	30.7*	54.9*	22.2	21.0	24.7*	20.6*
Without injury	58.4	60.2	49.1	37.3*	48.1	50.9	37.4	64.9*
Simple assault	50.8	51.1	51.4	39.3	26.2	26.7	23.8	23.8*
With injury	37.5	38.0	36.4	27.2*	14.1	13.7	14.0*	38.2*
Without injury	51.1	50.8	51.4	59.0*	27.4	27.9	25.7	22.5*
Verbal threat of assault	55.8	56.6	57.2	24.0*	33.1	33.7	30.8	15.1*

Source: National Crime Victimization Survey, 1993 preliminary data from: Bureau of the Census. 1995. *National crime victimization survey, 1992–1993.* [Computer files]. Suitland, Md. [See appendix entry 28]

Note: Table includes series crimes. Series crime and other crime types are defined in the appendix. Data for 1993 are not comparable with earlier years due to changes in the survey. Aggravated assaults include all attacks (and attempted attacks) with weapons or, if no weapon was involved, those that result in serious injury. Simple assaults are attacks (and attempted attacks) without weapons resulting in minor or undetermined injuries requiring less than two days of hospitalization.

*   Estimate is based on 10 or fewer sample cases.

2.86 Percentage of Single-Offender Assaults, by Victim-Offender Relationship, and by Type of Assault, 1993

	Aggravated Assault		Simple Assault		Verbal Threat of Assault
	With Injury	Without Injury	With Injury	Without Injury	
Related					
Spouse	5.3	0.9*	12.6	5.3	2.3
Ex-spouse	5.1	2.1*	2.7	1.4	2.0
Parent	1.1*	1.4*	3.4	0.4*	0.6*
Own child	1.0*	0.8*	1.9*	1.3	1.0*
Sibling	2.0*	0.6*	4.4	1.0*	0.8*
Other relative	2.4*	3.3	1.5*	1.1*	2.2
Well known, not related†	30.0	20.7	34.4	28.2	22.5
Casual acquaintance	19.2	16.5	16.3	20.1	21.2
Stranger	33.9	53.7	22.8	41.2	47.4

Source: National Crime Victimization Survey, 1993 preliminary data from: Bureau of the Census. 1995. *National crime victimization survey, 1992–1993.* [Computer files]. Suitland, Md. [See appendix entry 28]

Note: Table includes series crimes. Series crime and other crime types are defined in the appendix. Aggravated assaults include all attacks (and attempted attacks) with weapons or, if no weapon was involved, those that result in serious injury. Simple assaults are attacks (and attempted attacks) without weapons resulting in minor or undetermined injuries requiring less than two days of hospitalization. Data for 1993 are not comparable with earlier years due to changes in the survey.

* Estimate is based on 10 or fewer sample cases.

† Includes data on offenders well known to the victim whose relationship could not be ascertained.

2.87 Percentage of Multiple-Offender Assaults, by Victim-Offender Relationship, and by Type of Assault, 1993

	Aggravated Assault			Simple Assault			Verbal Threat of Assault
	Total	With Injury	Without Injury	Total	With Injury	Without Injury	
Related							
Spouse	0.5*	1.5*	0.0*	0.5*	0.0*	0.0*	1.3*
Ex-spouse	0.0*	0.0*	0.0*	0.2*	0.9*	0.0*	0.0*
Parent	0.2*	0.5*	0.0*	0.4*	0.0*	0.0*	1.1*
Own child	0.5*	1.5*	0.0*	0.2*	0.9*	0.0*	0.0*
Sibling	0.2*	0.5*	0.0*	0.3*	1.5*	0.0*	0.0*
Other relative	0.7*	0.0*	1.0*	2.2	1.9*	1.5*	2.5*
Well known, not related†	6.8	8.0*	6.3	10.0	12.2	11.1	8.1
Casual acquaintance	10.3	16.1	7.6	16.4	20.8	14.7	16.3
Stranger	68.1	53.1	75.0	61.3	55.8	63.2	62.2
Unknown/unspecified	12.7	18.8	10.1	8.5	6.0	9.5	8.5

Source: National Crime Victimization Survey, 1993 preliminary data from: Bureau of the Census. 1995. *National crime victimization survey, 1992–1993.* [Computer files]. Suitland, Md. [See appendix entry 28]

Note: Table includes series crimes. Series crime and other crime types are defined in the appendix. Aggravated assaults include all attacks (and attempted attacks) with weapons or, if no weapon was involved, those that result in serious injury. Simple assaults are attacks (and attempted attacks) without weapons resulting in minor or undetermined injuries requiring less than two days of hospitalization. Data for 1993 are not comparable with earlier years due to changes in the survey.

* Estimate is based on 10 or fewer sample cases.

† Includes data on offenders well known to the victim whose relationship could not be ascertained.

Weapons

2.88   Percentage of Assaults in Which Offenders Used Weapons, by Stranger/Nonstranger Classification, and by Type of Assault, 1993

Aggravated Assault	Total Victimizations	Weapon Victimizations	Weapon Victimizations Involving Strangers		Weapon Victimizations Involving Nonstrangers	
			Number	%	Number	%
With injury	611,530	467,890	178,720	38.2	289,180	61.8
Without injury	1,614,820	1,614,820	924,130	57.2	690,690	42.8

Source: National Crime Victimization Survey, 1993 preliminary data from: Bureau of the Census. 1995. *National crime victimization survey, 1992–1993.* [Computer files]. Suitland, Md. [See appendix entry 28]

Note: Table includes series crimes. Series crime and other crime types are defined in the appendix. Data for 1993 are not comparable with earlier years due to changes in the survey. Aggravated assaults are nonfatal attacks involving serious injury and/or the use of a weapon or other means capable of causing death or great bodily harm.

2.89   Percentage of Aggravated Assaults, by Injury, Strangers and Nonstrangers, and by Specific Weapon Used, 1993

	Aggravated Assaults With Injury	Aggravated Assaults Without Injury	Aggravated Assaults Involving Strangers	Aggravated Assaults Involving Nonstrangers
Total victimizations	611,530	1,614,820	1,152,450	1,073,910
Weapon victimizations	467,890	1,614,820	1,102,850	979,870
%	76.5	100.0	95.7	91.2
Handguns	61,960	524,980	329,030	257,910
%	13.5	32.3	29.6	26.4
Other guns	9,970*	107,280	60,590	56,660
%	2.2*	6.6	5.4	5.8
Knives	114,010	371,150	235,400	249,760
%	24.8	22.8	21.2	25.6
Other sharp objects	21,540*	64,920	38,900	47,560
%	4.7*	4.0	3.5	4.9
Blunt objects	94,340	257,890	191,330	160,900
%	20.5	15.9	17.2	16.5
Other weapons	158,430	298,320	254,430	202,330
%	34.4	18.3	22.9	20.7
Gun type unknown	1,910*	2,240*	2,240*	1,910*
%	0.4*	0.1*	0.2*	0.2*
Total number of weapons	460,260	1,626,770	1,111,920	975,110

Source: National Crime Victimization Survey, 1993 preliminary data from: Bureau of the Census. 1995. *National crime victimization survey, 1992–1993.* [Computer files]. Suitland, Md. [See appendix entry 28]

Note: Table includes series crimes. Series crime and other crime types are defined in the appendix. Aggravated assaults are nonfatal attacks involving serious injury and/or the use of a weapon or other means capable of causing death or great bodily harm. Data for 1993 are not comparable with earlier years due to changes in the survey.

*   Estimate is based on 10 or fewer sample cases.

Urban-Rural Location

2.90 Assaults, by Victim's Location of Residence, and by Type of Assault, 1993

	Metropolitan Areas								Non-metro Areas
	Outside of Central Cities			Central Cities					
	Not a Place	Under 50,000	50,000-249,000	Under 50,000	50,000-249,999	250,000-499,999	500,000-999,999	1,000,000 or More	
Aggravated assault									
With injury	95,170	136,300	44,860	26,560	80,510	42,560	55,180	58,720	120,030
Without injury	290,840	385,530	83,870	75,890	211,790	105,440	97,300	92,070	336,310
Simple assault									
With injury	235,540	267,880	74,770	52,880	231,390	91,340	85,950	86,140	250,740
Without injury	449,830	566,900	164,190	114,120	299,730	204,770	134,500	138,540	466,040
Verbal threat of assault	553,290	511,690	110,710	92,960	420,720	228,780	123,740	144,100	457,170

Source: National Crime Victimization Survey, 1993 preliminary data from: Bureau of the Census. 1995. *National crime victimization survey, 1992–1993.* [Computer files]. Suitland, Md. [See appendix entry 28]

Note: Table includes series crimes. Series crime and other crime types are defined in the appendix. "Not a Place" refers to areas that are neither incorporated (e.g., cities, towns, villages) nor otherwise defined as Census Designated Places (i.e., areas of discrete and/or concentrated settlement identifiable by name, but not legally incorporated). Data for 1993 are not comparable with earlier years due to changes in the survey. Aggravated assaults include all attacks (and attempted attacks) with weapons or, if no weapon was involved, those thatsesult in serious injury. Simple assaults are attacked (and attempted attacks) without weapons resulting in minor or undetermined injuries requiring less than two days of hospitalization.

2.91 Assault Rates, by Victim's Location of Residence, and by Type of Assault, 1993

	Metropolitan Areas								Non-metro Areas
	Outside of Central Cities			Central Cities					
	Not a Place	Under 50,000	50,000-249,000	Under 50,000	50,000-249,999	250,000-499,999	500,000-999,999	1,000,000 or More	
Aggravated assault									
With injury	2.0	2.9	3.9	4.3	3.5	4.0	6.0	4.7	2.5
Without injury	6.0	8.1	7.2	12.2	9.1	10.0	10.5	7.4	6.9
Simple assault									
With injury	4.9	5.6	6.4	8.5	10.0	8.7	9.3	6.9	5.2
Without injury	9.3	11.9	14.1	18.3	12.9	19.5	14.5	11.1	9.6
Verbal threat of assault	11.5	10.8	9.5	14.9	18.1	21.8	13.4	11.6	9.4

Source: National Crime Victimization Survey, 1993 preliminary data from: Bureau of the Census. 1995. *National crime victimization survey, 1992–1993*. [Computer files]. Suitland, Md. [See appendix entry 28]

Note: Rates are per 1,000 persons aged 12 years or more. Table includes series crimes. Series crime and other crime types are defined in the appendix. "Not a Place" refers to areas that are neither incorporated (e.g., cities, towns, villages) nor otherwise defined as Census Designated Places (i.e., areas of discrete and/or concentrated settlement identifiable by name, but not legally incorporated). Data for 1993 are not comparable with earlier years due to changes in the survey. Aggravated assaults include all attacks (and attempted attacks) with weapons or, if no weapon was involved, those that result in serious injury. Simple assaults are attacks (and attempted attacks) without weapons resulting in minor or undetermined injuries requiring less than two days of hospitalization.

Chapter 3
Groups and Situations

This chapter describes groups and situations that are at high risk for violence. Our approach is to present data from population groups or situations that are associated with high levels of violence or persons that are especially vulnerable to violence because they cannot effectively defend themselves. In this sense, risk reflects either higher-than-average occurrence of violence or lower-than-average ability to protect oneself, or both.

Thus, this chapter complements previous chapters on general population patterns of violence. By focusing on specific groups and situations at risk for violence, it provides a structure for addressing such topics as child abuse, violence against women, occupation-related violence, hate crime, recidivism, and the misuse of drugs, alcohol, and firearms.

DATA SOURCES

The data for this chapter are diverse and drawn from many sources. Whenever possible, multiple sources of data for the same topic are presented for purposes of contrast. Because there are too many sources to adequately discuss here, the reader is urged to consult the data source appendix entries for the tables and figures of interest. Sources vary considerably; appropriate interpretation requires some familiarity with the details of the data.

CHAPTER ORGANIZATION

The chapter is divided into two major sections. The first characterizes people who, because of their demographic characteristics or life situations, are especially vulnerable to violent victimization. The second characterizes groups and situations that have higher-than-average risks of committing or contributing to violence.

In the vulnerable groups and situations section, young people, elderly people, women, and members of certain minority and ethnic groups are described. The routines of daily life may also expose people to unusual risks of violence. Accordingly, we include data on workplaces and occupations, as well as economic status and daily involvement in organizations such as prisons and schools.

In the final section, tables and figures are presented on high-risk groups and situations. These include children and adolescents, police officers (who because of their duties may be required to engage in violence, for example, using deadly force to apprehend felons), and recidivists. The use of alcohol and drugs has been associated with violent behavior, as has the presence of firearms. Data on these factors can be found in the last tables and figures of this chapter.

In focusing on specific groups and situations in this chapter, we caution the reader not to ignore data on two of the highest risk groups for violence in America: males and African Americans. Since much of the basic incidence data is presented by race and gender in previous chapters, we do not repeat it here. However, the reader is urged to consult the index for further references throughout this volume on these important groups.

In the same vein, the index should be consulted to locate information on many other topics, such as family violence or stranger violence, that do not appear in distinct sections of this chapter. Of course, any system of organization will tend to emphasize certain aspects of the data while deemphasizing others. We hope the organizing structure we have selected for this chapter is helpful to most readers and that the index will also help in locating information of interest.

VULNERABLE GROUPS AND SITUATIONS: YOUTH

Children and Adolescents: Maltreatment and Abuse

3.1   Child Abuse and Child Abuse Rates, by Form of Abuse and Gender of Victim, 1986

	Number of Children		Rate	
	Male	Female	Male	Female
Physical abuse	123,100	145,400	3.8	4.7
Sexual abuse	28,400	90,200	0.9	2.9
Emotional abuse	68,700	86,000	2.1	2.8

Source: Study of National Incidence and Prevalence of Child Abuse and Neglect
1986 (NIS-2), adapted from: Sedlak, Andrea J. 1991. *National incidence
and prevalence of child abuse and neglect: 1988*. (Revised Report).
Rockville, Md.: Westat, Inc., p. 5-5, Table 5-2. Used with permission. [See appendix entry 44]

Note: Rates are per 1,000 children. The same child may be represented in more
than one abuse category. Therefore, adding different categories of abuse
results in counting the same child more than once and thus should be avoided.
See appendix for definitions of abuse categories. Children are defined as
persons under age 18.

3.2   Child Abuse and Neglect, by Age of Victim, 1986

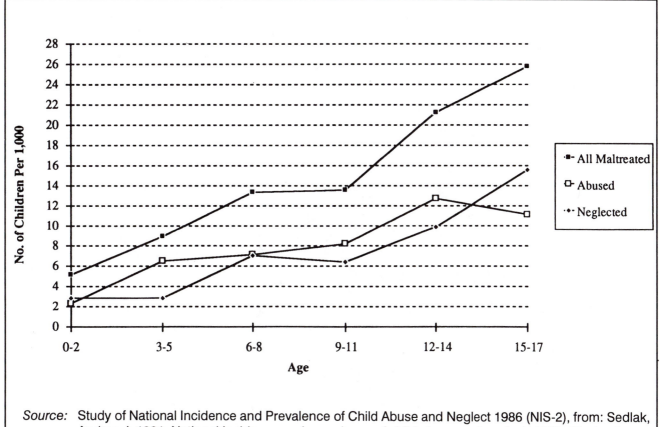

Source: Study of National Incidence and Prevalence of Child Abuse and Neglect 1986 (NIS-2), from: Sedlak, Andrea J. 1991. National Incidence and prevalence of child abuse and neglect: 1988. (Revised Report). Rockville, Md.: Westat, Inc., p. 5–11, Figure 5-1. Used with permission. [See appendix entry 44]

Note: The same child may be represented in more than one abuse category. Therefore, adding different categories of abuse results in counting the same child more than once and thus should be avoided. Children are defined as persons under age 18.

3.3 Child Abuse, by Age of Child, 1985

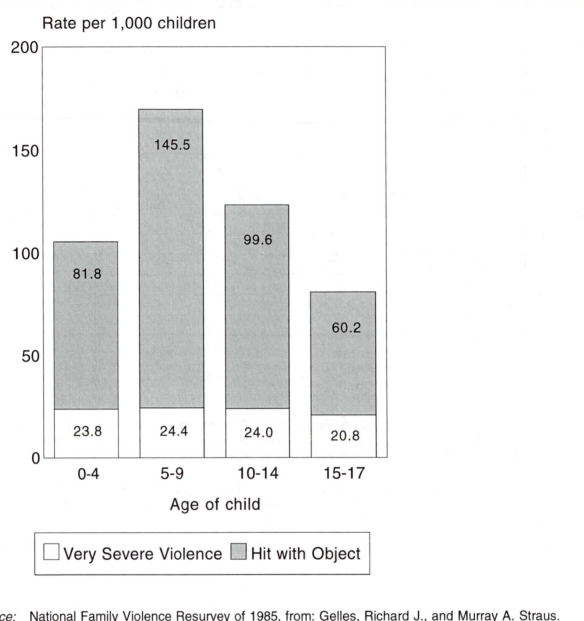

Source: National Family Violence Resurvey of 1985, from: Gelles, Richard J., and Murray A. Straus.
1989. *Physical violence in American families, 1985* [Computer file]. Ann Arbor, Mich.: Inter-
university Consortium for Political and Social Research. [See appendix entry 38]

Note: "Child abuse" in this figure is a category labeled "severe violence" (the sum of the two
categories shown) that was created by Gelles and Straus and documented in the codebook
distributed with the data (cited above).

Children and Adolescents: Punishment and Abuse

3.4   Annual Prevalence Rates of Child Maltreatment and Abuse, by Gender of Adult
Respondent, 1985

Type of Conflict Tactic	Total	Male	Female
Threatened to hit child or throw object	289.2	263.7	305.6
Threw, smashed object	108.9	91.2	120.4
Threw something at child	30.6	19.4	37.8
Pushed, grabbed, shoved child	281.8	277.3	284.7
Slapped or spanked child	556.8	529.3	574.5
Kicked, bit, hit child with fist	15.0	16.2	14.3
Hit, tried to hit child with object	97.6	92.1	101.1
Beat up child	6.8	6.9	6.8
Burned or scalded child	4.7	4.9	4.5
Threatened child with knife or gun	2.1	0.9	2.8
Used knife or gun on child	2.1	0.6	3.0

Source: National Family Violence Resurvey of 1985, from: Gelles, Richard J., and
Murray A. Straus. 1989. *Physical violence in American families, 1985* [Computer
file]. Ann Arbor, Mich.: Inter-university Consortium for Political and Social
Research. [See appendix entry 38]

Note: Annual prevalence rates are the number of children per 1,000 who have
experienced at least one instance of the specified "conflict tactic" by the parent
specified in the 12-month period preceding the interview. From the first row, for
example, 263.7 out of 1,000 children, in the year before the study, were said to
have been threatened with hitting or having objects thrown at them (at least
once) by adult males in their households. Adult females reported having been
responsible for this behavior at a rate of 305.6 per 1,000 children. Note that
only one adult per household was interviewed in the study.

3.5   Lifetime Prevalence Rates of Child Maltreatment, by Gender of Adult Respondent, 1985

Type of Conflict Tactic	Total	Male	Female
Threatened to hit child or throw object	339.4	312.8	356.5
Threw, smashed object	137.8	117.6	150.8
Threw something at child	45.5	30.2	55.3
Pushed, grabbed, shoved child	335.5	334.8	336.0
Slapped or spanked child	746.4	710.8	769.3
Kicked, bit, hit child with fist	20.7	20.0	21.2
Hit, tried to hit child with object	143.7	130.5	152.2
Beat up child	9.8	9.7	9.8
Burned or scalded child	6.3	6.1	6.5
Threatened child with knife or gun	2.7	0.9	3.8
Used knife or gun on child	2.1	0.6	3.0

Source: National Family Violence Resurvey of 1985, from: Gelles, Richard J., and Murray A. Straus. 1989. *Physical violence in American families, 1985* [Computer file]. Ann Arbor, Mich.: Inter-university Consortium for Political and Social Research. [See appendix entry 38]

Note: Lifetime prevalence rates are the number of children per 1,000 who have experienced at least one instance of the specified "conflict tactic" by the parent specified. From the first row, for example, 312.8 out of 1,000 children were said to have been threatened with hitting or having objects thrown at them, at least once in their lifetime by adult males in their households. Adult females reported having been responsible for this behavior at least once in the lifetime of a child living in their household, at a rate of 365.5 per 1,000 children. Note that only one adult per household was interviewed in the study.

3.6   Annual Prevalence Rates of Child Maltreatment and Abuse, by Gender and Occupation of Adult Respondent, 1985

Type of Conflict Tactic	Male		Female	
	Blue Collar	White Collar	Blue Collar	White Collar
Threatened to hit child or throw object	283	254	329	309
"Minor" violence	591	596	682	627
Threw or smashed object	92	89	132	108
Threw something at child	25	17	38	39
Pushed, grabbed, shoved child	263	306	278	293
Slapped or spanked child	562	518	624	555
"Severe" violence	119	89	127	107
Hit, tried to hit child with object	105	85	113	101
"Very severe"	30	15	31	17
Kicked, bit, hit child with fist	24	10	18	12
Beat up child	13	2	6	4
Burned or scalded child	7	4	2	4
Threatened child with knife or gun	1	1	2	1
Used knife or gun on child	0*	1	4	0*

Source: National Family Violence Resurvey of 1985, from: Gelles, Richard J., and Murray A. Straus. 1989. *Physical violence in American families, 1985* [Computer file]. Ann Arbor, Mich.: Inter-university Consortium for Political and Social Research. [See appendix entry 38]

Note: Annual prevalence rates are the number of children per 1,000 who have experienced at least one instance of the specified "conflict tactic" by the parent specified in the 12-month period preceding the interview. From the first row, for example, 283 out of 1,000 children, in the year before the study, were said to have been threatened with hitting or having objects thrown at them (at least once) by adult males with blue collar occupations. Adult males with white collar occupations reported having been responsible for this behavior at a rate of 254 per 1,000 children. Note that only one adult per household was interviewed in the study. The summary value for the "Severe" violence category includes at least one item under "Very severe" violence or "Hit, or tried to hit with object." The categories labeled "Minor," "Severe" and "Very severe" are those created by Gelles and Straus and are documented in the codebook distributed with the data (cited above).

*   Less than 0.5

3.7   Annual Prevalence Rates of Child Maltreatment and Abuse, by Gender and Race of Adult Respondent, 1985

Type of Conflict Tactic	Male				Female				Both Genders			
	White	Black	Hispanic	Other	White	Black	Hispanic	Other	White	Black	Hispanic	Other
Threatened to hit child or throw object	267	326	180	239	291	425	329	244	282	398	289	241
Minor violence	607	550	426	546	648	664	568	625	631	633	529	586
Threw or smashed object	93	97	70	77	125	106	120	99	112	103	106	88
Threw something at child	17	12	7	41	32	56	62	66	26	44	47	54
Pushed, grabbed, shoved child	299	256	188	152	294	285	282	197	296	277	257	175
Slapped or spanked child	542	516	384	532	575	610	523	611	561	584	485	572
Severe violence	97	200	100	82	103	187	147	122	101	190	134	102
Hit, tried to hit child with object	90	198	70	51	90	168	115	122	90	176	103	87
Very severe	18	29	46	45	21	40	50	15	20	37	49	30
Kicked, bit, hit child with fist	14	15	15	43	13	26	21	0*	13	23	19	21
Beat up child	5	21	17	14	2	19	35	15	3	20	30	14
Burned or scalded child	4	0*	12	17	5	0*	3	15	4	0*	5	16
Threatened child with knife or gun	1	0*	8	0*	3	0*	0*	15	2	0*	2	7
Used knife or gun on child	1	0*	0*	0*	4	0*	0*	0*	3	0*	0*	0*

Source: National Family Violence Resurvey of 1985, from: Gelles, Richard J., and Murray A. Straus. 1989. *Physical violence in American families, 1985* [Computer file]. Ann Arbor, Mich.: Inter-university Consortium for Political and Social Research. [See appendix entry 38]

Note.   Annual prevalence rates are the number of children per 1,000 who have experienced at least one instance of the specified "conflict tactic" by the parent specified in the 12-month period preceding the interview. From the first row, for example, 267 out of 1,000 children, in the year before the study, were said to have been threatened with hitting or having objects thrown at them (at least once) by adult white males in their households. Adult black males reported having been responsible for this behavior at a rate of 326 per 1,000 children. Note that only one adult per household was interviewed in the study. The categories labeled "Minor," "Severe," and "Very severe" are those created by Gelles and Straus and are documented in the codebook distributed with the data (cited above). The summary value for the "Severe" violence category includes at least one item under "Very severe" violence or "Hit, or tried to hit with object."

*   Less than 0.5

3.8   Lifetime Prevalence Rates of Child Maltreatment and Abuse, by Gender and Race of Adult Respondent, 1985

Type of Conflict Tactic	Male				Female				Both Genders			
	White	Black	Hispanic	Other	White	Black	Hispanic	Other	White	Black	Hispanic	Other
Threatened to hit child or throw object	318	402	187	277	344	466	362	337	333	448	315	307
Minor violence	764	693	519	630	810	778	642	832	792	755	608	731
Threw or smashed object	123	112	97	77	159	124	151	112	145	121	136	95
Threw something at child	29	19	7	48	49	69	82	95	41	55	61	71
Pushed, grabbed, shoved child	364	282	222	152	347	308	313	309	354	301	289	231
Slapped or spanked child	737	672	481	612	784	759	603	832	765	735	570	723
Severe violence	138	239	117	109	154	228	182	189	147	231	164	150
Hit, tried to hit child with object	130	229	86	78	142	211	152	179	137	216	134	129
Very severe violence	24	36	46	45	27	53	63	25	26	48	59	35
Kicked, bit, hit child with fist	18	22	15	43	21	30	26	10	20	28	23	26
Beat up child	8	21	17	14	4	27	44	15	6	25	37	14
Burned or scalded child	5	0*	12	17	7	3	5	15	6	2	7	16
Threatened child with knife or gun	1	0*	8	0*	4	2	0*	15	2	2	7	7
Used knife or gun on child	1	0*	0*	0*	4	0*	0*	0*	3	0*	0*	0*

Source: National Family Violence Resurvey of 1985, from: Gelles, Richard J., and Murray A. Straus. 1989. *Physical violence in American families, 1985* [Computer file]. Ann Arbor, Mich.: Inter-university Consortium for Political and Social Research. [See appendix entry 38]

Note: Lifetime prevalence rates are the number of children per 1,000 who have experienced at least one instance of the specified "conflict tactic" by the parent specified. From the first row, for example, 318 out of 1,000 children were said to have been threatened with hitting or having objects thrown at them, at least once in their lifetimes, by adult white males in their households. Adult black males reported having been responsible for this behavior, at least once in the lifetime of a child living in their household, at a rate of 402 per 1,000 children. Note that only one adult per household was interviewed in the study. The categories labeled "Minor," "Severe," and "Very severe" violence are those created by Gelles and Straus and are documented in the codebook distributed with the data (cited above). The summary value for the "Severe" violence category includes at least one item under "Very severe" violence or "Hit, or tried to hit with object."

*   Less than 0.5

3.9   "In the past 12 months, how often would you say you ... spanked or hit your child(ren), kicked, bit, or punched your child(ren), hit or tried to hit your child with something?" Percentage, by Age, Sex, and Race of Parent, and by Age of Children, 1994

Percentage	Parent's Age				Sex		Race			Children's Age				
	18-24	25-34	35-54	55 +	Male	Female	White	Black	Hispanic	<1	1-5	6-10	11-13	14-17
Spanked or hit														
More than 11 times a year	3	2	*	0	1	1	1	0	0	0	2	2	1	1
Often, 6 to 11 times a year	10	5	2	0	2	4	3	7	3	0	7	3	1	0
Occasionally, 3 to 5 times a year	20	17	9	25	11	14	12	23	11	20	22	17	10	5
Hardly ever, once or twice a year	20	38	29	0	30	33	30	30	44	16	38	39	33	23
Never	47	37	59	75	55	48	53	39	42	64	31	39	55	70
Refused any answer	0	1	*	0	*	*	1	0	0	0	0	1	0	0
Kicked, bit, or punched														
More than 11 times year	0	0	0	0	0	0	0	0	0	0	0	0	0	0
Often, 6 to 11 times a year	0	0	0	0	0	0	0	0	0	0	0	0	0	0
Occasionally, 3 to 5 times a year	0	0	0	0	0	0	0	0	0	0	0	0	0	0
Hardly ever, once or twice a year	0	1	3	0	2	2	2	4	3	2	1	2	1	1
Never	100	99	97	100	98	98	98	96	97	98	99	98	99	99
Refused any Answer	0	0	0	0	0	0	0	0	0	0	0	0	0	0
Hit, or tried to hit, with something														
More than 11 times a year	3	0	0	0	*	0	0	0	0	0	0	1	0	0
Often, 6 to 11 times a year	3	1	0	0	0	1	*	2	0	0	1	1	1	0
Occasionally, 3 to 5 times a year	0	3	2	10	3	2	1	11	0	2	4	4	4	1
Hardly ever, once or twice a year	3	5	6	0	6	5	4	11	8	0	6	7	6	4
Never	90	92	91	90	91	92	94	77	92	98	88	88	90	95
Refused any answer	0	0	0	0	0	0	0	0	0	0	0	0	0	0

Source: National Child Abuse Survey, adapted from: National Committee to Prevent Child Abuse. 1994. Unpublished data, tables generated by National Committee to Prevent Child Abuse, Chicago, Ill. Used with permission. [See appendix entry 27]

Note: Asked of those who have children under age 18 living at home. Column percentages may not add up to 100 due to rounding.

*   Less than one percent.

Children and Adolescents: General Victimization

3.10   Rape, Robbery, and Assault Victimization Rates, by Age of Victim, 1992

	12–15	16–19	20–24	25–34	35–49	50–64	65 & Over
Rape	1.1*	1.6*	2.6	0.5*	0.4*	0.1*	0.2*
Robbery	9.8	15.4	11.4	7.7	3.8	2.8	1.5
Completed	6.1	8.6	7.2	5.1	3.0	2.0	1.0*
With injury	2.1*	2.8*	3.0	2.5	1.2	0.9*	0.5*
From serious assault	1.1*	2.0*	1.5*	1.5	0.4*	0.3*	0.2*
From minor assault	1.0*	0.8*	1.5*	0.9*	0.8	0.6*	0.2*
Without injury	3.9	5.9	4.2	2.6	1.8	1.1*	0.5*
Attempted	3.7	6.7	4.2	2.7	0.8	0.8*	0.6*
With injury	0.6*	2.3*	0.8*	0.8*	0.1*	0.4*	0.0*
From serious assault	0.0*	2.1*	0.6*	0.2*	0.0*	0.2*	0.0*
From minor assault	0.6*	0.2*	0.2*	0.6*	0.1*	0.2*	0.0*
Without injury	3.1	4.5	3.4	1.9	0.7	0.4*	0.6*
Assault	64.8	60.9	56.0	29.4	17.1	7.1	3.1
Aggravated	20.1	26.3	18.1	9.3	6.8	2.3	1.3*
Completed with injury	7.4	10.2	6.6	3.0	2.3	0.9*	0.4*
Attempted with weapon	12.7	16.1	11.5	6.2	4.5	1.4	0.9*
Simple	44.7	34.5	38.0	20.1	10.2	4.8	1.8
Completed with injury	13.7	8.7	10.6	6.4	2.1	0.2*	0.3*
Attempted without weapon	31.0	25.9	27.4	13.7	8.1	4.6	1.4

Source: National Crime Victimization Survey, 1992 from: Bureau of Justice Statistics. 1993. *Criminal victimization in the United States, 1992*. Washington, D.C., p. 23, Table 4. [See appendix entry 28]

Note: Rates are per 1,000 persons in each age group. Table excludes series crimes. Series crimes and other crime types are defined in the appendix. "Serious assault" and minor assault" are defined in the appendix.

*   Estimate is based on 10 or fewer sample cases.

3.11   Serious Violent Crime and Handgun Crime Rates, by Age of Victim, 1987–1992

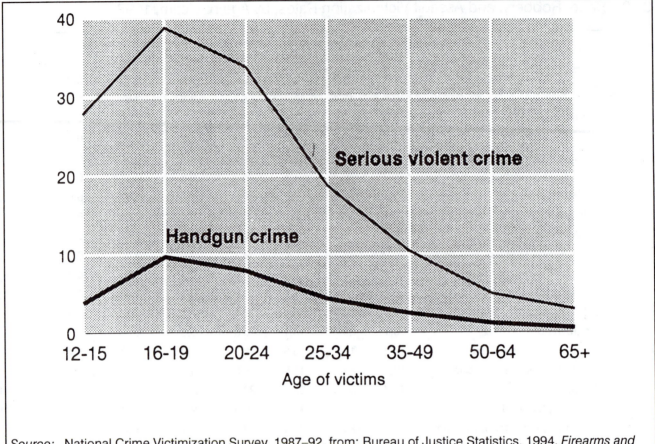

Source: National Crime Victimization Survey, 1987–92, from: Bureau of Justice Statistics, 1994. *Firearms and crimes of violence.* Washington, D.C., p. 5. [See appendix entry 28]

Note: Rates are per 1,000 residents aged 12 and older. Excludes series crimes. Series crimes and other crime types are defined in the appendix.

3.12   Percentage of Children Victimized, by Type of Victimization and Gender of Victim, 1992

Type of Victimization	Percent Ever		Percent in Last Year	
	Girls	Boys	Girls	Boys
Any victimizations (excluding corporal punishment)				
Attempted and completed	44.8	57.6	32.1	42.0
Completed only	26.1	43.9	18.5	32.1
Nonfamily assault				
Attempted and completed	22.8	42.0	14.3	30.0
Completed only	11.9	32.2	7.7	23.4
Family assault				
Attempted and completed	14.4	11.6	8.9	8.2
Completed only	8.3	6.7	5.7	4.8
Nonparent family perpetrator				
Attempted and completed	8.8	8.0	6.1	6.2
Completed only	5.5	4.7	4.2	3.9
Parent perpetrator				
Attempted and completed	5.6	3.4	2.5	1.7
Completed only	2.6	1.9	1.1	0.7
Corporal punishment	71.4	77.5	27.3	29.6
Sexual abuse				
Attempted and completed	15.3	5.9	10.2	3.4
Attempted only	8.2	3.7	5.8	1.9
Serious noncontact only	3.9	1.2	2.9	0.9
Contact only	5.6	1.0	3.2	0.6
Rape (completed only)	1.3	0.0	1.0	0.0
Violence to genitals				
Attempted and completed	1.7	16.2	1.0	9.2
Completed only	1.3	13.5	0.8	7.5
Kidnapping				
Attempted and completed	8.0	4.2	3.4	1.0
Completed only	0.4	0.0	0.0	0.0

Source: Finkelhor, David, and Jennifer Dziuba-Leatherman. 1994. Children as victims of violence: A national survey. *Pediatrics* 94, no. 4: 415, Table 2. Used with permission. [See appendix entry 8]

Note: Interviews were conducted during December 1992 and January 1993. Children were defined as persons of age 10–16 years.

3.13   Percentage of Children Victimized, by Family Income, Racial/Ethnic Background, Region, Type of Area, and Type of Victimization, 1992

	Any Victimization	Nonfamily Assault	Family Assault	Kidnapping	Sexual Abuse	Genital Violence
Income						
< $20,000	57.0	32.7	18.4	5.6	12.2	12.5
$20,000-50,000	49.7	32.3	11.6	6.9	10.2	8.7
> $50,000	50.2	31.0	12.7	5.2	10.3	7.7
Race/ethnicity						
Black	59.0	31.2	16.1	10.4	18.8	8.5
White	49.4	31.8	12.1	5.4	9.4	8.9
Hispanic*	54.3	37.8	14.8	5.4	8.2	11.2
Other	50.6	34.8	10.4	3.3	10.5	7.4
Region						
New England	48.5	28.3	10.5	11.1	9.6	11.7
Mid-Atlantic	54.4	35.1	16.9	5.5	10.6	7.4
South Atlantic	46.5	28.5	12.1	5.9	8.5	5.9
East North Central	46.4	32.1	11.5	4.3	9.3	7.4
East South Central	48.6	28.6	7.5	7.3	11.6	14.8
West North Central	50.6	31.2	12.2	6.3	9.5	10.9
West South Central	49.0	33.4	13.0	5.3	6.2	8.6
Mountain	64.6	38.8	15.8	5.9	17.8	15.5
Pacific	62.7	38.0	15.5	7.7	17.5	10.2
Metro area						
Large city	59.6	35.3	16.2	11.3	12.4	9.0
Suburb	53.6	31.5	15.2	5.7	13.1	11.1
Large town	47.9	31.2	11.9	5.2	8.3	11.0
Small town	50.3	32.1	13.1	5.9	11.7	7.7
Rural	46.3	31.8	9.2	3.6	7.0	7.8

Source: Finkelhor, David, and Jennifer Dziuba-Leatherman. 1994. Children as victims of violence: A national survey. *Pediatrics* 94, no. 4: 417, Table 5. Used with permission. [See appendix entry 8]

Note: Interviews were conducted during December 1992 and January 1993. All numbers represent percentage "ever" victimized, and include both attempted and completed episodes. Children were defined as persons of age 10–16 years.

*   Includes all Hispanics, regardless of racial identification.

3.14 Percentages of Stereotypical and Nonstereotypical Nonfamily Abductions, by Victim and Offender Characteristics, 1988

	Stereotypical	Nonstereotypical
Victim characteristics		
Gender		
Male	29.2	18.6
Female	70.8	81.4
Race		
White	41.5	23.5
Black	16.7	40.6
Hispanic	39.2	31.8
Other	2.5	4.1
Age		
12 or under	37.5	28.3
Over 12	62.5	71.7
Offender characteristics		
Gender		
Male	95.0	97.3
Female	5.0	2.7
Race		
White	40.2	19.9
Black	27.4	51.8
Hispanic	32.4	24.7
Other	0.0	3.6
Age		
15 or under	0.0	3.4
16 - 20	17.6	29.6
21 - 30	42.8	24.5
31 - 40	27.2	10.9
41 or over	12.5	31.6
Number of offenders		
One	49.1	70.8
More than one	50.9	29.2

Source: National Incidence Study of Missing, Abducted, Runaway, and Thrownaway Children, 1988, from: Asdigan, Nancy, David Finkelhor, and Gerald Hotaling. 1993. *Varieties of non-family abduction: Additional analyses from NISMART.* Durham, N.H.: Family Research Laboratory, p. 28, Table 2. Used with permission. [See appendix entry 31]

Note: Legal definition nonfamily abduction—the coerced and unauthorized *taking* of a child into a building, a vehicle, or a distance of more than 20 feet; the *detention* of a child for a period of more than an hour; the *luring* of a child for the purposes of committing another crime (these are also called nonstereotypical abductions).

Stereotypical abductions—in addition to meeting the criteria for abduction under legal definitions, the following also apply: the offender is a stranger (someone whom the child had not met or known before the day of the abduction) and the child is either (1) detained overnight; or (2) killed; or (3) transported 50 miles or more from the scene of the abduction; or (4) ransomed; or (5) the offender evidenced an intent to keep the child permanently.

For stereotypical, n = 32; for nonstereotypical, n = 364.

Children and Adolescents: Rape

3.15   Cumulative Percentages of Nonvoluntary Sexual Intercourse Among the Young, by Age, Race, and Gender, 1987

Age	Females		Males	
	White	Black	White	Black
14 and under	5.8	2.9	0.3	0.0
15	6.3	3.2	0.4	1.4
16	7.5	3.5	0.4	4.8
17	9.1	5.1	0.4	5.6
18	10.8	5.6	0.4	6.1
19	11.9	6.0	1.9	6.1
20	12.7	8.0	1.9	6.1

Source: National Survey of Children from: Moore, Kristen A., and James L. Peterson. 1989. *The consequences of teenage pregnancy.* Washington, D.C.: Child Trends, Inc., p. 15, Table 4. Used with permission. [See appendix entry 32]

3.16 Percentage of Rape Victims in 15 Reporting States, by Age of Victim, 1992

State	Number of Female Victims of Forcible Rape*	Age at Time of Rape: Cumulative Percentage of Female Victims of Forcible Rape								
		Under 10	Under 11	Under 12	Under 13	Under 14	Under 15	Under 16	Under 17	Under 18
Alabama	1,404	4	6	7	10	17	24	30	35	38
Arkansas	986	9	-	-	-	24	-	-	-	44
Delaware	783	22	-	-	29	-	50	61	66	71
District of Columbia	205	-	-	5	-	-	-	22	28	32
Florida	7,280	-	14	-	-	-	-	-	-	46
Idaho	221	5	-	-	9	-	20	24	29	35
Kansas	1,013	1	-	-	-	-	12	-	-	-
Michigan	4,731	25	28	31	35	41	49	58	64	68
Nebraska	290	-	6	-	-	-	-	31	-	42
North Carolina	2,397	-	5	-	-	-	-	20	-	-
North Dakota	124	-	25	30	35	44	48	50	52	57
Pennsylvania	2,996	-	9	-	14	-	25	32	37	42
Rhode Island	490	-	-	-	-	49	-	-	-	70
South Carolina	2,193	9	-	-	16	-	-	-	40	-
Wisconsin	1,314	4	6	8	10	14	22	29	37	42

Source: Bureau of Justice Statistics state survey of rapes reported to law enforcement agencies in 1992, from: Langan, Patrick A., and Caroline Wolf Harlow. 1994. *Child rape victims, 1992.* Washington, D.C.: Bureau of Justice Statistics, p. 1. [See appendix entry 7]

Note: Dashes indicate detail was not reported. Cumulative percentages represent the percentage of rape victims who were raped by the time they had reached a specified age. For example, in the first row, 4 percent of Alabama rape victims had been victimized under the age of 10 years, 6 percent had been raped under age 11, and so on.

* Excludes victims of unknown age.

Children and Adolescents: Homicide

3.17   Child Murder Victims, by Victim-Offender Relationship, 1992

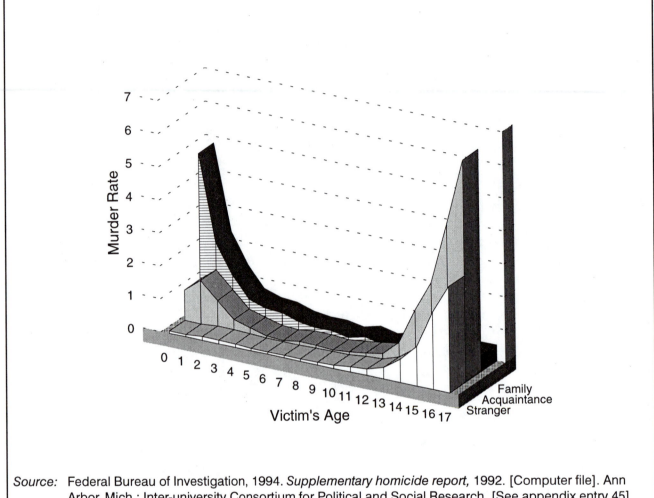

Source: Federal Bureau of Investigation, 1994. *Supplementary homicide report,* 1992. [Computer file]. Ann Arbor, Mich.: Inter-university Consortium for Political and Social Research. [See appendix entry 45]

3.18   Fatalities from Child Abuse, by Race and Ethnicity of Victim, 1986

Race and Ethnicity	Frequency	Rate per 1,000
Whites and Hispanics	600	0.01
Blacks	500	0.05
Others	0	0.00

Source: Adapted from: Sedlak, Andrea J. 1991. *National incidence and prevalence of child abuse and neglect: 1988.* (Revised Report). Rockville, Md.: Westat, Inc., p. 5–25, Table 5–5. Used with permission. [See appendix entry 44]

Note: Children are defined as persons under age 18.

3.19   Average Annual Murder Rates of Children Abducted by Strangers, by Age, Gender, Race of Victim, and Region, 1980–1987

	Excluding Undetermined Circumstances†	Including Undetermined Circumstances†
Age		
0 - 4	0.3	0.8
5 - 9	0.5	1.0
10 - 13	0.5	1.4
14 - 17	1.5	6.5
Sex		
Male	0.4	2.6
Female	0.9	2.0
Race		
White	0.6	1.6
Black	1.0	6.0
Asian‡	1.8	5.2
Native American‡	1.1*	2.2
Region		
Northeast	0.3	4.0
Midwest	0.4	1.7
South	0.4	1.8
West	1.8	2.3

Source: Supplementary Homicide Reports, 1980–1987 from: Finkelhor, David, Gerald Hotaling, and Andrea Sedlak. 1990. *Missing, abducted, runaway, and thrownaway children in America. First report: Numbers and characteristics, national incidence studies.* Washington, D.C.: Office of Juvenile Justice and Delinquency Prevention, p. 79, Table NFA-5. [See appendix entry 31]

Note: Rates are per 1 million children. Numerators derived from a reanalysis of Federal Bureau of Investigation Supplementary Homicide Report data. Average population estimates for the years 1980–1987 used in the calculation of age, gender, and race-specific rates and in child population data by region. Population data reported in U.S. Bureau of the Census, *Statistical Abstract of the United States*, 1981, 1982, 1983, 1984, 1985, 1986, 1987, 1988, 1989 (103rd–111th editions), Washington D.C.

*   Estimate is based on 10 or fewer sample cases.

†   Criminal/determined circumstances include rape, other sexual offense, other felony types, and other suspected felonies. Undetermined circumstances include those cases that cannot be identified as falling into a known category.

‡   Population estimates based on 1980 data, U.S. Bureau of the Census, *Statistical Abstract of the United States*, 1981 (103rd edition), Washington D.C.

3.20   Annual Stranger Abduction Homicides, Stranger Abduction Homicide Rates, and All Child Homicides and Homicide Rates, 1976–1987

Year	Number of Stranger Abduction Homicides	Stranger Abduction Homicide Rates	Number of All Child Homicides*	Rates for All Child Homicides
1976	120	1.8	1446	22.2
1977	126	2.0	1625	25.3
1978	177	2.7	1647	26.0
1979	166	2.7	1682	26.3
1980	110	1.7	1731	27.2
1981	177	2.8	1547	24.5
1982	212	3.4	1594	25.4
1983	134	2.1	1510	24.1
1984	156	2.5	1431	22.8
1985	147	2.3	1452	23.0
1986	114	1.8	1599	25.3
1987	126	2.0	1516	23.9

Source: Finkelhor, David, Gerald Hotaling, and Andrea Sedlak. 1990. *Missing, abducted, runaway, and thrownaway children in America. First report: Numbers and characteristics, national incidence studies.* Washington, D.C.: Office of Juvenile Justice and Delinquency Prevention, p, 80, Table NFA-6. [See appendix entry 31]

Note: Rates are per 1 million children. Children are defined as persons under age 18.

* From 1976 through 1984, the number of homicides of persons under 18 was estimated by Finkelhor, Hotaling, and Sedlak (1990, p. 80) based on figures reported in the Federal Bureau of Investigation's annual *Crime in the United States*; from 1985 through 1987, the FBI's own estimates were used.

3.21   Average Annual Stranger Abduction Homicides, by Criminal Circumstance, 1976–1987

Criminal Circumstance	Average Annual Cases 1976-1987	Average Annual Rate
Rape	14	0.2
Other sexual offense	3	0.0
Other felony types	7	0.1
Other suspected felonies	19	0.3
Undetermined	104	1.6
Total, excluding "undetermined" cases	43	0.7
Total, including "undetermined" cases	147	2.3

Source: Finkelhor, David, Gerald Hotaling, and Andrea Sedlak. 1990. *Missing, abducted, runaway, and thrownaway children in America. First report: Numbers and characteristics, national incidence studies.* Washington, D.C.: Office of Juvenile Justice and Delinquency Prevention, p. 73, Table NFA-2. [See appendix entry 31]

Note: Rates are per 1 million children.

VULNERABLE GROUPS AND SITUATIONS: ELDERLY

3.22   Rape, Robbery, and Assault Victimization Rates, by Age of Victim, 1987–1990

Violent Crimes	Age of Victim			
	12-24	25-49	50-64	65 or Older
All violent crimes	64.6	27.2	8.5	4.0
Rape	1.5	0.6	0.1*	0.9*
Robbery	10.0	5.3	2.4	1.5
Assault	53.1	21.2	5.9	2.3
Aggravated	18.4	7.5	2.2	1.1
Simple	34.6	13.7	3.7	1.3

Source: National Crime Victimization Survey, 1987–1990, from: Bachman, Ronet. 1992. *Elderly victims.* Washington, D.C.: Bureau of Justice Statistics, p. 2, Table 1. [See appendix entry 28]

Note: Detail may not add up to total because of rounding. Rates are the annual average (1987–1990) of the number of victimizations per 1,000 persons in each age group. Annual averages are computed by summing victimizations across years and dividing by the sum of respective populations across years. Table excludes series crimes. Series crime and other crime types are defined in the appendix.

*   Estimate is based on 10 or fewer sample cases.

3.23   Percentage of Violent Crimes, Robberies, and Assaults for Persons Over and Under 65, by Victim-Offender Relationship, and by Place of Occurrence, 1987–1990

	Crimes of Violence (%)		Robbery (%)		Assault (%)	
	Under 65	65 or Older	Under 65	65 or Older	Under 65	65 or Older
Offenders were:						
Relatives	8	8	5	3	9	13
Acquaintances	33	20	17	5	36	32
Strangers	56	64	74	83	52	47
Relationship not ascertained	3	8	4	9	3	8
Place of occurrence						
Total	100	100	100	100	100	100
At home	14	25	13	20	14	27
Near home	11	25	9	21	12	29
On the street	39	31	52	37	36	27
In commercial or public establishment	21	9	16	13	21	7
Elsewhere	15	10	10	10	15	10

Source: National Crime Victimization Survey, 1987–1990, from: Bachman, Ronet. 1992. *Elderly victims.* Washington, D.C.: Bureau of Justice Statistics, p. 3, Table 3 and Table 4. [See appendix entry 28]

Note: Table excludes series crimes. Series crime and other crime types are defined in the appendix.

3.24 Average Annual Robbery, and Assault and Violent Victimization Rates for Persons Over Age 65, by Gender, Race, and Marital Status, and by Location of Residence, Home Ownership, and Type of Crime, 1987–1990

	Crimes of Violence*	Robbery	Assault	
			Aggravated	Simple
Gender				
Male	4.9	2.0	1.4	1.4
Female	3.4	1.2	0.8	1.2
Race				
White	3.6	1.2	1.1	1.2
Black	7.6	4.4	1.4	1.4
Marital status				
Never married	3.0	1.2	0.8	0.9
Widowed	4.2	1.7	0.9	1.4
Married	7.6	5.1	1.5	0.7
Divorced/separated	11.3	1.7	4.8	4.4
Locality of residence				
City	7.1	3.5	1.4	1.9
Suburb	2.9	0.9	0.8	1.1
Nonmetro area	2.2	0.4	1.0	0.7
Home ownership				
Own	3.1	1.1	1.0	1.0
Rent	7.7	3.6	1.6	2.2

Source: National Crime Victimization Survey, 1987–1990, from: Bachman, Ronet. 1992. *Elderly victims*. Washington, D.C.: Bureau of Justice Statistics, p. 5, Table 9 and Table 10. [See appendix entry 28]

Note: Rates are the annual average (1987–1990) of the number of victimizations per 1,000 persons aged 65 years or older. Annual averages are computed by summing victimizations across years and dividing by the sum of respective populations across years. Table excludes series crimes. Series crime and other crime types are defined in the appendix. Aggravated assaults include all attacks (and attempted attacks) with weapons or, if no weapon was involved, those that result in serious injury. Simple assaults are attacks (and attempted attacks) without weapons resulting in minor or undetermined injuries requiring less than two days of hospitalization.

* Includes rapes, not shown separately.

3.25 Percentage of Elder Abuse Types, 29 States (FY 1990), 30 States (FY 1991)

Type of Maltreatment	Fiscal Year 1990	Fiscal Year 1991
Physical abuse	20.3	19.1
Sexual abuse	0.6	0.6
Psychological/emotional abuse	11.6	13.8
Neglect	46.6	45.2
Financial/material exploitation	17.4	17.1
All other types	3.3	4.0
Unknown/missing data	0.2	0.2
Total	100.0	100.0

Source: Tatara, Toshio. 1993. *Summaries of the statistical data on elder abuse in domestic settings for FY 90 and FY 91.* Washington, D.C.: National Aging Resource Center on Elder Abuse, p. 20. [See appendix entry 52]

Note: Includes only substantiated reports involving abuse victims and does not include abusive or neglectful conduct of an older person directed at himself/herself that threatens his/her safety.

VULNERABLE GROUPS AND SITUATIONS: WOMEN

3.26 Nonfatal Victimization of Females Aged 12 Years or More, by Demographic Characteristics, 1993

Characteristic	Total	Rape	Other Sexual Attacks	Unwanted Sexual Contact	Robbery	Aggravated Assault	Simple Assault	Verbal Assault Threats
Race								
White	3,890,100	215,140	126,970	153,320	293,170	588,840	1,483,540	1,029,140
Black	802,530	58,200	6,210*	16,610*	113,370	215,980	284,920	107,240
Other	117,690	5,710*	4,360*	6,570*	9,340*	28,390	42,980	20,340*
Ethnicity								
Hispanic	447,180	20,480*	12,510*	4,770*	52,030	100,270	144,970	112,140
Not Hispanic	4,363,140	258,570	125,020	171,730	363,850	732,930	1,666,470	1,044,570
Age (years)								
12-15	749,080	36,330	33,890	25,620*	56,080	118,690	323,610	154,870
16-19	671,530	54,530	28,570	30,560	39,060	112,180	240,430	166,200
20-24	798,390	62,530	33,500	51,010	69,160	167,560	253,570	161,070
25-34	1,057,000	59,370	20,260*	33,650	107,830	204,630	372,340	258,910
35-49	1,184,200	56,190	19,280*	25,560	104,020	150,640	515,680	312,830
50-64	227,480	2,080*	2,030*	10,100*	22,570*	44,890	75,210	70,610
65 and older	122,640	8,030*	0*	0	17,160*	34,620	30,600	32,220
Education								
Some high school or less	1,784,060	101,410	54,860	67,540	148,860	360,600	693,510	357,280
High school graduate	1,174,170	63,130	32,170	17,490*	123,970	202,780	449,710	284,920
Some college	1,146,090	88,950	36,800	42,240	86,820	183,460	418,480	289,320
College graduate or more	672,150	25,570	13,690*	43,040	53,560	81,860	235,810	218,640
Not stated	33,850	0*	0*	6,180*	2,670*	4,510*	13,930*	6,560*
Family income								
Under $9,999	1,099,730	85,780	37,090	26,120	133,420	202,540	415,740	199,040
$10,000-$19,999	944,670	61,540	24,680	30,530	56,720	197,770	349,370	224,070
$20,000-$29,999	754,400	30,940	21,680*	28,460	47,030	135,670	305,660	184,960
$30,000-$49,999	948,480	61,100	22,590*	35,070	80,414	155,200	324,270	269,830
$50,000 or more	682,370	17,570*	24,930	25,680*	57,970	80,450	268,510	207,270
Not stated	380,680	22,120*	6,570*	30,640*	40,330	61,570	147,890	71,560

See notes at end of table.

3.26   Nonfatal Victimization of Females Aged 12 Years or More, by Demographic Characteristics, 1993 (continued)

Characteristic	Total	Rape	Other Sexual Attacks	Unwanted Sexual Contact	Robbery	Aggravated Assault	Simple Assault	Verbal Assault Threats
Marital status								
Married	1,115,770	36,960	13,400*	43,600	109,120	188,590	401,880	322,220
Widowed	150,160	0*	2,080*	0*	25,910	38,110	42,690	41,370
Divorced/separated	1,116,190	79,610	26,470	22,370*	93,120	193,510	460,240	240,880
Never married	2,415,310	162,480	95,570	110,520	187,730	413,000	900,310	545,700
Not stated	12,880	0*	0*	0*	0*	0*	6,330*	6,560*
Location of residence								
Central city	1,937,230	128,560	60,920	62,870	215,050	354,150	714,570	401,110
Suburban	2,015,900	74,540	60,530	845,100	158,600	334,290	798,090	505,350
Nonmetro area	857,180	75,960	16,090*	29,120	42,230	144,760	298,790	250,250

Source: National Crime Victimization Survey, 1993 preliminary data from: Bureau of the Census. 1995. National crime victimization survey, 1992-1993. [Computer files]. Suitland, Md. [See appendix entry 28]

Note: Verbal assault threats include verbal threats to rape, or other sexual attack, in addition to verbal threats of nonsexual assault. Table includes series crimes. Series crime and other crime types are defined in the appendix. Detail may not add up to totals due to rounding. National Crime Victimization Survey data for 1993 are not comparable with earlier years due to changes in the survey. Aggravated assaults include all attacks (and attempted attacks) with weapons or, if no weapon was involved, those that result in serious injury. Simple assaults are attacks (and attempted attacks) without weapons resulting in minor or undetermined injuries requiring less than two days of hospitalization.

*   Estimate is based on 10 or fewer sample cases.

3.27 Nonfatal Victimization Rates of Females Aged 12 Years or More, by Demographic Characteristics, 1993

Characteristic	Total	Rape	Other Sexual Attack	Unwanted Sexual Contact	Robbery	Aggravated Assault	Simple Assault	Verbal Assault Threats
Race								
White	42.4	2.3	1.4	1.7	3.2	6.4	16.2	11.2
Black	58.5	4.2	0.5*	1.2*	8.3	15.8	20.8	7.8
Other	31.2	1.5*	1.2*	1.7*	2.5*	7.5	11.4	1.5
Ethnicity								
Hispanic	50.3	2.3*	0.1*	0.1*	5.8	11.3	16.3	8.2
Not Hispanic	43.5	2.6	1.4	1.9	3.6	7.3	16.6	76.2
Age (years)								
12-15	102.3	5.0	0.4	0.3	7.7	16.2	44.2	11.3
16-19	97.9	8.0	0.3	0.3	5.7	16.4	35.1	12.1
20-24	85.1	6.7	0.4	0.6	7.4	17.9	27.0	11.7
25-34	49.8	2.8	0.2*	0.4	5.1	9.6	17.6	18.9
35-49	40.8	1.9	0.2*	0.3	3.6	5.2	17.7	22.8
50-64	13.1	0.1*	0.0*	0.1*	1.3*	2.6	4.3	5.1
65 or more	6.8	0.4*	0.0*	0.0*	1.0*	1.9	1.7	2.4
Education								
Some high school or less	60.9	3.5	0.6	0.7	5.1	12.3	23.7	26.1
High school graduate	32.1	1.7	0.4	0.2*	3.4	5.5	12.3	20.8
Some college	48.4	3.8	0.4	0.5	3.7	7.7	17.7	21.1
College graduate or more	36.4	1.4	0.1*	0.5	2.9	4.4	12.8	15.9
Not stated	29.6	0.0*	0.0*	0.1*	2.3*	3.9*	12.2*	0.5*
Family income								
Under $10,000	69.2	5.4	0.4	0.3*	8.4	12.7	26.2	14.5
$10,000-$19,999	48.9	3.2	0.3	0.3	2.9	10.2	18.1	16.3
$20,000-$29,999	47.9	2.0	0.2*	0.3	3.0	8.6	19.4	13.5
$30,000-$49,999	39.2	2.5	0.2*	0.4	3.3	6.4	13.4	19.7
$50,000 or more	31.7	0.8*	0.3	0.3*	2.7	3.7	12.5	15.1
Not stated	30.5	1.8*	0.1*	0.3*	3.2	4.9	11.9	5.2
Marital status								
Married	20.3	0.7	0.1*	0.5	2.0	3.4	7.3	23.5
Widowed	13.4	0.0*	0.0*	0.0*	2.0	3.4	3.8	3.0
Divorced/separated	86.2	6.1	0.3	0.2*	7.2	14.9	35.5	17.6
Never married	81.2	5.5	1.0	1.2	6.3	13.9	30.3	39.8
Not stated	52.0	0.0*	0.0*	0.0*	0.0*	0.0*	25.5*	0.5*
Location of residence								
Central city	59.6	4.0	0.7	0.7	6.6	10.9	22.0	29.3
Suburban	38.9	1.4	0.7	0.9	3.1	6.4	15.4	36.9
Nonmetro area	34.6	3.1	0.2*	0.3	1.7	5.8	12.0	18.3

Source: National Crime Victimization Survey, 1993, preliminary data from: Bureau of the Census. 1995. *National crime victimization survey, 1992–1993.* [Computer files]. Suitland, Md. [See appendix entry 28]

Note: Verbal assault threats include verbal threats to rape, or other sexual attack, in addition to verbal threat of nonsexual assault. Rates are per 1,000 females aged 12 years or more. Table includes series crimes. Series crime and other crime types are defined in the appendix. National Crime Victimization Survey data for 1993 are not comparable with earlier years due to changes in the survey. Aggravated assaults include all attacks (and attempted attacks) with weapons or, if no weapon was involved, those that result in serious injury. Simple assaults are attacks (and attempted attacks) without weapons resulting in minor or undetermined injuries requiring less than two days of hospitalization.

* Estimate is based on 10 or fewer sample cases.

3.28   Nonfatal Victimizations of Females by a Single Offender, by Race of Victim and Perceived Race of Offender, 1993

Types of Violence and Race of Victim	Perceived Race of Offender				
	White	Black	Other	Unknown	Not Applicable
Crimes of violence					
White	2,525,750	475,310	297,860	70,430	0*
Black	67,380	549,690	18,060*	21,990*	0*
Other	43,910	12,200*	31,220	0*	0*
Rape					
White	164,980	22,430	14,920*	6,260*	6,550*
Black	11,450*	30,500	2,450*	0*	13,810*
Other	5,710*	0*	0*	0*	0*
Other sexual attack					
White	84,610	10,180*	11,730*	6,190*	14,260*
Black	0*	6,210*	0*	0*	0*
Other	4,360*	0*	0*	0*	0*
Unwanted sexual contact					
White	94,100	16,590*	22,030*	10,460*	10,140*
Black	0*	14,200*	0*	2,410*	0*
Other	4,290*	0*	2,280*	0*	0*
Robbery					
White	115,980	53,630	42,680	2,110*	78,770
Black	5,280*	65,630	0*	4,280*	38,170
Other	1,930*	2,060*	0*	0*	5,350*
Aggravated assault					
White	328,350	68,480	55,690	16,080*	120,230
Black	12,410*	162,790	8,020*	0*	32,770
Other	2,180*	5,920*	6,240*	0*	14,050*
Simple assault					
White	1,059,670	157,770	100,310	16,130	149,660
Black	28,500	188,420	2,730*	15,300*	49,970
Other	16,310	2,170*	20,500	0*	4,000*
Verbal assault threats					
White	679,920	146,240	50,500	13,200*	139,280
Black	9,750*	81,940	4,870*	0*	10,680*
Other	9,130*	2,050*	2,220*	0*	6,950*

Source: National Crime Victimization Survey, 1993 preliminary data from: Bureau of the Census. 1995. *National crime victimization survey, 1992–1993.* [Computer files]. Suitland, Md. [See appendix entry 28]

Note: "Not Applicable" includes victimizations in which the respondent either reported multiple offenders were involved, or did not know how many offenders were involved, or could not recall any other details about an offender. "Verbal assault threats" include threats of rape and other sexual attacks in addition to verbal threats of nonsexual assault. Detail may not add up to totals due to rounding. Table includes series crimes. Series crime and other crime types are defined in the appendix. National Crime Victimization Survey data for 1993 are not comparable with earlier years due to changes in the survey. Aggravated assaults include all attacks (and attempted attacks) with weapons or, if no weapon was involved, those that result in serious injury. Simple assaults are attacks (and attempted attacks) without weapons resulting in minor or undetermined injuries requiring less than two days of hospitalization.

*   Estimate is based on 10 or fewer sample cases.

3.29 Percentage of Victimizations of Females by Single Offenders, by Race of Victim and Perceived Race of Offender, 1993

Type of Violence and Race of Victim	White	Black	Other	Unknown	Not Applicable
	\multicolumn{5}{c}{Perceived Race of Offender}
Crimes of violence					
White	75.0	14.1	8.8	2.1	0.0
Black	10.3	83.7	2.7	3.3	0.0
Other	50.3	14.0	35.8	0.0	0.0
Rape					
White	76.7	10.4	6.9	2.9	3.0
Black	19.7	52.4	4.2	0.0	23.7
Other	100.0	0.0	0.0	0.0	0.0
Other sexual attack					
White	66.6	8.0	9.2	4.9	11.2
Black	0.0	100.0	0.0	0.0	0.0
Other	100.0	0.0	0.0	0.0	0.0
Unwanted sexual contact					
White	61.4	10.8	14.4	6.8	6.6
Black	0.0	85.5	0.0	14.5	0.0
Other	65.3	0.0	34.7	0.0	0.0
Robbery					
White	39.6	18.3	14.6	0.7	26.9
Black	4.7	57.9	0.0	3.8	33.7
Other	20.6	22.1	0.0	0.0	57.3
Aggravated assault					
White	55.8	11.6	9.5	2.7	20.4
Black	5.7	75.4	3.7	0.0	15.2
Other	7.7	20.8	22.0	0.0	49.5
Simple assault					
White	71.4	10.6	6.7	1.1	10.1
Black	10.0	66.1	1.0	5.4	17.5
Other	37.9	5.0	47.7	0.0	9.3
Verbal assault threats					
White	66.1	14.2	4.9	1.3	13.5
Black	9.1	76.4	4.5	0.0	10.0
Other	44.9	10.1	10.9	0.0	34.1

Source: National Crime Victimization Survey, 1993 preliminary data from: Bureau of the Census. 1995. *National crime victimization survey, 1992–1993.* [Computer files]. Suitland, Md. [See appendix entry 28]

Note: Percentages computed across rows. Detail may not add up to totals due to rounding. Victims were females aged 12 years or more. "Not Applicable" includes victimizations in which the respondent either reported multiple offenders were involved, or did not know how many offenders were involved, or could not recall any other details about an offender. "Verbal assault threats" include threats of rape and other sexual attacks in addition to verbal threats of nonsexual assault. Table includes series crimes. Series crime and other crime types defined in appendix. National Crime Victimization Survey data for 1993 are not comparable with earlier years due to changes in the survey. Aggravated assaults include all attacks (and attempted attacks) with weapons or, if no weapon was involved, those that result in serious injury. Simple assaults are attacks (and attempted attacks) without weapons resulting in minor or undetermined injuries requiring less than two days of hospitalization.

3.30   Single-Offender Victimizations of Females, by Victim-Offender Relationship and Demographic Characteristics of Victim, 1993

		Victim-Offender Relationship			
Characteristic	Total	Intimate[a]	Other Relative[b]	Acquaintance[c]	Stranger[d]
Race					
White	3,369,350	673,780	64,800	1,686,890	923,640
Black	657,130	70,960	36,760*	344,210	202,410
Other	87,330	6,270*	2,800*	53,470	24,790
Ethnicity					
Hispanic	348,270	95,130	6,640*	153,070	93,430
Not Hispanic	3,765,540	655,890	97,720	1,931,490	1,057,410
Age (years)					
12-15	548,770	33,530	4,600*	398,020	112,630
16-19	566,500	58,670	8,330*	350,630	148,870
20-24	720,090	84,360	46,870	387,130	192,910
25-34	937,790	210,090	24,970	387,500	307,520
35-49	1,032,790	319,390	4,210*	439,360	263,360
50-64	195,660	35,230	13,490*	68,940	78,000
65 and over	112,200	9,760*	1,910*	52,980	47,560
Education					
Some high school or less	1,421,810	192,460	53,020	851,160	325,160
High school graduate	1,044,020	253,910	21,540	480,280	278,330
Some college	1,025,410	213,250	27,800	438,610	336,930
College graduate+	588,720	79,560	2,000*	299,670	203,260
Not stated	33,850	11,840*	0*	14,850*	7,160*
Family income					
Under $10,000	954,030	183,800	45,870	526,640	197,720
$10,000-$19,999	828,220	191,770	21,550	375,670	230,890
$20,000-$29,999	663,040	141,620	6,260*	325,540	189,630
$30,000-$49,999	789,040	117,240	25,660*	416,210	227,150
$50,000 or more	565,950	70,310	5,030*	290,110	196,260
Not stated	313,540	46,280	0*	150,400	109,180
Marital status					
Married	943,260	209,020	32,790	326,290	370,220
Widowed	139,350	0*	0*	80,280	56,840
Divorced/separated	1,034,500	420,490	48,110	397,850	168,050
Never married	1,983,810	117,260	23,460*	1,273,710	553,530
Not stated	12,880*	4,240*	0*	6,440*	2,200*
Location of residence					
Central city	1,615,060	242,930	64,660	768,510	523,650
Suburban	1,759,040	377,940	19,440*	868,300	485,640
Nonmetro area	739,710	130,140	20,260	447,760	141,550

Source: National Crime Victimization Survey, 1993 preliminary data from: Bureau of the Census. 1995. *National crime victimization survey, 1992–1993*. [Computer files].
Suitland, Md. [See appendix entry 28]

Note: Victimization in this table includes rape, other sexual attacks, robbery, assault (including verbal threats of rape, other sexual attack, or nonsexual assault), and unwanted sexual contact without the use of force. Victims were females aged 12 years or more. Table includes series crimes. Series crime and other crime types are defined in the appendix. National Crime Victimization Survey data for 1993 are not comparable with earlier years due to changes in the survey.

*   Estimate is based on 10 or fewer sample cases.

[a]   Includes spouses, ex-spouses, parents, stepparents, children, stepchildren, and siblings.

[b]   Includes all other relatives.

[c]   Includes boyfriends, girlfriends, ex-boyfriends, ex-girlfriends, friends, ex-friends, roommates, boarders, schoolmates, neighbors, and other nonrelatives known to the victim.

[d]   Includes either someone the victim identified as a stranger, or someone whom the victim would not be able to recognize, or someone whom the victim knew by sight only.

3.31   Single-Offender Victimization Rates of Females, by Victim-Offender Relationship and Demographic Characteristics of Victim, 1993

| Characteristic | Total | Victim-Offender Relationship | | | |
		Intimate[a]	Other Relative[b]	Acquaintance[c]	Stranger[d]
Race					
White	36.7	7.3	0.7	18.4	10.1
Black	47.9	5.2	2.7	25.1	14.8
Other	23.1	1.7*	0.7*	14.2	6.6
Ethnicity					
Hispanic	39.1	10.7	0.7*	17.2	10.5
Not Hispanic	37.6	6.5	1.0	19.3	10.5
Age (years)					
12-15	75.0	4.6	0.6*	54.4	15.4
16-19	82.6	8.6	1.2*	51.1	21.7
20-24	76.7	9.0	5.0	41.2	20.6
25-34	44.2	9.9	1.2	18.3	14.5
35-49	35.5	11.0	0.1*	15.1	9.1
50-64	11.3	2.0	0.8*	4.0	4.5
65 and over	6.2	0.5*	0.1*	2.9	2.6
Education					
Some high school or less	48.6	6.6	1.8	29.1	11.1
High school graduate	28.5	6.9	0.6	13.1	7.6
Some college	43.3	9.0	1.2	18.5	14.2
College graduate or more	31.9	4.3	0.1*	16.2	11.0
Not stated	29.6	10.3	0.0*	13.0	6.3
Family income					
Under $10,000	60.0	11.6	2.9	33.1	12.4
$10,000-$19,999	42.8	9.9	1.1	19.4	11.9
$20,000-$29,999	42.1	9.0	0.4*	20.7	12.0
$30,000-$49,999	32.6	4.8	1.1*	17.2	9.4
$50,000 or more	26.3	3.3	0.2*	13.5	9.1
Not stated	25.1	3.7	0.0*	12.1	8.7
Marital status					
Married	17.1	3.8	0.6	5.9	6.7
Widowed	12.5	0.0*	0.0*	7.2	5.1
Divorced/separated	79.9	32.5	3.7	30.7	13.0
Never married	66.7	3.9	0.8*	42.8	18.6
Not stated	52.0*	17.1*	0.0*	26.0*	8.9*
Location of residence					
Central city	49.7	7.5	2.0	23.6	16.1
Suburban	33.9	7.3	0.4*	16.7	9.4
Nonmetro area	29.8	5.2	0.8	18.1	5.7

Source: National Crime Victimization Survey, 1993 preliminary data from: Bureau of the Census. 1995. *National crime victimization survey, 1992–1993.* [Computer files]. Suitland, Md. [See appendix entry 28]

Note: Rates are per 1,000 females aged 12 years or more. Victimization in this table includes rape, other sexual attacks, robbery, assault (including verbal threats to rape or other sexual attack), and unwanted sexual contact without the use of force. Table includes series crimes. Series crime and other crime types are defined in the appendix. National Crime Victimization Survey data for 1993 are not comparable with earlier years due to changes in the survey.

*   Estimate is based on 10 or fewer sample cases.

[a]   Includes spouses, ex-spouses, parents, stepparents, children, stepchildren, and siblings.

[b]   Includes all other relatives.

[c]   Includes boyfriends, girlfriends, ex-boyfriends, ex-girlfriends, friends, ex-friends, roommates, boarders, schoolmates, neighbors, and other nonrelatives known to the victim.

[d]   Includes either someone the victim identified as a stranger, or someone whom the victim would not be able to recognize, or someone whom the victim knew by sight only.

3.32 Rapes and Sexual Attacks of Females Reported to Police, by Offender Weapon Presence, Victim-Offender Relationship, Injury Status, Medical Care Received, Number of Offenders, and Place of Occurrence, 1993

Characteristic	Total	Reported to Police	
		Number	Percentage
Total rapes/sexual attacks	416,580	129,900	31.2
Type of assault			
Completed rape	173,910	63,740	36.7
Attempted rape	105,150	34,520	32.8
Other sexual attack with injury	53,800	13,000*	24.2*
Other sexual assault without injury	83,730	18,640*	22.3*
Weapon			
Weapon present	34,100	16,980*	49.8*
No weapon present	382,480	112,920	29.5
Victim-offender relationship			
Unknown	4,700*	2,570*	54.6*
Stranger	74,470	30,110	40.4
Nonstranger	337,410	97,220	28.8
Physical injury status			
Not injured	144,750	36,160	25.0
No additional injuries sustained†	157,730	39,400	25.0
Additional injuries sustained	114,100	54,340	47.6
Medical care received			
No medical care received	332,600	86,040	25.9
Medical care received	83,990	43,860	52.2
Number of offenders			
Single offenders	381,970	112,020	29.3
Multiple offenders	29,920	15,310*	51.2*
Unknown	4,700*	2,570*	54.6*
Place of occurrence			
At/near own home	194,810	59,940	30.8
At/near friend's home	87,920	28,490	32.4
Commercial place or school	30,740	5,600*	18.2*
Public parking lot/garage	24,350*	9,570*	39.3*
Open or public area	43,270	19,980*	46.2*
Other	35,510	6,330*	17.8*

Source: National Crime Victimization Survey, 1993 preliminary data from: Bureau of the Census. 1995. *National crime victimization survey, 1992–1993*. [Computer files]. Suitland, Md. [See appendix entry 28]

Note: Detail may not add up to totals due to rounding. Percentages computed on unrounded estimates. Rape/sexual attack in this table includes completed and attempted rapes and other (nonrape) sexual attacks invoving the use or threat of force. Victims were females aged 12 years or more. Table includes series crimes. National Crime Victimization Survey data for 1993 are not comparable with earlier years due to changes in the survey.

* Estimate is based on 10 or fewer sample cases.

† Includes responses only of "Rape" or "Other sexual assault" to the question, "What were the injuries you suffered, if any?"

3.33   Offender Weapon Use, Victim Self-Protection, Injury Status, and Medical Care Received in Single-Offender Rape/Sexual Attack Victimizations, by Victim-Offender Relationship, 1993

Characteristic	Total	Percent	Stranger		Nonstranger	
			Number	Percent	Number	Percent
Total rapes/sexual assaults	416,580	100.0	74,470	100.0	337,410	100.0
Type of assault						
Completed rape	173,910	41.7	28,250*	37.9*	143,100	42.4
Attempted rape	105,150	25.2	19,400*	26.1*	85,740	25.4
Other sexual attack with injury	53,800	12.9	14,890*	20.0*	38,920	11.5
Other sexual assault without injury	83,730	20.1	11,940*	16.0*	69,660	20.6
Weapon						
Weapon present	34,100	8.2	14,230*	19.1*	19,880*	5.9*
No weapon present	382,480	91.8	60,240	80.9	317,530	94.1
Type of weapon						
Handgun	21,610*	5.2*	9,700*	13.0*	11,910*	3.5*
Knife or sharp instrument	7,960*	1.9*	2,210*	3.0*	5,740*	1.7*
Other weapon	4,540*	1.1*	2,320*	3.1*	2,230*	0.7*
No weapon present	382,480	91.8	60,240	80.9	317,530	94.1
Type of self-protection						
Active/physical	193,320	46.4	29,740	39.9	163,580	48.5
Passive/verbal	138,400	33.2	31,860	42.8	106,530	31.6
None	84,870	20.4	12,860*	17.3*	67,300	19.9
Self-protection helped						
Action helped	196,250	47.1	34,130	45.8	162,130	48.1
Action didn't helped	122,150	29.3	27,480	36.9	94,670	28.1
Don't know if helped	13,320*	3.2*	0*	0.0*	13,320*	3.9*
No self-protection	84,870	20.4	12,860*	17.3*	67,300	19.9
Self-protection hurt						
Made situation worse	75,640	18.2	13,220*	17.8*	62,420	18.5
Didn't make it worse	228,700	54.9	41,210	55.3	187,490	55.6
Don't know if made worse	27,380	6.6	7,180*	9.6*	20,210*	6.0*
No self-protection	84,870	20.4	12,860*	17.3*	67,300	19.9
Time of self-protection						
Before injury	40,480	9.7	7,320*	9.8*	33,160	9.8
After injury	7,010*	1.7*	4,780*	6.4*	2,230*	0.7*
Same time as injury	89,430	21.5	20,060*	26.9*	69,370	20.6
Not applicable	279,670	67.1	42,300	56.8	232,660	69.0
Physical injury status						
Not injured	144,750	34.7	26,050*	35.0*	116,130	34.4
No additional injuries sustained†	157,730	37.9	26,850	36.0	128,750	38.2
Additional injuries sustained	114,100	27.4	21,570*	29.0*	92,530	27.4
Medical care received						
No medical care received	332,600	79.8	49,170	66.0	278,730	82.6
Received medical care	83,990	20.2	25,310*	34.0*	58,680	17.4
Hospital care received						
No hospital care received	414,290	99.5	74,470	100.0	335,120	99.3
Received hospital care	2,290*	0.5*	0*	0.0*	2,290*	0.7*

Source: National Crime Victimization Survey, 1993 preliminary data from: Bureau of the Census. 1995. *National crime victimization survey, 1992–1993.* [Computer files]. Suitland, Md.[See appendix entry 28]

Note: Percentages calculated down columns for each group of characteristics. Detail may not add to totals due to rounding. Percentages computed on unrounded estimates. Rape/sexual attack in this table includes completed and attempted rapes and other (non-rape) sexual attacks that involved the use or threat of force. Table includes series crimes. Series crime and other crime types are defined in the appendix. National Crime Victimization Survey data for 1993 are not comparable with earlier years due to changes in the survey.

* Estimate is based on 10 or fewer sample cases.
† Includes only responses of "Rape" or "Other sexual assault" to the question, "What were the injuries you suffered, if any?"

3.34   Annual Prevalence Rates of Violence Against Women by Males in Intimate Relationships, by Race, Gender, Occupation, Family Income, and Education of Respondent, 1985

	Total		Minor Violence		Severe Violence	
	Male	Female	Male	Female	Male	Female
Race						
White	101	117	99	108	11	45
Black	188	166	178	157	46	81
Hispanic	148	181	142	160	41	86
Other	128	110	128	90	9	49
Unknown	45	89	45	63	0	62
Occupation						
Blue collar	123	138	123	128	13	64
White collar	102	115	96	104	14	43
Income						
Less than $10,000	112	200	113	187	24	110
$10,000–$19,999	149	104	149	94	21	57
$20,000–$29,999	117	137	116	128	9	56
$30,000–$39,999	97	114	93	104	17	40
$40,000–$49,999	82	124	71	129	12	35
$50,000 and over	89	109	88	91	3	26
Unknown	79	80	65	58	18	34
"Husband's" Education						
Less than 8th grade	53	91	53	82	0	61
Some high school	116	154	117	138	27	88
High school graduate	127	141	124	130	14	59
Some college	106	121	101	121	14	21
College graduate & up	100	93	96	77	12	34
Unknown	0	144	0	125	0	123
"Wife's" Education						
Less than 8th grade	61	72	61	54	0	40
Some high school	134	120	134	113	23	64
High school graduate	117	130	116	121	15	54
Some college	113	125	101	113	19	40
College graduate & up	85	118	82	108	5	45
Unknown	121	0	121	0	0	0

Source: National Family Violence Resurvey of 1985, from: Gelles, Richard J. and Murray A. Straus. 1989. *Physical violence in American families, 1985* [Computer file]. Ann Arbor, Mich.: Inter-university Consortium for Political and Social Research. [See appendix entry 38]

Note: Annual prevalence rates represent at least one instance per 1,000 couples in the 12-month period preceding the interview. All rates refer to violence by males against females. Male responses refer to the respondent's own acts; female responses refer to acts by their male partners. From the first row, for example, 101 out of 1,000 couples, in the year before the study, were said to have experienced an act of male-against-female violence (at least once) according to males in the study who were white. Females who were white reported being victims of male acts of violence at a rate of 117 per 1,000 couples. Note that only one person per couple was interviewed. "Minor" and "Severe" violence categories represent scales constructed by Gelles and Straus from the conflict tactics items. "Husband" and "Wife" refer to the male and female partners in cohabiting relationships regardless of whether the couple was legally married.

3.35   Annual Prevalence Rates of Violence Against Women by Males in Intimate Relationships, by Gender and Income of Respondent, 1985

Family Income	Threatened to Hit or Throw	Threw or Smashed Object	Threw Something at Partner	Pushed, Grabbed, or Shoved	Slapped	Kicked, Bit, Hit with Fist	Hit, Tried to Hit With Object	Beat Up	Choked	Threatened With Knife or Gun	Used Knife or Gun
Male respondent											
Less than $10,000	94	147	35	92	45	11	4	11	9	0	9
$10,000–$19,999	93	192	26	133	49	7	14	2	0	1	0
$20,000–$29,999	57	139	20	97	26	6	4	2	3	0	0
$30,000–$39,999	62	157	11	91	10	4	7	4	2	0	6
$40,000–$49,999	45	136	6	66	13	2	2	6	1	0	0
$50,000 and over	52	121	10	77	16	2	1	0	2	0	0
Unknown	54	81	8	61	21	0	0	4	0	0	14
Female respondent											
Less than $10,000	143	179	74	178	94	45	72	30	15	13	2
$10,000–$19,999	99	166	32	90	36	30	31	20	14	11	4
$20,000–$29,999	90	177	49	105	43	25	34	10	13	10	0
$30,000–$39,999	78	163	36	81	19	17	28	4	4	2	0
$40,000–$49,999	80	157	48	115	31	16	19	2	9	0	0
$50,000 and over	39	125	24	76	19	10	8	10	10	3	1
Unknown	29	46	11	58	16	12	20	10	14	14	0

Source: National Family Violence Resurvey of 1985, from: Gelles, Richard J., and Murray A. Straus. 1989. *Physical violence in American families, 1985* [Computer file]. Ann Arbor, Mich.: Inter-university Consortium for Political and Social Research. [See appendix entry 38]

Note: Annual prevalence rates represent at least one instance per 1,000 couples in the 12-month period preceding the interview.   All rates refer to violence by males against females.   Male responses refer to the respondent's own acts; female responses refer to acts by their male partners.   From the first column, for example, 94 out of 1,000 couples, in the year before the study, were said to have had the male threaten to hit or throw an object at the female (at least once) according to males in the study whose income was less than $10,000.   Females, whose income was less than $10,000, reported being victims of male threats to hit them or to have an object thrown at them at a rate of 143 per 1,000 couples.   Note that only one person per couple was interviewed.

3.36   Annual Prevalence Rates of Violence Against Women by Males in Intimate Relationships, by Gender and Occupation of Respondent, 1985

Type of Conflict Tactic	Male		Female	
	Blue Collar	White Collar	Blue Collar	White Collar
Threatened to hit or throw	75	60	108	66
Minor violence	123	96	128	104
Threw or smashed object	159	140	165	153
Threw something at partner	26	10	40	38
Pushed, grabbed, shoved	103	92	109	91
Slapped	35	15	55	24
Severe violence	13	14	64	43
Hit, tried to hit with object	5	6	40	22
Kicked, bit, hit with fist	7	3	34	16
Beat up	4	2	17	9
Choked	2	2	13	10
Threatened with knife or gun	0	0	9	6
Used knife or gun	3	3	1	1

Source: National Family Violence Resurvey of 1985, from: Gelles, Richard J., and Murray A. Straus. 1989. *Physical violence in American families, 1985* [Computer file]. Ann Arbor, Mich.: Inter-university Consortium for Political and Social Research. [See appendix entry 38]

Note: Annual prevalence rates represent at least one instance per 1,000 couples in the 12-month period preceding the interview.   All rates refer to violence by males against females.   Male responses refer the respondent's own acts; female responses refer to acts by their male partners.   From the first row, for example, 75 out of 1,000 couples, in the year before the study, were said to have had the male threaten to hit or throw an object at the female (at least once) according to males who were in blue collar occupations.   Males in white collar occupations reported threatening to hit or throw an object at the female, at least once in the previous year, at a rate of 60 per 1,000 couples.   Note that only one person per couple was interviewed.   "Blue Collar" and "White Collar" classifications are those created by Gelles and Straus and are documented in the codebook to the data (cited above).

3.37   Past Year and Lifetime Prevalence Rates and Estimates of Rape and Aggravated Assault, for Women, 1989 and 1990

	Completed Rape	Aggravated Assault	Rape or Aggravated Assault
Lifetime prevalence rate	126.5	102.8	195.0
Estimated victims (lifetime)*	12,100,000	9,800,000	18,700,000
Past year prevalence rate	7.1	18.0	25.2
Estimated victims (past year)†	683,000	1,733,000	2,426,000

Source: National Women's Study, from: Kilpatrick, Dean G., Heidi S. Resnick, Benjamin E. Saunders, Connie L. Best. 1994. *Survey research on violence against women: Measuring violent assaults against women.* Paper presented at the 46th annual meeting of the American Society of Criminology, November 11, Miami, Florida, Tables 1 and 2. Used with permission. [See appendix entry 35]

Note: Prevalence rates refer to the number of victims either in the past 12-months ("Past year prevalence rate") or ever ("Lifetime prevalence rate") who report being raped or assaulted per 1,000 adult women aged 18 years or more. From the first row, for example, 126.5 adult women for every 1,000 reported being victims of a completed rape at some point in their lifetimes.

*   Based on U.S. Bureau of Census estimate that U.S. residential adult (18 and over) female population in 1989 was 96,056,000. Estimate rounded down to nearest 100,000. Lifetime rates and estimates are based on Wave 1, 1989 data (n=4,008) and are unbounded.

†   Based on U.S. Bureau of Census estimate that residential adult female population in 1990 was 96,298,000. Estimate rounded to nearest thousand. Past year rates and estimates are based on Wave 2, 1990 (n=3,220) and are considered bounded estimates.

3.38   Past Year Prevalence of Rape and Aggravated Assault, by Age of Victim at Time of Assault, Victim's Relationship to Perpetrator, and Life Threat and Degree of Physical Injury, Percentages of Women, 1989–1990

Characteristic	Rape	Aggravated Assault
Age		
18-25	40.0	22.8
26-35	30.0	25.4
36 and over	30.0	51.8
Victim-offender relationship		
Stranger	24.4	26.1
Husband/ex-husband	21.9	32.2
Boyfriend	19.5	9.6
Other relative	9.8	23.4
Friend	9.8	4.3
Other nonrelative	14.6	4.3
Perceived life threat	58.5	74.8
Degree of physical injury		
Serious	9.8	28.7
Minor	46.3	43.5
None	43.9	27.8

Source: National Women's Study, from: Kilpatrick, Dean G., Heidi S. Resnick, Benjamin E. Saunders, Connie L. Best. 1994. *Survey research on violence against women: Measuring violent assaults against women.* Paper presented at the 46th annual meeting of the American Society of Criminology, November 11, Miami, Florida, Figures 5, 6, and 7.   Used with permission. [See appendix entry 35]

Note: Past year prevalence rates refer to the number of adult female victims per 1,000 women aged 18 or older who reported being raped or assaulted at least once in the 12 months preceding the interview. From the first row, for example, 40 women aged 18-25 per 1,000 reported being victims of a completed rape within the previous 12 months. Numbers in table are based on data from Waves 2 and 3 of the survey that were conducted in the fall of 1990 and 1991, respectively. 83.8 percent (n=3,359) of Wave 1 respondents completed a Wave 2 or Wave 3 interview. The recall period for respondents (i.e., "in the past year") is "bounded" by the experience of being interviewed in Wave 1 and is generally considered more reliable than estimates from single wave studies. The number of sample cases for rape=41; aggravated assault=115.

VULNERABLE GROUPS AND SITUATIONS: MINORITY GROUPS

Native Americans

3.39   Homicide and Legal Intervention Rates for American Indians and Alaskan Natives, by Age and Gender of Victim, 1980–82, 1985–87, 1989–91

Age	Both Genders			Male			Female		
	1980–82	1985–87	1989–91	1980–82	1985–87	1989–91	1980–82	1985–87	1989-91
15–24	20.7	19.4	17.9	31.6	29.1	27.5	9.5	9.2	7.7
25–44	22.2	19.4	18.3	32.7	31.4	28.2	12.1	7.9	8.6
45–64	15.8	11.0	10.1	24.2	17.7	15.1	8.1	4.7*	5.4

Source: National Vital Statistics System, selected years 1980-1991, from: National Center for Health Statistics. 1994. *Health, United States, 1993.* Hyattsville, Md.: Public Health Service, p. 108, Table 37. [See appendix entry 34]

Note: Rates are per 100,000 residents. Includes International Classification of Diseases (Ninth Revision) codes E960–E978 (defined in the appendix). Interpretation of trends should take into account that population estimates for American Indians increased by 45 percent between 1980 and 1990, partly due to better enumeration techniques in the 1990 decennial census and to the increased tendency for people to identify themselves as American Indian in 1990. Persons identified as American Indian in Bureau of the Census data are sometimes misreported as white on death certificates, causing death rates to be underestimated by 22-30 percent (Sorlie, P. D., E. Rogot, and N. J. Johnson. 1992. Validity of demographic characteristics on the death certificate. *Epidemiology* 3(2): 181–184).

*   Based on 20 or fewer deaths.

3.40   Percentage of Deaths Due to Homicide for American Indians and Alaska Natives, by Age and Gender of Victim, and by Firearm, 1981–1985

	Under 5	5 - 14	15 - 24	25 - 34	35 - 44	45 - 54	55 - 64	65 & over
Males								
All homicides	10.1	6.6	13.2	15.5	14.5	14.9	9.8	7.0
By firearms	1.1	2.8	5.4	7.7	7.1	6.2	3.5	1.2
By other means	9.0	3.8	7.8	7.8	7.4	8.7	6.3	5.8
Females								
All homicides	10.2	5.4	13.4	17.3	19.6	18.3	10.2	4.8
By firearms	0.0	2.7	4.7	7.9	8.4	7.2	2.8	1.2
By other means	10.2	2.7	8.7	9.4	11.2	11.1	7.4	3.6

Source: National Vital Statistics System data, from: Indian Health Service. 1990. *Injuries among American Indians, Alaska Natives.* Washington, D.C.: Department of Health and Human Services, pp. 45 and 46, Tables 3 and 4. [See appendix entry 34]

3.41 Average Annual Homicide Rates Among American Indians and Alaska Natives, by Age, Gender, and Indian Health Service Area, 1981–1985

Service Area	Age of Victim							
	Under 5	5-14	15-24	25-34	35-44	45-54	55-64	65 & over
Aberdeen								
Male	12.1	2.2	55.7	81.9	41.7	68.5	51.0	28.2
Female	3.9	2.2	28.1	34.9	31.6	33.5	11.7	11.5
Alaska								
Male	4.8	5.0	26.2	40.2	63.0	29.8	11.6	38.2
Female	10.3	0.0	12.2	18.4	11.7	7.7	23.9	0.0
Albuquerque								
Male	6.1	0.0	41.1	41.9	0.0	40.9	20.8	19.3
Female	6.2	0.0	16.0	9.8	15.8	0.0	0.0	36.0
Bemidji								
Male	7.9	0.0	23.0	51.3	8.5	0.0	56.0	0.0
Female	7.6	0.0	15.2	10.6	8.2	11.9	0.0	0.0
Billings								
Male	7.6	8.5	78.0	85.2	42.5	107.9	0.0	0.0
Female	15.4	0.0	13.0	25.0	30.2	0.0	0.0	21.1
California								
Male	0.0	0.0	25.1	18.4	28.1	6.6	9.5	13.9
Female	0.0	3.1	2.6	5.9	8.7	0.0	0.0	0.0
Nashville								
Male	0.0	12.5	34.6	51.0	33.3	15.9	44.3	25.6
Female	14.0	0.0	0.0	14.5	0.0	44.5	38.2	0.0
Navajo								
Male	11.6	1.0	40.0	28.8	26.7	30.1	31.9	23.1
Female	0.0	1.0	6.2	10.0	7.6	10.6	0.0	5.3
Oklahoma City								
Male	8.5	0.0	11.8	38.0	20.6	32.6	16.7	13.7
Female	0.0	0.0	4.1	12.6	8.1	2.5	2.9	0.0
Phoenix								
Male	4.6	6.9	65.5	67.1	70.7	46.9	29.7	24.0
Female	14.3	0.0	15.2	20.2	26.1	24.5	0.0	9.7
Portland								
Male	8.5	0.0	30.2	43.9	24.7	36.4	37.0	0.0
Female	0.0	0.0	8.0	28.7	16.1	17.8	26.6	0.0
Tucson								
Male	0.0	0.0	101.8	50.1	105.3	37.6	0.0	51.2
Female	0.0	0.0	9.7	31.2	23.1	0.0	0.0	0.0

Source: National Vital Statistics System data, from: Indian Health Service. 1990. *Injuries among American Indians, Alaska Natives.* Washington, D.C.: Department of Health and Human Services, pp. 58–92, Tables 16-50. [See appendix entry 34]

Note: Average annual rates are calculated as the sum of homicides between 1981–1985 divided by the sum of 1981–1985 population multiplied by 100,000. Indian Health Service areas cover the following states (postal codes in parentheses): Aberdeen (ND, SD, NE, IA), Alaska (AK), Albuquerque (CO, NM), Bemidji (MN, WI, MI), Billings (MT, WY), California (CA), Nashville (ME, MA, NY, RI, CT, PA, TN, NC, AL, FL, MS, LA), Navajo (northeastern AZ), Oklahoma City (KS, OK), Phoenix (NV, UT, central AZ), Portland (WA, OR, ID), Tucson (southern AZ). The state of Texas is jointly administered by the Nashville, Oklahoma City, and Albuquerque areas. States not listed above are outside of Indian Health Service areas (AR, DE, GA, HI, IL, IN, KY, MD, MO, NJ, NH, OH, SC, VA, VT, and WV).

Hispanics

3.42   Homicide and Legal Intervention Rates for Hispanics, by Age and Gender of Victim, 1989–1992

Age	1989		1990		1991		1992	
	Male	Female	Male	Female	Male	Female	Male	Female
15–24	45.5	6.0	56.2	8.1	63.4	8.5	68.0	7.0
25–44	43.7	6.8	47.2	6.1	44.4	6.4	42.0	7.0
45–64	21.5	3.4	20.9	3.3	21.9	3.8	17.6	2.9

Source: National Vital Statistics System, 1989–1992, from: National Center for Health Statistics. 1995. *Health, United States, 1994.* Hyattsville, Md.: Public Health Service, pp. 133–134, Table 47. [See appendix entry 34]

Note: Rates are per 100,000 residents. Includes International Classification of Diseases (Ninth Revision) codes E960–E978. For 1989, rates exclude data from states lacking an Hispanic-origin item on their death certificates or those with Hispanic-origin items that were less than 90 percent complete: only Connecticut, Louisiana, Maryland, New Hampshire, Oklahoma, and Virginia were not included in the reporting area. In 1990, criteria for reporting area inclusion changed to include states with data that were 80 percent complete. In 1990, Maryland, Virginia, and Connecticut were included. In 1991, Louisiana was added to the reporting area.

3.43 Rape, Robbery, and Assault Rates for Hispanics and Non-Hispanics Aged 12 Years and Over, by Gender of Victim, 1992

	Hispanic		Non-Hispanic	
	Male	Female	Male	Female
Crimes of violence	48.5	27.9	37.6	25.7
Completed	16.6	12.9	13.6	9.3
Attempted	31.9	15.0	24.0	16.3
Rape	0.6*	0.7*	0.6	0.8
Robbery	15.7	5.6	7.2	3.8
Completed	8.2	4.3*	4.8	2.6
With injury	2.8*	2.2*	1.7	1.4
From serious assault	0.9*	0.4*	1.0	0.7
From minor assault	1.9*	1.7*	0.6	0.7
Without injury	5.4	2.1*	3.2	1.1
Attempted	7.5	1.3*	2.4	1.2
With injury	1.5*	0.7*	0.7	0.2*
From serious assault	1.0*	0.4*	0.4*	0.1*
From minor assault	0.5*	0.3*	0.2*	0.2*
Without injury	6.1	0.6*	1.7	1.0
Assault	32.1	21.6	29.8	21.1
Aggravated	16.0	4.1*	11.6	6.3
Completed with injury	3.7*	0.4*	4.6	2.1
Attempted with weapon	12.3	3.7*	7.1	4.2
Simple	16.1	17.6	18.1	14.8
Completed with injury	4.7	7.8	4.0	4.4
Attempted without weapon	11.4	9.7	14.2	10.4

Source: National Crime Victimization Survey, 1992, from: Bureau of Justice Statistics. 1994. *Criminal victimization in the United States, 1992.* Washington, D.C., p. 27, Table 9. [See appendix entry 28]

Note: Rates are per 1,000 persons aged 12 years or more. "Hispanic" includes all individuals of the following Spanish origins regardless of racial identity: Mexican American, Chicano, Mexican, Puerto Rican, Cuban, Central or South American, and any other Spanish origin. "Non-Hispanic" includes individuals of any other origin including those for whom origin was not known or not ascertained. Table excludes series crimes. Series crime and other crime types are defined in the appendix. "Serious assault" and "minor assault" are defined in the apppendix. Aggravated assaults include all attacks (and attempted attacks) with weapons or, if no weapon was involved, those that result in serious injury. Simple assaults are attacks (and attempted attacks) without weapons resulting in minor or undetermined injuries requiring less than two days of hospitalization.

* Estimate is based on 10 or fewer sample cases.

3.44   Violent Victimization Rates, by Ethnicity and Location of Residence, and by Home Ownership, 1979–1986

Type of Crime and Ethnicity	Location of Residence			Household Owned	Household Rented
	Central City	Suburban Area	Non-metro Area		
Crimes of violence*					
Hispanic	45.7	34.1	32.3	28.4	50.5
Non-Hispanic	48.5	33.9	26.0	23.8	63.2
Robbery					
Hispanic	14.8	7.5	3.4	5.6	15.4
Non-Hispanic	11.7	5.0	2.7	3.5	12.4
Aggravated assault					
Hispanic	12.9	10.6	12.2	9.2	14.7
Non-Hispanic	13.1	9.1	7.7	6.5	17.6
Simple assault					
Hispanic	17.0	15.5	16.0	13.3	19.2
Non-Hispanic	22.2	19.0	14.9	13.4	31.2

Source: National Crime Victimization Survey, 1979-1986, from: Bastian, Lisa D. 1990. *Hispanic victims*. Washington, D.C.: Bureau of Justice Statistics, p. 5, Tables 7 and 8. [See appendix entry 28]

Note: Rates are average annual victimizations per 1,000 persons aged 12 years and over between 1979 and 1986. "Hispanic" includes all individuals of the following Spanish origins regardless of racial identity: Mexican American, Chicano, Mexican, Puerto Rican, Cuban, Central or South American, and any other Spanish origin. "Non-Hispanic" includes individuals of any other origin including those for whom origin was not known or not ascertained. Table excludes series crimes. Series crime and other crime types are defined in the appendix. Aggravated assaults include all attacks (and attempted attacks) with weapons or, if no weapon was involved, those that result in serious injury. Simple assaults are attacks (and attempted attacks) without weapons resulting in minor or undetermined injuries requiring less than two days of hospitalization.

*   Includes data on rape not shown as a separate category.

3.45   Robbery and Assault Rates, by Ethnicity and Educational Attainment of Victim, 1979–1986

| | Elementary School | High School | | College | |
	0-8 Years	9-11 Years	12 Years	1-3 Years	4 or More Years
Crimes of violence*					
Hispanic	31.7	53.6	37.1	53.8	30.5
Non-Hispanic	32.7	45.1	31.7	43.6	27.7
Robbery					
Hispanic	11.0	12.4	8.9	12.1	5.6
Non-Hispanic	6.8	8.0	5.4	6.4	4.5
Aggravated assault					
Hispanic	7.8	18.1	12.7	15.6	9.4
Non-Hispanic	7.5	13.6	9.4	12.0	6.4
Simple assault					
Hispanic	12.3	21.9	15.0	24.7	15.3
Non-Hispanic	17.6	22.2	16.1	23.9	16.3

Source: National Crime Victimization Survey, 1979–1986, from: Bastian, Lisa D. 1990. *Hispanic victims*. Washington, D.C.: Bureau of Justice Statistics, p. 4, Table 5. [See appendix entry 28]

Note: Rates are average annual victimizations per 1,000 persons aged 12 years and over between 1979 and 1986. "Hispanic" includes all individuals of the following Spanish origins regardless of racial identity: Mexican American, Chicano, Mexican, Puerto Rican, Cuban, Central or South American, and any other Spanish origin. "Non-Hispanic" includes individuals of any other origin including those for whom origin was not known or not ascertained. Table excludes series crimes. Series crime and other crime types are defined in the appendix. Aggravated assaults include all attacks (and attempted attacks) with weapons or, if no weapon was involved, those that result in serious injury. Simple assaults are attacks (and attempted attacks) without weapons resulting in minor or undetermined injuries requiring less than two days of hospitalization.

*   Includes data on rape not shown as a separate category.

Asians and Pacific Islanders

3.46   Homicide and Legal Intervention Rates for Asians and Pacific Islanders, by Age and Gender of Victim, 1980–1982, 1985–1987, 1989–1991

| | Both Genders | | | Male | | | Female | | |
Age	1980-82	1985-87	1989-91	1980-82	1985-87	1989-91	1980-82	1985-87	1989-91
15-24	7.6	8.5	8.3	10.5	12.1	12.6	4.7	4.5	3.6
25-44	8.1	6.5	6.7	10.5	8.9	9.4	6.0	4.3	4.1
45-64	8.8	8.0	7.6	10.1	10.4	10.3	7.7	5.9	5.3
65 and over	13.7	15.9	13.2	18.5	22.5	18.5	9.4	10.4	8.9

Source: National Vital Statistics System, selected years 1980–1991, from: National Center for Health Statistics. 1994. *Health, United States, 1993*. Hyattsville, Md.: Public Health Service, p. 107, Table 37. [See appendix entry 34]

Note: Rates are per 100,000 residents. Includes International Classification of Diseases (Ninth Revision) codes E960–E978, (defined in the appendix). Interpretation of trends should take into account that the Asian population in the United States more than doubled between 1980 and 1990, primarily due to immigration. Also, persons identified in Bureau of the Census data as Asian are sometimes misreported as white on death certificates, causing Asian death rates to be underestimated by about 12 percent (Sorlie, P. D., E. Rogot, and N. J. Johnson. 1992. Validity of demographic characteristics on the death certificate. *Epidemiology* 3(2): 181–184).

3.47   Rape, Robbery, and Assaults of Asians and Pacific Islanders Aged 12 Years or Older, by Gender of Victim, 1987–1991

Type of Violence	Male	Female
Rapes, total	0*	7,660*
Completed	0*	1,870*
Attempted	0*	5,790*
Robberies, total	94,360	44,470
Completed	76,400	33,370
With injury	27,390	2,650*
From serious assault	11,700*	1,760*
From minor assault	15,690*	900*
Without injury	49,020	30,710
Attempted	17,950*	11,100*
With injury	3,910*	1,820*
From serious assault	1,770*	0*
From minor assault	2,140*	1,820*
Without injury	14,050*	9,280*
Assaults, total	244,800	99,140
Aggravated	100,170	18,800
Completed with injury	9,140*	580*
Attempted with weapon	91,040	18,220
Simple	144,630	80,340
Completed with injury	23,080	24,400
Attempted without weapon	121,550	55,940

Source: National Crime Victimization Survey, 1987–1991, from: Bureau of Justice Statistics. 1992. *National crime surveys: National sample, 1986–1991 [near-term data]*. [Computer files]. 4th ICPSR ed. Ann Arbor, Mich.: Inter-university Consortium for Political and Social Research. [See appendix entry 28]

Note: Estimates are for the entire five year-period (1987–1991); divide by five to determine the average annual number of victimizations. "Serious assault" and "minor assault" are defined in the appendix. Aggravated assaults include all attacks (and attempted attacks) with weapons or, if no weapon was involved, those that result in serious injury. Simple assaults are attacks (and attempted attacks) without weapons resulting in minor or undetermined injuries requiring less than two days of hospitalization.

*   Estimate based on 10 or fewer sample cases.

Hate Crimes

3.48   Hate Crime Offense Type for Reporting States, 1990

State and Offense	Number of Offenses	Percent	State and Offense	Number of Offenses	Percent
Connecticut			**Maryland**		
Total*	69	99.8	Total	792	100.0
Robbery	2	2.9	Assault	225	28.4
Assault	13	18.8	Arson	3	0.4
Arson	1	1.4	Destruction/damage/vandalism	188	23.7
Criminal mischief	25	36.2	Cross burnings	12	1.5
Threats	5	7.2	Threats	99	12.5
Other	23	33.3	Other	265	33.5
Florida			**Massachusetts**		
Total†	306	100.0	Total*	348	99.9
Murder	2	0.7	Aggravated assault	107	30.7
Sex offense	3	1.0	Simple assault	54	15.5
Robbery	4	1.3	Destruction/damage/vandalism	86	24.7
Aggravated assault	102	33.3	Harassment	40	11.5
Burglary	4	1.3	Threats	26	7.5
Larceny/theft	3	1.0	Arson	6	1.7
Arson	2	0.7	Larceny/theft	4	1.1
Simple assault	50	16.3	Other	25	7.2
Intimidation	50	16.3			
Destruction/damage/vandalism	85	27.8			
Other	1	0.3			

See notes at end of table.

3.48   Hate Crime Offense Type for Reporting States, 1990 *(continued)*

State and Offense	Number of Offenses	Percent	State and Offense	Number of Offenses	Percent
Minnesota			**New York**		
Total*	309	99.7	Total*	1,130	100.2
Criminal sexual conduct	2	0.6	Homicide	3	0.3
Robbery	7	2.3	Robbery	29	2.6
Aggravated assault	44	14.2	Assault‡	247	21.9
Burglary	2	0.6	Burglary	7	0.6
Larceny/theft	2	0.6	Larceny/theft	3	0.3
Arson	2	0.6	Arson	7	0.6
Simple assault	82	26.5	Criminal mischief	272	24.1
Destruction/damage/vandalism	43	13.9	Harassment	508	45.0
Cross burnings	8	2.6	Other	54	4.8
Harassment	97	31.4	**Oregon**		
Other	20	6.4	Total*	343	100.1
New Jersey			Robbery	64	18.7
Total*	824	99.9	Aggravated assault	10	2.9
Murder	1	0.1	Burglary/theft	3	0.9
Sex offense (except rape)	2	0.2	Simple assault	68	19.8
Robbery	8	1.0	Destruction/damage/vandalism	65	19.0
Aggravated assault	60	7.3	Threats	49	14.3
Burglary	9	1.1	Other	84	24.5
Larceny/theft	6	0.7	**Pennsylvania**		
Arson	3	0.4	Total	194	100.0
Simple assault	105	12.7	Robbery	3	1.5
Destruction/damage/vandalism	38	4.6	Aggravated assault	36	18.6
Criminal mischief	176	21.4	Burglary	1	0.5
Harassment	255	30.9	Simple assault	38	19.6
Threats	89	10.8	Intimidation	1	0.5
Other	72	8.7	Destruction/damage/vandalism	1	0.5
			Criminal mischief	42	21.7
			Harassment	46	23.7
			Threats	15	7.7
			Other	11	5.7

See notes at end of table.

3.48   Hate Crime Offense Type for Reporting States, 1990 *(continued)*

State and Offense	Number of Offenses	Percent	State and Offense	Number of Offenses	Percent
Rhode Island			**Virginia**		
Total	43	100.0	Total	91	100.0
Rape	1	2.3	Aggravated assault	4	4.4
Aggravated assault	2	4.6	Arson	1	1.1
Simple assault	12	27.9	Simple assault	10	11.0
Destruction/damage/vandalism	12	27.9	Destruction/damage/vandalism	31	34.0
Harassment	6	14.0	Cross burnings	13	14.3
Threats	2	4.7	Harassment	9	9.9
Other	8	18.6	Threats	10	11.0
			Other	13	14.3

Source: Federal Bureau of Investigation. 1992. *Hate crime statistics, 1990: A resource book.* Washington, D.C.: U.S. Government Printing Office, pp. 12, 17, 30, 37, 44, 50, 56, 61, 65, and 69, Tables 1.1, 2.1, 3.1, 4.1, 5.1, 6.1, 7.1, 8.1, 9.1, 10.1, and 11.1. [See appendix entry 19]

Note: Crime type not listed in table if no incidents were reported. Aggravated assaults include all attacks (and attempted attacks) with weapons or, if no weapon was involved, those that result in serious injury. Simple assaults are attacks (and attempted attacks) without weapons resulting in minor or undetermined injuries requiring less than two days of hospitalization.

*   The sum of the percentages do not equal 100 percent because of rounding.

†   Florida counts crimes against the person per victim, not per incident. Therefore, Florida had 258 incidents of hate crimes but 306 total offenses.

‡   Includes both aggravated and simple assaults.

3.49   Hate Crime Bias Motivation for Reporting States, 1990

State and Bias	Number of Offenders	Percent	State and Bias	Number of Offenders	Percent
Connecticut			New Jersey		
Total	69	100.0	Total*	824	100.1
Racial	41	59.4	Race	485	58.9
Ethnicity/national origin	2	2.9	Ethnicity/national origin	116	14.1
Religious	16	23.2	Religious	214	26.0
Sexual orientation	10	14.5	Sexual orientation	9	1.1
Florida			New York		
Total*	306	100.2	Total	1,100	100.0
Racial	220	71.9	Race	496	45.1
Ethnicity/national origin	28	9.3	Ethnicity/national origin	91	8.3
Religious	58	19.0	Religious	334	30.4
Maryland			Sexual orientation	160	14.5
Total	792	100.0	Multiple types	11	1.0
Racial	618	78.0	Other	8	0.7
Ethnicity/national origin	50	6.3	Oregon		
Religious	124	15.7	Total*	343	99.9
Massachusetts			Racial	222	64.7
Total	348	100.0	Ethnicity/national origin	56	16.3
Racial	222	63.8	Religious	19	5.5
Ethnicity/national origin	47	13.5	Sexual orientation	35	10.2
Religious	39	11.2	Political	10	2.9
Sexual orientation	34	9.8	Labor Union	1	0.3
Handicap	6	1.7	Rhode Island		
Minnesota			Total	43	100.0
Total	309	100.0	Racial	28	65.1
Racial	257	83.2	Ethnicity/national origin	1	2.3
Ethnicity/national origin	4	1.3	Religious	11	25.6
Religious	24	7.8	Unknown	3	7.0
Sexual orientation	22	7.1			
Disability	2	0.6			

Source: Federal Bureau of Investigation. 1992. *Hate crime statistics, 1990: A resource book.* Washington, D.C.: U.S. Government Printing Office, pp. 12, 17, 24, 30, 37, 44, 50, 56, and 65, Tables 1.3, 2.3, 3.2, 4.2, 5.3, 6.3, 7.2, 8.2, and 10.3. [See appendix entry 19]

Note: Each state defines hate crime bias, and no consistent definition exists. In general, "bias motivation" is a characteristic of the victim, or a group to which the victim belonged, which was a factor in the offender's decision to commit the crime. Pennsylvania and Virginia did not report bias motivation.

*   The sum of the percentages do not equal 100 percent because of rounding.

VULNERABLE GROUPS AND SITUATIONS: WORKPLACE

General Workplace Violence: Fatal Violence

3.50   Occupational Homicides, by State, 1980–1989

State	Frequency	State	Frequency	State	Frequency
Alabama	211	Kentucky	110	North Dakota	2
Alaska	25	Louisiana	275*	Ohio	2
Arizona	19	Maine	14	Oklahoma	121*
Arkansas	77	Maryland	180	Oregon	46
California	1,325	Massachusetts	47	Pennsylvania	261
Colorado	88	Michigan	313	Rhode Island	10
Connecticut	50	Minnesota	41	South Carolina	161
Delaware	18	Mississippi	141	South Dakota	10
Dist. of Columbia	70	Missouri	191	Tennessee	180
Florida	764	Montana	21	Texas	969
Georgia	352	Nebraska	9	Utah	25
Hawaii	35	Nevada	66	Vermont	3
Idaho	18	New Hampshire	10	Virginia	195
Illinois	496	New Jersey	164	Washington	79
Indiana	144	New Mexico	59	West Virginia	37
Iowa	29	New York	867*	Wisconsin	99
Kansas	64	North Carolina	220	Wyoming	14

Source: National Traumatic Occupational Fatalities Surveillance Systems, 1980–1989, from: National Institute for Occupational Safety and Health. 1994. *National traumatic occupational fatalities surveillance systems.* Unpublished data, prepared by National Institute for Occupational Safety and Health, Division of Safety Research. [See appendix entry 33]

Note: Occupational homicides are homicides (ICD-9 codes E960–E969) of persons aged 16 years or more for which the death certificate indicated occurrence "at work." Includes military and civilian workers.

*   Estimated; state was unable to provide data on work-related homicides for the entire period of the study.

3.51   Occupational Homicides and Occupational Homicide Rates, 1980–1989 (Annual)

Year	Homicides	Rate
1980	914	1.10
1981	939	1.13
1982	851	1.03
1983	720	0.89
1984	659	0.76
1985	754	0.84
1986	682	0.74
1987	678	0.71
1988	712	0.73
1989	694	0.68

Source: National Traumatic Occupational Fatalities Surveillance Systems, 1980–1989, from: National Institute for Occupational Safety and Health. 1994. *National traumatic occupational fatalities surveillance systems*. Unpublished data, prepared by National Institute for Occupational Safety and Health, Division of Safety Research. [See appendix entry 33]

Note: Rates are per 100,000 workers. Includes data only on occupational homicides for which a death certificate was collected; no estimates are included. Occupational homicides are homicides (ICD-9 codes E960–E969) of persons aged 16 years or more for which the death certificate indicated occurrence "at work."

3.52   Occupational Homicide Rates, by Industry Division, and by Occupation Division, 1980–1989

Industry Division	Rate	Occupation Division	Rate
Total*	0.85	Executives/administrators/ managers	0.90
Agriculture/forestry/fishing	0.57	Professional specialties	0.26
Mining	0.48	Technicians/related support	0.12
Construction	0.65	Sales	1.36
Manufacturing	0.27	Clerical	0.18
Transportation/communication/ public utilities	1.47	Service	0.97
Wholesale trade	0.19	Farmers/foresters/fishers	0.49
Retail trade	1.66	Precision production/craft/repair	0.42
Finance/insurance/real estate	0.39	Machine operators	0.20
Services	0.61	Transportation/material movers	1.50
Public administration	1.54	Laborers	1.48

Source: National Traumatic Occupational Fatalities Surveillance Systems, 1980–1989, from: National Institute for Occupational Safety and Health. 1994. *Fatal injuries to workers in the United States, 1980–1989: A decade of surveillance.* Morgantown, W.Va.: Centers for Disease Control, p. 10, Table US-2; p. 19, Table US-4. [See appendix entry 33]

Note: Industry divisions are from Standard Industrial Classification (SIC) system, and Occupational divisions are from Bureau of the Census system. Rates are per 100,000 workers. Data for New York, Oklahoma, Louisiana, and Nebraska are not available for earlier years. Occupational homicides are homicides (ICD-9 codes E960–E969) of persons aged 16 years or more for which the death certificate indicated occurrence "at work."

*   Total includes cases for which industry could not be classified (7 percent).

3.53   Traumatic Occupational Fatalities, by Manner of Death, Race, and Gender of Victim, 1980–1989

Gender and Race	Manner of Death			
	Accident	Homicide	Suicide	Unknown
Male				
White	44,561 (74.6)	4,487 (7.5)	1,722 (2.9)	763 (1.3)
Black	4,999 (8.4)	1,239 (2.1)	116 (0.2)	113 (0.2)
Other	869 (1.5)	373 (0.6)	54 (0.1)	26 (0.0)
Unknown	396 (0.7)	29 (0.1)	4 (0.0)	20 (0.0)
Total	50,825 (85.0)	6,128 (10.3)	1,896 (3.2)	922 (1.5)
Female				
White	1,786 (46.8)	1,221 (32.0)	147 (3.9)	59 (1.6)
Black	193 (5.1)	234 (6.1)	16 (0.4)	10 (0.3)
Other	41 (1.1)	79 (2.1)	6 (0.2)	1 (0.0)
Unknown	17 (0.5)	6 (0.2)	1 (0.0)	1 (0.0)
Total	2,037 (53.4)	1,540 (40.3)	170 (4.5)	71 (1.9)

Source: National Traumatic Occupational Fatalities Surveillance Systems, 1980–1989, from: National Institute for Occupational Safety and Health. 1994. *National traumatic occupational fatalities surveillance systems.* (Unpublished Data), prepared by National Institute for Occupational Safety and Health, Division of Safety Research. [See appendix entry 33]

Note: Values in parentheses are percentages. Traumatic occupational fatalities are deaths of persons aged 16 years or older by other than natural causes for which the death certificate indicated occurrence "at work."

3.54   Occupational Homicides, by High-Risk Industries and Occupations, and by Race and Gender of Victim, 1980–1989

	Total		Male		Female		Blacks		Nonblacks	
	Number	Rate	Number	Rate	Number	Rate	Number	Rate	Number	Rate
Industry										
Taxicab service	287	26.87	279	29.40	8	*	114	41.89	173	19.59
Liquor stores	115	7.96	97	10.40	18	3.53	19	13.98	96	6.35
Gasoline stations	304	5.56	266	6.11	38	3.41	44	10.65	260	3.77
Detective and protective services	152	4.96	143	5.78	9	*	41	5.13	111	3.88
Justice, public order, and safety	640	3.42	614	4.54	26	0.60	79	3.09	561	3.47
Grocery stores	806	3.24	562	4.31	244	2.06	82	3.88	724	2.87
Jewelry stores	56	3.22	46	6.63	10	0.96	1	*	55	2.69
Hotels and motels	153	1.54	106	2.52	47	0.82	20	1.15	133	1.43
Barber shops	14	1.48	14	1.78	0	*	7	*	7	*
Eating and drinking places	734	1.45	518	2.42	216	0.74	128	2.09	606	1.17
Occupation										
Taxicab drivers and chauffeurs	197	15.11	193	14.80	4	*	79	27.62	118	11.59
Sheriffs, bailiffs, and other law enforcement officers	73	10.86	72	12.37	1	*	6	*	67	11.13
Police detectives, public service	267	8.96	256	9.37	11	4.44	32	8.89	235	8.97
Hotel clerks	29	5.10	18	10.84	11	2.74	3	*	26	4.94
Garage and service station related occupations	83	4.46	76	4.36	7	*	13	7.07	70	4.17
Guards and police, except public service	160	3.57	153	3.97	7	*	49	5.13	111	3.14
Stock handlers and baggers	189	3.13	102	2.17	87	6.55	13	1.91	176	3.29
Supervisors and proprietors, sales occupations	662	2.75	555	3.37	107	1.41	57	5.90	605	2.62
Supervisors, police and detectives	12	2.21	12	2.35	0	*	1	*	11	2.23
Barbers	14	2.19	13	2.44	1	*	7	*	7	*
Bartenders	49	2.13	31	2.66	18	1.59	7	*	42	1.89
Correctional institution officers	19	1.51	17	1.63	2	*	4	*	15	1.55

Source: National Traumatic Occupational Fatalities Surveillance Systems, 1980–1989, from: Castillo, Dawn N., and E. Lynn Jenkins. 1994. Industries and occupations at high risk for work-related homicide. *Journal of Occupational Medicine* 36 no. 2 (February): p. 128 and 129, Tables 2 and 5. Used with permission. [See appendix entry 33]

Note: Uses Standard Industrial Classification (SIC) for industries and Bureau of the Census (BOC) classifications for occupation. Rates are per 100,000 workers in each classification. High risk has at least twice the average annual work-related homicide rate for all workers (0.71 per 100,000). For race of the victim within industry division, frequency is for 1980–1989; rate is for 1983–1989.

*   Not determined due to the instability of rates based on small frequencies.

3.55   Percentage of All Occupational Fatalities Due to Homicides, by Weapon and Gender of Victim, 1992

		Percent of All Occupational Fatalities		
	Number	Total	Male	Female
Homicides	1,004	17	15	40
Shootings	822	14	12	29
Stabbings	82	1	1	5

Source: National Census of Fatal Occupational Injuries, 1992, from: Bureau of Labor Statistics. 1994. *Fatal workplace injuries in 1992: A collection of data analysis.* Washington, D.C.: Department of Labor, p. 13, Table 1. [See appendix entry 5]

Note: Total number of male occupational fatalities=5,657; females = 426. Occupational injuries were included in this source if two or more independent sources substantiated the classification of "work-related."

3.56   Work-Related Homicides, by Circumstance, and by Victim-Offender Relationship, 1993

Circumstance/Victim-Offender Relationship	Homicides	Percentage
Robberies and miscellaneous crimes	793	75
Work associates	106	10
Co-worker, former co-worker	(59)	(6)
Customer, client	(43)	(4)
Police in the line of duty	67	6
Security guard in the line of duty	52	5
Personal acquaintance	45	4
Victim's husband, ex-husband	(15)	(1)
Boyfriend, ex-boyfriend	(11)	(1)
Other relative	(6)	(1)
Other acquaintance	(11)	(1)
Total	1,063	100

Source: National Census of Fatal Occupational Injuries, 1993, from Toscano, Guy, and Janice Windau. 1994. The changing character of fatal work injuries. *Monthly Labor Review* 117, no.10 (October): p. 18. [See appendix entry 5]

Note: Occupational injuries were included in this source if two or more independent sources substantiated the classification of "work-related." Indented rows and values in parentheses represent subgroups of the general category under which they are listed. General categories sum to the totals at the bottom of the table.

3.57   Occupational Homicides, by Employee Status, Gender, Age, Race, and Ethnicity of Victim, 1992

Characteristic	Number	Percentage
Total	1,004	100
Employee status		
Wage and salary workers	764	76
Self-employed*	240	24
Gender		
Male	832	83
Female	172	17
Age		
Under 20	33	3
20 to 24	100	10
25 to 34	258	26
35 to 44	264	26
45 to 54	178	18
55 to 64	114	11
65 and over	57	6
Race		
White	688	69
Black	183	18
Asian or Pacific Islander	83	8
Other	50	5
Hispanic†	123	12

Source: National Census of Fatal Occupational Injuries, 1992, from: Bureau of Labor Statistics. 1994. *Fatal workplace injuries in 1992: A collection of data analysis.* Washington, D.C.: Department of Labor, p. 14, Table 2. [See appendix entry 5]

Note: Percentages may not add up to totals because of rounding. Occupational injuries were included in this source if two or more independent sources substantiated the classification of "work-related."

*   Includes paid and unpaid family workers, and may include owners of incorporated businesses, or members of partnerships.

†   Persons identified as Hispanic may be of any race.

3.58   Occupational Homicides, by Occupational Classification, 1992

Occupation	Frequency	Percentage
Total	1,004	100
Managerial and professional specialty	177	18
Executive, administrative, and managerial	134	13
Managers, food service and lodging establishments	59	6
Professional specialty	43	4
Health diagnosing, assessment and treating occupations	8	1
Teachers, except postsecondary	7	1
Social, recreation, and religious workers	7	1
Lawyers and judges	6	1
Writers, artists, entertainers and athletes	8	1
Technical, sales, and administrative support	335	33
Technicians and related support	5	*
Sales occupations	296	29
Supervisors and proprietors	156	16
Sales representatives, finance and business services	10	1
Sales workers, retail and personal services	128	13
Sales workers, motor vehicles and boats	6	1
Sales counter clerks	14	1
Cashiers	77	8
Administrative support occupations, including clerical	34	3
Service occupations	225	22
Protective services	117	12
Supervisors	5	*
Firefighters and fire prevention	—	—
Police and detectives	58	6
Guards	54	5
Service occupations except protective and household	108	11
Food preparation and service	64	6
Health service	5	*
Cleaning and building service occupations, except household	24	2
Personal service occupations	15	1
Farming, forestry, and fishing	14	1
Farming occupations	12	1
Precision production, craft, and repair	41	4
Mechanics and repairers	15	1
Construction trades	11	1
Operators, fabricators, and laborers	202	20
Machine operators, assemblers, and inspectors	7	1
Transportation and material moving operators	135	13
Motor vehicle operators	132	13
Truck drivers	29	3
Driver-sales workers	12	1
Taxicab drivers and chauffeurs	86	9
Handlers, equipment cleaners, helpers, and laborers	60	6
Freight, stock, and material handlers	26	3
Garage and service station-related occupations	15	1
Laborers, except construction	9	1
Military occupations	3	*

Source: National Census of Fatal Occupational Injuries, 1992, from: Bureau of Labor Statistics. 1994. *Fatal workplace injuries in 1992: A collection of data analysis.* Washington, D.C.: Department of Labor, p. 15, Table 3. [See appendix entry 5]

Note: Occupational classification system is from the Bureau of the Census. Occupational injuries were included in this source if two or more independent sources substantiated the classification of "work-related." Percentages may not add up to total due to rounding. Indented rows are subgroups of the more general category appearing above them.

*   Less than 0.5 percent.

—   Indicates no data reported or data that did not meet publication guidelines of the Bureau of Labor Statistics.

3.59   Work-Related Homicides, by Industry, and by Gender of Victim, 1992

Industry	Frequency	Percentages		
		Total	Male	Female
Total	1,004	100	100	100
Private Industry	904	90	90	89
Agriculture, forestry and fishing	14	1	1	–
Construction	19	2	2	–
Manufacturing	32	3	4	–
Transportation and public utilities	115	11	13	–
Local and interurban passenger transportation	91	9	11	–
Taxicabs	86	9	10	–
Trucking and warehousing	14	1	2	–
Trucking and courier services, except air	14	1	2	–
Wholesale trade	22	2	3	–
Durable goods	14	1	2	–
Retail trade	484	48	47	53
General merchandise stores	15	1	1	–
Food stores	176	18	17	19
Grocery stores	160	16	16	18
Automotive dealers and service stations	55	5	6	–
Gasoline service stations	38	4	4	–
Apparel and accessory stores	18	2	1	–
Eating and drinking places	143	14	14	16
Eating places	81	8	7	12
Drinking places	31	3	3	–
Miscellaneous retail	73	7	7	6
Liquor stores	17	2	2	–
Used merchandise stores	15	1	1	–
Miscellaneous shopping goods stores	25	2	3	–
Retail stores, not elsewhere classified	10	1	–	–
Finance, insurance, and real estate	36	4	3	6
Depository institutions	10	1	–	–
Real estate	18	2	2	–
Services	165	16	15	22
Hotels and other lodging places	19	2	1	–
Personal services	24	2	2	6
Business services	51	5	6	–
Detective, guard, and armored car services	23	2	3	–
Automotive repair, services, and parking	18	2	2	–
Health services	14	1	–	–
Other or nonclassifiable	12	1	1	–
Government	100	10	10	11
Federal	10	1	1	3
State	11	1	1	1
Local	77	8	8	7
Police protection	46	5	5	1

Source: National Census of Fatal Occupational Injuries, 1992, from: Bureau of Labor Statistics. 1994. *Fatal workplace injuries in 1992: A collection of data analysis.* Washington, D.C.: Department of Labor, p. 16, Table 4. [See appendix entry 5]

Note: The number of male work-related homicides in this table is 832; the number of female work-related homicides is 172. Industry divisions come from the Standard Industrial Classification system. Occupational injuries were included in this source if two or more independent sources substantiated the classification of "work-related." Percentages may not add up to total due to rounding.

   – Indicate no data reported or data that did not meet publication guidelines of the Bureau of Labor Statistics.

3.60   Percentages of Job-Related Homicides, by Worker Traits and Weapon, 1993

Characteristic	Percentage
Employment type	
Wage and salary workers	73
Self-employed	27
Gender	
Male	82
Female	18
Age	
Under 20	4
20 to 24	8
25 to 34	27
35 to 44	27
45 to 54	18
55 and over	16
Weapon/event	
Shooting	82
Stabbing	9
Beating	3
Other	6

Source: National Census of Fatal Occupational Injuries, 1993, from: Bureau of Labor Statistics. 1994. *News.* Washington, D.C.: Department of Labor, p. 3, Table B. [See appendix entry 5]

Note: Occupational homicides were included in this source if two or more independent sources substantiated the classification of "work-related."

3.61   Homicides at Work, by Offender's Motive, Victim's Activity, and Time, 1993

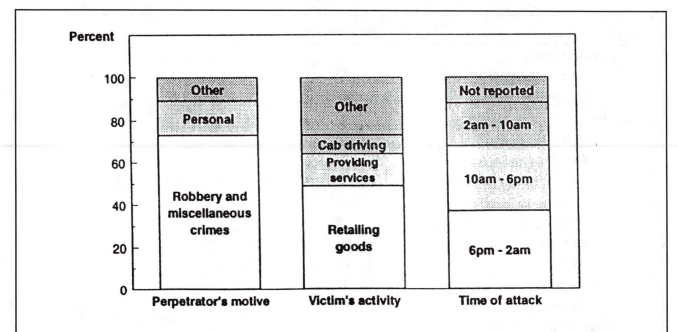

Source: National Census of Fatal Occupational Injuries, 1993, from: Bureau of Labor Statistics, 1994. *Issues in labor statistics.* Washington, D.C.: Department of Labor, p. 1. [See appendix entry 5]

General Workplace Violence: Other Interpersonal Violence

3.62   Victimizations and Victimization Rates at Work, by Occupation Type, 1993

Occupation Group	Aggravated Assault	Simple Assault	Crimes of Violence†
Health	36,060	198,320	263,390
	(3.0)	(16.7)	(22.2)
Education	7,000*	152,580	176,920
	(0.9*)	(19.5)	(22.7)
Law enforcement	51,930	283,450	343,710
	(18.8)	(102.7)	(124.6)
Retail sales	58,820	220,260	311,090
	(4.0)	(15.1)	(21.3)
Transportation	18,000*	46,850	78,670
	(3.7*)	(9.7)	(16.3)
Other	169,650	496,730	763,520
	(1.9)	(5.4)	(8.4)

Source: National Crime Victimization Survey, 1993 preliminary data, from: Bureau of the Census. 1995. *National crime victimization survey, 1992–1993.* [Computer files]. Suitland, Md. [See appendix entry 28]

Note: Values in parentheses are rates per 1,000 employed residents aged 16 years or more. "Health" includes physicians, nurses, medical technicians, other medical workers, mental health services professionals, custodial care, and other mental health workers. "Education" includes teachers or other professionals employed in schools or special educational facilities. "Law enforcement" includes police officers, prison or jail guards, security guards, and other law enforcement personnel. "Retail sales" include convenience or liquor store clerks, gas station attendants, bartenders, and other retail sales personnel. "Transportation" includes bus drivers, taxi cab drivers, and other transportation workers. "Simple Assault" in this table includes verbal threats of assault, rape, and other (nonrape) sexual attack in addition to actual attacks involving no weapon and at most, only minor injury. Table includes series crimes. Series crime and other crime types are defined in the appendix. National Crime Victimization Survey data for 1993 are not comparable to earlier years due to changes in the survey.

* Estimate is based on 10 or fewer cases.

† Includes rape, other sexual attack, robbery, and unwanted sexual contact without force, in addition to aggravated assault, and simple assault.

3.63   Victimizations, by Occupation of Victim, 1993

Occupation Type	All Violence	Rape	Sexual Assault	Robbery	Aggravated Assault	Simple Assault
Health	722,990	22,520*	35,830	54,700	120,230	489,710
Education	347,660	8,430*	10,850*	27,920*	46,350	254,120
Law enforcement	451,890	5,140*	2,230*	5,640*	85,780	353,100
Retail sales	899,810	22,900*	15,510*	98,010	170,740	592,650
Transportation	231,180	2,930*	0*	30,590*	55,860	141,810
Other	3,767,860	90,430	134,690	503,760	877,050	2,161,930
Not applicable	2,674,450	109,800	90,290	338,000	677,520	1,458,850

Source: National Crime Victimization Survey, 1993 preliminary data, from: Bureau of the Census. 1995. *National crime victimization survey, 1992–1993*. [Computer files]. Suitland, Md. [See appendix entry 28]

Note: Includes all victimizations, regardless of whether they occurred at work. "Health" includes physicians, nurses, medical technicians, other medical workers, mental health services professionals, custodial care, and other mental health workers. "Education" includes teachers or other professionals employed in schools or special educational facilities. "Law enforcement" includes police officers, prison or jail guards, security guards, and other law enforcement personnel. "Retail sales" include convenience or liquor store clerks, gas station attendants, bartenders, and other retail sales personnel. "Transportation" includes bus drivers, taxi cab drivers, and other transportation workers. "Not applicable" includes persons aged 16 years or more who were not employed at time of incident—i.e., those either looking for work, keeping house, going to school, unable to work, retired, or others not employed. "Sexual Assault" in this table includes nonrape sexual attacks, with and without injury, and unwanted sexual contact without force. "Simple Assault" in this table includes verbal threats of assault, rape, and other sexual attack in addition to actual attacks involving no weapon and at most, only minor injury. Table includes series crimes. Series crime and other crime types are defined in the appendix. National Crime Victimization Survey data for 1993 are not comparable to earlier years due to changes in the survey.

*   Estimate is based on 10 or fewer cases.

3.64 Victimization Rates, by Occupation of Victim, 1993

Occupation Group	All Violence	Rape	Sexual Assault	Robbery	Aggravated Assault	Simple Assault
Health	61.1	1.9*	3.0	4.6	10.2	41.4
Education	44.5	1.1*	1.4*	3.6*	5.9	32.5
Law enforcement	163.8	1.9*	0.8*	2.0*	31.1	128.0
Retail sales	61.5	1.6*	1.1*	6.7	11.7	40.5
Transportation	47.8	0.6*	0.0*	6.3*	11.5	29.3
Other	41.2	1.0	1.5	5.5	9.6	23.7
Not applicable	42.2	1.7	1.4	5.3	10.7	23.0

Source: National Crime Victimization Survey, 1993 preliminary data, from: Bureau of the Census. 1995. *National crime victimization survey, 1992–1993.* [Computer files]. Suitland, Md. [See appendix entry 28]

Note: Rates are per 1,000 residents aged 16 years or more. Includes all victimizations, regardless of whether they occurred at work. "Health" includes physicians, nurses, medical technicians, other medical workers, mental health services professionals, custodial care, and other mental health workers. "Education" includes teachers or other professionals employed in schools or special educational facilities. "Law enforcement" includes police officers, prison or jail guards, security guards, and other law enforcement personnel. "Retail sales" include convenience or liquor store clerks, gas station attendants, bartenders, and other retail sales personnel. "Transportation" includes bus drivers, taxi cab drivers, and other transportation workers. "Not applicable" includes those not employed at time of incident—i.e., those either looking for work, keeping house, going to school, unable to work, retired, or others not employed. "Sexual Assault" in this table includes nonrape sexual attacks, with and without injury, and unwanted sexual contact without force. "Simple Assault" in this table includes verbal threats of assault, rape, and other sexual attack in addition to actual attacks involving no weapon and at most, only minor injury. Table includes series crimes. Series crime and other crime types are defined in the appendix. National Crime Victimization Survey data for 1993 are not comparable to earlier years due to changes in the survey.

* Estimate is based on 10 or fewer cases.

Police Officers

3.65   Homicides of Police Officers, Total, and by Region, 1972–1993

Region	1972	1973	1974	1975	1976	1977	1978	1979	1980	1981	1982
Total	112	131	132	129	111	93	93	106	104	91	92
Northeast	14	17	14	19	15	11	12	13	23	13	7
New England	1	3	1	3	1	1	3	0	3	2	0
Middle Atlantic	13	14	13	16	14	10	9	13	20	11	7
Midwest	30	20	37	23	24	19	10	16	15	18	21
East North Central	19	15	34	20	15	8	5	13	8	10	15
West North Central	11	5	3	3	9	11	5	3	7	8	6
South	57	60	57	54	57	47	47	49	45	43	42
South Atlantic	27	26	35	23	29	24	15	23	21	18	18
East South Central	8	11	7	15	10	9	13	15	9	16	9
West South Central	22	23	15	16	18	14	19	11	15	9	15
West	11	30	20	22	10	14	20	23	14	14	18
Mountain	3	12	7	9	2	3	5	8	5	6	8
Pacific	8	18	13	13	8	11	15	15	9	8	10

See notes at end of table.

3.65 Homicides of Police Officers, Total, and by Region, 1972–1993 *(continued)*

Region	1983	1984	1985	1986	1987	1988	1989	1990	1991	1992	1993
Total	80	72	78	66	74	78	66	66	71	62	70
Northeast	5	10	11	6	12	7	9	7	7	8	9
New England	1	1	4	0	2	2	1	1	2	1	1
Middle Atlantic	4	9	7	6	10	5	8	6	5	7	8
Midwest	13	10	14	11	17	12	8	14	20	8	11
East North Central	9	9	7	10	13	10	4	10	12	5	8
West North Central	4	1	7	1	4	2	4	4	8	3	3
South	37	37	36	32	28	38	32	31	29	28	31
South Atlantic	14	17	17	16	15	13	14	16	12	14	14
East South Central	9	7	7	8	5	7	6	9	5	7	3
West South Central	14	13	12	8	8	18	12	6	12	7	14
West	18	13	10	13	16	19	9	9	7	13	11
Mountain	6	3	1	7	7	10	3	3	4	4	3
Pacific	12	10	9	6	9	9	6	6	3	9	8

Source: Federal Bureau of Investigation. 1992 (Annual). *Law enforcement officers killed and assaulted.* Washington, D.C.: U.S. Government Printing Office, page numbers and table numbers vary by year. [See appendix entry 22]

Note: For 1972–1983, the North Central region is equivalent to the Midwest region. "Total" includes U.S. territories, such as Puerto Rico, U.S. Virgin Islands, Guam, American Samoa, and Mariana Islands.

3.66   Characteristics of Homicides of Police Officers, 1972–1993

Characteristics of Victim	1972	1973	1974	1975	1976	1977	1978	1979
Percent white	92	89	89	90	90	90	91	88
Percent black	8	10	11	9	8	10	9	9
Percent other race	0	1	0	1	2	0	0	3
Percent male	100	100	99	100	100	99	100	99
Percent female	0	0	1	0	0	1	0	1
Percent under 25 years of age*	16	15	12	11	11	11	14	9
Percent 25-30 years of age*	25	30	31	36	32	40	30	20
Percent 31-40 years of age	22	28	35	31	28	23	30	41
Percent over 40 years of age	37	27	22	22	29	27	26	30
Average years of law enforcement service†‡			5	5	5.5	5.5	8	8
Percent 1 year or less of service‡			17	11	13	13	10	10
Percent less than 5 years of service‡			45	48	43	41	39	34
Percent 5 through 10 years of service‡			33	28	28	38	30	40
Percent over 10 years of service‡			22	24	29	21	31	26
Percent in uniform‡			68	69	71	81	80	71

See notes at end of table.

3.66   Characteristics of Homicides of Police Officers, 1972–1993 (continued)

Characteristics of Victim	1980	1981–1985	1986–1990	1990	1991	1992	1993
Percent white	87	87	88	80	87	82	86
Percent black	13	13	11	18	13	16	14
Percent other race	0	0	0	2	0	2	0
Percent male	99	97	98	98	96	100	94
Percent female	1	3	2	2	4	0	6
Percent under 25 years of age*	11	9	9	5	7	6	6
Percent 25-30 years of age*	26	26	21	14	27	21	37
Percent 31-40 years of age	43	41	37	41	37	39	33
Percent over 40 years of age	19	24	33	40	29	34	21
Average age§					36	38	34
Average years of law enforcement service†‡	8	8	9	10	8	10	9
Percent less than 1 year of service‡	2	6	4	3	6	6	3
Percent 1-4 years of service‡	29	29	28	26	38	23	34
Percent 5-10 years of service‡	42	34	27	26	24	24	24
Percent over 10 years of service‡	27	31	41	45	31	44	34
Percent years of service not reported§					1	3	4
Percent wearing uniform	69	70	69	63	73	65	81
Percent wearing protective body armor**		19	26	25	34	27	56

Source: Federal Bureau of Investigation. 1973-1993 (Annual). *Law enforcement officers killed and assaulted* [Title varies]. Washington, D.C.: U.S. Government Printing Office, page numbers and table numbers vary by year.

* For 1972–1973, these age ranges are Up to 25 and 26–30, respectively.

† From 1972–1977, the average years of law enforcement service was the median years of law enforcement service.

‡ This information was not included in 1972–1973.

§ This category was not included for 1972–1990.

** This category was not included for 1972–1980.

3.67   Homicide of Police Officers, by Circumstances, 1973–1993

Circumstance	1973-1982	1983	1984	1985	1986	1987	1988	1989	1990	1991	1992	1993
Disturbance calls	135	15	8	13	7	23	7	13	10	17	11	10
Arrest situations	483	31	33	29	26	27	33	24	30	14	26	29
Burglaries in progress/pursuing burglary suspects	69	4	2	4	1	6	3	0	1	3	5	1
Robberies in progress/pursuing robbery suspects	191	11	9	12	9	4	7	8	13	4	10	10
Drug-related matters	56	6	4	6	7	4	12	7	5	3	3	3
Attempting other arrests	167	10	18	7	9	13	11	9	11	4	8	15
Civil disorders (mass disobedience, riot, etc.)	2	0	0	0	0	0	0	0	0	0	0	0
Handling, transporting, custody of prisoners	45	3	3	4	5	6	2	6	2	6	2	1
Investigating suspicious persons/ circumstances	106	10	12	9	11	5	23	10	9	10	7	15
Ambush situations	84	9	8	7	4	4	6	4	8	11	6	4
Mentally deranged individuals	25	1	0	0	3	1	1	2	1	0	0	1
Traffic pursuits/stops	143	11	8	16	10	8	6	7	6	13	10	10

Source: Federal Bureau of Investigation. 1973–1993 (Annual). *Law enforcement officers killed and assaulted* [Title varies]. Washington, D.C.: U.S. Government Printing Office, page numbers and table numbers vary by year. [See appendix entry 22]

Note: For 1973–1982, there were 62 officers killed while answering domestic disturbance calls. This type of circumstance was not reported for any other years.

3.68 Homicides of Police Officers, by Type of Firearm, Whether Killed With Own Weapon, and Wearing of Body Armor, 1990–1993

Firearms used	1990			1991			1992			1993		
	Total slain with firearms	Slain with own weapon	Slain wearing body armor	Total slain with firearms	Slain with own weapon	Slain wearing body armor	Total slain with firearms	Slain with own weapon	Slain wearing body armor	Total slain with firearms	Slain with own weapon	Slain wearing body armor
Total	56	3	15	68	8	24	53	4	18	67	5	37
Handgun total	48	3	13	50	8	16	42	4	14	50	5	27
.22 Caliber	2	0	0	3	0	1	1	0	1	3	0	1
.22 Magnum	1	0	1	0	0	0	0	0	0	0	0	0
.25 Caliber	0	0	0	3	0	2	2	0	1	1	0	0
.32 Caliber	2	0	0	3	0	1	0	0	0	0	0	0
.38 Caliber	18	2	4	10	1	1	13	1	4	11	0	6
.357 Magnum	10	0	3	12	2	4	9	2	3	5	1	3
.380 Caliber	0	0	0	1	0	1	2	0	1	9	0	6
9mm	8	0	3	12	4	5	8	1	2	11	1	6
.40 Caliber	0	0	0	0	0	0	0	0	0	3	1	3
.44 Caliber/Magnum	1	0	0	0	0	0	1	0	0	0	0	0
.45 Caliber	2	1	1	4	1	1	2	0	1	3	2	2
Caliber not reported	4	0	1	2	0	0	4	0	1	4	0	0
Rifle total	7	0	2	14	0	8	9	0	4	14	0	9
.22 Caliber	1	0	0	6	0	2	2	0	1	2	0	0
.223 Caliber	0	0	0	3	0	2	1	0	1	3	0	3
.240 Caliber	0	0	0	0	0	0	0	0	0	1	0	0
.270 Caliber	1	0	0	0	0	0	0	0	0	0	0	0
.30 Caliber	1	0	0	1	0	1	2	0	2	1	0	1
.308 Caliber	0	0	0	0	0	0	0	0	0	2	0	1
.25-20	0	0	0	0	0	0	0	0	0	1	0	1
.30-06	2	0	0	2	0	2	1	0	0	0	0	0
.30-30	1	0	1	0	0	0	0	0	0	1	0	1
.300 Magnum	0	0	0	0	0	0	1	0	0	0	0	1
7 mm	0	0	0	1	0	1	1	0	0	0	0	0
8 mm	0	0	0	1	0	0	0	0	0	0	0	0
7.62 x 39 mm	1	0	1	0	0	0	2	0	0	0	0	0
Caliber not reported	0	0	0	0	0	0	0	0	0	2	0	1
Shotgun total	1	0	0	4	0	0	2	0	0	3	0	1
20 gauge	0	0	0	1	0	0	1	0	0	0	0	0
12 gauge	1	0	0	3	0	0	1	0	0	3	0	1

Source: Federal Bureau of Investigation. 1986–1993 (Annual). *Law enforcement officers killed and assaulted* [Title varies]. Washington, D.C.: U.S. Government Printing Office, pages and tables vary by year. [See appendix entry 22]

3.69   Assaults of Police Officers, Total, With Injuries, and by Region, 1982–1993

	1982		1983		1984		1985		1986		1987	
	Total	With injury	Total	With injury	Total	With injury	Total	With Injury	Total	With Injury	Total	With Injury
Total	55,775	17,116	62,324	20,807	60,153	20,205	61,724	20,817	64,259	21,639	63,842	21,273
Northeast	13,217	4,560	16,296	7,405	15,364	7,653	15,322	7,454	14,867	7,657	15,272	7,895
New England	4,084	1,547	4,233	1,444	4,029	1,347	3,823	1,312	3,474	1,113	3,498	1,036
Middle Atlantic	9,133	3,013	12,063	5,961	11,335	6,306	11,499	6,142	11,393	6,544	11,774	6,859
Midwest*	9,057	3,594	9,912	3,776	9,096	3,274	9,902	3,949	10,669	4,170	9,321	3,611
East North Central	5,552	2,523	5,629	2,601	4,814	2,078	6,216	2,817	6,949	3,084	6,087	2,614
West North Central	3,505	1,071	4,283	1,175	4,282	1,196	3,686	1,132	3,720	1,086	3,234	997
South	21,254	4,673	22,734	4,975	22,054	4,903	22,829	5,238	24,418	5,397	24,885	5,564
South Atlantic	14,288	2,775	14,997	2,925	14,684	2,852	15,534	3,025	16,376	3,219	17,109	3,335
East South Central	1,297	373	1,237	322	1,075	298	983	320	1,128	381	849	270
West South Central	5,669	1,525	6,500	1,728	6,295	1,753	6,312	1,893	6,914	1,797	6,927	1,959
West	12,247	4,289	13,382	4,651	13,639	4,375	13,671	4,176	14,305	4,415	14,364	4,203
Mountain	3,131	949	3,369	1,026	3,603	889	3,889	850	4,338	1,042	4,300	1,075
Pacific	9,116	3,340	10,013	3,625	10,036	3,486	9,782	3,326	9,967	3,373	10,064	3,128

See notes at end of table.

3.69   Assaults of Police Officers, Total, With Injuries, and by Region, 1982–1993 (continued)

	1988		1989		1990		1991		1992		1993	
	Total	With injury	Total	With injury	Total	With injury	Total	With injury	Total	With injury	Total	With injury
Total	58,752	21,015	62,172	21,893	71,794	26,031	62,852	23,650	81,252	29,673	66,975	24,031
Northeast	15,493	8,225	16,489	8,828	17,630	9,412	14,331	8,035	18,491	9,572	14,733	7,899
New England	3,726	1,197	3,194	1,023	3,456	1,172	2,725	765	4,348	1,246	3,316	976
Middle Atlantic	11,767	7,028	13,295	7,805	14,174	8,240	11,606	7,270	14,143	8,326	11,417	6,923
Midwest*	10,437	4,216	10,732	4,053	10,755	3,841	9,684	3,747	12,667	4,635	9,801	3,448
East North Central	7,048	3,161	6,781	2,985	6,549	2,758	6,726	2,859	8,314	3,535	6,665	2,668
West North Central	3,389	1,055	3,951	1,068	4,206	1,083	2,958	888	4,353	1,100	3,136	780
South†	17,629	4,232	19,378	4,614	28,530	8,497	27,226	8,407	33,365	10,532	29,141	9,016
South Atlantic	11,082	2,207	10,947	2,023	19,665	5,805	18,845	5,766	23,179	7,187	19,444	6,006
East South Central	848	276	1,086	381	1,014	418	732	333	1,184	394	1,276	394
West South Central	5,699	1,749	7,345	2,210	7,851	2,274	7,649	2,308	9,002	2,951	8,421	2,616
West	15,193	4,342	15,573	4,398	14,879	4,281	11,611	3,461	16,729	4,934	13,300	3,668
Mountain	4,677	994	4,303	853	4,038	785	1,879	435	4,551	1,068	3,545	780
Pacific	10,516	3,348	11,270	3,545	10,841	3,496	9,732	3,026	12,178	3,866	9,755	2,888

Source: Federal Bureau of Investigation. 1982–1993 (Annual). *Law enforcement officers killed and assaulted* [Title varies]. Washington, D.C.: U.S. Government Printing Office, pages vary, Table 1. [See appendix entry 22]

*   For 1982–1983, the North Central region is equivalent to the Midwest region.

†   Florida and Kentucky did not furnish data for 1988 and are excluded.

3.70   Assaults of Police Officers, by Type of Weapon and Region, 1982–1993

Year	Weapon	All Regions	Northeast	Midwest	South	West
1982	Firearm	2,642	263	544	1,208	627
	Knife or cutting instrument	1,452	255	202	634	361
	Other dangerous weapon	4,879	937	656	1,753	1,533
	Personal weapons*	46,802	11,762	7,655	17,659	9,726
1983	Firearm	3,067	617	517	1,216	717
	Knife or cutting instrument	1,829	526	212	652	439
	Other dangerous weapon	5,527	1,290	698	1,896	1,643
	Personal weapons*	51,901	13,863	8,485	18,970	10,583
1984	Firearm	2,654	556	307	1,176	615
	Knife or cutting instrument	1,662	401	197	605	459
	Other dangerous weapon	5,148	1,250	590	1,815	1,493
	Personal weapons*	50,689	13,157	8,002	18,458	11,072
1985	Firearm	2,793	563	417	1,126	687
	Knife or cutting instrument	1,715	361	255	652	447
	Other dangerous weapon	5,263	1,179	674	1,899	1,511
	Personal weapons*	51,953	13,219	8,556	19,152	11,026
1986	Firearm	2,852	606	479	1,215	552
	Knife or cutting instrument	1,614	339	219	649	407
	Other dangerous weapon	5,721	1,091	771	2,219	1,640
	Personal weapons*	54,072	12,831	9,200	20,335	11,706
1987	Firearm	2,789	602	367	1,234	586
	Knife or cutting instrument	1,561	376	175	601	409
	Other dangerous weapon	5,685	1,281	590	2,154	1,660
	Personal weapons*	53,807	13,013	8,189	20,896	11,709

See notes at end of table.

3.70 Assaults of Police Officers, by Type of Weapon and Region, 1982–1993 *(continued)*

		All Regions	Northeast	Midwest	South	West
1988	Firearm	2,759	755	377	888	739
	Knife or cutting instrument	1,367	347	209	413	398
	Other dangerous weapon	5,573	1,531	795	1,397	1,850
	Personal weapons*	49,053	12,860	9,056	14,931	12,206
1989	Firearm	3,154	949	517	871	817
	Knife or cutting instrument	1,379	318	198	463	400
	Other dangerous weapon	5,778	1,512	812	1,592	1,862
	Personal weapons*	51,861	13,710	9,205	16,452	12,494
1990	Firearm	3,662	1,036	635	1,318	673
	Knife or cutting instrument	1,641	376	233	706	326
	Other dangerous weapon	7,390	1,890	807	2,995	1,698
	Personal weapons*	59,101	14,328	9,080	23,511	12,182
1991	Firearm	3,532	1,031	591	1,285	625
	Knife or cutting instrument	1,493	331	186	689	287
	Other dangerous weapon	7,014	1,765	777	3,144	1,328
	Personal weapons*	50,813	11,204	8,130	22,108	9,371
1992	Firearm	4,455	1,010	657	1,649	1,139
	Knife or cutting instrument	2,095	395	228	902	570
	Other dangerous weapon	8,604	1,954	927	3,908	1,815
	Personal weapons*	66,098	15,132	10,855	26,906	13,205
1993	Firearm	4,002	1,045	521	1,479	957
	Knife or cutting instrument	1,574	300	191	734	349
	Other dangerous weapon	7,551	1,494	806	3,708	1,543
	Personal weapons*	53,848	11,894	8,283	23,220	10,451

Source: Federal Bureau of Investigation. 1983–1993 (Annual). *Law enforcement officers killed and assaulted* [Title varies]. Washington, D.C.: U.S. Government Printing Office, pages vary, Table 3. [See appendix entry 22]

Note: For 1982–1983, the North Central region is equivalent to the Midwest region.
* Hands, feet, fists, etc.

Postal Workers

3.71   Workplace-Related Homicides of Postal Workers, by Gender of Victim and Job Type, 1980–1989

	Homicides	Percentage
Gender		
Male	26	65
Female	14	35
Total	40	100
Job		
Mail carrier	17	43
Postal clerk	9	23
Postmaster and mail superintendent	5	13
Other (specified)	3	8
Other (unknown or unspecified)	6	15
Total	40	100

Source: National Traumatic Occupational Fatalities Surveillance System, from: Centers for Disease Control. 1994. Occupational injury deaths of postal workers—United States, 1980–1989. *Morbidity and Mortality Weekly Report* 43, no. 32 (August): p. 587. [See appendix entry 33]

3.72   Occupational Injury Death Rates Among Postal Service Employees, by Causes, 1983–1989

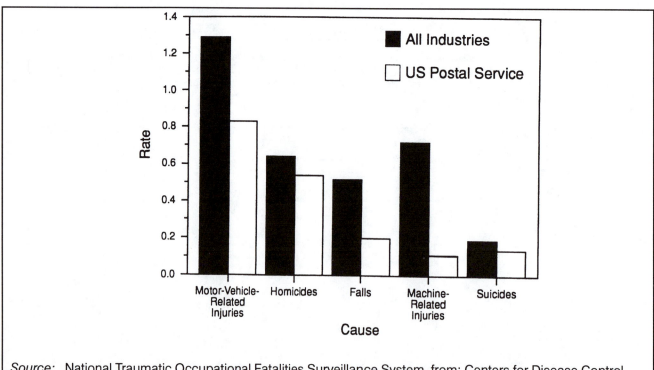

Source: National Traumatic Occupational Fatalities Surveillance System, from: Centers for Disease Control. 1994. Occupational injury deaths of postal workers—United States, 1980–1989. *Morbidity and Mortality Weekly Report* 43, no. 32 (August): p. 593, Figure 1. [See appendix entry 33]

Note: Rates are per 100,000 workers.

3.73   Number of Occupational Injury Deaths Among Postal Service Employees, by Causes, 1980–1989

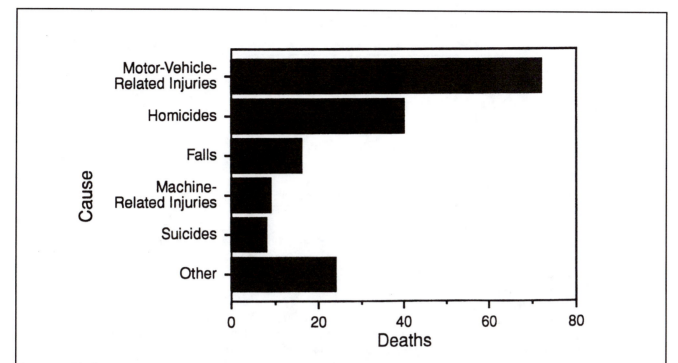

Source: National Traumatic Occupational Fatalities Surveillance System, from: Centers for Disease Control. 1994. Occupational injury deaths of postal workers—United States, 1980–1989. *Morbidity and Mortality Weekly Report* 43, no. 32 (August): p. 593, Figure 2. [See appendix entry 33]

Health Care Workers

3.74   Workplace-Related Homicides of Health Care Workers, by Occupational Category, Weapon, and Gender of Victim, 1980–1990

Occupational Category	Gender of Victim		Weapon		
	Male	Female	Firearm	Cutting instrument	Other
Pharmacist	24	3	24	2	1
Physician	23	3	19	3	4
Registered nurse	3	15	13	4	1
Nurse's aide	2	15	9	4	4
Other*	12	6	13	2	3
Total	64	42	78	15	13

Source: National Traumatic Occupational Fatalities Surveillance System, from: Goodman, Richard A., Lynn Jenkins, and James A. Mercy. 1994. Workplace-related homicide among health care workers, 1980 through 1990. *Journal of the American Medical Association* 272, no. 21 (December): p. 1687, Table 2. Used with permission. [See appendix entry 33]

   *   This category includes health aides except nurses (4), dentists (2), health technicians not classified elsewhere (2), optometrists (2), physical therapists (2), radiologic technicians (2), clinical laboratory technicians (1), health records technicians (1), licensed practical nurses (1), and physician assistants (1).

3.75   Workplace-Related Homicides and Homicide Rates of Health Care Workers, by Occupational Category and Gender of Victim, 1983–1990

Occupational Category	Gender of Victim			Rate		
	Male	Female	Total	Male	Female	Total
Pharmacist	14	2	16	1.54	*	1.21
Physician	12	3	15	0.35	0.40	0.36
Registered nurse	1	13	14	*	0.11	0.12
Nurse's aide	1	10	11	*	0.10	0.10
Other†	9	4	13	0.19	0.03	0.07
Total	37	32	69	0.34	0.09	0.15

Source: National Traumatic Occupational Fatalities Surveillance System, from: Goodman, Richard A., Lynn Jenkins, and James A. Mercy. 1994. Workplace-related homicide among health care workers, 1980 through 1990. *Journal of the American Medical Association* 272, no. 21 (December): p. 1687, Table 3. Used with permission. [See appendix entry 33]

Note: Rates are per 100,000 workers.

   *   Rate not calculated; fewer than three cases.

   †   This category includes health aides except nurses, dentists, health technicians not classified elsewhere, optometrists, physical therapists, radiologic technicians, clinical laboratory technicians, health records technicians, licensed practical nurses, and physician assistants.

VULNERABLE GROUPS AND SITUATIONS: SOCIO-ECONOMIC STATUS

Income

3.76 Victimization Rates for Persons Aged 12 years and Over, Total, and by Race, Annual Family Income of Victims, and Type of Crime, 1992

Race and Type of Crime	Annual Family Income						
	Less than $7,500	$7,500-$9,999	$10,000-$14,999	$15,000-$24,999	$25,000-$29,999	$30,000-$49,999	$50,000 or More
All violent victimization	64.4	40.3	34.3	34.1	35.6	26.6	21.2
Completed violent victimization	25.5	16.3	14.6	12.2	13.4	9.0	5.9
Attempted violent victimization	38.9	24.0	19.6	21.9	22.2	17.6	15.4
Rape	1.3*	0.0*	0.5*	0.8*	0.0*	0.9	0.5*
Robbery	11.1	11.5	7.1	5.4	6.3	4.8	3.7
Completed	8.1	7.2	4.7	3.9	4.7	3.3	2.0
With injury	4.2	2.3*	2.0*	2.0	1.2*	0.8*	0.8*
From serious assault	2.5	1.0*	1.0*	0.9*	0.9	0.5*	0.2*
From minor assault	1.8*	1.2*	1.0*	1.1*	0.3*	0.3*	0.6*
Without injury	3.9	4.9*	2.7	1.9	3.5	2.5	1.2
Attempted	3.0	4.3*	2.4	1.5	1.6*	1.6	1.8
With injury	1.1*	1.2*	0.4*	0.3*	0.0*	0.3*	0.3*
From serious assault	0.3*	0.0*	0.4*	0.2*	0.0*	0.1*	0.1*
From minor assault	0.9*	1.2*	0.0*	0.1*	0.0*	0.1*	0.2*
Without injury	1.9*	3.1*	2.0*	1.2*	1.6*	1.3	1.5
Assault	52.0	28.8	26.6	27.8	29.3	20.9	16.9
Aggravated	23.1	9.3	9.0	9.7	6.3	6.6	5.5
Completed with injury	8.4	2.5*	4.1	2.9	2.3*	2.1	1.7
Attempted with weapon	14.7	6.8	4.9	6.9	4.1	4.4	3.8
Simple	28.8	19.5	17.6	18.1	23.0	14.3	11.4
Completed with injury	8.4	6.7	5.8	5.1	6.4	3.5	2.1
Attempted without weapon	20.5	12.8	11.8	13.0	16.6	10.8	9.3

See notes at end of table.

3.76 Victimization Rates for Persons Aged 12 and Over, Total, and by Race, Annual Family Income of Victims, and Type of Crime, 1992 (continued)

Race and Type of Crime	Annual Family Income						
	Less than $7,500	$7,500-$9,999	$10,000-$14,999	$15,000-$24,999	$25,000-$29,999	$30,000-$49,999	$50,000 or More
White							
All violent victimization	63.5	38.7	31.8	31.3	34.4	25.9	20.7
Completed violent victimization	23.0	15.7	13.9	10.5	12.2	8.8	5.4
Attempted violent victimization	40.5	23.0	17.9	20.8	22.2	17.1	15.4
Rape	1.0*	0.0*	0.6*	1.0*	0.0*	0.7*	0.5*
Robbery	8.2	8.8	6.2	4.5	4.0	4.2	2.8
With injury	4.7	1.5*	1.8*	1.5	1.1*	1.0	0.7*
Without injury	3.5	7.3	4.4	3.1	2.9*	3.2	2.1
Assault	54.3	29.9	24.9	25.9	30.4	21.0	17.4
Aggravated	21.3	8.0	6.8	8.7	6.1	6.4	5.7
Simple	33.0	21.9	18.1	17.2	24.4	14.6	11.8
Black							
All violent victimization	70.2	50.6	46.5	53.1	54.2	37.5	35.0
Completed violent victimization	32.8	22.8*	14.9	24.3	28.2	12.7	15.7*
Attempted violent victimization	37.4	27.8*	31.6	28.8	26.1	24.9*	19.3
Rape	2.4*	0.0*	0.0*	0.0*	0.0*	4.2*	1.6*
Robbery	20.0	20.9*	11.0*	13.4	29.0	13.7	17.6*
With injury	7.8*	13.7*	5.4*	9.6*	2.9*	1.2*	5.0*
Without injury	12.2	7.2*	5.6*	3.8*	26.1*	12.5	12.5*
Assault	47.9	29.7*	35.4	39.7	25.2	19.7	15.8*
Aggravated	28.9	17.3*	23.1	16.4	10.3*	8.8*	6.9*
Simple	19.0	12.4*	12.3*	23.4	14.9*	10.9*	8.9*

Source: National Crime Victimization Survey, 1992 from: Bureau of Justice Statistics. 1994. *Criminal victimization in the United States, 1992.* Washington, D.C., pp. 33–35, Tables 15 and 16. [See appendix entry 28]

Note: Table excludes series crimes. Series crime and other crime types are defined in the appendix. Aggravated assaults include all attacks (and attempted attacks) with weapons or, if no weapon was involved, those that result in serious injury. Simple assaults are attacks (and attempted attacks) without weapons resulting in minor or undetermined injuries requiring less than two days of hospitalization.

* Estimate is based on 10 or fewer sample cases.

3.77   Lifetime Prevalence Rates of Child Abuse by Fathers and Mothers, by Income, Occupational Group, and Employment Status, 1985

	By Father			By Mother		
Socioeconomic Status	Minor Violence	Severe Violence	Very Severe Violence	Minor Violence	Severe Violence	Very Severe Violence
Annual family income						
Under $10,000	609	162	47	787	210	59
$10,000-$19,999	726	156	25	795	169	28
$20,000-$29,999	758	134	19	817	150	30
$30,000-$39,999	729	125	23	813	167	35
$40,000-$49,999	783	139	20	789	234	22
$50,000 and over	757	137	49	764	118	13
Unknown	655	220	25	718	93	29
Occupation of respondent						
Blue collar	730	151	41	813	176	38
White collar	750	135	16	791	161	25
Husband's employment						
Full time	740	146	28	793	161	26
Part time	787	100	0	825	152	54
Unemployed	725	155	29	789	209	80
Other (retired, student, keep house, disabled)	668	73	39	817	128	0
Unknown	–	–	–	793	183	47
Wife's employment						
Full time	745	138	32	791	166	24
Part time	721	113	12	820	160	26
Unemployed	777	169	50	769	185	47
Other (retired, student, keep house, disabled)	718	139	21	794	161	41
Unknown	795	225	44	–	–	–

Source: National Family Violence Resurvey of 1985, from: Gelles, Richard J. and Murray A. Straus. 1989. *Physical violence in American families*, 1985. [Computer file]. Ann Arbor, Mich.: Inter-University Consortium for Political and Social Research. [See appendix entry 38]

Note: Lifetime prevalence rates are the number of children per 1,000 who have experienced at least one instance of the specified "conflict tactic" by the parent specified. From the first row, for example, 609 out of 1,000 children were said to have been threatened with hitting or having objects thrown at them, at least once in their lifetimes, by adult males in their households with incomes under $10,000. Adult females in the same income group reported having been responsible for this behavior, at least once in the lifetime of a child living in their household, at a rate of 787 per 1,000 children. Note that only one adult per household was interviewed in the study. See appendix for definitions of the Minor, Severe, and Very Severe Violence Conflict Tactic Scales and definitions of "blue collar" and "white collar."

–   No sample cases.

3.78   Child Maltreatment and Child Maltreatment Rates, by Type of Maltreatment and Family Income, 1986

	Family Income			
	Number of Children		Rate	
Type of Maltreatment	Less than $15,000	$15,000 or More	Less than $15,000	$15,000 or More
All maltreatment	487,500	253,700	29.3	5.5
All abuse	241,400	162,200	14.5	3.5
Physical abuse	118,800	92,200	7.1	2.0
Sexual abuse	69,200	32,600	4.2	0.7
Emotional abuse	68,700	47,600	4.1	1.0
All neglect	271,100	102,500	16.3	2.2
Physical neglect	105,000	33,100	6.3	0.7
Educational neglect	162,300	57,600	9.8	1.2
Emotional neglect	23,300	13,700	1.4	0.3
Serious injury/impairment	92,100	35,200	5.5	0.8
Moderate injury/impairment	339,400	195,000	20.4	4.2
Probable injury/impairment	55,400	23,200	3.3	0.5

Source: Study of National Incidence and Prevalence of Child Abuse and Neglect, 1986 (NIS-2), adapted from: Sedlak, Andrea J. 1991. *National incidence and prevalence of child abuse and neglect: 1988.* (Revised Report). Rockville, Md.: Westat, Inc., p. 5-27, Table 5-6. Used with permission. [See appendix entry 44]

Note: Rates represent number of victims per 1,000 children. The same child may be represented in more than one abuse category. Therefore, adding different categories of abuse results in counting the same child more than once and thus should be avoided. Children are defined as persons under age 18.

3.79   "In the past 12 months, how often would you say you . . . spanked or hit your child(ren), kicked, bit, or punched your child(ren), hit or tried to hit your child with something?" Percentage, by Income, 1994

	Income					
	Less Than $7500	$7500 - $14,999	$15,000 - $24,999	$25,000 - $34,999	$35,000 - $49,999	$50,000 or More
Spanked or hit						
More than 11 times a year	0	0	3	2	1	1
Often, 6 to 11 times a year	6	3	8	4	1	1
Occasionally, 3 to 5 times a year	17	29	11	11	14	11
Hardly ever, once or twice a year	39	26	33	34	38	27
Never	39	41	45	47	45	60
Refused any answer	0	0	0	1	1	0
Kicked, bit, or punched						
More than 11 times a year	0	0	0	0	0	0
Often, 6 to 11 times a year	0	0	0	0	0	0
Occasionally, 3 to 5 times a year	0	0	0	0	0	0
Hardly ever, once or twice a year	6	3	2	2	4	0
Never	94	97	98	98	96	100
Refused any answer	0	0	0	0	0	0
Hit, or tried to hit, with something						
More than 11 times a year	0	0	0	1	0	0
Often, 6 to 11 times a year	0	0	2	0	0	0
Occasionally, 3 to 5 times a year	0	0	2	3	1	5
Hardly ever, once or twice a year	11	6	9	8	6	2
Never	89	94	88	88	92	93
Refused any answer	0	0	0	0	0	0

Source: National Child Abuse Survey from: National Committee to Prevent Child Abuse. 1994. Unpublished Data, Tables Generated by National Committee to Prevent Child Abuse, Chicago, Ill. Used with permission. [See appendix entry 27]

Note: Asked of those who have children under 18 living at home.

Education

3.80   Rape, Robbery, and Assault Rates, by Level of Educational Attainment and Race of Victim, 1992

Education and Race of Victim	Violent Victimization			Rape	Robbery			Assault		
	All	Completed	Attempted		Total	With Injury	Without Injury	Total	Aggravated	Simple
Elementary school										
All races	43.9	18.2	25.7	0.4*	8.0	3.4	4.6	35.5	12.1	23.4
White	43.6	17.9	25.7	0.5*	7.7	2.3	5.3	35.4	10.7	24.6
Black	48.2	19.2	29.0	0.0*	9.8	8.2*	1.6*	38.4	21.6	16.8
0-4 years										
All races	17.4	6.3*	11.1	0.0*	2.2*	0.0*	2.2*	15.2	6.1*	9.0*
White	20.7	8.7*	12.0*	0.0*	3.0*	0.0*	3.0*	17.7	5.2*	12.4*
Black	12.3*	0.0*	12.3*	0.0*	0.0*	0.0*	0.0*	12.3*	12.3*	0.0*
5-7 years										
All races	50.7	21.7	29.0	0.6*	10.5	4.1	6.4	39.6	14.0	25.6
White	49.4	20.7	28.7	0.7*	10.3	2.6*	7.7	38.4	11.3	27.1
Black	56.2	23.0	33.2	0.0*	10.5*	8.7*	1.8*	45.7	28.7	17.0
8 years										
All races	44.1	17.7	26.4	0.3*	6.5	3.7*	2.8*	37.2	11.6	25.6
White	43.0	16.9	26.1	0.4*	5.6	2.7*	3.0*	36.9	11.7	25.3
Black	53.6	22.9*	30.7*	0.0*	14.0*	11.8*	2.2*	39.6	13.3*	26.3*
High school										
All races	31.8	11.7	20.1	0.5	6.0	2.3	3.8	25.3	9.2	16.1
White	28.8	10.2	18.6	0.4*	4.2	1.7	2.4	24.2	7.8	16.4
Black	52.5	22.2	30.3	0.7*	18.8	5.8	13.0	33.1	18.3	14.8
1-3 years										
All races	47.4	16.6	30.8	1.2*	8.7	3.6	5.0	37.6	13.6	24.0
White	41.5	14.7	26.8	1.3*	6.3	2.8	3.5	33.9	10.6	23.3
Black	78.4	28.4	49.9	0.8*	21.4	7.7*	13.7	56.2	29.2	27.0
4 years										
All races	25.7	9.8	16.0	0.2*	5.0	1.8	3.3	20.5	7.6	13.0
White	24.1	8.6	15.5	0.1*	3.4	1.3	2.0	20.6	6.8	13.8
Black	38.8	18.9	19.9	0.6*	17.4	4.8*	12.6	20.9	12.6	8.3

See notes at end of table.

3.80 Rape, Robbery, and Assault Rates, by Level of Educational Attainment and Race of Victim, 1992 *(continued)*

Education and Race of Victim	Violent Victimization			Rape	Robbery			Assault		
	All	Completed	Attempted		Total	With Injury	Without Injury	Total	Aggravated	Simple
College										
All races	27.2	8.7	18.5	1.1	4.9	1.4	3.5	21.3	7.1	14.1
White	25.9	7.7	18.2	0.9	4.0	1.0	3.0	21.0	6.8	14.2
Black	46.5	19.0	27.5	3.4*	14.2	6.0*	8.2	29.0	13.4	15.6
1-3 years										
All races	33.8	11.8	22.0	1.2	5.6	1.4	4.2	27.0	9.3	17.7
White	31.9	10.5	21.4	1.0*	4.6	1.0*	3.6	26.3	8.8	17.5
Black	49.8	20.7	29.1	3.2*	13.1	5.4*	7.7*	33.5	14.9	18.6
4 years										
All races	20.9	5.7	15.2	1.0*	4.2	1.4	2.8	15.7	5.0	10.7
White	20.1	5.0	15.1	0.8*	3.4	1.0*	2.4	15.9	4.9	11.0
Black	41.8	16.5	25.2	3.5*	15.7	6.8*	8.9*	22.5	11.2*	11.4*

Source: National Crime Victimization Survey, 1992 from: Bureau of Justice Statistics. 1994. *Criminal victimization in the United States, 1992.* Washington, D.C., pp. 36–37, Table 17. [See appendix entry 28]

Note: Rates are per 1,000 residents aged 12 years or more. Table excludes series crimes. Series crime and other crime types are defined in the appendix. Aggravated assaults include all attacks (and attempted attacks) with weapons or, if no weapon was involved, those that result in serious injury. Simple assaults are attacks (and attempted attacks) without weapons resulting in minor or undetermined injuries requiring less than two days of hospitalization.

* Estimate is based on 10 or fewer sample cases.

3.81   Homicides of Infants, by Race of Victim and Mother's Education, 1983–1985

Mother's Education	All Races*	Whites	Blacks
0-8 years	28	14	14
9-11 years	167	70	92
12 years	154	90	62
13-15 years	46	28	16
16+ years	22	18	4
Not stated	23	12	8

Source: Linked Birth and Infant Death data for 1983–85, from: Loftin, Colin, David McDowall, and Brian Wiersema. 1992. Economic risk factors for infant homicide. *Proceedings of the 1991 public health conference on records and statistics.* Hyattsville, Md.: National Center for Health Statistics, p. 274, Table 2. [See appendix entry 23]

Note: California, Texas, and Washington did not report maternal educational attainment.

*   Includes races other than blacks and whites.

3.82   Infant Homicide Rates, by Race of Victim and Mother's Education, 1983–1985

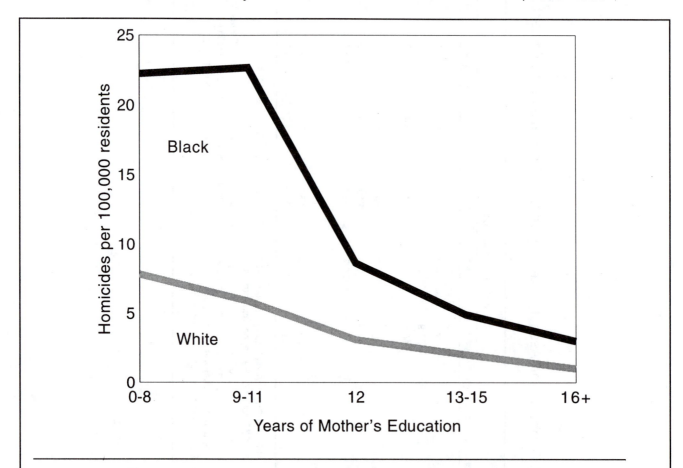

Source: Linked Birth and Infant Death data for 1983–85, from: Loftin, Colin, David McDowall, and Brian Wiersema. 1992. Economic risk factors for infant homicide. *Proceedings of the 1991 public health conference on records and statistics.* Hyattsville, Md.: National Center for Health Statistics, p. 275, Figure 1. [See appendix entry 23]

Note: California, Texas, and Washington did not report maternal educational attainment.

VULNERABLE GROUPS AND SITUATIONS: INSTITUTIONALIZED POPULATIONS

Prisoners

3.83   Homicides and Assaults in State and Federal Prisons, 1990

	Total	State Confinement	Federal Confinement
Homicide by other inmate(s)	65	57	3
Homicide-other	11	6	1
Assaults on staff	10,731	10,562	169
Assaults on inmates	21,590	21,184	406

Source: Stephan, James. 1992. *Census of state and federal correctional facilities, 1990*. Washington, D.C.: Bureau of Justice Statistics, p. 5, Tables 5 and 6. [See appendix entry 6]

Children in School

3.84   Percentage of Students Victimized at School, by Age, Race, Ethnicity, Gender, Family Income, Place of Residence, and Number of Times Family Moved in the Last 5 Years, Students Over 12 Years Old, 1989

Characteristic	Total Victimization (%)	Violent Victimization (%)
Sex		
Male	9	2
Female	9	2
Race		
White	9	2
Black	8	2
Other	10	2*
Hispanic origin		
Yes	7	3
No	9	2
Not ascertained	3*	–
Age		
12	9	2
13	10	2
14	11	2
15	9	3
16	9	2
17	8	1
18	5	1*
19	2*	–
Number of times family moved in last 5 years		
None	8	2
Once	9	2*
Twice	13	3*
3 or more	15	6
Not ascertained	5*	5*
Family income		
Less than $7,500	8	2
$7,500-$9,999	4	1*
$10,000-$14,999	9	3
$15,000-$24,999	8	1
$25,000-$29,999	8	2
$30,000-$49,999	10	2
$50,000 and over	11	2
Not ascertained	7	3
Place of residence		
Central city	10	2
Suburbs	9	2
Nonmetropolitan area	8	1

Source: National Crime Victimization Survey, 1989, from: Bastian, Lisa D., and Bruce M. Taylor. 1991. *School crime: A national crime victimization survey report.* Washington D.C.: Bureau of Justice Statistics, p. 1, Table 1. [See appendix entry 28]

Note: "Total" includes nonviolent or property offenses such as theft. Table excludes series crimes. Series crime and other crime types are defined in the appendix.

*   Estimate is based on 10 or fewer sample cases.

-   Less than .5%

3.85 Percentage of Students Victimized at School, by Type of School, and by School Security Measures, Students Over 12 Years Old, 1989

Characteristic	Total Victimization (%)	Violent Victimization (%)
Type of school		
Public	9	2
Private	7	1*
Not ascertained	6	3*
Teacher hall monitors		
Yes	9	2
No	10	2
Other hall monitors		
Yes	10	2
No	7	2
Visitors sign-in		
Yes	9	2
No	9	2*
Open school		
Yes	10	2
No	9	2
Only certain grades	10	3*

Source: National Crime Victimization Survey, 1989, from: Bastian, Lisa D., and Bruce M. Taylor. 1991. *School crime: A national crime victimization survey report.* Washington D.C.: Bureau of Justice Statistics, p. 2, Table 2; p. 13, Table 27. [See appendix entry 28]

Note: "Total" includes nonviolent or property offenses such as theft. Table excludes series crimes. Series crime and other crime types are defined in the appendix.

   * Estimate is based on 10 or fewer sample cases.

HIGH-RISK GROUPS AND SITUATIONS

Children and Adolescents

3.86   Arrest Rates for Murder, by Age of Arrestee, 1965, 1970, 1975, 1980, 1985, 1990, and 1992

Age Group	1965			1970		
	Total	Male	Female	Total	Male	Female
12 and under	0.1	0.1	*	0.1	0.2	*
13-14	2.0	3.7	0.2	2.5	4.2	0.6
15	4.6	8.7	0.4	9.5	17.2	1.4
16	8.1	15.1	0.8	14.3	26.8	1.3
17	10.0	17.7	2.1	18.0	32.9	2.6
18	11.5	20.7	2.3	25.6	46.5	4.5
19	15.1	26.2	4.3	24.2	44.3	4.5
20	14.6	24.9	4.7	24.1	42.6	6.7
21	15.5	27.0	4.5	27.1	50.3	5.9
22	14.7	26.1	3.7	24.8	44.7	6.0
23	18.3	32.8	4.6	23.9	42.3	6.3
24	17.9	30.2	6.2	25.9	45.5	7.1
25-29	15.6	25.7	5.9	21.3	36.1	6.9
30-34	12.5	19.2	6.1	17.0	27.7	6.6
35-39	10.4	16.2	4.9	13.9	22.2	6.0
40-44	7.9	12.5	3.6	10.8	16.9	5.0
45-49	6.0	9.7	2.4	8.0	13.3	3.1
50-54	4.9	8.2	1.8	6.1	10.2	2.2
55-59	3.3	6.2	0.7	4.7	8.1	1.6
60-64	2.5	4.7	0.5	3.0	5.9	0.5
65 and over	1.4	3.0	0.1	1.6	3.5	0.3

See notes at end of table.

3.86   Arrest Rates for Murder, by Age of Arrestee, 1965, 1970, 1975, 1980, 1985, 1990, and 1992 *(continued)*

Age Group	1975			1980		
	Total	Male	Female	Total	Male	Female
12 and under	0.1	0.2	*	0.1	0.1	0.1
13-14	2.0	3.6	0.3	2.6	4.4	0.7
15	8.5	14.9	1.8	7.5	13.5	1.2
16	13.9	24.9	2.5	13.5	24.6	2.0
17	16.6	29.2	3.5	21.0	38.2	2.9
18	23.8	41.5	5.8	25.3	45.0	5.0
19	25.1	43.7	6.3	26.7	48.7	4.4
20	26.1	44.9	7.1	25.6	45.3	5.7
21	25.6	44.7	6.5	25.6	45.0	6.2
22	25.5	44.2	6.9	25.1	44.6	5.5
23	26.4	44.5	8.5	24.7	43.6	5.8
24	27.1	48.3	6.1	25.2	44.1	6.3
25-29	21.5	36.9	6.4	19.6	34.4	5.0
30-34	16.0	26.5	5.8	16.0	28.0	4.3
35-39	13.3	21.7	5.2	13.1	22.5	4.1
40-44	10.7	17.3	4.4	9.2	15.6	3.0
45-49	7.1	11.5	2.9	6.8	11.7	2.2
50-54	4.9	7.8	2.2	4.6	7.9	1.5
55-59	3.5	6.2	1.1	3.5	6.2	1.1
60-64	3.1	5.8	0.8	2.3	4.5	0.5
65 and over	1.5	3.2	0.3	1.1	2.5	0.2

See notes at end of table.

3.86   Arrest Rates for Murder, by Age of Arrestee, 1965, 1970, 1975, 1980, 1985, 1990, and 1992 *(continued)*

Age Group	1985			1990		
	Total	Male	Female	Total	Male	Female
12 and under	0.1	0.1	*	0.1	0.1	*
13-14	2.3	4.0	0.6	4.9	8.8	0.8
15	6.8	11.8	1.7	16.8	31.0	1.8
16	12.5	22.4	2.1	30.4	56.5	2.8
17	19.1	34.5	3.0	39.1	72.4	3.6
18	23.6	42.7	3.8	47.7	88.2	5.1
19	23.9	43.0	4.5	39.2	71.7	5.2
20	22.1	39.9	4.2	33.9	61.8	4.8
21	24.5	43.9	5.0	31.9	58.6	4.1
22	21.5	38.6	4.4	29.5	52.1	6.0
23	21.5	38.3	4.8	26.0	46.1	5.1
24	19.9	35.3	4.4	23.7	41.3	5.7
25-29	17.4	30.4	4.5	18.0	31.4	4.5
30-34	13.0	22.3	3.8	12.5	21.2	3.9
35-39	9.9	16.9	3.2	9.3	15.7	3.0
40-44	7.7	13.5	2.1	6.7	11.9	1.7
45-49	5.4	9.7	1.8	5.1	9.0	1.5
50-54	4.4	7.9	1.2	3.4	6.0	0.9
55-59	3.3	6.0	0.9	2.4	4.3	0.6
60-64	1.9	3.7	0.5	1.8	3.3	0.5
65 and over	0.9	2.1	0.1	0.8	1.7	0.2

See notes at end of table.

3.86 Arrest Rates for Murder, by Age of Arrestee, 1965, 1970, 1975, 1980, 1985, 1990, and 1992 *(continued)*

Age Group	1992		
	Total	Male	Female
12 and under	0.1	0.1	*
13-14	4.9	8.7	0.9
15	15.7	28.4	2.2
16	29.8	55.2	3.0
17	41.2	76.5	3.6
18	52.0	96.8	4.9
19	44.8	83.7	4.3
20	38.4	70.4	5.0
21	36.0	66.6	4.0
22	31.1	55.8	5.2
23	27.8	49.7	5.0
24	23.3	42.3	3.7
25-29	17.0	30.0	3.9
30-34	10.7	18.2	3.3
35-39	7.8	13.3	2.4
40-44	5.6	9.5	1.8
45-49	4.6	8.1	1.3
50-54	3.3	5.6	1.1
55-59	2.2	4.0	0.6
60-64	1.4	2.7	0.3
65 and over	0.8	1.7	0.1

Source: Age, Sex, Race, and Ethnic Origin of Persons Arrested, 1965, 1970, 1975, 1980, 1985, 1990, and 1992, from: Federal Bureau of Investigation. 1993. *Age-specific arrest rates and race-specific arrest rates for selected offenses 1965–1992.* Washington, D.C.: U.S. Government Printing Office, pp. 21–25. [See appendix entry 1]

Note: Rates are per 100,000 persons.
    * Less than 0.05.

3.87   Arrest Rates for Murder, by Juvenile Status and Gender of Arrestee, 1965–1992

Year	Under Age 18			Age 18 and Over		
	Total	Male	Female	Total	Male	Female
1965	1.4	2.6	0.2	8.3	14.1	3.0
1966	1.6	2.9	0.3	8.6	14.9	2.9
1967	1.7	3.1	0.3	9.4	16.4	3.0
1968	2.2	4.0	0.3	10.7	18.8	3.5
1969	2.4	4.2	0.4	11.9	21.1	3.6
1970	2.7	5.0	0.4	12.2	21.5	3.8
1971	3.0	5.3	0.6	13.3	23.3	4.3
1972	3.9	6.4	1.3	12.8	22.5	4.0
1973	3.3	5.9	0.6	13.3	23.5	4.0
1974	3.3	6.0	0.6	14.2	25.2	4.1
1975	2.8	5.0	0.6	12.3	21.7	3.7
1976	3.0	5.3	0.7	12.3	22.1	3.4
1977	3.1	5.5	0.5	11.8	21.1	3.4
1978	3.0	5.4	0.6	12.0	21.5	3.4
1979	3.1	5.5	0.7	11.8	21.3	3.1
1980	3.1	5.6	0.5	11.9	21.8	3.0
1981	3.4	6.0	0.6	12.4	22.7	3.0
1982	3.1	5.6	0.5	12.4	22.4	3.3
1983	2.5	4.4	0.5	11.4	20.6	2.9
1984	2.5	4.4	0.4	10.8	19.6	2.8
1985	2.5	4.5	0.5	10.0	18.3	2.4
1986	2.8	5.2	0.4	10.4	19.0	2.6
1987	3.0	5.4	0.5	10.1	18.4	2.5
1988	3.7	6.7	0.5	10.5	19.2	2.6
1989	4.3	7.8	0.6	10.6	19.4	2.6
1990	5.1	9.4	0.5	11.0	20.3	2.4
1991	5.4	10.0	0.5	11.4	21.1	2.5
1992	5.0	9.3	0.6	10.4	19.4	2.0

Source: Age, Sex, Race, and Ethnic Origin of Persons Arrested, 1965–1992, from: Federal Bureau of Investigation. 1993. *Age-specific arrest rates and race-specific arrest rates for selected offenses 1965–1992.* Washington, D.C.: U.S. Government Printing Office, p. 158. [See appendix entry 1]

Note: Rates are per 100,000 persons.

3.88   Arrest Rates for Murder, by Juvenile Status and Race of Arrestee, 1965–1992

Year	Under Age 18		Age 18 and Over	
	White	Nonwhite	White	Nonwhite
1965	0.5	5.1	3.7	44.7
1966	0.7	6.6	3.8	47.8
1967	0.7	7.4	4.0	51.4
1968	0.8	9.7	4.5	60.2
1969	0.6	12.0	4.8	66.4
1970	0.9	13.4	5.5	66.0
1971	0.9	12.7	5.3	74.5
1972	1.5	16.7	5.4	68.3
1973	1.1	13.0	5.8	67.9
1974	1.4	12.2	6.4	71.2
1975	1.5	8.7	6.2	54.9
1976	1.5	10.2	6.1	56.2
1977	1.8	9.8	6.1	54.0
1978	1.7	9.5	6.3	52.9
1979	1.9	8.9	6.7	47.7
1980	2.1	8.0	6.9	46.5
1981	2.0	9.8	7.2	47.7
1982	1.8	9.1	7.0	48.3
1983	1.5	6.9	6.4	43.6
1984	1.6	6.4	6.4	39.1
1985	1.5	7.1	5.7	37.0
1986	1.7	7.8	5.9	38.5
1987	1.6	9.1	5.4	38.7
1988	1.8	11.0	5.4	40.3
1989	2.0	13.6	5.3	42.1
1990	2.5	15.5	5.6	41.4
1991	2.7	15.3	5.8	42.1
1992	2.7	15.8	5.5	41.5

Source: Age, Sex, Race, and Ethnic Origin of Persons Arrested, 1965–1992, from: Federal Bureau of Investigation. 1993. *Age-specific arrest rates and race-specific arrest rates for selected offenses 1965–1992*. Washington, D.C.: U.S. Government Printing Office, p. 182. [See appendix entry 1]

Note: Rates are per 100,000 persons.

3.89   Annual Prevalence Rate of Injury in Physical Fights Between Youths, by Age, Gender, and Race of Respondent, 1992

	Male		Female	
Age	White	Nonwhite	White	Nonwhite
12	43.2	26.5*	17.9*	20.0*
13	22.4	40.3*	12.7*	78.0*
14	43.8	18.9*	15.5*	40.6*
15	29.5	108.9*	18.4*	26.6*
16	58.0	85.5*	21.1	23.7*
17	47.2	71.6	31.9*	23.5*
18	33.1	104.0*	11.2*	13.5*
19	47.1	95.1*	29.0	84.4*
20	39.3	55.1*	22.9	30.9*
21	30.8	60.6*	8.0*	32.4*
12 - 17	40.6	58.5	19.5	33.7
18 - 21	37.6	78.5	18.0	41.2
Overall	39.5	66.1	18.9	36.7

Source: Youth Risk Behavior Supplement to the National Health Interview Survey, 1992, from: National Center for Health Statistics. 1994. *National health interview survey: 1992 youth risk behavior survey public use data file.* [Computer file]. Hyattsville, Md.: Public Health Service. [See appendix entry 30]

Note: Annual prevalence rates are the number of youths per 1,000 in the population who report being injured, at least once, in physical fights in the 12 months preceding the interview.

*   Estimate is based on 10 or fewer sample cases.

3.90   Medically Treated Injuries in Youth Fights in the Past Year, by Gender and Race of Respondent, and by Number of Fights, 1992

Number of Times Injured In Fights	Male				Female			
	White	(%)	Nonwhite	(%)	White	(%)	Nonwhite	(%)
No fights in last year	7,228,750	52.7	1,711,690	48.2	9,858,610	72.9	2,075,630	60.2
Injured 0 times	5,943,360	43.3	1,608,190	45.2	3,405,390	25.2	1,243,690	36.1
Injured 1 time	477,290	3.5	180,900	5.1	224,750	1.7	102,800	3.0
Injured 2 or more times	63,820	0.5	54,090	1.5	30,810*	0.2*	23,760*	0.7*
Total	13,713,210	100.0	3,554,880	100.0	13,519,570	100.0	3,445,880	100.0

Source: Youth Risk Behavior Supplement to the National Health Interview Survey, 1992, from: National Center for Health Statistics. 1994. *National health interview survey: 1992 youth risk behavior survey public use data file.* [Computer file]. Hyattsville, Md.: Public Health Service. [See appendix entry 30]

*   Estimate is based on 10 or fewer sample cases.

3.91   Youth Weapon Carrying in the Past 30 Days, by Gender, Age, and Race of Respondent, by Number of Days Carried Weapon, and by Type of Weapon Carried Most Often, 1992

	Male				Female			
	Age 12-17 Years		Age 18-21 Years		Age 12-17 Years		Age 18-21 Years	
	White	Nonwhite	White	Nonwhite	White	Nonwhite	White	Nonwhite
Number of days carried a weapon								
0	6,034,000	1,737,000	4,070,400	1,056,150	7,617,980	1,841,290	5,182,250	1,225,330
1	443,420	141,890	174,000	48,680	134,500	88,520	36,610	23,660
2 or 3	633,970	95,690	226,770	72,030	106,000	35,790	31,110	19,500*
4 or 5	227,560	34,200*	94,180	8,990*	18,820*	17,630*	12,890*	10,440*
6 or more	892,410	118,540	655,950	159,760	123,080	47,620	157,700	92,720
Total	8,231,350	2,127,310	5,221,290	1,345,610	8,000,380	2,030,840	5,420,560	1,371,650
Type of weapon carried most often								
Didn't carry weapon	6,034,000	1,737,000	4,070,400	1,056,150	7,617,980	1,841,290	5,182,250	1,225,330
Handgun	140,050	68,870	163,170	109,750	16,340*	16,950*	30,180	42,800
Other gun	292,310*	22,750*	164,990	6,110*	14,860*	3,400*	16,450*	0*
Knife/razor	1,365,140	165,440	589,510	114,710	264,670	115,330	122,560	93,900
Club/stick/bat/pipe	268,660	90,060	162,620	27,560*	34,630	25,740*	31,600	6,850*
Other weapon	127,540	43,190	54,270	29,280*	50,510	28,140*	37,510	2,780*
Total	8,227,710	2,127,310	5,204,960	1,343,560	7,998,990	2,030,840	5,420,560	1,371,650

Source: Youth Risk Behavior Supplement to the National Health Interview Survey, 1992, from: National Center for Health Statistics. 1994. *National health interview survey: 1992 youth risk behavior survey public use data file.* [Computer file]. Hyattsville, Md.: Public Health Service. [See appendix entry 30]

Note: Percentages may not add to 100 because of rounding.
*   Estimate is based on 10 or fewer sample cases.

3.92   Percentage of Youths Who Report Carrying Weapons in the Past 30 Days, by Gender and Race of Respondent, by Number of Days Carried Weapon, and by Type of Weapon Carried Most Often, 1992

	Male				Female			
	Age 12-17 Years		Age 18-21 Years		Age 12-17 Years		Age 18-21 Years	
	White	Nonwhite	White	Nonwhite	White	Nonwhite	White	Nonwhite
Number of days carried a weapon								
0	73.3	81.7	77.9	78.5	95.2	90.7	95.6	89.3
1	5.4	6.7	3.3	3.6	1.7	4.3	0.7	1.7
2 or 3	7.7	4.5	4.3	5.3	1.3	1.8	0.6	1.4*
4 or 5	2.8	1.6*	1.8	0.7*	0.2*	0.9*	0.2*	0.8*
6 or more	10.8	5.6	12.6	11.9	1.5	2.3	2.9	6.7
Total	100.0	100.1	99.9	100.0	99.9	100.0	100.0	99.9
Type of weapon carried most often								
Didn't carry weapon	73.3	81.7	78.2	78.6	95.2	90.7	95.6	89.3
Handgun	1.7	3.2	3.1	8.2	0.2*	0.8*	0.5	3.1
Other gun	3.5	1.1*	3.2	0.5*	0.2*	0.2*	0.3*	0.0*
Knife/razor	16.6	7.8	11.3	8.5	3.3	5.7	2.3	6.8
Club/stick/bat/pipe	3.3	4.2	3.1	2.1*	0.4	1.3*	0.6	0.5*
Other weapon	1.6	2.0	1.0	2.2*	0.6	1.4*	0.7	0.2*
Total	100.0	100.0	99.9	100.1	99.9	100.1	100.0	99.9

Source: Youth Risk Behavior Supplement to the National Health Interview Survey, 1992, from: National Center for Health Statistics. 1994. *National health interview survey: 1992 youth risk behavior survey public use data file*. [Computer file]. Hyattsville, Md.: Public Health Service. [See appendix entry 30]

*   Estimate is based on 10 or fewer sample cases.

3.93 Physical Fights by 12- to 21-Year-Olds, by Gender, Race, and Person Last Fought, and by Number of Fights in the Last Year, 1992

	Male				Female			
	Age 12-17 Years		Age 18-21 Years		Age 12-17 Years		Age 18-21 Years	
	White	Nonwhite	White	Nonwhite	White	Nonwhite	White	Nonwhite
Persons fought in last fight								
Never in a fight	3,314,620	696,090	2,638,320	606,850	5,076,460	957,750	4,048,270	826,630
Stranger	618,990	176,210	715,570	167,580	126,080	96,610	115,210	42,600
Friend	2,359,670	882,570	965,350	294,830	728,050	462,320	326,020	161,600
Boyfriend/girlfriend/date	88,420	35,650	45,610	29,890	183,750	59,510	388,280	163,590
Family member	656,390	111,360	261,810	64,260	1,176,150	235,680	293,970	59,700
Other	352,270	99,720	196,960	19,550*	91,420	39,880	56,650	37,700
More than one of above	983,880	195,060	468,250	166,620	607,490	188,410	226,880	101,580
Total	8,374,240	2,196,650	5,291,860	1,349,570	7,989,410	2,040,170	5,455,270	1,393,390
Number of times in fights								
No fights in last year	3,878,310	882,320	3,350,440	829,380	5,432,050	1,110,540	4,426,560	965,090
1 time	1,587,560	495,710	871,270	202,950	903,550	390,810	506,930	224,110
2 or 3 times	1,621,540	406,120	674,490	188,120	973,280	323,720	353,030	124,540
4 or 5 times	548,850	200,850	184,500	44,370	300,880	139,060	120,840	38,180
6 or 7 times	202,780	72,780	64,590	25,610*	105,850	31,840*	34,140	15,700*
8 or 9 times	149,060	43,260	31,270*	13,140*	91,050	7,180*	11,850*	11,670*
10 or 11 times	57,950	23,010*	45,870	11,570*	26,760*	8,540*	4,120*	9,270*
12 or more times	320,460	76,490	87,010	36,060*	168,490	27,270	13,820*	7,060*
Total	8,366,510	2,200,530	5,309,440	1,351,190	8,001,910	2,038,970	5,471,300	1,395,630

Source: Youth Risk Behavior Supplement to the National Health Interview Survey, 1992, from: National Center for Health Statistics. 1994. *National health interview survey: 1992 youth risk behavior survey public use data file.* [Computer file]. Hyattsville, Md.: Public Health Service. [See appendix entry 30]

* Estimate is based on 10 or fewer sample cases.

3.94   Percentage of Physical Fights by 12- to 21-Year-Olds, by Gender, Race, and Person Last Fought, and by Number of Fights in the Last Year, 1992

| | Male | | | | Female | | | |
| | Age 12-17 Years | | Age 18-21 Years | | Age 12-17 Years | | Age 18-21 Years | |
	White	Nonwhite	White	Nonwhite	White	Nonwhite	White	Nonwhite
Persons fought in last fight								
Never in a fight	39.6	31.7	49.9	45.0	63.5	46.9	74.2	59.3
Stranger	7.4	8.0	13.5	12.4	1.6	4.7	2.1	3.1
Friend	28.2	40.2	18.2	21.8	9.1	22.7	6.0	11.6
Boyfriend/girlfriend/date	1.1	1.6	0.9	2.2	2.3	2.9	7.1	11.7
Family member	7.8	5.1	4.9	4.8	14.7	11.6	5.4	4.3
Other	4.2	4.5	3.7	1.4*	1.1	2.0	1.0	2.7
More than one of above	11.7	8.9	8.8	12.3	7.6	9.2	4.1	7.3
Total	100.0	100.0	99.9	99.9	99.9	100.0	99.9	100.0
Number of times in fights								
No fights in last year	46.4	40.1	63.1	61.4	67.9	54.5	80.9	69.1
1 time	19.0	22.5	16.4	15.0	11.3	19.2	9.3	16.1
2 or 3 times	19.4	18.5	12.7	13.9	12.2	15.9	6.5	8.9
4 or 5 times	6.6	9.1	3.5	3.3	3.8	6.8	2.2	2.7
6 or 7 times	2.4	3.3	1.2	1.9*	1.3	1.6*	0.6	1.1*
8 or 9 times	1.8	2.0	0.6*	1.0*	1.1	0.3*	0.2*	0.8*
10 or 11 times	0.7	1.0*	0.9	0.9*	0.3*	0.4*	0.1*	0.7*
12 or more times	3.8	3.5	1.6	2.7*	2.1	1.3	0.3*	0.5*
Total	100.1	100.0	100.0	100.1	100.0	100.0	100.1	99.9

Source: Youth Risk Behavior Supplement to the National Health Interview Survey, 1992, from: National Center for Health Statistics. 1994. *National health interview survey: 1992 youth risk behavior survey public use data file.* [Computer file]. Hyattsville, Md.: Public Health Service. [See appendix entry 30]

Note: Percentages may not add up to 100 because of rounding.
  *   Estimate is based on 10 or fewer cases.

3.95 Annual Prevalence Rates of Physical Fights by Youth, by Age, Gender, and Race of Respondent, 1992

Age	Male		Female	
	White	Nonwhite	White	Nonwhite
12	585.2	640.7	345.1	516.5
13	629.7	677.9	324.5	447.3
14	546.3	619.8	380.8	497.1
15	499.1	629.9	311.2	422.8
16	499.2	439.4	290.4	472.5
17	446.8	580.1	269.8	362.6
18	407.5	529.3	208.0	356.9
19	416.5	424.9	221.1	344.0
20	342.7	244.1	183.4	294.4
21	311.4	345.6	153.4	252.3
12–17	536.4	599.0	321.2	455.3
18–21	369.0	386.2	190.9	308.5
Overall	471.4	518.1	268.3	395.7

Source: Youth Risk Behavior Supplement to the National Health Interview Survey, 1992, from: National Center for Health Statistics. 1994. *National health interview survey: 1992 youth risk behavior survey public use data file.* [Computer file]. Hyattsville, Md.: Public Health Service. [See appendix entry 30]

Note: Annual prevalence rates are the number of youths per 1,000 in the population who report being involved in physical fights, at least once, in the 12 months preceding the interview.

3.96   Percentage of Self-Reported Serious Violent Offenders, by Age, Race, and Gender of Respondent, 12- to 27-Year-Olds, 1976–1989

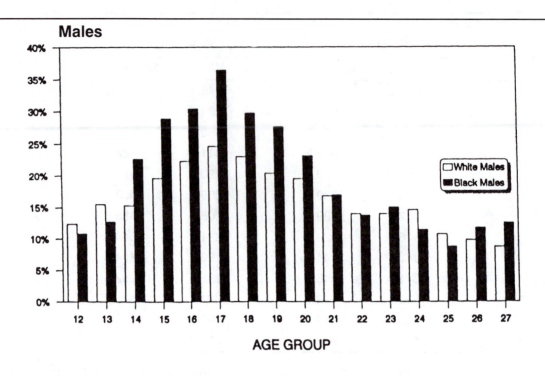

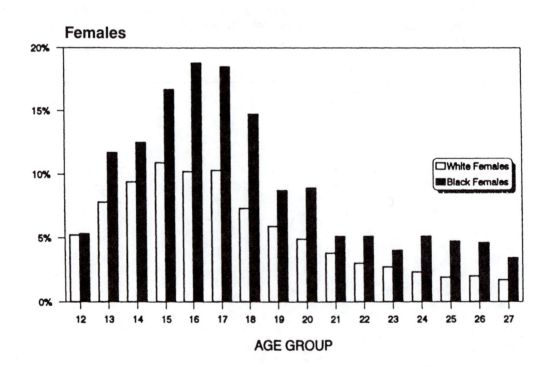

Source: National Youth Survey, 1976–1989, from: Elliott, Delbert S. 1994. 1993 Presidential Address: Serious violent offenders: Onset, developmental course, and treatment. *Criminology* 32, no. 1 (February): p. 6, Figures 1 and 2. Used with permission. [See appendix entry 36]

Note: Values are percentages of all persons in the specified group who reported at least one act of serious violence in that year.

Police

3.97   Legal Interventions by Police, 1976–1990 (Annual)

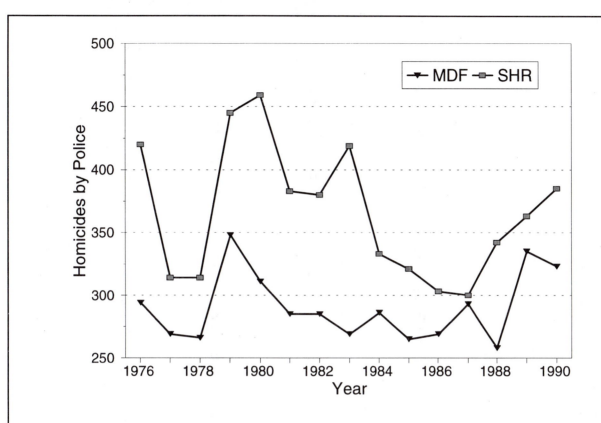

Sources: Federal Bureau of Investigation. 1993. *Supplementary homicide report, 1976-1990*. [Computer files]. Ann Arbor, Mich.: Inter-university Consortium for Political and Social Research. National Center for Health Statistics. *Mortality detail files, 1976-1990*. [Computer files]. Ann Arbor, Mich.: Inter-university Consortium for Political and Social Research. [See appendix entry 34 and 45]

Note: "MDF" stands for Mortality Detail Files and represents data on *Legal Interventions* (ICD-9 E970–E977) from the national vital statistics data system classified by place of occurrence. Legal intervention in this figure includes only fatal injuries inflicted by the police or other law enforcement agents in the course of arresting or attempting to arrest law breakers, suppressing disturbances, maintaining order, and other legal action. Legal executions are excluded. "SHR" stands for Supplementary Homicide Report data submitted to the FBI on justifiable homicides by police that occurred in the line of duty. See appendix for additional information about the two different data collection systems.

3.98   Legal Interventions by Police, by State, 1976–1990

State	MDF Totals	SHR Totals	Difference (SHR–MDF)	Ratio (SHR/MDF)
Alabama	53	69	16	1.30
Alaska	6	6	0	1.00
Arizona	115	102	-13	0.89
Arkansas	45	39	-6	0.87
California	653	1308	655	2.00
Colorado	64	84	20	1.31
Connecticut	40	20	-20	0.50
Delaware	9	8	-1	0.89
Florida	178	321	143	1.80
Georgia	115	90	-25	0.78
Hawaii	3	13	10	4.33
Idaho	13	11	-2	0.85
Illinois	118	245	127	2.08
Indiana	104	52	-52	0.50
Iowa	29	17	-12	0.59
Kansas	42	35	-7	0.83
Kentucky	56	37	-19	0.66
Louisiana	119	133	14	1.12
Maine	6	3	-3	0.50
Maryland	101	138	37	1.37
Massachusetts	52	34	-18	0.65
Michigan	216	258	42	1.19
Minnesota	19	33	14	1.74
Mississippi	63	44	-19	0.70
Missouri	65	109	44	1.68
Montana	13	1	-12	0.08
Nebraska	6	14	8	2.33
Nevada	70	47	-23	0.67
New Hampshire	9	7	-2	0.78
New Jersey	95	140	45	1.47
New Mexico	58	35	-23	0.60
New York	305	431	126	1.41
North Carolina	93	56	-37	0.60
North Dakota	9	1	-8	0.11
Ohio	205	188	-17	0.92
Oklahoma	149	135	-14	0.91
Oregon	61	60	-1	0.98
Pennsylvania	101	185	84	1.83
Rhode Island	18	5	-13	0.28
South Carolina	23	45	22	1.96
South Dakota	4	2	-2	0.50
Tennessee	65	101	36	1.55
Texas	324	515	191	1.59
Utah	25	11	-14	0.44
Vermont	2	1	-1	0.50
Virginia	113	105	-8	0.93
Washington	60	55	-5	0.92
Washington, D.C.	68	65	-3	0.96
West Virginia	26	16	-10	0.62
Wisconsin	36	46	10	1.28
Wyoming	8	5	-3	0.63
Total U.S.	4230	5481	1251	1.30

Source: Federal Bureau of Investigation. 1994. *Supplementary homicide report, 1976–1992.* [Computer file]. Ann Arbor, Mich.: Inter-university Consortium for Political and Social Research; National Center for Health Statistics. 1993. *Public-use data tape and documentation: Mortality detail, 1991 data.* [Computer file]. Hyattsville, Md.: Public Health Service. [See appendix entry 45 and 34]

Note: These data come from two national data sources, the Supplementary Homicide Report (SHR) of the FBI, and the Mortality Detail File (MDF) of the National Center for Health Statistics. See appendix for a description of their differences. Legal interventions in this table includes only fatal injuries inflicted by the police or other law enforcement agents in the course of arresting or attempting to arrest law breakers, suppressing disturbances, maintaining order, and other legal action. Legal executions are excluded. Place of occurrence used to classify MDF deaths geographically.

3.99   Reported Rates of Police Use of Force, by Agency Type, 1991

Type of Force	Agency Type			
	Sheriff	County Police	City Police	State Agencies
Civilians shot and killed	0.2	0.8	0.9	0.4
Civilians shot and wounded but not killed	0.2	1.6	0.2	0.4
Civilians shot at but not hit	8.1	5.8	3.0	1.8
Electrical devices (e.g., Taser)	10.3	13.3	5.4	0.4
Chemical agents (e.g., Mace, Capstun)	49.3	22.3	36.2	6.9
Batons	12.8	16.6	36.0	2.8
Other impact devices (e.g., saps, soft projectiles, rubber bullets)	0.3	0.3	2.4	1.5
Flashlight	4.8	11.6	21.7	0.7
Twist lock/wrist lock	11.8	1.8	80.9	4.2
Bodily force (e.g., arm, foot, leg, etc.)	177.0	164.7	272.2	200.5
Unholstering weapon	193.4	19.3	129.9	9.9
Swarm	19.1	2.5	126.7	0.0
Firm grip	19.6	4.3	57.7	0.0
Neck restraints/unconsciousness-rendering holds	1.1	0.2	1.4	0.9
Handcuff/leg restraints	195.1	73.9	490.4	7.7
Come-alongs	113.3	0.9	226.8	1.5
Dog attacks or bites	18.3	15.4	6.5	2.6
Vehicle ramming	4.7	0.1	1.0	3.7

Source: The Law Enforcement Agency Survey, from: Pate, Antony M., and Lorie A. Fridell. 1993. *Police use of force: Official reports, citizens complaints, and legal consequences.* Vol. 1. Washington D.C.: Police Foundation, p. 74, Table 6.1. Used with permission. [See appendix entry 39]

Note: Rates are incidents per 1,000 sworn officers, weighted by agency size for standardization and comparison purposes.

Recidivists

3.100   Recidivism to 1987 for Prisoners Released in 1983, by Most Serious Offense for Which Released

Most Serious Offense for Which Released	Percent of All Released Prisoners	Percentage of Released Prisoners Who Within 3 Years Were:		
		Rearrested	Reconvicted	Reincarcerated
All violent offenses	34.6	59.6	41.9	36.5
Murder*	3.1	42.1	25.2	20.8
Negligent manslaughter	1.4	42.5	27.9	21.8
Kidnapping	0.6	54.5	35.7	31.3
Rape	2.1	51.5	36.4	32.3
Other sexual assault	2.1	47.9	32.6	24.4
Robbery	18.7	66.0	48.3	43.2
Assault	6.4	60.2	40.4	33.7
Other violence	0.4	50.1	33.2	31.4

Source: Beck, Allen J., and Bernard E. Shipley. 1989. *Recidivism of prisoners released in 1983*. Washington, D.C.: Bureau of Justice Statistics, p. 5, Table 8. [See appendix entry 41]

*   Includes non-negligent manslaughter.

3.101   Violent Criminal Arrest Charges of State Prisoners Released in 1983, by Type of Charge

Arrest Charge	Number of Adult Arrest Charges	
	Prior to Release	After Release, 1983-1986
Total violent offenses	214,778	50,121
Homicide*	12,185	2,282
Kidnapping	5,622	1,451
Rape	8,922	1,291
Other sexual assault	10,335	2,626
Robbery	84,166	17,060
Assault	84,497	22,633
Other violence	9,051	2,778

Source: Beck, Allen J., and Bernard E. Shipley. 1989. *Recidivism of prisoners released in 1983*. Washington, D.C.: Bureau of Justice Statistics, p. 3, Table 3. [See appendix entry 41]

Note: "Prior to Release" includes the time prior to most recent incarceration. It represents the entire adult criminal history of serious misdemeanor and felony charges of prisoners released in 1983. Table includes data from 11 states on prisoners released in 1983 (57 percent of the total state prison population) who were still alive in 1987. See appendix for further information.

*   Homicide includes murder, non-negligent manslaughter, and negligent manslaughter.

3.102 Percentage of Index Crime Arrests of Persons Who Were Released from Prison in 1983, by Type of Charge and Year (Through 1986)

Rearrest Charge, Index Crime	Year of Arrest				
	Total 1983-86	1983	1984	1985	1986
Murder and non-negligent manslaughter	2.3	3.1	2.5	2.0	1.9
Rape	1.8	3.8	2.4	0.9	1.1
Robbery	5.0	6.6	6.4	4.1	3.7
Aggravated assault	2.4	3.0	2.7	2.5	1.7
Burglary	4.8	6.8	5.9	4.3	3.4
Larceny/theft	2.0	2.8	2.3	1.8	1.5
Motor vehicle theft	3.3	4.6	3.7	3.3	2.3

Source: Beck, Allen J., and Bernard E. Shipley. 1989. *Recidivism of prisoners released in 1983*. Washington, D.C.: Bureau of Justice Statistics, p. 4, Table 6. [See appendix entry 41]

Note: Table includes data from 11 states on prisoners released in 1983 (57 percent of the total state prison population) who were still alive in 1987. Percentages are computed as follows: the numerator is the number of arrests for the seven Uniform Crime Report Index crimes among prisoners released in 1983 (multiplied by 100), and the denominator is the estimated number of arrests for Index crimes among all offenders in the 11 states. Percentages for 1983 were adjusted for partial-year exposure to rearrest. From the first row, for example, 2.3 percent of arrests for murder or non-negligent manslaughter between 1983 and 1986 in the 11 states were those of persons who were released from state prison in 1983. Of all arrests in these states for murder and non-negligent manslaughter in just 1983, 3.1 percent were of persons released from state prison that year. The same group comprised 2.5 percent of 1984 murder arrests, 2.0 percent of 1985 murder arrests, and 1.9 percent of 1986 murder arrests.

3.103 Percentage of Prisoners Rearrested Within 3 Years of Release, by Most Serious Offense at Release and Charge at Rearrest, 1987

		Most Serious Offense for Which Released											
		Violent Offense					Property Offense						
Rearrest Charges	Total, All Offenses	Total	Murder*	Rape	Robbery	Assault	Total	Burglary	Larceny/ Theft	Motor Vehicle Theft	Fraud	Drug Offense	Public Order Offense
All charges	62.5	59.6	42.1	51.5	66.0	60.2	68.1	69.5	67.3	78.4	60.9	50.4	54.6
Violent offenses	22.7	30.4	21.6	27.5	33.3	31.5	19.7	20.9	19.5	23.0	11.5	12.2	19.3
Homicide†	1.6	2.8	6.6	2.8	2.9	1.7	1.1	1.1	0.8	1.4	1.1	0.3	0.9
Rape	0.9	1.7	0.8	7.7	1.4	1.2	0.5	0.7	0.4	0.1	0.4	0.4	0.8
Robbery	9.9	14.1	7.0	8.5	19.6	9.1	8.4	9.1	8.7	12.8	3.5	4.2	5.9
Assault	12.6	15.7	10.5	10.7	15.8	21.9	11.1	11.9	10.8	13.1	6.9	7.8	13.4
Property offenses	39.7	32.1	16.8	25.0	38.9	28.9	49.8	50.4	50.3	54.7	47.4	22.9	28.2
Burglary	18.4	12.6	6.4	12.7	15.4	10.7	25.2	31.9	17.5	23.7	16.2	8.2	10.3
Larceny/theft	21.2	16.3	7.4	7.4	21.0	14.4	27.2	25.3	33.5	26.3	26.0	12.2	14.9
Motor vehicle theft	5.5	4.0	2.5	0.7	5.0	3.7	7.2	6.0	8.2	18.6	5.1	2.3	3.7
Fraud	6.5	4.2	2.3	1.8	5.5	2.9	8.6	6.0	8.7	8.5	21.6	4.3	5.7
Drug offenses	16.6	14.8	9.1	11.3	18.0	13.8	16.2	17.7	15.1	17.1	14.8	24.8	14.0
Public order offenses	29.9	29.0	19.2	22.3	32.0	30.9	31.0	32.1	30.5	39.0	24.3	23.0	33.7
Number of released prisoners	106,216	36,769	3,258	2,214	19,815	6,756	51,332	27,416	11,896	2,785	5,809	10,104	6,826

Source: Beck, Allen J., and Bernard E. Shipley. 1989. *Recidivism of prisoners released in 1983.* Washington, D.C.: Bureau of Justice Statistics, p. 6, Table 9. [See appendix entry 41]

Note: Includes data from 11 states on prisoners released in 1983 (57 percent of the total state prison population) who were still alive in 1987. Percentages are computed as follows: the numerator is the number of released prisoners who were rearrested for a new charge between 1983 and 1986 (multiplied by 100), and the denominator is the number of all prisoners released in the 11 states. From the first row, for example, 62.5 percent of all persons released from prison in the 11 states in 1983 were rearrested within three years. 42.1 percent of released murder convicts, 51.5 percent of released rapists, 66.0 percent of released robbers, and 60.2 percent of released assault convicts were similarly rearrested. From the second row, 22.7 percent of all released prisoners were rearrested for a violent offense, 30.4 percent of released prisoners, whose most serious offense prior to release was a violent offense, were rearrested for a new violent offense, and so on. Detail may not add up to total because persons may be rearrested for more than one type of charge.

* Includes negligent manslaughter.

† Includes murder, non-negligent manslaughter, and negligent manslaughter.

3.104 Odds of Rearrest for Offense Similar to Release Charge, Relative to Odds of Rearrest for Offense Different from Release Charge, by Rearrest Charge, 1987

Rearrest Charge	Odds Ratio
Violent Offenses	1.9
Homicide	4.9
Rape	10.5
Other sexual assault	7.5
Robbery	2.9
Assault	2.1

Source: Beck, Allen J., and Bernard E. Shipley. 1989. *Recidivism of prisoners released in 1983*. Washington, D.C.: Bureau of Justice Statistics, p. 6, Table 10. [See appendix entry 41]

Note: Includes data from 11 states on prisoners released in 1983 (57 percent of the total state prison population) who were still alive in 1987. For each type of rearrest charge, the numerator is the odds of rearrest for that charge among prisoners released for the same type of offense; the denominator is the odds of rearrest for that charge among prisoners released for a different type of offense. Each ratio expresses the odds of rearrest among prisoners released on a similar offense relative to the odds of rearrest among those released on a different type of offense. For example, a released violent offender was 1.9 times likelier to be rearrested for a new violent offense than to be rearrested for a nonviolent offense. A released homicide convict was 4.9 times likelier to be rearrested for another homicide than to be rearrested on some other charge. A released rapist was 10.5 times likelier to be rearrested for rape than a nonrape offense, and so on.

3.105   Percentage of Prisoners Released in 1983 and Rearrested Within 3 Years, by Most Serious Offense for Which Released, and by Selected Characteristics of Prior Record, 1987

Characteristics of Prior Record	Percent of All Releases	Most Serious Offense for Which Released				
		All Offenses	Violent	Property	Drugs	Public Order
Prior arrest for a violent offense						
Yes	52.1	68.3	63.5	75.8	64.4	59.1
No	47.9	56.2	53.1	61.8	39.4	48.1
Prior incarceration						
Yes	67.1	69.1	67.3	72.7	62.8	57.7
No	32.9	49.1	47.6	56.7	29.3	45.8
Prior escape or revocation of probation or of parole*						
Yes	39.9	73.1	70.3	76.1	67.8	68.3
No	60.1	55.5	54.8	61.2	41.3	44.4
Prior arrest for a drug offense†						
Yes	37.9	68.6	69.1	75.3	53.2	65.1
No	62.1	58.8	55.2	64.2	40.0†	49.4

Source: Beck, Allen J., and Bernard E. Shipley. 1989. *Recidivism of prisoners released in 1983.* Washington, D.C.: Bureau of Justice Statistics, p. 10, Table 19. [See appendix entry 41]

Note: "Prior Record" refers to events before the crime for which the prisoner was released in 1983. Except for the column titled "Percent of All Releases," values refer to percentages of released prisoners with a specifed prior record characteristic who were rearrested within three years of release. From the first rows, for example, 63.5 percent of prisoners released after a violent offense conviction, who also had a prior arrest for a violent offense, were rearrested within three years; in comparison, 53.1 percent of first-time violent offenders (i.e., those with no prior record of violent offenses) were rearrested in the same period of time. Table includes data from 11 states on prisoners released in 1983 (57 percent of the total state prison population) who were still alive in 1987 (n = 108,580).

*   Includes escape, absconding, absent without leave, revocation of parole, mandatory release, furlough, other conditional release or probation, and flight to avoid prosecution.

†   Prisoners whose most serious offense when released was a drug offense were coded "no" if there was no prior drug arrest.

Alcohol and Drugs

3.106   Drug-Related Homicides, 1986–1992

Year	Total Homicides	Percent Drug Related
1986	19,257	3.9
1987	17,963	4.9
1988	17,971	5.6
1989	18,954	7.4
1990	20,273	6.7
1991	21,676	6.2
1992	22,540	5.7

Source: Supplementary Homicide Report of the Uniform Crime Reports, 1986–1992 from: Bureau of Justice Statistics. 1993. *Drugs and crime facts, 1993.* Washington, D.C., p. 8. [See appendix entry 45]

Note: Includes only those homicides where circumstances were known.

3.107 Percentage of Rapes, Robberies, and Assaults in Which Victim Perceived the Offender to be Under the Influence of Drugs or Alcohol, 1992

| Type of Crime | Total | Perceived to be Under the Influence of Drugs or Alcohol | | | | | | |
		Under the Influence of Alcohol	Under the Influence of Drugs	Under the Influence of Both Drugs and Alcohol	Under the Influence of One, Not Sure Which	Not Available Whether Drugs or Alcohol	Not on Alcohol or Drugs	Don't Know or Not Ascertained
Crimes of violence	30.2	18.0	4.3	6.1	1.6	0.2*	20.8	49.0
Rape	38.6	18.2	8.0	12.4*	0.0*	0.0*	23.1*	38.3
Robbery	24.9	10.8	5.4	6.1	2.6*	0.0*	15.2	59.9
Assault	31.2	19.7	3.9	5.9	1.4	0.2*	22.1	46.7
Aggravated	31.4	16.7	4.3	8.2	1.8*	0.5*	12.7	55.9
Simple	31.1	21.3	3.7	4.7	1.2	0.1*	27.2	41.8

Source: National Crime Victimization Survey, 1992, from: Bureau of Justice Statistics. 1993. Criminal victimization in the United States, 1992. Washington, D.C., p.58, Table 42. [See appendix entry 28]

Note: Detail may not add up to total shown because of rounding. Table excludes series crimes. Series crime and other crime types are defined in the appendix. Aggravated assaults include all attacks (and attempted attacks) with weapons or, if no weapon was involved, those that result in serious injury. Simple assaults are attacks (and attempted attacks) without weapons resulting in minor or undetermined injuries requiring less than two days of hospitalization.

* Estimate is based on 10 or fewer sample cases.

3.108   Percentage of Booked Arrestees Testing Positive for Drugs, by Charge at Arrest and Gender of Arrestee, in 24 Cities, 1991

Charge	Male (%)	Female (%)
Drug sale/possession	79	79
Burglary	68	63
Robbery	65	76
Larceny/theft	64	58
Probation/parole violation	61	60
Stolen property	58	74
Fraud/forgery	56	51
Flight/escape/warrant	52	66
Other	51	46
Weapons	49	62
Public peace/disturbance	48	61
Homicide	48	65
Assault	48	50
Prostitution	47	85
Damage/destruction of property	45	57
Traffic offense	42	48
Family offense	40	38
Sex offense	37	68

Source: National Institute of Justice, Drug Use Forecasting, 1991 Annual Report, from: Bureau of Justice Statistics. 1993. *Drugs and crime data fact sheet: Drug related crime.* Washington, D.C., p. 2, Table 2. [See appendix entry 10]

Note: Positive by urinalysis. Drug tests were designed to detect cocaine, opiates, PCP, marijuana, amphetamines, methadone, methaqualone, benzodiazepines, barbiturates, and propoxyphene. Female arrestees were not tested in three cities. See appendix for cities included in the study.

3.109 Percentage of State Prison Inmates Reporting That They or Their Victims Were Under the Influence of Alcohol or Drugs at the Time of the Offense, by Type of Offense, 1991

Offense	Under Influence of Alcohol or Drugs		
	Inmate	Victim	Inmate or Victim
Violent offenses	50	30	61
Homicide	52	46	70
Sexual assault	42	19	47
Robbery	52	19	61
Assault	50	42	68

Source: Bureau of Justice Statistics. 1993. *Survey of state prison inmates, 1991*. Washington, D.C., p. 18, Figure 39. [See appendix entry 49]

3.110 Percentage of State Prison and Local Jail Inmates Who Used Drugs at the Time of the Offense, 1989, 1991

Drug Type	Jail Inmates (1989) (%)	Prison Inmates (1991) (%)
Any drug	27	31
Marijuana	9	11
Cocaine/crack	14	14
Heroin/opiates	5	6

Source: Drugs and Jail Inmates, 1989, and Survey of State Prison Inmates, 1991, from: Bureau of Justice Statistics. 1993. *Drugs and Crime Facts, 1993*. Washington, D.C., p. 5, Table 2. [See appendix entry 49 and 51]

3.111 Percentage of State Prison Inmates Who Reported Using Drugs in the Month Prior to Offense, by Type of Drug and Type of Violent Offense, 1991

Offense	Type of Drug Used in Month Before Offense			
	Crack	Powder Cocaine	Another Drug	No Drug
Violent offenses	33	39	48	51
Homicide	5	10	14	14
Sexual assault	4	5	7	13
Robbery	19	17	17	12
Assault	5	6	8	10
Property offenses	31	25	26	23
Drug offenses	32	30	20	17
Public order offenses	4	5	5	9
Current offense	100	100	100	100

Source: Adapted from Bureau of Justice Statistics. 1993. *Survey of state prison inmates, 1991.* Washington, D.C., p. 23, Figure 50. [See appendix entry 49]

Note: Percentages computed down columns. From the first column, for example, 33 percent of inmates who said they used crack in the month before their offense were imprisoned for a violent offense; 5 percent of such crack users were imprisoned for homicide, 4 percent for sexual assault, and so on.

3.112 Percentage of State Prison and Local Jail Inmates Who Committed Their Offense to Get Money for Drugs, by Type of Offense, 1989, 1991

Most Serious Offense	Local Jail Inmates (1989)	State Prison Inmates (1991)
All offenses	13	17
Violent offenses	12	12
Homicide	3	5
Sexual assault	2	2
Robbery	32	27
Assault	3	6

Source: Survey of State Prison Inmates, 1991, and Drugs and Jail inmates, 1989, from: Bureau of Justice Statistics. 1994. *Fact sheet: Drug related crime.* Washington, D.C., p. 3, Table 3. [See appendix entry 49 and 50]

3.113   Percentage of State Prison Inmates Who Reported They Were Under the Influence of Drugs Only, or Alcohol Only, or Both, at the Time of Offense, by Type of Offense, 1991

Type of Offense	Alcohol Only	Drugs Only	Both Alcohol and Drugs
All offenses	18	17	14
Violent offenses	21	12	16
Homicide	25	10	17
Sexual assault	22	5	14
Robbery	15	19	18
Assault	27	8	14

Source: Bureau of Justice Statistics. 1993. *Survey of state prison inmates, 1991.* Washington, D.C., p. 26. [See appendix entry 49]

3.114   Percentage of Violent Offenses Committed Under the Influence of Drugs, or to Get Money for Drugs, by Type of Offense of Sentenced Federal and State Prison Inmates, 1991

Type of Offense	Committed Offense Under the Influence of Drugs		Committed Offense to Get Money for Drugs	
	Federal	State	Federal	State
All violent offenses	24.9	28.3	18.0	11.6
Homicide	18.0	27.7	2.7	5.3
Sexual assault	10.3	19.8	0.0	2.4
Robbery	29.3	37.5	26.6	26.7
Assault	19.8	23.1	2.3	5.6
Other violence	15.4	23.8	2.6	6.8

Source: Survey of Inmates in State Correctional Facilities, 1991 from: Harlow, Caroline Wolf. 1994. *Comparing federal and state prison inmates, 1991.* Washington, D.C.: Bureau of Justice Statistics, p. 9, Table 14; p. 10, Table 15. [See appendix entry 48 and 49]

3.115 Percentage of Juveniles in Long-Term, State-Operated Juvenile Institutions Reporting Drug and Alcohol Use at Time of the Offense, by Type of Violent Offense, 1987

Current Offense	Not Under the Influence	Under the Influence of:			
		Either Drugs or Alcohol	Drugs Only	Alcohol Only	Both Drugs and Alcohol
Violent offenses	55.4	44.6	12.1	8.2	24.2
Murder*	57.5	42.5	15.2	17.3	10.0
Rape	65.8	34.2	3.6	6.2	24.5
Other sexual assault	76.7	23.3	5.9	8.1	9.3
Robbery	48.8	51.2	13.8	6.8	30.6
Assault	51.4	48.6	14.6	8.5	25.5

Source: Beck, Allen J., Susan A. Kline, and Lawrence A. Greenfeld. 1988. *Survey of Youth in Custody, 1987*. Washington, D.C.: Bureau of Justice Statistics, p. 8, Table 13. [See appendix entry 53]

* Includes non-negligent manslaughter.

Firearms

3.116 Homicides, Rapes, Robberies, and Assaults Committed with Handguns, 1987–1992

Crime Type	1992	Annual Average, 1987–1991
Handgun crimes	930,700	667,000
Homicide	13,200	10,600
Rape	11,800	14,000
Robbery	339,000	225,100
Assault	566,800	417,300

Source: Supplementary Homicide Report of the Uniform Crime Reports, 1987–1992 (homicide), and National Crime Victimization Survey, 1987–1992 (rape, robbery, and assault), from: Rand, Michael R. 1994. *Guns and crime*. Washington, D.C.: Bureau of Justice Statistics, p. 1. [See appendix entry 28 and 45]

Note: Detail may not add up to total because of rounding. Data on rape, robbery, and assault exclude series crimes. Series crime and other crime types are defined in the appendix.

3.117   Nonlethal Handgun Victimization Rates, by Age, Race, and Gender of Victim, 1987–1992

Age	Male			Female		
	Total	White	Black	Total	White	Black
All ages	4.9	3.7	14.2	2.1	1.6	5.8
12 - 15	5.0	3.1	14.1	2.5	2.1	4.7
16 - 19	14.2	9.5	39.7	5.1	3.6	13.4
20 - 24	11.8	9.2	29.4	4.3	3.5	9.1
25 - 34	5.7	4.9	12.3	3.1	2.1	9.0
35 - 49	3.3	2.7	8.7	1.7	1.4	3.3
50 - 64	1.5	1.2	3.5	0.8	0.7	1.6
65 or older	0.8	0.6	3.7	0.3	0.2	2.3

Source: National Crime Victimization Survey, 1987–1992, from: Rand, Michael R. 1994. *Guns and crime.* Washington, D.C.: Bureau of Justice Statistics, p. 1. [See appendix entry 28]

Note: Rates are per 1,000 persons aged 12 years or older in each age category. Rates do not include murder or non-negligent manslaughter committed with handguns. The totals include persons of other races not shown separately. Table excludes series crimes. Series crime and other crime types are defined in the appendix.

3.118   Percentage of Nonlethal Handgun Victimizations, by Whether Offender Shot at the Victim, 1987–1992

Offender Action	Percentage
Shot at victim	16.6
Hit victim	3.0
Missed victim	13.6
Non-gunshot injury	1.6
No physical injury	12.0
Did not shoot at victim	83.4
Other attack/attempt	19.9
Verbal threat of attack	15.4
Weapon present	46.8
Other threat	0.8
Unknown action	0.5
Average annual number of nonlethal handgun victimizations	699,900

Source: National Crime Victimization Survey, 1987–1992, from: Rand, Michael R. 1994. *Guns and crime.* Washington, D.C.: Bureau of Justice Statistics, p. 2. [See appendix entry 28]

Note: Excludes homicides and series crimes. Series crime and other crime types are defined in the appendix.

3.119 Number of Homicides Each Month, by Firearms and Other Means, January 1962–December 1991

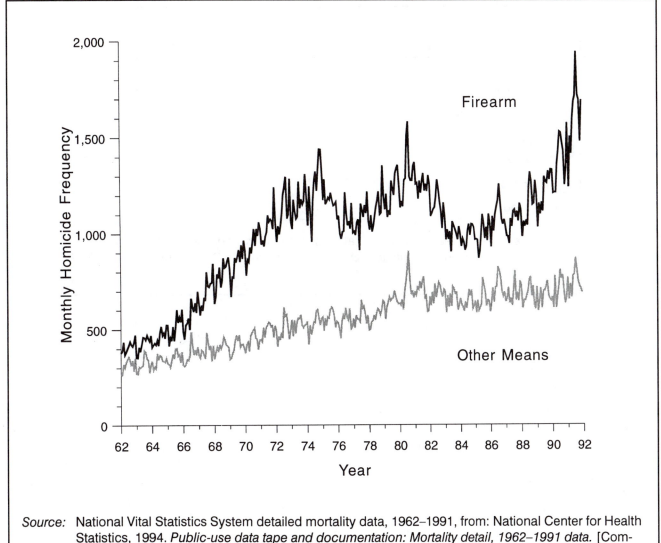

Source: National Vital Statistics System detailed mortality data, 1962–1991, from: National Center for Health Statistics, 1994. *Public-use data tape and documentation: Mortality detail, 1962–1991 data.* [Computer files]. Hyattsville, Md.: Public Health Service. [See appendix entry 34]

Note: For 1962–1967, firearm homicide includes ICD-8 code E981, and homicide by other means includes ICD-8 codes E980, E982, and E983. For 1968–1991, firearm homicide includes ICD-9 code E965, and homicide by other means is defined by ICD-9 codes E960–E964 and E966–E969

3.120   Manner in Which Violent, Armed State Prison Inmates Used Weapons in Commission of Their Crime, Percentages by Type of Weapon, 1991

How Weapon Was Used	Gun	Knife	Other Weapon
To kill the victim	14	15	11
To injure the victim	11	18	23
To scare the victim	54	51	43
For protection	30	29	27
To get away	12	14	15
Other reasons	6	5	6
Not used	8	9	11

Source: Bureau of Justice Statistics. 1993. *Survey of state prison inmates, 1991*. Washington, D.C., p. 18, Figure 38. [See appendix entry 49]

3.121 Murders, Robberies, and Aggravated Assaults in Which Firearms Were Used, Estimated Numbers of Offenses and Per Capita Rates, 1980–1992

Year	Total Estimated Firearm Crimes		Murders With Firearms*		Robberies With Firearms		Aggravated Assaults With Firearms	
	Frequency	Rate	Frequency	Rate	Frequency	Rate	Frequency	Rate
1980	392,083	174.0	14,377	6.4	221,170	98.1	156,535	69.5
1981	396,197	172.9	14,052	6.1	230,226	100.5	151,918	66.3
1982	372,477	160.9	12,648	5.5	214,219	92.5	145,609	62.9
1983	330,419	141.2	11,258	4.8	183,581	78.5	135,580	57.9
1984	329,232	139.4	10,990	4.7	173,634	73.5	144,609	61.2
1985	340,942	142.8	11,141	4.7	175,748	73.6	154,052	64.5
1986	376,064	156.0	12,181	5.1	186,174	77.2	177,710	73.7
1987	365,709	150.3	11,879	4.9	170,841	70.2	182,989	75.2
1988	385,934	157.0	12,553	5.1	181,352	73.8	192,029	78.1
1989	410,039	165.2	13,416	5.4	192,006	77.3	204,618	82.4
1990	492,671	198.1	15,025	6.0	233,973	94.1	243,673	98.0
1991	548,667	217.6	16,376	6.5	274,404	108.8	257,887	102.3
1992	565,575	221.7	16,204	6.4	271,009	106.2	278,362	109.1

Source: Uniform Crime Reports, 1980–1992, from: Bureau of Justice Statistics. 1994. *Firearms and crimes of violence.* Washington, D.C., p. 13, Table 1. [See appendix entry 26]

Note: Rates are per 100,000 residents. Aggravated assaults are nonfatal attacks involving serious injury and/or the use of a weapon or other means capable of causing death or great bodily harm.

* Includes non-negligent manslaughter.

3.122   Percentage of Murders, Robberies, and Aggravated Assaults in Which Firearms Were Used, 1980–1992

Year	Total for Selected Crimes		Murders*		Robberies		Aggravated Assaults	
	Number	Percent with Firearms	Number	Percent with Firearms	Number	Percent with Firearms	Number	Percent with Firearms
1980	1,226,810	32.0	23,040	62.4	548,810	40.3	654,960	23.9
1981	1,240,370	31.9	22,520	62.4	574,130	40.1	643,720	23.6
1982	1,207,942	30.8	21,010	60.2	536,890	39.9	650,042	22.4
1983	1,159,060	28.5	19,310	58.3	500,220	36.7	639,530	21.2
1984	1,189,050	27.7	18,690	58.8	485,010	35.8	685,350	21.1
1985	1,240,100	27.5	18,980	58.7	497,870	35.3	723,250	21.3
1986	1,397,710	26.9	20,610	59.1	542,780	34.3	834,320	21.3
1987	1,392,890	26.3	20,100	59.1	517,700	33.0	855,090	21.4
1988	1,473,740	26.2	20,680	60.7	542,970	33.4	910,090	21.1
1989	1,551,540	26.4	21,500	62.4	578,330	33.2	951,710	21.5
1990	1,717,570	28.7	23,440	64.1	639,270	36.6	1,054,860	23.1
1991	1,805,170	30.4	24,700	66.3	687,730	39.9	1,092,740	23.6
1992	1,823,210	31.0	23,760	68.2	672,480	40.3	1,126,970	24.7

Source: Uniform Crime Reports, 1980–92, from: Bureau of Justice Statistics. 1994. *Firearms and crimes of violence.* Washington, D.C., p. 13, Table 2. [See appendix entry 26]

Note: Aggravated assaults are nonfatal attacks involving serious injury and/or the use of a weapon or other means capable of causing death or great bodily harm.

*   Includes non-negligent manslaughter.

3.123   Handgun Victimization and Total (Nonlethal) Victimization, 1979–1992

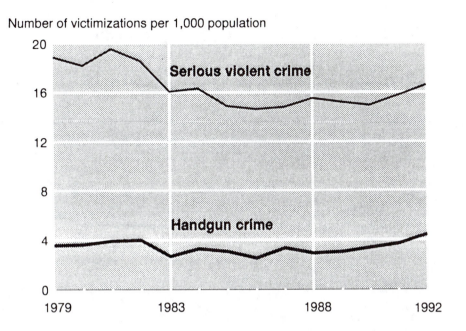

Number of victimizations per 1,000 population

Source: National Crime Victimization Survey, 1979–1992, from: Rand, Michael R. 1994. *Guns and crime.*
Washington, D.C.: Bureau of Justice Statistics, p. 1. [See appendix entry 28]

Note: Serious violent crime includes rape, robbery, and aggravated assault. Excludes series crimes. Series
crime and other crime types are defined in the appendix.

3.124   Percentage of Violent Crime Involving a Firearm, 1980–1992

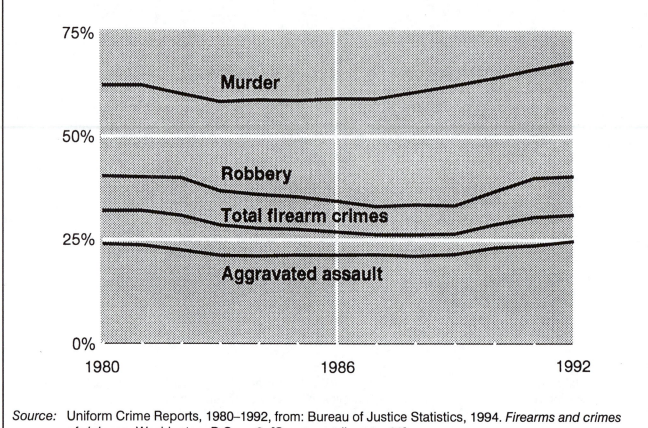

Source: Uniform Crime Reports, 1980–1992, from: Bureau of Justice Statistics, 1994. *Firearms and crimes of violence.* Washington, D.C., p. 3. [See appendix entry 26]
Note: "Total firearm crimes" refers to the percentage of all violent crimes that involved a firearm. "Murder" refers to the percentage of murders and non-negligent manslaughters that involved a firearm, and so on.

3.125 Rate of Violent Crimes Involving a Firearm, 1980–1992

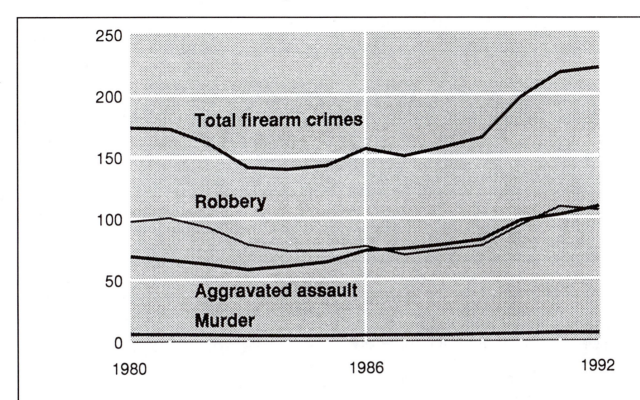

Source: Uniform Crime Reports, 1980–1992, from: Bureau of Justice Statistics, 1994. *Firearms and crimes of violence.* Washington, D.C., p. 4. [See appendix entry 26]

Note: Rates are the number of firearm crimes reported to the police per 100,000 persons.

Chapter 4
Impact of Violence

The impact of violence on American society is enormous but very difficult to quantify. Some of these societal costs include operating the criminal justice system, fear of crime, civil litigation, victim compensation payments, the emergency medical and other health care systems, private security devices and services, higher consumer costs, lower property values, moving costs, and insurance costs. Even if we could estimate the total amount of a societal cost—say, for example, the cost of operating the criminal justice system—the portion that is attributable to violence remains unknown.

The impact of violence on victims is also enormous. Violence imposes three types of costs on victims: out-of-pocket expenses such as medical bills and property losses; reduced productivity at work, home, and school; and non-monetary losses such as fear, pain, suffering, and lost quality (and in the case of death, potential years) of life. Intangible losses such as pain, suffering, and reduced quality of life are real, but they are much more difficult to quantify than direct, tangible losses. Nevertheless, even though we cannot measure the impact of intangible costs either on victims or society, they are pervasive and devastating. There is every likelihood that they overshadow other more easily quantified impacts.

CHAPTER FOCUS

The focus in this chapter is on tangible losses and other measurable consequences directly attributable to violence. Even so, there are considerable data gaps for these categories of impacts. Not very much is currently known about the nature and extent of even the most basic consequences of violence such as injury, medical costs, and loss of productivity. Perhaps the most important consequence of violence may be psychological trauma and the costs associated with it. Yet, there are no comprehensive national data available on the psychological effects of violence or the mental health care costs directly attributable to violence.

CHAPTER ORGANIZATION

We have organized the chapter to address five impacts of violence: psychological trauma resulting from violence; physical injury sustained in violent crimes; economic costs including medical costs due to violence; loss of productivity and wages; and the impact of violence on life expectancy and the risk of death.

PSYCHOLOGICAL TRAUMA

4.1 Percentage of Adult Women Meeting Diagnostic Criteria for Prior or Current Post-Traumatic Stress Disorder, by Type of Trauma Experienced, 1989

Event Type	Percent of Sample	Estimated Population	Lifetime PTSD (%)	Current PTSD (%)
Completed rape	12.65	12,151,084	32.0	12.4
Other sexual assault	14.32	13,755,219	30.8	13.0
Physical assault	10.28	9,874,557	38.5	17.8
Homicide of family or close friend	13.37	12,842,687	22.1	8.9
Any crime victimization	35.58	34,176,724	25.8	9.7
Noncrime trauma only (disaster/accident/other)	33.31	31,996,253	9.4	3.4
Any trauma	68.89	66,172,978	17.9	6.7
Total sample			12.3	4.6

Source: National Women's Study, adapted from: Resnick, Heidi S., Dean G. Kilpatrick, Bonnie S. Dansky, Benjamin E. Saunders, and Connie L. Best. 1993. Prevalence of civilian trauma and post-traumatic stress disorder in a representative national sample of women. *Journal of Consulting and Clinical Psychology* 61, no. 6: 987–988, Tables 1 and 2. Copyright © 1993 by the American Psychological Association. Used with permission. [See appendix entry 35]

Note: Post-traumatic stress disorder (PTSD) is a clinical psychological diagnosis that applies to individuals who have experienced a traumatic event, but who also report certain specific kinds of psychological distress following the trauma. "Current PTSD" in this table includes individuals who met diagnostic criteria for PTSD within the six months prior to the study. "Lifetime PTSD" includes individuals who would, at any point in their past, have met diagnostic criteria for PTSD.

4.2   Percentage of Adult Women Meeting Diagnostic Criteria for Post-Traumatic Stress Disorder Who Reported Ever Experiencing a Sexual or Physical Assault or Rape, by Threat and/or Injury, 1989

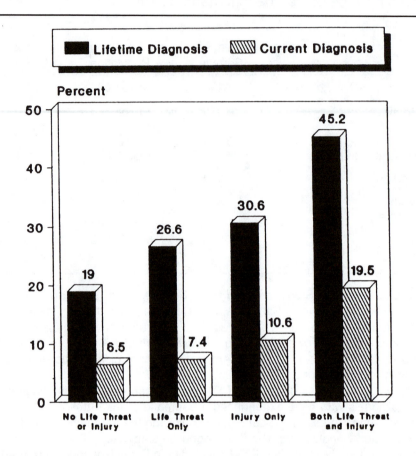

Source: National Women's Study from: Resnick, Heidi S., Dean G. Kilpatrick, Bonnie S. Dansky, Benjamin E. Saunders, and Connie L. Best. 1993. Prevalence of civilian trauma and post-traumatic stress disorder in a representative national sample of women. *Journal of Consulting and Clinical Psychology* 61, no. 6: 989, Figure 2. Copyright 1993 by the American Psychological Association. Used with permission. [See appendix entry 35]

Note: Post-traumatic stress disorder (PTSD) is a clinical psychological diagnosis that applies to individuals who have experienced a traumatic event, but who also report certain specific kinds of psychological distress following the trauma. "Current PTSD" in this table includes individuals who met diagnostic criteria for PTSD within the six months prior to the study. "Lifetime PTSD" includes individuals who would, at any point in their past, have met diagnostic criteria for PTSD.

4.3 Percentage of Homicide Survivors Meeting Diagnostic Criteria for Post-Traumatic Stress Disorder, 1987

	Criminal Homicide	Alcohol-Related Vehicular Homicide	Both Groups
Lifetime PTSD			
Intrusions	37.4	44.0	40.7
Avoidance	40.0	41.8	40.9
Arousal	47.8	52.7	50.2
All criteria	19.1	27.5	23.3
Current PTSD			
Intrusions	15.7	14.3	15.0
Avoidance	13.0	7.7	10.4
Arousal	22.6	22.0	22.3
All criteria	5.2	4.4	4.8
Sample n	115	91	206
Total estimated adult survivors	6,700,000	9,700,000	16,400,000

Source: Table adapted from: Amick-McMullan, Angelynne, Dean G. Kilpatrick, and Heidi S. Resnick. 1991. Homicide as a risk factor for PTSD among surviving family members. *Behavior Modification* 15, no. 4 (October):551, 552, copyright © 1991 by Sage Publications. Used with permission of Sage Publications, Inc. [See appendix entry 20]

Note: A homicide survivor is one who is either an immediate family member, other relative, or close friend of a homicide victim. Post-traumatic stress disorder (PTSD) is a clinical psychological diagnosis that applies to individuals who have experienced a traumatic event, but who also report certain specific kinds of psychological distress following the trauma. "Intrusions," "Avoidance," and "Arousal" are three of the major criterion events that can contribute to a clinical diagnosis of PTSD.

PHYSICAL INJURY SUSTAINED IN VIOLENT CRIME

4.4   Percentage of Robbery and Assault Victimizations in Which Victims Sustained Physical Injury, by Age, Race, Gender, Victim-Offender Relationship, and Income of Victim, 1992

Characteristics	Robbery and Assault	Robbery	Assault
Sex			
Both sexes	30.9	35.7	29.7
Male	28.9	30.6	28.4
Female	33.6	45.4	31.5
Age			
12-15	32.0	28.3*	32.5
16-19	31.4	32.9	31.0
20-24	31.0	32.8	30.6
25-34	34.3	42.5	32.2
35-49	27.1	32.3	26.0
50-64	24.1	46.3	15.3*
65 and over	25.3*	30.3*	22.8*
Race			
White	30.2	33.1	29.6
Black	32.4	39.7	29.0
Victim-offender relationship			
Strangers	27.7	36.1	24.9
Nonstrangers	35.7	34.1	35.8
Income			
Less than $7,500	35.1	48.4	32.3
$7,500-$9,999	31.4	30.5*	31.7
$10,000-$14,999	36.7	34.7	37.3
$15,000-$24,999	31.1	43.6	28.7
$25,000-$29,999	27.7	19.0*	29.6
$30,000-$49,999	25.9	21.7	26.9
$50,000 or more	23.8	29.5	22.6

Source: National Crime Victimization Survey, 1992, from: Bureau of Justice Statistics. 1993. *Criminal victimization in the United States, 1992*. Washington, D.C., p. 88, Table 80. [See appendix entry 28]

Note: Victims were directly asked if they were physically injured. Affirmative responses are included here. Rape is not shown above because all victims of completed rape were considered, by definition, to have suffered physical injury. Table excludes data on persons whose income level was not ascertained. Table excludes series crimes. Series crime and other crime types are defined in the appendix.

*   Estimate is based on 10 or fewer sample cases.

4.5   Percentage of Violent Victimizations in Which Victims Received Hospital Care, by Age, Race, Gender of Victim, and Victim-Offender Relationship, 1992

Characteristics	Crimes of Violence†	Robbery	Assault
Sex			
Both sexes	7.7	7.7	7.3
Male	8.4	8.6	8.2
Female	6.7	6.0*	6.0
Age			
12-19	5.9	3.1*	6.1
20-34	8.3	9.3	7.3
35-49	8.4	6.6*	9.0
50-64	11.4*	14.0*	10.6*
65 and over	7.3*	15.8*	3.6*
Race			
White	6.3	5.5	5.9
Black	13.9	13.2	14.3
Victim-offender relationship			
Strangers	8.0	8.4	7.3
Nonstrangers	7.2	4.7*	7.3

Source: National Crime Victimization Survey, 1992, from: Bureau of Justice Statistics. 1993. *Criminal victimization in the United States, 1992.* Washington, D.C., p. 91, Table 86. [See appendix entry 28]

Note: Table excludes series crimes. Series crime and other crime types are defined in the appendix.

   *   Estimate is based on 10 or fewer sample cases.

   †   Includes data on rape, not shown separately.

4.6   Percentage of Violent Victimizations in Which Injured Victims Received Hospital Care, by Age, Race, Gender of Victim, and Victim-Offender Relationship, 1992

Characteristics	Crimes of Violence†	Robbery	Assault
Sex			
Both sexes	24.6	21.6	24.5
Male	29.2	28.0	29.0
Female	19.3	13.2*	19.2
Age			
12-19	18.3	9.8*	19.1
20-34	24.8	24.0	23.2
35-49	31.0	20.5*	34.8
50-64	47.9*	30.3*	69.2*
65 and over	30.5*	52.4*	15.8*
Race			
White	20.6	16.7	20.0
Black	42.4	33.2	49.5
Victim-offender relationship			
Strangers	28.5	23.3	29.4
Nonstrangers	20.1	13.8*	20.2

Source: National Crime Victimization Survey, 1992, from: Bureau of Justice Statistics. 1993. *Criminal victimization in the United States, 1992.* Washington, D.C., p. 91, Table 87. [See appendix entry 28]

Note: Table excludes series crimes. Series crime and other crime types are defined in the appendix.

*   Estimate is based on 10 or fewer sample cases.

†   Includes data on rape, not shown separately.

4.7 Percentage of Single-Offender Violent Crime Victimizations Resulting in Injuries, Medical Care, and Hospital Care for Female Victims, by Victim-Offender Relationship, 1993

Relationship	Injury			Received Medical Care		Received Hospital Care	
	None	Minor	Serious	No	Yes	No	Yes
Total	3,365,660	883,500	583,220	4,214,050	596,270	4,767,690	42,630
%	70.4	17.4	12.2	87.6	12.4	99.1	0.9
Single-offender victimizations	2,837,100	759,210	491,950	3,605,670	508,140	4,085,060	28,750
%	69.4	18.6	12.0	87.6	12.4	99.3	0.7
Intimate	365,330	250,170	128,840	614,040	136,980	746,520	4,490*
%	49.1	33.6	17.3	81.8	18.2	99.4	0.6*
Other relative	84,720	4,830*	13,670*	94,730	9,630*	99,540	4,820*
%	82.1	4.7*	13.2*	90.8	9.2*	95.4	4.6*
Acquaintance	1,431,460	361,190	279,030	1,810,480	274,090	2,072,200	12,370*
%	69.1	17.4	13.5	86.9	13.1	99.4	0.6*
Stranger	940,230	135,340	70,410	1,066,190	84,650	1,143,770	7,070*
%	82.0	11.8	6.1	92.6	7.4	99.4	0.6*

Source: National Crime Victimization Survey, 1993 preliminary data, from: Bureau of the Census. 1995. *National crime victimization survey, 1992–1993.* [Computer files]. Suitland, Md. [See appendix entry 28]

Note: "Serious injuries are broken bones, loss of teeth, internal injuries, loss of consciousness, rape or attempted rape injuries, and undetermined injuries requiring two or more days of hospitalization. "Minor" injuries are bruises, black eyes, cuts, scratches, swelling, or undetermined injuries requiring less than two days of hospitalization. "Not stated" responses are not shown or included in percentages. Detail may not add up to totals due to rounding. Table includes series crimes. Series crime and other crime types are defined in the appendix.

4.8   Percentage of Injuries, Medical Treatment, and Hospital Care Received by Violent Crime Victims, for Ages Over and Under 65, 1987–1990

Outcome	Under 65	65 or Older
Injured	31	33
Serious	5	9
Minor	26	24
Received medical care	15	19
Hospital care	8	14

Source: National Crime Victimization Survey, 1987–1990, from: Bachman, Ronet. 1992. *Elderly victims.* Washington, D.C.: Bureau of Justice Statistics, p. 4, Table 5. [See appendix entry 28]

Note: "Serious" injuries are broken bones, loss of teeth, internal injuries, loss of consciousness, rape or attempted rape injuries, or undetermined injuries requiring two or more days of hospitalization. "Minor" injuries are bruises, black eyes, cuts, scratches, swelling, or undetermined injuries requiring less than two days of hospitalization. Table excludes series crimes. Series crime and other crime types are defined in the appendix.

4.9   Average Annual Injuries Sustained in Violent Crime, by Type of Crime, 1987–1990

Type of Injury	Rape	Robbery	Assault
Raped†	53,370	-	-
Attempted rape†	12,320	-	-
Knife wounds	1,850*	22,070	54,540
Gunshot wounds	0*	5,620*	12,770
Broken bones, teeth loss	2,640*	25,220	101,640
Internal injuries	6,330	13,960	44,010
Knocked unconscious	1,240*	24,300	49,380
Bruises, cuts, swelling, etc.	46,930	336,640	1,299,020
Other	13,110	66,590	26,140
None	84,180	398,550	1,545,530
Any injury	142,650	1,135,360	5,124,680

Source: National Crime Victimization Survey, 1987–1990, from: Bureau of Justice Statistics. 1992. *National crime surveys: national sample, 1986–1991 [near-term data].* [Computer files]. 4th ICPSR ed. Ann Arbor, Mich.: Inter-university Consortium for Political and Social Research. [See appendix entry 28]

Note: Respondents were encouraged to state all types of injury in the incident; therefore injury types do not sum to equal "Any injury" total. A dash indicates not applicable. Table includes series crimes. Series crime and other crime types are defined in the appendix.

†   Recorded as injuries if respondents mentioned these when asked how they were injured.

*   Estimate based on 10 or fewer sample cases.

4.10 Average Annual Injuries in Order of Seriousness, by Type of Violence, 1987–1990

Type of Injury	Rape	Robbery	Assault
Gunshot wound	0*	5,620*	12,770
Broken bones and internal injury	470*	2,340*	7,810
Internal injury	5,860*	11,620	35,390
Broken bones	2,170*	22,410	93,830
Knife wound	1,850*	19,960	49,770
Knocked unconscious	1,240*	15,300	33,810
Other injury	10,710	52,620	217,040
Bruises, cuts, scratches	32,460	264,690	1,071,910
Rape only	28,970	-	-
Not specified	440*	3,990*	23,210

Source: National Crime Victimization Survey, 1987–1990, from: Bureau of Justice Statistics. 1992. *National crime surveys: national sample, 1986–1991 [near-term data].* [Computer files]. 4th ICPSR ed. Ann Arbor, Mich.: Inter-university Consortium for Political and Social Research. [See appendix entry 28]

Note: Incidents involving injury are listed only once if multiple injuries were sustained. Order of seriousness defined by average expected medical costs associated with the injury. A dash indicates not applicable. Table includes series crimes. Series crimes and other crime types are defined in the appendix.

* Estimate based on 10 or fewer sample cases.

4.11 Annual Estimates of Nonfatal Gun-Related Injuries, U.S., by Type of Weapon and Wound, and by Severity, 1992

Type of Weapon and Wound	Total	Admitted to Hospital	Emergency Department Only	Percent Admitted
All gun related	151,373	59,525	91,848	39.3
Gunshot	130,572	58,538	72,034	44.8
Firearm	99,025	56,491	42,534	57.0
BB/Pellet	31,547	2,047	29,500	6.5
Other gun†	20,801	987*	19,814	4.7*

Source: Annest, Joseph L., James A. Mercy, Delinda R. Gibson, and George W. Ryan. 1995. National estimates of nonfatal firearm-related injuries: beyond the tip of the iceberg. *Journal of the American Medical Association* 273, no. 22 (June 14): 1751, Table 2. Used with permission. [See appendix entry 29]

* Estimate is based on fewer than 50 injured persons.

† Includes non-gunshot wounds; e.g., powder burn, struck with a firearm, injury from recoil of a firearm.

4.12   Nonfatal Firearm-Related Injury Rates, by Age, Gender, and Race, 1992

Characteristic	Number	Rate
Total	99,025	38.6
Gender		
Male	86,000	68.7
Female	13,008	9.9
Age		
0-14	3,768	6.7
15-24	43,382	119.5
25-34	27,420	64.4
35-44	15,528	38.7
45 and over	8,680	10.7
Race		
Black	47,663	149.4
White*	30,444	15.9
Hispanic	11,122	45.2
Type of injury		
Assault/legal intervention	58,485	22.8
Unintentional	19,727	7.7
Suicide attempt	5,197	2.0

Source: Annest, Joseph L., James A. Mercy, Delinda R. Gibson, and George W. Ryan. 1995. National estimates of nonfatal firearm-related injuries: beyond the tip of the iceberg. *Journal of the American Medical Association* 273, no. 22 (June 14): p. 1752, Table 3. Used with permission. [See appendix entry 29]

Note: Rates are per 100,000 residents.
   *   Nonfatal injuries exclude those who were of Hispanic origin; nonfatal injury rates were calculated using white, non-Hispanic population estimates.

4.13   Injury and Impairment from Child Abuse, 1980, 1986

Severity	1980 Number	1980 Rate	1986 Number	1986 Rate
Fatal	1,000	0.02	1,100	0.02
Serious	131,200	2.1	141,700	2.2
Moderate	393,400	6.2	682,700	10.8
Probable	97,500	1.5	105,500	1.7
Unknown*	2,000	0.0	-	-
Total	625,100	9.8	931,000	14.8

Source: Study of National Incidence and Prevalence of Child Abuse and Neglect, 1986 (NIS-2), from: Sedlak, Andrea J. 1991. *National incidence and prevalence of child abuse and neglect: 1988.* (Revised Report). Rockville, Md.: Westat, Inc., p. 3-11, Table 3-5. Used with permission. [See appendix entry 44]

Note: Rates are per 1,000 children. Serious injury/impairment was defined as either involving a life-threatening condition, representing a long-term impairment of physical, mental, or emotional capacities, or requiring professional treatment aimed at preventing such long-term impairment. Moderate injuries/impairment were those which persisted in observable form (including pain or impairment) for at least 48 hours. Probable injuries/impairment were inferred from the nature of maltreatment rather than direct evidence, but they should not be considered less serious than "moderate" because many types of maltreatment, e.g., abandonment, incest, extreme close confinement, could reasonably lead to serious injury or impairment. Numbers of children rounded to the nearest 100, not adjusted by population totals. A dash represents no sample cases.

*   For 0.31 percent of all maltreated children in the 1980 survey, severity of injury/impairment was unknown.

4.14 Moderate Injuries from Child Abuse, by Age, 1986

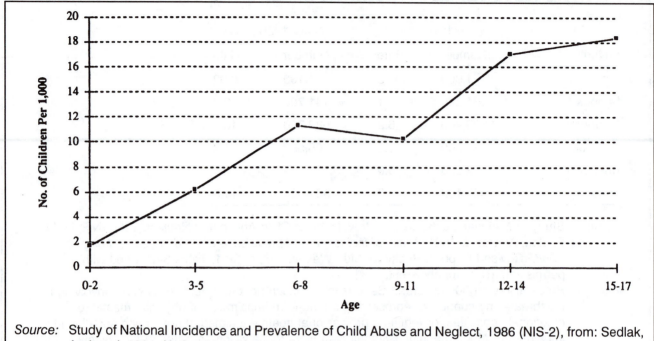

Source: Study of National Incidence and Prevalence of Child Abuse and Neglect, 1986 (NIS-2), from: Sedlak, Andrea J. 1991. *National incidence and prevalence of child abuse and neglect: 1988.* (Revised Report). Rockville, Md.: Westat, Inc., p. 5-16, Figure 5-5. Used with permission. [See appendix entry 44]

Note: Moderate injuries/impairment were those which persisted in observable form (including pain or impairment) for at least 48 hours. Includes only cases of demonstrable harm.

4.15   Severity of Injury or Impairment, by Type of Child Abuse, 1986

	Total	Fatal	Serious	Moderate	Inferred
Physical abuse	269,700	600	12,000	257,100	†
Sexual abuse	119,200	*	6,700	51,500	61,100
Intrusion	40,400	*	*	15,400	20,500
Genital molestation	53,100	*	*	19,400	31,800
Other/unknown	25,800	*	*	16,600	8,800
Emotional injury	155,200	*	15,100	115,500	24,600
Verbal assault	106,600	*	14,100	77,000	15,600
Close confinement	8,700	*	*	*	*
Other/unknown	46,700	*	*	37,800	*

Source: Second National Incidence Study of Child Abuse and Neglect, 1986, from: Sedlak, Andrea J. 1991. *Supplementary analyses of data on the national incidence of child abuse and neglect.* Rockville, Md.: Westat, Inc., p. 2-6, Table 2-2. Used with permisssion. [See appendix entry 44]

Note: "Abuse" includes mainly physical injury, but a small proportion of "mental injury" is also included. Abuse types are not mutually exclusive and thus table columns do not sum to the total number of children affected. Serious injury/impairment was defined as either involving a life-threatening condition, representing a long-term impairment of physical, mental, or emotional capacities, or requiring professional treatment aimed at preventing such long-term impairment. Moderate injuries/impairment were those which persisted in observable form (including pain or impairment) for at least 48 hours. Probable injuries/impairment were inferred from the nature of maltreatment rather than direct evidence, but they should not be considered less serious than "moderate" because many types of maltreatment, e.g., abandonment, incest, extreme close confinement, could reasonably lead to serious injury or impairment.

*   Fewer than 20 cases with which to calculate estimate; estimate too unreliable to be presented.

†   Severity level not relevant for this form of maltreatment.

4.16   Nature of Injury or Impairment, by Severity Levels in Child Abuse, 1986

	Total	Fatal	Serious	Moderate	Inferred
Physical abuse	269,700	600	12,000	257,100	†
Physical injury	225,100	600	10,900	213,500	†
Mental injury	44,600	†	*	43,600	†
Sexual abuse	119,200	*	6,700	51,400	61,100
Physical injury	5,600	*	*	4,900	†
Mental injury	113,600	†	6,000	46,500	61,100
Emotional injury	155,200	*	15,100	115,500	24,600
Physical injury	8,300	*	*	7,300	†
Mental injury	147,000	†	14,900	108,200	23,900

Source: Second National Incidence Study of Child Abuse and Neglect, 1986, from: Sedlak, Andrea J. 1991. *Supplementary analyses of data on the national incidence of child abuse and neglect.* Rockville, Md.: Westat, Inc., p. 2-20, Table 2-6. Used with permission. [See appendix entry 44]

Note: "Abuse" includes mainly physical injury, but a small proportion of "mental injury" is also included. Abuse types are not mutually exclusive and thus table columns do not sum to the total number of children affected. Serious injury/impairment was defined as either involving a life-threatening condition, representing a long-term impairment of physical, mental, or emotional capacities, or requiring professional treatment aimed at preventing such long-term impairment. Moderate injuries/impairment were those which persisted in observable form (including pain or impairment) for at least 48 hours. Probable injuries/impairment were inferred from the nature of maltreatment rather than direct evidence, but they should not be considered less serious than "moderate" because many types of maltreatment, e.g., abandonment, incest, extreme close confinement, could reasonably lead to serious injury or impairment.

*   Fewer than 20 cases with which to calculate estimate; estimate too unreliable to be presented.

†   This severity level not relevant for this form of maltreatment.

4.17 Nature of Injury or Impairment, by Type of Maltreatment of Children, 1986

	Total	Fatal	Serious	Moderate	Inferred
Abused	507,700	600	32,700	393,400	81,000
Physical injury	238,900	600	11,800	225,700	†
Mental injury	293,000	†	20,900	188,100	84,000
Neglected	474,800	*	114,100	323,300	37,000
Physical injury	88,400	*	60,400	27,500	†
Mental injury	390,300	†	54,500	298,500	37,200
Total	931,000	1,100	141,700	682,700	105,500
Physical injury	324,000	1,100	69,700	252,500	†
Mental injury	644,100	†	73,100	460,200	110,900

Source: Second National Incidence Study of Child Abuse and Neglect, 1986, from: Sedlak, Andrea J. 1991. *Supplementary analyses of data on the national incidence of child abuse and neglect.* Rockville, Md.: Westat, Inc., p. 2-18, Table 2-5. Used with permission. [See appendix entry 44]

Note: Abuse and neglect types are not mutually exclusive and thus table columns do not sum to the total number of children affected.

* Fewer than 20 cases with which to calculate estimate; estimate too unreliable to be given.

† This severity level not relevant for this form of maltreatment.

ECONOMIC COSTS TO VICTIMS

4.18 Assaults and Other Violent Acts Resulting in Days Away from Work, Selected Characteristics, Private Industry, 1992

Violent Act	Total Cases	Women as a Percent of Total	Median Days Away From Work
Total	22,396	56	5
Hitting/kicking/beating	10,425	55	5
Squeezing/pinching/ scratching/twisting	2,457	84	4
Biting	901	53	3
Stabbing	598	7	28
Shooting	560	3	30
All other specified acts (e.g.,rape, threats)	5,157	60	5
Unspecified acts	2,301	46	6

Source: Survey of Occupational Injuries and Illnesses, 1992, from: Bureau of Labor Statistics. 1994. *Issues in labor statistics.* Washington, D.C.: U.S. Department of Labor, p. 2. [See appendix entry 51]

4.19   Mean Short-Term Loss Per Violent Crime, 1992

	Dollar Amount
Crimes of violence	206
Rape	234
Robbery	555
Assault	124

Source: National Crime Victimization Survey, 1992, from: Klaus, Patsy A. 1994. *The costs of crime to victims.* Washington, D.C.: Bureau of Justice Statistics, p. 1. [See appendix entry 28]

Note: "Loss" includes all forms of economic loss recorded by the NCVS: property loss, medical expenses, and time lost from work. "Short-Term" is defined as no more than six months from the time of victimization (a period determined by the six-month recall interval of the NCVS design). The NCVS does not specifically ask respondents about psychological counseling costs although some victims may have included these among "medical costs." Increases to insurance premiums as a result of filing claims, decreased productivity at work, moving costs incurred when moving as a result of victimization, intangible costs of pain and suffering, and other similar costs are also not included in the NCVS. Table excludes series crimes. Series crime and other crime types are defined in the appendix.

4.20 Mean Short-Term Loss Per Violent Crime, 1975–1992

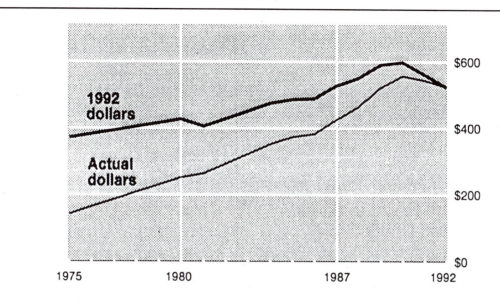

Source: National Crime Victimization Survey, 1992, from: Klaus, Patsy A. 1994. *The costs of crime to victims.* Washington, D.C.: Bureau of Justice Statistics, p. 1. [See appendix entry 28]

Note: During the 1975–92 period, according to the Current Population Survey, household money income adjusted for inflation remained relatively unchanged. Data are interpolated for 1976–79 and 1982–83. "Loss" includes all forms of economic loss recorded by the NCVS: property loss, medical expenses, and time lost from work. "Short-Term" is defined as no more than six months from the time of victimization (a period determined by the six-month recall interval of the NCVS design). The NCVS does not specifically ask respondents about psychological counseling costs although some victims may have included these among "medical costs." Increases to insurance premiums as a result of filing claims, decreased productivity at work, moving costs incurred when moving as a result of victimization, intangible costs of pain and suffering, and other similar costs are also not included in the NCVS. Excludes series crimes. Series crime and other crime types are defined in the appendix.

4.21 Amount of Loss, Based Upon Violent Crimes Involving Economic Loss, 1992

	Crimes of Violence†	Robbery	Assault
Total victimizations	13,371,440	876,800	639,170
No monetary value (%)	5.3	1.3*	10.3
$1-$249 (%)	57.3	60.0	55.4
$250-$499 (%)	8.6	9.1	7.6
$500 or more (%)	12.7	17.7	4.0
Don't know (%)	16.2	11.6	22.8

Source: National Crime Victimization Survey, 1992, from: Klaus, Patsy A. 1994. *The costs of crime to victims.* Washington, D.C.: Bureau of Justice Statistics, p. 2, Table 4. [See appendix entry 28]

Note: NCVS excludes losses incurred by commercial establishments in robbery. Percentages may not sum to 100 due to rounding. Table excludes series crimes. Series crime and other crime types are defined in the appendix.

* Estimate based on 10 or fewer sample cases.

† Includes rape, not shown separately.

4.22 Percentage of Victimizations Resulting in Economic Loss, by Race of Victim, Type of Violence, and Value of Loss, 1992

	Number of Victimizations	No Monetary Value	Less Than $50	$50-$99	$100-$249	$250-$499	$500 or More	Not Known and Not Available
All races†								
Crimes of violence‡	1,548,680	5.3	25.6	12.3	19.4	8.6	12.7	16.2
Completed	1,166,730	2.4*	31.5	13.0	19.2	7.5	13.4	13.1
Attempted	381,940	14.0	7.7*	10.3*	19.9	12.0	10.5	25.6
Robbery	876,800	1.3*	28.3	12.0	19.7	9.1	17.9	11.6
Completed	806,460	0.0*	30.5	12.5	20.2	9.5	17.7	9.7
With injury	334,040	0.0*	22.5	12.3	20.5	11.2*	23.1	10.3*
Without injury	472,420	0.0*	36.1	12.6	19.9	8.4*	13.8	9.2
Attempted	70,340	16.6*	4.0*	6.8*	14.6*	4.5*	20.2*	33.3*
With injury	26,160*	30.8*	0.0*	18.2*	18.9*	0.0*	20.5*	11.8*
Without injury	44,170	8.2*	6.4*	0.0*	12.1*	7.1*	20.1*	46.0*
Assault	639,170	10.3	22.3	13.3	19.8	7.6	4.0*	22.8
Aggravated	319,570	3.5*	17.8	14.9	22.2	7.1*	6.1*	28.3
Simple	319,590	17.0	26.7	11.6*	17.5	8.0*	1.9*	17.3

See notes at end of table.

4.22 Percentage of Victimizations Resulting in Economic Loss, by Race of Victim, Type of Violence, and Value of Loss, 1992 (continued)

	Number of Victimizations	No Monetary Value	Less Than $50	$50-$99	$100-$249	$250-$499	$500 or More	Not Known and Not Available
White								
Crimes of violence‡	1,086,570	5.3	28.9	11.9	19.1	9.1	8.8	17.0
Completed	786,320	2.9*	37.6	13.3	16.7	8.4	7.8	13.2
Attempted	300,240	11.3*	6.1*	8.0*	25.3	11.0*	11.4*	26.7
Robbery	561,860	1.2*	33.2	13.6	19.3*	10.3	10.0	12.4
Completed	513,820	0.0*	35.7	14.9	19.1	10.7	9.3	10.3
With injury	202,250	0.0*	26.8	12.3*	19.3	16.1*	15.2*	10.3*
Without injury	311,560	0.0*	41.5	16.6	18.9	7.2*	5.5*	10.3*
Attempted	48,040	13.8*	5.9*	0.0*	21.4*	6.6*	17.4*	34.9*
With injury	16,340*	18.3*	0.0*	0.0*	30.2*	0.0*	32.7*	18.8*
Without injury	31,690*	11.5*	9.0*	0.0*	16.8*	10.0*	9.6*	43.2*
Assault	497,480	9.2	24.9	10.5	20.0	7.2*	5.1*	23.1
Aggravated	226,370	3.2*	20.7	11.8*	21.0	5.7*	8.6*	29.0
Simple	271,100	14.3*	28.5	9.4*	19.2	8.4*	2.3*	18.1

See notes at end of table.

4.22   Percentage of Victimizations Resulting in Economic Loss, by Race of Victim, Type of Violence, and Value of Loss, 1992 (continued)

	Number of Victimizations	No Monetary Value	Less Than $50	$50-$99	$100-$249	$250-$499	$500 or More	Not Known and Not Available
Black								
Crimes of violence‡	439,480	5.6*	18.0	12.9	20.2	7.9*	22.1	13.2
Completed	357,780	1.5*	19.0	11.6	24.8	6.2*	25.6	11.3
Attempted	81,690	23.9*	13.4*	18.5*	0.0*	15.5*	7.1*	21.5*
Robbery	295,610	1.7*	21.0	8.1*	20.8	7.5*	32.9	8.0*
Completed	273,310	0.0*	22.7	7.1*	22.5	8.1*	33.5	6.2*
With injury	117,240	0.0*	17.7*	13.8*	22.4*	4.2*	37.1	4.7*
Without injury	156,070	0.0*	26.4	2.0*	22.6*	11.0*	30.8	7.3*
Attempted	22,290*	22.7*	0.0*	21.3*	0.0*	0.0*	26.2*	29.8*
With injury	9,810*	51.6*	0.0*	48.4*	0.0*	0.0*	0.0*	0.0*
Without injury	12,470*	0.0*	0.0*	0.0*	0.0*	0.0*	46.7*	53.3*
Assault	138,380	14.2*	10.8*	23.6*	19.8*	9.1*	0.0*	22.4*
Aggravated	93,190	4.3*	10.8*	22.6*	25.3*	10.3*	0.0*	26.7*
Simple	45,190	34.6*	10.9*	25.7*	8.4*	6.7*	0.0*	13.6*

Source: National Crime Victimization Survey, 1992, from: Bureau of Justice Statistics. 1993. *Criminal victimization in the United States, 1992.* Washington, D.C., pp. 94–95, Table 91. [See appendix entry 28]

Note: Table excludes series crimes. Series crime and other crime types are defined in the appendix. Details may not sum to totals due to rounding.

* Estimate is based on 10 or fewer sample cases.

† Includes data on "other" races, not shown separately.

‡ Includes data on rape, not shown separately.

4.23 Percentage of Victimizations in Which Victims Incurred Medical Expenses, by Selected Characteristics of Victim and Type of Violence, 1992

Characteristic	Crimes of Violence† (%)	Robbery (%)	Assault (%)
Race			
All races‡	9.3	11.4	8.4
White	7.9	6.9	7.4
Black	16.1	22.2	13.8
Victim-offender relationship			
Strangers	9.8	11.3	8.6
Nonstrangers	8.6	11.6*	8.2

Source: National Crime Victimization Survey, 1992, from: Bureau of Justice Statistics. 1993. *Criminal victimization in the United States, 1992.* Washington, D.C., p. 89, Table 82. [See appendix entry 28]

Note: Table excludes series crimes. Series crime and other crime types are defined in the appendix.

   * Estimate is based on 10 or fewer sample cases.
   † Includes data on rape, not shown separately.
   ‡ Includes data on "other" races, not shown separately.

4.24   Percentage of Victimizations in Which Injured Victims Incurred Medical Expenses, by Race of Victim, Victim-Offender Relationship, and Type of Violence, 1992

Characteristic	Number of Victimizations	Less Than $50 %	$50-$249 %	$250 or More %	Amount Not Known %
Race					
All races†					
Crimes of violence‡	617,460	7.8	14.7	42.2	35.3
Robbery	139,410	14.0*	15.2*	45.0	25.8*
Assault	443,930	6.5*	14.6	40.5	38.4
White					
Crimes of violence‡	412,760	10.1	14.6	44.8	30.6
Robbery	56,570	23.0*	14.3*	49.5*	13.2*
Assault	322,070	8.9*	14.7	43.1	33.2
Black					
Crimes of violence‡	193,230	3.3*	15.8*	37.0	43.9
Robbery	82,830	7.8*	15.8*	42.0*	34.4*
Assault	110,390	0.0*	15.7	33.3*	51.0
Victim-offender relationship					
Involving strangers					
Crimes of violence‡	389,760	8.7*	14.0	47.0	30.3
Robbery	112,160	7.2*	18.9*	49.9	24.1*
Assault	251,340	10.2*	11.5*	46.7	31.6
Involving nonstrangers					
Crimes of violence‡	227,690	6.3*	15.8*	33.9	43.9
Robbery	27,240*	41.8*	0.0*	25.2*	33.0*
Assault	192,590	1.6*	18.7*	32.5	47.3

Source: National Crime Victimization Survey, 1992, from: Bureau of Justice Statistics. 1993. *Criminal victimization in the United States, 1992*. Washington, D.C., p. 90, Table 84. [See appendix entry 28]

Note: Detail may not add up to total shown because of rounding.   Table excludes series crimes.   Series crime and other crime types are defined in the appendix.

*   Estimate is based on 10 or fewer sample cases.
†   Includes data on "other" races, not shown separately.
‡   Includes data on rape, not shown separately.

4.25 Mean Medical Expense (in 1990 Dollars), by Most Serious Injury in Violent Crime, 1987–1990

Most Serious Injury	Mean Expense ($)	Number Reporting Expenses	Injured, No Cost	Injured, Unknown Cost	No Medical Care Received
Gunshot wound	8,725	34,380	2,000*	33,700	3,480*
Broken bones and internal injury	6,605	27,050	0*	13,410*	2,010*
Internal injury	5,047	110,610	25,430	36,990	38,430
Broken bones	2,084	258,470	47,290	128,330	39,570
Knife wound	2,794	113,650	67,360	70,410	34,930
Knocked unconscious	1,033	79,160	47,320	38,170	36,760
Other injury	810	261,570	190,360	144,670	524,870
Bruises, cuts, scratches	377	653,890	1,209,690	418,690	3,194,000
Rape only	451	25,380	8,750*	23,390	58,350
Injury not specified	256	6,450*	9,650*	8,040*	86,400

Source: National Crime Victimization Survey, 1987–1990, from: Bureau of Justice Statistics. 1992. *National crime surveys: national sample, 1986–1991 [near-term data]*. [Computer files]. (4th ICPSR ed.). Ann Arbor, Mich.: Inter-university Consortium for Political and Social Research. [See appendix entry 28]

Note: Four years of rapes, robberies, and assaults are pooled together in this table to more reliably estimate medical expenses due to injury in violence. To estimate the annual number of incidents in each of the four rightmost columns, divide by four. Respondents are asked to report the total amount of medical expenses, including hospital and doctor bills, medicine, therapy, braces, and other injury-related expenses resulting from the incident, including expense covered by insurance. Table includes series crimes. Series crime and other crime types are defined in the appendix. "Mean expense" is a per-incident cost.

*   Estimate based on 10 or fewer sample cases.

4.26 Percentage of Victimizations in Which Injured Victims Received Hospital Care, by Gender, Race of Victim, Victim-Offender Relationship, and Type of Crime, 1992

Characteristic and Type of Crime	Number of Victimizations	Emergency Room Care	Inpatient Care				
			Total	Under 1 Day	1-3 Days	4 Days or More	Not Available
Gender							
Both genders							
Crimes of violence†	509,600	60.6	39.4	18.0	10.2	10.8	0.4*
Robbery	94,260	62.9	37.1*	11.8*	17.8*	7.5*	0.0*
Assault	382,870	61.1	38.9	18.0	9.3*	11.2	0.5*
Male							
Crimes of violence†	324,860	58.1	41.9	13.4	15.2	13.3	0.0*
Robbery	68,890	49.2*	50.8*	16.2*	24.3*	10.3*	0.0*
Assault	246,260	61.0	39.0	11.0*	13.3*	14.7*	0.0*
Female							
Crimes of violence†	184,740	65.1	34.9	26.1	1.4*	6.2*	1.1*
Robbery	25,360*	100.0*	0.0*	0.0*	0.0*	0.0*	0.0*
Assault	136,600	61.3	38.7	30.4	2.0*	4.8*	1.5*
Race							
White							
Crimes of violence†	330,920	66.5	33.5	19.2	6.3*	7.5*	0.6*
Robbery	45,100	69.6*	30.4*	14.2*	8.2*	8.0*	0.0*
Assault	256,600	68.6	31.4	17.6	6.6*	6.3*	0.8*
Black							
Crimes of violence†	167,220	48.7	51.3	14.5*	18.8*	18.0*	0.0*
Robbery	49,150	56.7*	43.3*	9.6*	26.6*	7.1*	0.0*
Assault	114,800	43.8	56.2	17.1*	16.0*	23.1*	0.0*
Victim-offender relationship							
Involving strangers							
Crimes of violence†	318,060	55.5	44.5	16.8	15.6	12.1*	0.0*
Robbery	83,250	58.0	42.0*	13.4*	20.1*	8.5*	0.0*
Assault	213,460	57.9	42.1	14.3*	15.3*	12.4*	0.0*
Involving nonstrangers							
Crimes of violence†	191,530	69.1	30.9	19.9*	1.4*	8.4*	1.1*
Robbery	11,000*	100.0*	0.0*	0.0*	0.0*	0.0*	0.0*
Assault	169,400	65.1	34.9	22.5*	1.6*	9.5*	1.2*

Source: National Crime Victimization Survey, 1992, from: Bureau of Justice Statistics. 1993. *Criminal victimization in the United States, 1992.* Washington, D.C., p. 91, Table 88. [See appendix entry 28]

Note: Detail may not add up to total shown because of rounding. Table excludes series crimes. Series crime and other crime types are defined in the appendix.

* Estimate is based on 10 or fewer sample cases.

† Includes data on rape, not shown separately.

4.27   Mean Hospital Days, by Most Serious Injury in Violent Crime, 1987–1990

Most Serious Injury	Mean Hospital Days	Overnight Hospital Care Received	No Overnight Hospital Care Received
Gunshot wound	8.2	33,420	45,280
Broken bones and internal injury	4.0	14,640*	35,910
Internal injury	13.1	37,550	197,670
Broken bones	4.1	86,550	473,980
Knife wound	6.3	42,450	270,540
Knocked unconscious	3.2	21,580*	189,450
Other injury	5.8	34,180	1,166,670
Bruises, cuts, scratches	2.2	20,920*	5,631,520
Rape only	3.4	4,060*	115,770
Not specified	2.0	2,010*	112,660

Source: National Crime Victimization Survey, 1987–1990, from: Bureau of Justice Statistics. 1992. *National crime surveys: national sample, 1986–1991 [near-term data].* [Computer files]. 4th ICPSR ed. Ann Arbor, Mich.: Inter-university Consortium for Political and Social Research. [See appendix entry 28]

Note: Four years of rapes, robberies, and assaults are pooled together to more reliably estimate number of days spent in the hospital due to injury in violence. The two rightmost columns include the number of victimizations between 1987 and 1990, inclusive. To estimate the annual number of incidents in these columns, divide by four. "Mean Hospital Days" are based on the column labeled "Overnight Hospital Care Received." Victimizations in this table are counted only once even though some involve multiple injuries. In the case of multiple injuries, the victimization is classified by the most serious injury. Table includes series crimes. Series crime and other crime types are defined in the appendix.

*   Estimate based on 10 or fewer sample cases.

LOSS OF PRODUCTIVITY

4.28   Percentage of Victims Who Lost Time from Work, by Race, 1992

	White	Black
Any time lost	5	6
1-5 days lost	43	67

Source: National Crime Victimization Survey, 1992, from: Klaus, Patsy A. 1994. *The costs of crime to victims.* Washington, D.C.: Bureau of Justice Statistics, p. 2. [See appendix entry 28]

Note: Losing 1–5 days is conditioned on having lost any time. In other words, of those who lost any time from work due to rape, robbery, assault, or personal theft, 43 percent of whites and 67 percent of blacks lost between 1 and 5 days. Table excludes series crimes. Series crime and other crime types are defined in the appendix.

4.29 Mean Work Days Lost, by Most Serious Injury and Type of Violent Crime, 1987–1990

Most serious injury	Pay Loss			No Pay Loss			No Time Lost	Not Applicable
	Mean Workdays	Frequency	Number of Days Unknown	Mean Workdays	Frequency	Number of Days Unknown		
Gunshot wound	55.4	22,620	0*	10.4	9,650*	1,800*	4,440*	39,480
Broken bones and internal injury	20.9	15,850*	2,330*	55.0	5,830*	1,880*	3,540*	16,590*
Internal injury	13.4	70,850	0*	35.5	28,890	0*	34,710	110,030
Broken bones	24.4	139,720	5,990*	14.4	50,220	3,940*	76,100	273,790
Knife wound	19.0	46,480	3,740*	2.8	19,650*	0*	91,780	214,590
Knocked unconscious	15.1	57,750	0*	1.0	2,060*	2,680*	66,460	137,050
Other injury	7.7	110,410	1,980*	9.3	100,470	7,460*	420,230	891,710
Bruises, cuts, scratches	5.8	369,120	9,930*	5.5	184,640	15,930*	2,353,520	4,812,570
Rape only	2.7	7,120*	2,150*	0.0	0*	0*	32,400	106,590
Not specified	2.0	2,060*	1,760*	3.0	2,110*	0*	16,420*	76,280

Source: National Crime Victimization Survey, 1987–1990, from: Bureau of Justice Statistics. 1992. *National crime surveys: national sample, 1986–1991 [near-term data].* [Computer files]. 4th ICPSR ed. Ann Arbor, Mich.: Inter-university Consortium for Political and Social Research. [See appendix entry 28]

Note: Four years of rapes, robberies, and assaults are pooled together to more reliably estimate number of days lost from work due to injury from victimization. To estimate the annual number of incidents in all but the "Mean Workdays" columns, divide by four. Victimizations in this table are counted only once even though some involve multiple injuries. In the case of multiple injuries, the victimization is classified by the most serious injury. "Pay Loss" indicates days lost from work that were not covered by vacation, sick time, or other paid leave; i.e., that involved direct loss of pay to the victim. The "Not Applicable" category includes victimizations of persons either not injured or not employed at the time of the incident. Table includes series crimes. Series crime and other crime types are defined in the appendix.

*   Estimate based on 10 or fewer sample cases.

4.30 Mean Wages Lost (in 1990 Dollars), by Most Serious Injury, 1987–1990

Most Serious Injury	Mean Pay Lost ($)	Pay Lost, Amount Known	No Pay Lost	Pay Lost, Amount Unknown	Not Injured and/or Not Employed
Gunshot wound	2,289	18,620*	11,450*	3,990*	50,940
Broken bones and internal injury	1,315	10,160*	7,700*	8,010*	24,290
Internal injury	642	63,510	28,890	7,340*	140,610
Broken bones	748	118,900	54,160	26,810	327,950
Knife wound	749	41,960	19,650*	8,260*	236,130
Knocked unconscious	866	57,750	4,740*	0*	143,660
Other injury	402	99,920	107,920	12,460*	1,009,090
Bruises, cuts, scratches	255	344,320	200,570	34,730	5,097,210
Rape only	70	4,440*	0*	4,830*	106,590
Not specified	2	2,060*	2,110*	30,100	78,390

Source: National Crime Victimization Survey, 1987–1990, from: Bureau of Justice Statistics. 1992. *National crime surveys: national sample, 1986–1991 [near-term data].* [Computer files]. Ann Arbor, Mich.: Inter-university Consortium for Political and Social Research. [See appendix entry 28]

Note: Four years of rapes, robberies, and assaults are pooled together to more reliably estimate mean wages lost due to injury from victimization. To estimate the annual number of incidents in the four rightmost columns, divide by four. Victimizations in this table are counted only once even though some involve multiple injuries. In the case of multiple injuries, the victimization is classified by the most serious injury. Table includes series crimes. Series crime and other crime types are defined in the appendix.

* Estimate based on 10 or fewer sample cases.

PREMATURE MORTALITY

4.31 Years of Potential Life Lost Before Age 65 from Homicide and Legal Intervention (Per 100,000 Population), by Gender and Race, Selected Years: 1970, 1980, 1984–1992 (Annual)

Years	Male		Female	
	White	Black	White	Black
1970	201.9	2,234.6	69.7	460.3
1980	365.4	2,274.9	109.3	492.0
1984	278.6	1,664.0	100.1	421.3
1985	275.0	1,689.1	98.1	399.8
1986	292.6	1,956.0	102.7	447.7
1987	265.4	1,924.0	100.3	467.4
1988	267.8	2,148.2	99.7	495.8
1989	279.9	2,287.7	97.6	481.4
1990	313.3	2,580.7	97.5	509.8
1991	327.0	2,712.3	101.7	534.9
1992	321.6	2,567.5	96.3	498.8

Source: National Vital Statistics System data, selected data years 1970–1992, from: National Center for Health Statistics. 1995. *Health, United States, 1994.* Hyattsville, Md.: Public Health Service, pp. 99–100. [See appendix entry 34]

Note: "Years of Potential Life Lost" (YPLL) is a measure of premature mortality that is calculated over the age range from birth to 65 years using seven age groups (under 1, 1–14, 15–24, 25–34, 35–44, 45–54, and 55–64 years). The number of deaths for each age group is multiplied by the years of life lost, calculated as the difference between 65 years and the midpoint of the age group. YPLL is derived by summing years of life lost over all age groups and dividing by the annual population estimate for the race/gender group multiplied by 100,000. Annual population values are intercensal estimates computed by the U.S. Bureau of the Census, Population Estimates Branch. For more information, see Centers for Disease Control. 1986. *Mortality and morbidity weekly report* 35: (December 19): Supp. 2S. Note also that YPLL is a measure only of excess mortality for a single cause of death and does not account for competing risks or causes of death.

4.32 Life Expectancy at Birth (in Years) of Homicide Victims and the General Population, by Gender and Race, 1992

Gender and Race	General Population	Homicide Victims
Male	72.1	34.0
White	73.0	36.3
Black	64.7	32.9
Other races	78.8	38.4
Female	79.1	38.3
White	79.7	40.6
Black	74.0	36.0
Other races	85.5	51.5
All whites	76.4	37.3
All blacks	69.4	33.4
All other races	82.1	42.2
All races and genders	75.7	34.8

Source: National Vital Statistics Mortality data, 1992, from: National Center for Health Statistics. 1995. *Compressed mortality file, 1992.* [Computer files]. Accessed via CDC Wonder. Atlanta, Ga.: Centers for Disease Control and Prevention. [See appendix entry 34]

Note: Life expectancy is the average length of life (in years) that would be expected for persons born in 1992 if death rates for specific age-race-gender groups were to remain at their 1992 levels. Calculations based on abridged life tables using the following age intervals: under 1, 1–4, 5–9, 10–14, 15–19, 20–24, 25–29, 30–44, 45–54, 55–64, 65–74, 75–84, 85 and over. Computed using Survival 3.0 software for DOS by David P. Smith, School of Public Health, University of Texas Health Science Center, Houston, Texas 77225. For more information about life expectancy and life table construction, generally, see Namboodiri, Krishnan. 1991. *Demographic analysis: a stochastic approach.* San Diego, Calif.: Academic Press.

4.33   Years of Potential Gain in Lifetime if Major Causes of Death Were Eliminated, Adjusted for Differential Life Expectancies, by Gender and Race, 1992

Cause of Death	Both Sexes				Male				Female			
	White	Black	Other	All	White	Black	Other	All	White	Black	Other	All
Homicide (E960–E978)	**0.18**	**1.05**	**0.20**	**0.30**	**0.26**	**1.71**	**0.31**	**0.47**	**0.09**	**0.37**	**0.10**	**0.13**
Malignant neoplasms (140–208)	3.00	3.71	1.99	3.05	3.29	4.32	2.27	3.36	2.75	3.18	1.74	2.77
Diabetes mellitus (250)	0.24	0.53	0.24	0.27	0.25	0.48	0.24	0.27	0.23	0.58	0.24	0.26
Diseases of the heart (390–398, 402, 404–429)	2.78	3.99	1.81	2.89	3.64	4.70	2.39	3.73	1.92	3.33	1.28	2.07
Cerebrovascular (430–438)	0.41	0.82	0.42	0.45	0.44	0.92	0.49	0.49	0.38	0.74	0.37	0.42
Pneumonia and influenza (480–487)	0.22	0.36	0.21	0.24	0.27	0.48	0.27	0.29	0.18	0.26	0.15	0.19
Chronic obstructive pulmonary diseases (490–496)	0.44	0.35	0.19	0.42	0.52	0.46	0.26	0.51	0.37	0.26	0.13	0.36
HIV (042*–044*)	0.30	1.03	0.08	0.38	0.53	1.63	0.14	0.64	0.05	0.43	0.02	0.10
Accidents and adverse effects (E810–E949)	0.82	0.99	0.73	0.84	1.15	1.42	0.99	1.17	0.47	0.56	0.47	0.49
Suicide (E950–E959)	0.33	0.18	0.21	0.31	0.52	0.30	0.30	0.49	0.14	0.06	0.11	0.13
All other causes	2.20	4.22	1.83	2.47	2.55	4.75	2.07	2.82	1.86	3.69	1.61	2.11
Residual	0.16	0.47	0.06	0.18	0.33	0.98	0.11	0.36	0.08	0.22	0.03	0.09
Total potential gain	10.91	17.23	7.91	11.61	13.40	21.16	9.72	14.24	8.42	13.46	6.22	9.00
Life expectancy to age 85 net of potential gain	74.09	67.77	77.09	73.39	71.60	63.84	75.28	70.76	76.54	71.54	78.78	76.00

Source: National Vital Statistics Mortality data, 1992, from: National Center for Health Statistics. 1995. *Compressed mortality file, 1992.* [Computer files]. Accessed via CDC Wonder. Atlanta, Ga.: Centers for Disease Control and Prevention. [See appendix entry 34]

Note: Life expectancy, as defined here, is the average length of life (in years) that would be expected for persons born in 1992 if death rates for specific age-race-gender groups were to remain at their 1992 levels. Potential gain in life expectancy is the number of years added to life expectancy if the specified cause of death or group of causes could be eliminated. Numbers in parentheses are ICD-9-CM cause of death codes. Estimates based on abridged life tables using the following age intervals: under 1, 1–4, 5–9, 10–14, 15–19, 20–24, 25–29, 30–44, 45–54, 55–64, 65–74, and 75–84. Differential life expectancies across race/gender groups standardized to the interval of 0–85 years for purposes of comparison and to limit measurement error associated with an open-ended age interval. Computed using Survival 3.0 software for DOS by David P. Smith, School of Public Health, University of Texas Health Science Center, Houston, Texas 77225.

*   HIV not a part of ICD-9. Added by the United States in 1987.

4.34 Lifetime Chances of Becoming a Homicide Victim, Given All Other Causes of Death, by Gender and Race, 1992

Gender and Race	Lifetime Chance
Male	1 in 99
White	1 in 170
Black	1 in 26
Other races	1 in 152
Female	1 in 355
White	1 in 503
Black	1 in 125
Other races	1 in 407
All whites	1 in 253
All blacks	1 in 44
All other races	1 in 222
All races and genders	1 in 154

Source: National Vital Statistics Mortality data, 1992, from: National Center for Health Statistics. 1995. *Compressed mortality file, 1992.* [Computer files]. Accessed via CDC Wonder. Atlanta, Ga.: Centers for Disease Control and Prevention. [See appendix entry 34]

Note: "Lifetime chance" is defined as 1 divided by the conditional probability of dying from homicide between ages 0 and 85, given survival probabilities for all other causes of death.

4.35 Cumulative Odds of Being a Homicide Victim Given All Other Causes of Death, by Age, Race, and Gender, 1992

By Age	Both Sexes				All Races		Male			Female		
	All	White	Black	Other	Females	Males	White	Black	Other	White	Black	Other
1	12,500	16,667	5,263	20,000	14,286	11,111	16,667	4,762	20,000	20,000	5,882	25,000
5	5,263	7,692	2,041	6,250	5,882	4,762	6,667	1,961	5,000	9,091	2,174	8,333
10	4,348	6,250	1,724	4,348	4,762	4,000	5,882	1,613	3,571	7,143	1,818	5,556
15	2,857	4,348	1,064	2,941	3,448	2,439	3,704	926	2,174	5,263	1,250	4,762
20	769	1,408	225	1,149	1,818	498	980	137	730	2,703	671	2,857
25	397	769	107	645	1,099	248	508	63	412	1,695	373	1,639
30	298	562	79	500	794	186	369	47	319	1,250	255	1,205
45	202	356	55	330	508	127	235	32	214	769	166	725
55	177	302	49	275	439	112	200	29	179	645	148	595
65	165	276	47	251	405	105	183	28	165	588	139	515
75	158	262	45	229	377	101	175	27	153	541	132	444
85	154	253	44	222	355	99	170	26	152	503	125	407

Source: National Vital Statistics Mortality data, 1992, from: National Center for Health Statistics. 1995. *Compressed mortality file, 1992.* [Computer files]. Accessed via CDC Wonder. Atlanta, Ga.: Centers for Disease Control and Prevention. [See appendix entry 34]

Note: Numbers in the table are interpreted as odds of becoming a homicide victim by the time the specified age is reached. For example, in the last row of the table, the chance that a person of any sex or race will become a homicide victim by the time he or she reaches age 85 is 1 in 154 persons, assuming mortality patterns are identical to those in 1992. "Cumulative odds" is calculated as 1 divided by the conditional cumulative probability of dying from homicide by the time an individual reaches a specified age interval, given survival probabilities for all other causes of death. Computed using Survival 3.0 software for DOS by David P. Smith, School of Public Health, University of Texas Health Science Center, Houston, Texas 77225.

4.36 Differences in Average Life Expectancy (in Years) Between Whites and Blacks and Between Females and Males, by Cause of Death, 1992

Cause of Death	White – Black			Other – Black			White – Other			Female – Male			
	Male	Female	Both Sexes	Male	Female	Both Sexes	Male	Female	Both Sexes	White	Black	Other	All Races
Homicide (E960–E978)	**1.30**	**0.26**	**0.80**	**1.32**	**0.26**	**0.81**	**0.03**	**0.01**	**0.02**	**0.17**	**1.21**	**0.20**	**0.32**
Malignant neoplasms (140–208)	1.13	0.59	0.85	2.10	1.50	1.79	-0.99	-0.98	-0.98	0.66	1.17	0.56	0.70
Diabetes mellitus (250)	0.18	0.29	0.24	0.23	0.32	0.28	-0.03	-0.00	-0.01	0.04	0.00	0.02	0.03
Diseases of the heart (390–398, 402, 404–429)	1.27	1.35	1.26	2.40	1.99	2.17	-1.20	-0.63	-0.93	1.64	1.51	1.08	1.60
Cerebrovascular (430–438)	0.38	0.32	0.35	0.42	0.37	0.39	0.01	-0.02	-0.01	0.08	0.21	0.13	0.10
Pneumonia and influenza (480–487)	0.19	0.09	0.14	0.22	0.11	0.16	-0.02	-0.03	-0.02	0.08	0.18	0.11	0.09
Chronic obstructive pulmonary diseases (490–496)	0.03	-0.05	-0.01	0.19	0.13	0.16	-0.20	-0.21	-0.21	0.13	0.14	0.12	0.14
Accidents and adverse effects (E810–E949)	0.32	0.11	0.20	0.51	0.13	0.32	-0.19	-0.02	-0.12	0.64	0.77	0.51	0.65
Suicide (E950–E959)	-0.13	-0.06	-0.11	0.04	-0.04	-0.00	-0.21	-0.03	-0.12	0.35	0.21	0.18	0.33
HIV (042*–044*)	1.00	0.36	0.67	1.38	0.39	0.89	-0.36	-0.03	-0.20	0.44	1.07	0.12	0.50
All other causes	2.10	1.78	1.93	2.66	2.08	2.38	-0.53	-0.28	-0.41	0.74	1.23	0.49	0.78
Residual (distribution among causes)	-0.03	-0.01	-0.01	-0.15	-0.03	-0.07	0.01	0.00	0.00	-0.02	-0.06	-0.01	-0.02
Total difference (in years)	7.77	5.03	6.33	11.45	7.24	9.33	-3.68	-2.21	-3.00	4.97	7.71	3.50	5.24

Source: National Vital Statistics Mortality data, 1992, from: National Center for Health Statistics. 1995. *Compressed mortality file, 1992.* [Computer files]. Accessed via CDC Wonder. Atlanta, Ga.: Centers for Disease Control and Prevention. [See appendix entry 34]

Note: Life expectancy, as defined here, is the average length of life (in years) that would be expected for persons born in 1992 if death rates for specific age-race-gender groups were to remain at their 1992 levels. This table presents differences in life expectancies between pairs of race-gender groups for specific causes of death, given competing causes. In the first column, for example, the life expectancy of white males exceeds that of black males by a total of 7.77 years; of that, homicide contributes 1.3 years to the difference. Negative differences indicate higher black than white, higher black than other, higher other than white, or higher male than female, life expectancy. Life expectancy to age 85 is 71.6 years for white males, 76.6 for white females, 63.8 for black males, 71.5 for black females, 75.3 for males of other races, and 78.8 for females of other races. Life expectancy to age 85 is 74.1 for whites of both sexes, 67.8 for blacks of both sexes, 76.0 for females of all races, and 70.8 for males of all races. Estimates are based on abridged life tables using the following age intervals: under 1, 1–4, 5–9, 10–14, 15–19, 20–24, 25–29, 30–44, 45–54, 55–64, 65–74, and 75–84. Differential life expectancies across race/gender groups standardized to the interval of 0–85 years for purposes of comparison and to limit measurement error associated with an open-ended age interval. Numbers in parentheses are ICD-9-CM cause of death codes. Tables computed using Survival 3.0 software for DOS by David P. Smith, School of Public Health, University of Texas Health Science Center, Houston, Texas 77225. For more information on methodology and interpretation, see Verna M. Keith and David P. Smith, (1988), The current differential in black and white life expectancy, *Demography* 25(4): 625–632.

* HIV not a part of ICD-9. Added by the United States in 1987.

4.37   Ten Leading Causes of Death in Rank Order, by Age Group, 1992

Age Groups

Rank	<1	1-4	5-9	10-14	15-24	25-34	35-44	45-54	55-64	65+	Total
1	Congenital Anomalies 7,449	Unintentional Injuries 2,467	Unintentional Injuries 1,628	Unintentional Injuries 1,760	Unintentional Injuries 13,662	Unintentional Injuries 13,798	Malignant Neoplasms 16,882	Malignant Neoplasms 41,206	Malignant Neoplasms 91,609	Heart Disease 595,313	Heart Disease 717,706
2	SIDS 4,891	Congenital Anomalies 856	Malignant Neoplasms 557	Malignant Neoplasms 548	Homicide 8,019	HIV 10,426	HIV 14,203	Heart Disease 31,413	Heart Disease 72,516	Malignant Neoplasms 362,060	Malignant Neoplasms 520,578
3	Short Gestation 4,035	Malignant Neoplasms 479	Congenital Anomalies 245	Homicide 441	Suicide 4,693	Homicide 7,343	Heart Disease 12,698	Unintentional Injuries 7,485	Bronchitis Emphysema Asthma 10,098	Cerebro-vascular 125,392	Cerebro-vascular 143,769
4	Respiratory Distress Synd. 2,063	Homicide 430	Homicide 146	Suicide 304	Malignant Neoplasms 1,809	Suicide 6,172	Unintentional Injuries 12,010	HIV 5,575	Cerebro-vascular 9,709	Bronchitis Emphysema Asthma 78,182	Bronchitis Emphysema Asthma 91,938
5	Maternal Complications 1,461	Heart Disease 286	Heart Disease 130	Congenital Anomalies 203	Heart Disease 968	Malignant Neoplasms 5,303	Suicide 6,009	Cerebro-vascular 4,791	Diabetes 7,109	Pneumonia & Influenza 67,489	Unintentional Injuries 86,777
6	Placenta Cord Membranes 993	Pneumonia & Influenza 188	HIV 72	Heart Disease 154	HIV 578	Heart Disease 3,423	Homicide 4,460	Liver Disease 4,569	Unintentional Injuries 6,397	Diabetes 37,328	Pneumonia & Influenza 75,719
7	Perinatal Infections 901	HIV 161	Benign Neoplasms 53	Bronchitis Emphysema Asthma 62	Congenital Anomalies 450	Cerebro-vascular 796	Liver Disease 3,608	Suicide 4,018	Liver Disease 5,780	Unintentional Injuries 26,633	Diabetes 50,067
8	Unintentional Injuries 819	Perinatal Period 113	Pneumonia & Influenza 53	Pneumonia & Influenza 51	Pneumonia & Influenza 229	Liver Disease 765	Cerebro-vascular 2,591	Diabetes 3,203	Pneumonia & Influenza 3,453	Nephritis 18,711	HIV 33,566
9	Intrauterine Hypoxia 613	Septicemia 77	Bronchitis Emphysema Asthma 38	Benign Neoplasms 44	Cerebro-vascular 197	Diabetes 658	Diabetes 1,600	Bronchitis Emphysema Asthma 2,274	Suicide 3,105	Athero-sclerosis 15,995	Suicide 30,484
10	Pneumonia & Influenza 600	Anemias 65	Anemias 30	Cerebro-vascular 37	Bronchitis Emphysema Asthma 189	Pneumonia & Influenza 654	Pneumonia & Influenza 1,350	Homicide 2,046	HIV 1,785	Septicemia 15,884	Homicide 25,488

Source: National Vital Statistics Mortality data, 1992 from: National Center for Injury Prevention and Control, Centers for Disease Control and Prevention. 1995. Unpublished. [See appendix entry 34]

Note: Numbers shown in boxes are the total number of deaths that occurred in 1992 within the specified age group. For persons aged 15–24 years, homicide was the nation's second leading cause of death in 1992; across all ages, it was the tenth leading cause of death.

Chapter 5
Opinions About Violence

The impact of violence is not limited to its direct effects on victims and offenders. The whole community reacts to violence, not only because it demands a moral stance, but also because it raises anxiety about personal security. Violence leads people who have never personally experienced it to alter their perceptions of their social environment, to make choices about appropriate social policy, and to change their own behavior.

This chapter uses data drawn from national surveys to document reactions of Americans to violence. We have organized the chapter around four general questions:

1. When and under what conditions is violent behavior justified?
2. What are the effects of violence on beliefs and behavior?
3. What do people think communities and governments should do about violence?
4. What are the causes of violence?

We have selected items from many different surveys that we think address these general questions. Most of the surveys are recent, but in a few cases trend data are available to show how reactions have changed over time. Where the data are available, the distribution of responses are presented for major demographic groups.

The surveys, though diverse in terms of methodological detail, all use modern probability sampling designs to produce statistical estimates for the nation as a whole. As with all estimates based on samples, the results are subject to sampling errors. In most cases, these errors are quite small relative to the differences between demographic groups or responses to different questions. Sampling error, however, is only one source of potential error in surveys. The appendix provides more detailed information about the methods used in the surveys.

WHEN IS VIOLENCE JUSTIFIED?

5.1   "Are there any situations that you can imagine in which you would approve of a man punching an adult male stranger?" Percentages by Race and Gender, 1994

	White		Black	
	Male	Female	Male	Female
Generally				
Yes	64.7	66.0	58.8	41.3
No	32.4	30.0	35.3	44.0
Not sure	2.9	4.0	5.9	14.7
"If the stranger was drunk and bumped into the man and his wife on the street?"				
Yes	5.3	5.7	2.9	5.3
No	92.0	92.1	97.1	94.7
Not sure	2.7	2.2	0.0	0.0
"If the stranger had hit the man's child after the child accidentally damaged the stranger's car?"				
Yes	63.4	56.1	44.1	57.3
No	35.6	42.2	55.9	42.7
Not sure	1.1	1.7	0.0	0.0
"If the stranger was beating up a woman and the man saw it?"				
Yes	84.5	83.9	58.8	72.0
No	14.4	13.9	29.4	18.7
Not sure	1.1	2.2	11.8	9.3
"If the stranger broke into the man's house?"				
Yes	84.2	83.4	79.4	90.7
No	15.8	16.1	20.6	9.3
Not sure	0.0	0.5	0.0	0.0

Source: Davis, James A., and Tom W. Smith. 1994. *General social surveys, 1972–1994*. [Computer file]. NORC ed. Chicago, Ill.: National Opinion Research Center [producer]; Storrs, Conn.: Roper Center for Public Opinion Research [distributor]. [See appendix entry 18]

5.2   "Are there any situations you can imagine in which you would approve of a policeman striking an adult male citizen?" Percentages by Race and Gender, 1994

	White		Black	
	Male	Female	Male	Female
Generally				
Yes	83.3	69.4	66.3	32.7
No	15.5	27.5	27.5	59.4
Not sure	1.3	3.1	6.2	8.0
If he "said vulgar and obscene things to the policeman?"				
Yes	11.5	7.0	7.3	3.2
No	87.7	92.4	91.2	96.0
Not sure	0.8	0.6	1.6	0.8
If he "was attempting to escape from custody?"				
Yes	84.3	73.2	62.7	53.4
No	13.9	22.1	28.0	41.4
Not sure	1.8	4.7	9.3	5.2

Source: Davis, James A., and Tom W. Smith. 1994. *General social surveys, 1972–1994.* [Computer file]. NORC ed. Chicago, Ill.: National Opinion Research Center [producer]; Storrs, Conn.: Roper Center for Public Opinion Research [distributor]. [See appendix entry 18]

5.3   "Do you strongly agree, agree, disagree, or strongly disagree that it is sometimes necessary to discipline a child with a good, hard spanking?" Percentages, by Race and Gender, 1994

	White		Black	
	Male	Female	Male	Female
Strongly agree	27.9	20.8	41.6	42.0
Agree	48.0	45.6	42.7	44.5
Disagree	16.9	21.2	10.8	11.7
Strongly disagree	5.8	10.8	2.7	1.8
Don't know	0.7	1.5	1.1	0.0

Source: Davis, James A., and Tom W. Smith. 1994. *General social surveys, 1972–1994.* [Computer file]. NORC ed. Chicago, Ill.: National Opinion Research Center [producer]; Storrs, Conn.: Roper Center for Public Opinion Research [distributor]. [See appendix entry 18]

5.4   "Do you strongly agree, agree, disagree, or strongly disagree that it is sometimes necessary to discipline a child with a good, hard spanking?" Percentages by Race, 1986–1994

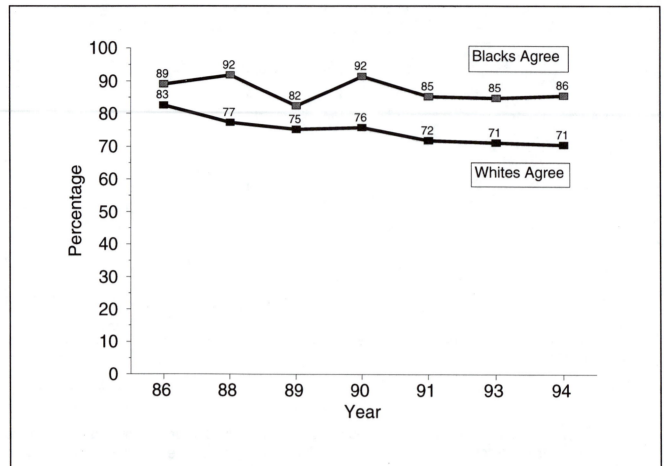

Source: Davis, James A., and Tom W. Smith. 1994. *General social surveys, 1972–1994.* [Computer file]. NORC ed. Chicago, Ill.: National Opinion Research Center [producer]; Storrs, Conn.: Roper Center for Public Opinion Research [distributor]. [See appendix entry 18]

5.5   "Do you strongly agree, agree, disagree, or strongly disagree that it is sometimes necessary to discipline a child with a good, hard spanking?" Percentages by Gender, 1986–1994

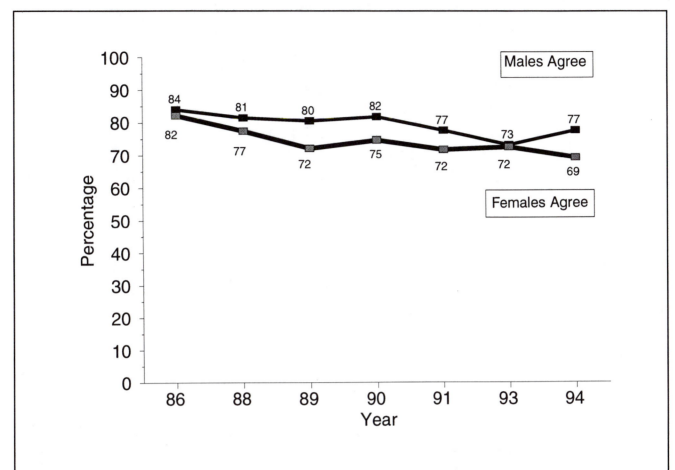

Source: Davis, James A., and Tom W. Smith. 1994. *General social surveys, 1972–1994.* [Computer file]. NORC ed. Chicago, Ill.: National Opinion Research Center [producer]; Storrs, Conn.: Roper Center for Public Opinion Research [distributor]. [See appendix entry 18]

5.6   "There has been a lot of talk about crime increasing in this country and the fears people have about police not being around to protect them when they are needed. Do you think the situation has reached the point where it is necessary for citizens to take the law into their own hands in order to protect themselves from attack in any way they can, or do you think it is wrong for people to take the law into their own hands under such circumstances?" Percentages by Demographic Characteristics, 1992

Characteristic	Yes, Necessary to Take Law into Own Hands	No, Wrong to Take Law into Own Hands	Don't Know
Total	26	66	8
Gender			
Male	30	62	8
Female	22	71	8
Age			
18 to 29	26	65	9
30 to 44	30	63	7
45 to 59	26	67	7
60 and older	19	72	9
Region			
Northeast	17	77	6
Midwest	25	66	9
South	31	60	9
West	27	66	7
Education			
College graduate	23	71	6
Some college	25	69	6
High school graduate	27	65	8
Less than high school graduate	26	61	12
Politics			
Democrat	25	68	6
Republican	23	69	7
Income			
$50,000 and over	23	71	6
$30,000 to $49,000	29	66	5
$15,000 to $29,000	21	70	9
Under $15,000	31	62	7
Occupation			
Executive/professional	27	66	7
White collar	25	67	8
Blue collar	29	62	9
Homemaker	19	75	6

Source: Roper Organization data from: Maguire, Kathleen, Ann L. Pastore, and Timothy J. Flanagan, eds. 1993. *Sourcebook of criminal justice statistics, 1992.* Washington, D.C.: Bureau of Justice Statistics, p. 194, Table 2.42. Used with permission. [See appendix entry 42]

Note: Totals may not add up to 100 because of rounding.

5.7 Approval of a Wife Slapping Her Husband, But Not the Reverse, Percentages by Gender and Age, 1994

Age	Male	Female
18 - 30	15	27
31 - 50	16	7
51 and over	11	17
Total	14	13

Source: Moore, David W. 1994. Approval of husband slapping wife continues to decline. *The Gallup Monthly Poll* 341 (February): p. 2. Used with permission. [See appendix entry 16]

Note: The questions for these items are: "Are there any situations that you can imagine in which you would approve of a husband slapping his wife's face?" and "Are there any situations that you can imagine in which you would approve of a wife slapping her husband's face?" The approval for males and females of all ages is 14 percent.

5.8 "Now I would like to ask you a few questions about the outbreak of violence in Los Angeles last night [April 29, 1992] after the verdict [of not guilty] in the Rodney King case was announced [where four Los Angles police officers were videotaped beating Rodney king, a black man]. How much of that violence do you feel was justified by the anger that blacks in Los Angeles felt over the verdict in the trial? Was the violence completely justified, somewhat justified, somewhat unjustified, or completely unjustified?" Percentages by Race, 1992

	Total	Whites	Blacks
Completely justified	5	4	15
Somewhat justified	14	14	14
Somewhat unjustified	14	14	20
Completely unjustified	60	63	42
Not sure	7	5	9

Source: Time/CNN. 1992. *Latest Time/CNN poll*, Yankelovich, Clancy, Shulman, p. 10. Used with permission. [See appendix entry 55]

Note: The sample included an oversample of blacks; however the results in the "Total" column are weighted so that the number of blacks is representative of the proportion in the general population.

5.9   "Some jurors say they found the police officers not guilty because circumstances not seen on the videotape justified the use of that amount of force against Rodney King. Do you think there are any circumstances in which police officers should be allowed to use the amount of force the videotape [of the four Los Angeles police officers beating Rodney King, a black man] shows, or would you consider that amount of force to be excessive under any circumstances?" Percentages by Race, 1992

	Total	Whites	Blacks
Justified in some circumstances	15	16	4
Excessive under any circumstances	74	72	92
Not sure	11	12	4

Source: Time/CNN. 1992. *Latest Time/CNN poll*, Yankelovich, Clancy, Shulman, p. 2. Used with permission. [See appendix entry 55]

Note: The sample included an oversample of blacks; however the results in the "Total" column are weighted so that the number of blacks is representative of the proportion in the general population.

WHAT ARE THE EFFECTS OF VIOLENCE ON BELIEFS AND BEHAVIOR?

Precautions Taken to Limit Victimization

5.10   "Did you stay away from any of the following places because you thought someone might attack or harm you at school?" Percentage of Students Older Than 12 Years, 1989

Place Avoided	Percentage
Shortcut	1.5
Inside school	
Entrance	1.3
Hallways	2.1
Cafeteria	1.6
Rest room	2.7
Other places	1.1
Outside school	
Parking lot	1.3
Other places	1.7

Source: National Crime Victimization Survey, 1989, from: Bastian, Lisa D., and Bruce M. Taylor. 1991. *School crime: A national crime victimization survey report.* Washington D.C.: Bureau of Justice Statistics, p. 9, Table 20. [See appendix entry 28]

Note: Table excludes series crimes. Series crime and other crime types are defined in the appendix.

5.11   Percentage of Students Older Than 12 Avoiding Places at School Out of Fear, by Violent Victimization During Previous 6 Months, 1989

Type of Victimization at School	Percentage Avoiding Places
Any victimization	
Yes	12
No	5
Any violent victimization	
Yes	25
No	5

Source: National Crime Victimization Survey, 1989, from: Bastian, Lisa D., and Bruce M. Taylor. 1991. *School crime: A national crime victimization survey report.* Washington D.C.: Bureau of Justice Statistics, p. 9, Table 19. [See appendix entry 28]

Note: Table excludes series crimes. Series crime and other crime types are defined in the appendix.

5.12   Reported Behavior Changes Because of Fear of Crime, Percentages by Race, 1991

	Yes	No	Not Sure
Limit the places or times that you go shopping	32	68	0
White	30	70	0
Black	44	56	0
Hispanic	37	61	1
Limit the places or times that you work	22	76	2
White	19	78	2
Black	33	65	3
Hispanic	37	63	0
Limit the places you will go by yourself	60	40	1
White	60	40	1
Black	63	37	0
Hispanic	64	36	0
Purchase a weapon for self-protection	18	82	0
White	16	84	0
Black	27	72	1
Hispanic	25	75	0
Install a home security system	25	75	1
White	22	77	1
Black	34	66	0
Hispanic	41	58	2

Source: National Victim Center data from: Maguire, Kathleen, Ann L. Pastore, and Timothy J. Flanagan, eds. 1993. *Sourcebook of criminal justice statistics, 1992.* Washington, D.C.: Bureau of Justice Statistics, p. 192, Table 2.37. Used with permission. [See appendix entry 2]

Note: "Has fear of crime caused you to . . . limit the places or times that you go shopping, limit the places or times that you work, limit the places that you will go by yourself, purchase a weapon for self-protection, install a home security system?" Percentages calculated within rows and may not add up to 100 because of rounding.

5.13 "I'm going to read some things people do because of their concern over crime. Please tell me which, if any, of these things you, yourself, do or have done." Percentages, 1981, 1993

Precautions	1981	1993
Had special locks installed	13	43
Walk only with others in your neighborhood at night	20	40
Keep a dog for protection	20	38
Bought a gun for protection of yourself or your home	16	30
Carry a weapon or other instrument for defense	NA	27
Had a burglar alarm installed	5	18
Carry a whistle on yourself or in your car	5	10

Source: McAnney, Leslie. 1993. The Gallup Poll on crime. *The Gallup Poll Monthly* 339 (December):22. Used with permission. [See appendix entry 13]

Note: "NA" stands for not asked.

5.14 "I'm going to read some things people do because of their concern over crime. Please tell me which, if any, of these things you, yourself, do or have done." Percentages by Demographic Characteristics, 1993

Characteristic	Special Locks		Not Walk Alone		Dog for Protection		Bought a Gun		Carry a Weapon		Burglar Alarm		Carry Whistle	
	Yes	No	Yes	No	Yes	No	Yes	No	Yes	No	Yes	No	Yes	No
Total	43	57	40	57	38	62	30	69	27	72	18	82	10	90
Gender														
Male	40	60	23	75	35	65	36	63	31	68	20	80	4	96
Female	46	54	56	40	41	59	24	75	25	75	16	84	16	84
Age														
18 - 29	39	62	50	50	39	61	32	68	30	70	18	82	10	90
30 - 49	46	54	41	57	45	55	33	67	33	67	20	80	10	90
50 - 64	46	53	40	58	36	63	31	67	23	76	18	81	11	89
65 and older	39	61	28	63	21	79	20	79	16	83	11	89	10	90
Region														
East	36	64	40	57	39	61	18	82	23	76	17	83	8	92
Midwest	39	61	35	61	29	71	23	76	18	81	14	85	10	90
South	50	50	43	54	40	60	40	59	33	67	21	78	10	90
West	45	55	42	55	44	56	38	62	37	63	18	82	14	86
Community														
Urban	53	47	48	49	35	65	25	74	29	71	26	74	12	88
Suburban	44	56	36	60	34	66	30	69	28	71	19	80	13	87
Rural	31	69	37	61	44	56	35	65	25	75	7	93	5	95
Race														
White	42	58	40	57	39	61	30	69	27	72	16	83	10	90
Black*	48	52	41	55	27	73	31	68	29	70	25	75	12	88
Education														
College postgrad.	54	45	34	64	33	66	26	73	29	71	32	68	16	83
College graduate	56	44	39	58	35	65	24	75	25	75	30	69	16	84
College incomplete	42	58	40	59	34	66	26	73	35	65	20	80	13	87
No college	39	61	41	55	41	59	33	66	25	74	12	88	7	93
Politics														
Republican	45	55	44	53	39	61	33	66	32	68	20	79	10	90
Democrat	42	58	42	54	34	66	27	73	21	79	16	83	11	89
Independent	42	58	37	61	40	60	31	68	30	69	17	83	10	90
Ideology														
Liberal	42	58	39	57	30	70	21	79	18	82	17	83	9	91
Moderate	44	56	41	57	37	63	27	72	26	73	15	84	10	90
Conservative	42	58	42	55	41	59	34	66	32	68	20	80	11	89
Fear of Crime														
Most fearful	61	36	68	28	43	57	37	63	41	59	22	78	15	85
All others	37	64	31	67	36	64	27	72	23	76	16	83	9	91
Income														
$50,000 and over	50	50	35	63	36	64	27	72	29	70	27	73	13	87
$30,000 - $49,999	44	56	33	67	37	63	31	69	29	71	17	83	11	89
$20,000 - $29,000	38	62	48	51	43	57	32	67	25	74	14	86	8	92
Under $20,000	41	59	46	47	37	63	31	69	27	73	14	86	10	90

Source: McAnney, Leslie. 1993. The Gallup Poll on crime. *The Gallup Poll Monthly* 339 (December):25. Used with permission. [See appendix entry 13]

Note: "No opinion" responses omitted. Percentages are calculated within rows.

* Includes oversample of 235 respondents.

5.15   Percentage of Students Older Than 12 Reporting That They Had Taken Something to School to Protect Themselves, by Demographic Characteristics, 1989

Characteristic	Percentage
Gender	
Male	3
Female	1
Race	
White	2
Black	2
Other	2
Hispanic origin	
Yes	2
No	2
Place of residence	
Central city	3
Suburbs	2
Non-metropolitan area	1

Source: National Crime Victimization Survey, 1989, from: Bastian, Lisa D., and Bruce M. Taylor. 1991. *School crime: A national crime victimization survey report.* Washington D.C.: Bureau of Justice Statistics, p. 12, Table 25. [See appendix entry 28]

Note: Table excludes series crimes. Series crime and other crime types are defined in the appendix.

5.16   Estimates of Firearm Ownership for Self-Defense, 1989, 1993

Measure of Defensive Ownership	Percentage of All Adults	Percentage of All Gun Owners	Percentage of Handgun Owners
Respondent reports owning a gun in part for protection from crime			
Gallup, 1993	18.2	58.8	73.5
Yankelovich, 1989	*	62.1	79.3
Respondent reports owning a gun only for protection from crime			
Gallup, 1993	6.2	20.0	26.2
Respondent reports protection from crime is main reason for owning gun			
Yankelovich, 1989	*	27.1	38.9
Respondent reports owning a gun that is currently loaded			
Gallup, 1993	11.1	35.8	45.1
Yankelovich, 1989	*	30.9	44.8

Source: Gallup Organization. 1993. *Gallup/CNN/USA Today poll: December 1993, wave 1.* [Computer file]. Princeton, N.J., [producer]; Storrs, Conn.: Roper Center for Public Opinion Research [distributor]. [See appendix entry 13]; Yankelovich, Clancy, Shulman, Inc. 1993. *Time soundings #25404.* [Computer file]. Norwalk, Conn., [producer]; Storrs, Conn.: Roper Center for Public Opinion Research [distributor]. [See appendix entry 54]

   *   Not applicable: survey of gun owners only.

5.17   Based on handgun and rifle/shotgun owners, "Please tell me whether you own your gun for each of the following reasons: for hunting, for target shooting, for protection against crime." Percentages, 1993

	Percentage
Handgun owners	
For hunting	28
For target shooting	62
For protection against crime	78
Rifle/shotgun owners	
For hunting	77
For target shooting	59
For protection against crime	40

Source: McAnney, Leslie. 1993. The Gallup Poll on crime. *The Gallup Poll Monthly* 339 (December):54. Used with permission. [See appendix entry 13]

5.18   Based on gun owners, 841 respondents, "Have you ever bought a gun just to protect yourself against crime?" Percentages, 1993

	All Gun Owners	All Handgun Owners	Long-Gun Owners Only
Yes	29	41	7
No	71	59	93
No opinion	0	0	0

Source: McAnney, Leslie. 1993. The Gallup Poll on crime. *The Gallup Poll Monthly* 339 (December):54. Used with permission. [See appendix entry 13]

5.19   Based on those who bought a gun just for protection, 240 respondents, "Did you buy it because of a particular incident that happened to you or someone you know, or was this not the reason?" Percentages, 1993

	All Gun Owners
Yes	34
No	60
No opinion	*

Source: McAnney, Leslie. 1993. The Gallup Poll on crime. *The Gallup Poll Monthly* 339 (December):54. Used with permission. [See appendix entry 13]

   *   Less than 0.5 percent.

5.20   Based on those who bought a gun just for protection, "Do you ever carry a gun on your person for protection against crime?" Percentages by Type of Gun Owner, 1993

	All Gun Owners	Handgun Owners	Long-Gun Owners
Yes	16.5	20.9	15.9
No	82.5	79.1	82.9
No opinion	1.0	0.0	1.1

Source: Gallup Organization. 1993. *Gallup/CNN/USA Today poll: December 1993, wave 1.* [Computer file]. Princeton, N.J., [producer]; Storrs, Conn.: Roper Center for Public Opinon Research [distributor]. [See appendix entry 13]

5.21   Based on gun owners who carry guns for protection against crime, "How often do you carry a gun on your person?" Percentages by Gun Type Owned, 1993

	All Gun Owners	Handgun Owners	Long-Gun Owners
Always	23.3	47.5	19.0
Fairly often	26.7	0.0	31.5
Not too often	32.6	52.5	29.0
Not often at all	17.4	0.0	20.5

Source: Gallup Organization. 1993. *Gallup/CNN/USA Today poll: December 1993, wave 1.* [Computer file]. Princeton, N.J., [producer]; Storrs, Conn.: Roper Center for Public Opinon Research [distributor]. [See appendix entry 13]

5.22   "Do you ever carry a gun in your car or truck for protection against crime?" Percentages by Gun Type Owned, 1993

	All Gun Owners	Handgun Owners	Long-Gun Owners
Yes	24.7	25.0	24.6
No	74.6	75.0	74.6
No opinion/not applicable	0.7	0.0	0.8

Source: Gallup Organization. 1993. *Gallup/CNN/USA Today poll: December 1993, wave 1.* [Computer file]. Princeton, N.J., [producer]; Storrs, Conn.: Roper Center for Public Opinon Research [distributor]. [See appendix entry 13]

5.23   Based on those who carry a gun in their car or truck for protection against crime, "How often do you carry a gun in your car or truck?" Percentages by Gun Type Owned, 1993

	All Gun Owners	Handgun Owners	Long-Gun Owners
Always	30.7	48.1	28.3
Fairly often	23.4	0.0	26.6
Not too often	30.0	36.8	29.1
Not often at all	15.0	7.8	16.0
No opinion	0.9	7.3	0.0

Source: Gallup Organization. 1993. *Gallup/CNN/USA Today poll: December 1993, wave 1.* [Computer file]. Princeton, N.J., [producer]; Storrs, Conn.: Roper Center for Public Opinon Research [distributor]. [See appendix entry 13]

Perceptions of Risk and Safety

5.24   "Is there any area right around here—that is, within a mile—where you would be afraid to walk alone at night?" Percentages by Race and Gender, 1994

	White		Black	
	Male	Female	Male	Female
Yes	27.2	57.4	45.4	65.0
No	72.2	41.7	54.6	35.0
Don't know	0.5	1.0	0.0	0.0

Source: Davis, James A., and Tom W. Smith. 1994. *General social surveys, 1972–1994*. [Computer file]. NORC ed. Chicago, Ill.: National Opinion Research Center [producer]; Storrs, Conn.: Roper Center for Public Opinion Research [distributor]. [See appendix entry 18]

5.25   "Is there any area right around here—that is, within a mile—where you would be afraid to walk alone at night?" Percentages by Race, 1973–1994

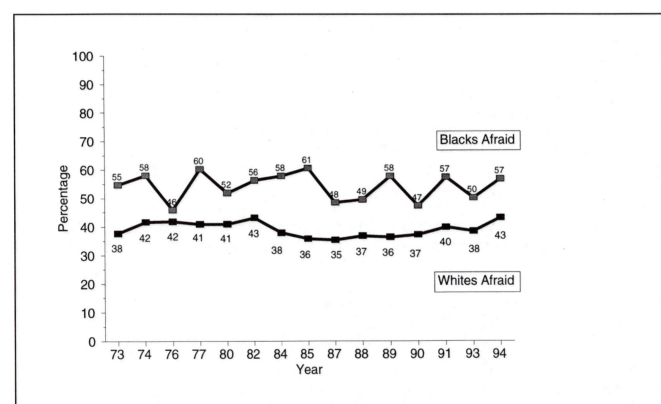

Source: Davis, James A., and Tom W. Smith. 1994. *General social surveys, 1972–1994*. [Computer file]. NORC ed. Chicago, Ill.: National Opinion Research Center [producer]; Storrs, Conn.: Roper Center for Public Opinion Research [distributor]. [See appendix entry 18]

5.26   "Is there any area right around here—that is, within a mile—where you would be afraid to walk alone at night?" Percentages by Gender, 1973–1994

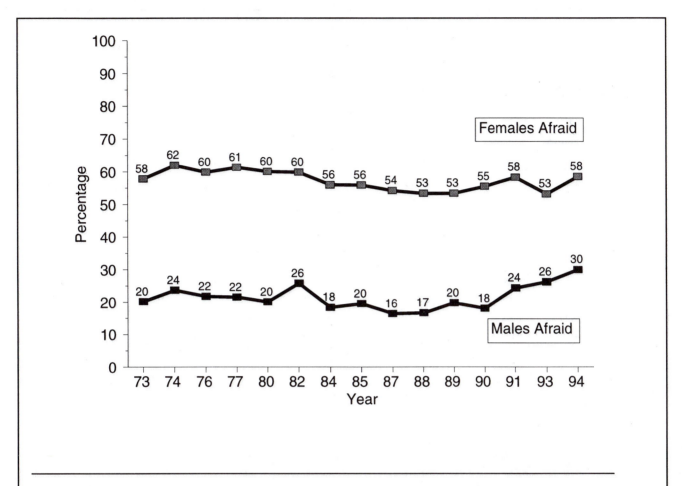

Source: Davis, James A., and Tom W. Smith. 1994. *General social surveys, 1972–1994.* [Computer file]. NORC ed. Chicago, Ill.: National Opinion Research Center [producer]; Storrs, Conn.: Roper Center for Public Opinion Research [distributor]. [See appendix entry 18]

5.27   "Do you, personally, feel any sense of danger from gun violence where you live and work, or not?" Percentages by Demographic Characteristics, 1993

		Yes	No	No Opinion
Total		36	64	*
Gender				
	Male	34	66	*
	Female	36	63	1
Age				
	18 - 29	36	64	0
	30 - 49	39	61	*
	50 and older	31	68	1
Region				
	East	35	65	0
	Midwest	29	71	0
	South	37	62	1
	West	41	58	1
Race				
	White	34	66	*
	Black	46	54	0
	Nonwhite†	45	55	*
Education				
	College graduate	42	58	0
	College incomplete	44	56	*
	No college	28	71	1
Politics				
	Republican	31	69	0
	Democrat	42	58	0
	Independent	33	66	1
Income				
	$50,000 and over	42	58	*
	$30,000 - $49,999	34	66	0
	$20,000 - $29,000	35	65	0
	Under $20,000	31	69	0
Community				
	Urban area	50	50	0
	Suburban area	32	68	*
	Rural area	29	70	1

Source: Gallup Organization data from: Maguire, Kathleen, Ann L. Pastore, and Timothy J. Flanagan, eds. 1993. *Sourcebook of criminal justice statistics, 1992.* Washington, D.C.: Bureau of Justice Statistics, p. 186, Table 2.28. Used with permission. [See appendix entry 13]

Note: Percentages are calculated within rows.
*   Percentages are less than 1 percent.
†   Includes black respondents.

5.28 "How afraid are you of being attacked or robbed? Are you very fearful, somewhat fearful, a little fearful, or not at all fearful of being attacked or robbed?" Percentages by Location, 1991

Location	Very Fearful	Somewhat Fearful	A Little Fearful	Not Fearful	Not Sure
At home in your house or apartment	9	21	30	40	0
On the streets in your community during the day	6	13	22	59	0
Out alone at night in your neighborhood	16	19	26	37	1
Out with other people at night in your neighborhood	3	13	21	62	1
Travelling on vacation or for business	10	38	24	25	3

Source: National Victim Center data from: Maguire, Kathleen, Ann L. Pastore, and Timothy J. Flanagan, eds. 1993. *Sourcebook of criminal justice statistics, 1992.* Washington, D.C.: Bureau of Justice Statistics, p. 186, Table 2.29. Used with permission. [See appendix entry 2]

Note: Percentages may not add up to 100 because of rounding.

5.29 Percentage of Students Older Than 12 Fearing Violent Crime, by Location, and by Whether Victimized by Violent Crime During Previous 6 Months, 1989

Location of Feared Attack and Whether Victim of Violent Crime	Total	Fear Violent Crime			
		Never	Almost Never	Sometimes	Most Times
At school					
Violent crime victims	100	47	28	18	7
Non-victims	100	81	15	4	*
In travel to and from school					
Violent crime victims	100	74	15	8	3
Non-victims	100	87	10	3	*

Source: National Crime Victimization Survey, 1989, from: Bastian, Lisa D., and Bruce M. Taylor. 1991. *School crime: A national crime victimization survey report.* Washington D.C.: Bureau of Justice Statistics, p. 9, Table 18. [See appendix entry 28]

Note: Table excludes series crimes. Series crime and other crime types are defined in the appendix.

    * Less than 0.5 percent.

5.30   "Is teenage violence something you personally fear, or not?" Percentages, 1989 and 1994

	June 1989	June 1994
Yes, personally fear	35	37
No, do not fear	63	63
Not sure	2	0

Source: Time/CNN. 1994. *Time/CNN poll, June 15–16, 1994*, Yankelovich, Clancy, Shulman, p. 15, Q.19. Used with permission. [See appendix entry 56]

Note: Based on adults in U.S. households equipped with telephones.

5.31   "We'd like to know how safe you feel your children are from violent crime in each of the following places. (First), in general, do you feel your children are very safe, somewhat safe, or not safe from violent crime . . . ?" Percentages, 1993.

	Very Safe	Somewhat Safe	Not Safe	Don't Know
At home at night	80	19	1	*
When walking in your neighborhood after dark	31	52	14	3
When travelling to school	57	38	5	*
At school	45	48	6	1

Source: Princeton Survey Research Associates. 1993. *Children's defense fund/Newsweek national poll of children and parents: Final top-line questionnaire*, October 18–November 7, 1993, p. 6, Q. 10. Used with permission. [See appendix entry 9]

*   Less than 0.5 percent.

5.32   Fear of Specific Crimes, "How often do you, yourself, worry about the following things . . . ?" Percentages by Race, 1993

	Very Frequently	Pretty Frequently	Pretty Seldom	Very Seldom	No Opinion
"Yourself or someone in your family getting sexually assaulted or raped?"					
Total	15	23	22	39	1
Whites	13	24	23	40	*
Blacks	22	18	23	36	1
"Your home being burglarized when you're not there?"					
Total	14	21	22	42	1
Whites	13	22	23	41	1
Blacks	20	15	17	48	0
"Being attacked while driving your car?"					
Total	12	16	22	47	3
Whites	10	17	23	48	2
Blacks	21	15	14	41	9
"Getting mugged?"					
Total	11	15	23	51	*
Whites	9	15	23	52	1
Blacks	15	18	20	47	0
"Getting beaten up, knifed, shot?"					
Total	11	12	24	53	*
Whites	10	12	25	52	1
Blacks	15	10	16	58	1
"Your home being burglarized when you are there?"					
Total	9	12	22	56	1
Whites	8	12	22	57	1
Blacks	11	14	22	53	0
"Getting murdered?"					
Total	8	11	18	62	1
Whites	7	11	19	63	*
Blacks	13	15	14	57	1

Source: McAnney, Leslie. 1993. The Gallup Poll on crime. *The Gallup Poll Monthly* 339 (December):21. Used with permission. [See appendix entry 13]
   *   Less than 0.5 percent.

5.33   "Do you think most children in America are physically safe going to and from school, live in homes safe from violence, live in safe neighborhoods, are safe from violence in the schools?" Percentages by Young People and Parents, 1993.

	Agreement Among Young People	Agreement Among Parents
Most are physically safe going to and from school	30	38
Most live in homes safe from violence	23	28
Most live in safe neighborhoods	22	21
Most are safe from violence in the schools	21	24

Source: LH Research Inc. 1993. *A survey of experiences, perceptions, and apprehensions about guns among young people in America.* (Unpublished). Prepared for the Harvard School of Public Health (June): p. 2. Used with permission. [See appendix entry 47]

5.34   Asked of those who carry a firearm outside the home, "Does carrying that firearm outside your home make you feel safer from crime, or does it make you feel less safe, or doesn't it have much effect on how safe you feel?" Percentages, 1994

	Percentage
Safer	59
Less safe	1
Not much effect	35
Don't know	5

Source: Los Angeles Times. 1994. *Los Angeles Times poll: Survey #334—National Issues.* April, 1994, p. 9, Q. 57.   Used with permission. [See appendix entry 25]

5.35   Asked of gun owners, "Does having a gun in your house make you feel more safe from crime, less safe, or doesn't it make any difference?" Percentages, 1989.

	Percentage
More safe	42
Less safe	2
No difference	56
Not sure	*

Source: Time/CNN. 1992. *Time/CNN poll, December, 1989,* Yankelovich, Clancy, Shulman, p. 11. Used with permission. [See appendix entry 54]
  *   Less than 0.5 percent.

5.36   Neighborhood Crime, Percentages by Race, 1993

	Total	Whites	Blacks
"Just your impression, does your neighborhood have more violent crime than the average, an average amount of violent crime, less than average amount of violent crime, or none?"			
More than average	5	4	11
Average amount	10	10	18
Less than average	57	57	53
None	27	28	17
No opinion	1	1	1
"During the last 12 months, have there been any violent crimes in your neighborhood?"			
Yes	31	30	41
No	68	69	57
No opinion	1	1	2

Source: McAnney, Leslie. 1993. The Gallup Poll on crime. *The Gallup Poll Monthly* 339 (December):20, 23. Used with permission. [See appendix entry 13]

5.37   "How safe do you feel being . . . out alone at night using public transportation, out alone at night walking in your neighborhood, alone at night in your home, out alone at night driving a car in your neighborhood?" Percentages by Race, 1993

	Very Safe	Somewhat Safe	Somewhat Unsafe	Very Unsafe	Not Applicable (Volunteered)	No Opinion
At home						
Total	61	29	6	4	*	*
Whites	63	28	6	3	*	*
Blacks	49	32	9	9	1	*
Driving						
Total	51	29	11	5	3	1
Whites	53	29	9	5	3	1
Blacks	36	30	17	10	7	0
Walking						
Total	36	32	14	15	3	*
Whites	38	31	14	13	4	*
Blacks	20	36	13	26	4	1
On public transportation						
Total	11	22	22	23	19	3
Whites	12	22	22	21	19	4
Blacks	8	21	19	36	14	2

Source: McAnney, Leslie. 1993. The Gallup Poll on crime. *The Gallup Poll Monthly* 339 (December):22. Used with permission. [See appendix entry 13]

*   Less than 0.5 percent.

5.38   Feelings of Safety and Guns, Percentages by Gun Owners and Type of Gun Owned, 1993

	Total*	All Gun Owners	All Handgun Owners	Long-gun Only Owners
"Suppose a law were passed making it illegal for all citizens other than the police to have a gun. Would you feel more safe or less safe, or wouldn't it make any difference?"				
More	25	11	10	12
Less	39	63	66	55
No difference	34	25	23	31
No opinion	2	1	1	2
"Which of the following comes closer to your view: having a gun in the house makes it a safer place to be because you can protect yourself from violent intruders, or having a gun in the house makes it a *more dangerous* place to be because you increase the risk from gun accidents and domestic violence?"				
Safer	42	76	80	66
More dangerous	52	16	13	23
Mixed (volunteered)	5	6	6	8
No opinion	1	2	1	3

Source: McAnney, Leslie. 1993. The Gallup Poll on crime. *The Gallup Poll Monthly* 339 (December):50, 51. Used with permission. [See appendix entry 13]

Note: Includes oversample of 742 gun households.

*   Total includes people who do not own any guns.

5.39   Percentage of Victimizations in Which Victims Took Self-Protective Measures, by Type of Crime and Victim-Offender Relationship, 1992

Type of Crime	All Victimizations	Involving Strangers	Involving Nonstrangers
Crimes of violence	71.7	69.9	74.3
Completed	68.6	61.6	78.8
Attempted	73.4	74.5	71.6
Rape	80.1	84.3	76.2
Robbery	59.4	54.9	78.8
Completed	47.5	43.4	68.0
With injury	63.5	58.6	87.8
From serious assault	67.9	63.4	100.0*
From minor assault	58.7	52.7	80.5*
Without injury	36.2	32.7	53.8
Attempted	82.5	79.1	93.0
With injury	86.1	86.2	85.7*
From serious assault	85.0	88.7*	71.5*
From minor assault	87.4	83.2*	100.0*
Without injury	81.3	76.8	95.3
Assault	74.3	74.6	73.8
Aggravated	71.9	71.3	73.0
Completed with injury	74.6	74.4	75.0
Attempted with weapon	70.3	70.0	71.3
Simple	75.6	77.1	74.1
Completed with injury	82.1	80.8	82.8
Attempted without weapon	73.2	76.1	69.9

Source: National Crime Victimization Survey, 1992, from: Bureau of Justice Statistics. 1993. *Criminal victimization in the United States, 1992.* Washington, D.C., p. 84, Table 73. [See appendix entry 28]

Note: Self-protective measures were defined as the following victim actions in response to attacks or threats: used physical force toward the offender, resisted or captured the offender, scared or warned the offender, persuaded or appeased the offender, escaped or got away, got help or gave alarm, reacted to pain or emotion or "other" measures. Table excludes series crimes. Series crime and other crime types are defined in the appendix.

*   Estimate is based on 10 or fewer sample cases.

5.40   Percentage of Victimizations in Which Victims Took Self-Protective Measures, by Characteristics of Victim and Crime Type, 1992

Characteristic	Crimes of Violence	Completed Violent Crimes	Attempted Violent Crimes	Rape	Robbery			Assault		
					Total	With Injury	Without Injury	Total	Aggravated	Simple
Gender										
Male	70.9	64.6	74.4	74.3	56.9	66.5	52.6	74.6	72.8	75.8
Female	72.7	73.9	72.0	84.1	64.3	71.7	58.2	73.8	70.1	75.3
Race										
White	71.2	68.1	72.8	77.9	59.8	65.3	57.1	73.1	70.6	74.3
Black	71.1	68.3	73.3	88.1*	56.8	76.3	43.9	77.2	74.2	80.8
Age										
12 - 19	73.3	73.3	73.3	83.4*	70.6	84.7	64.3	73.6	72.8	74.0
20 - 34	74.6	74.9	74.4	83.8	61.0	67.4	57.0	77.5	75.6	78.4
35 - 49	69.0	56.7	75.7	84.8*	49.9	58.1*	46.0	72.8	66.9	76.8
50 - 64	54.1	36.9*	61.9	100.0*	49.6	69.4*	32.6*	55.1	55.8	54.7
65 and over	51.9	27.3*	65.0	0.0*	21.2*	19.3*	22.0*	71.3	66.2*	75.1

Source: National Crime Victimization Survey, 1992, from: Bureau of Justice Statistics. 1993. *Criminal victimization in the United States, 1992.* Washington, D.C., p. 84, Table 74. [See appendix entry 28]

Note: Detail may not add up to total shown because of rounding. Self-protective measures were defined as the following victim actions in response to attacks or threats: used physical force toward the offender, resisted or captured the offender, scared or warned the offender, persuaded or appeased the offender, escaped or got away, got help or gave alarm, reacted to pain or emotion or "other" measures. Table excludes series crimes. Aggravated assaults include all attacks (and attempted attacks) with weapons or, if no weapons was involved, those that result in serious injury. Simple assaults are attacked (and attempted attacks) without weapons resulting in minor or undetermined injuries requiring less than two days of hospitalization. Series crime and other crime types are defined in the appendix.

*   Estimate is based on 10 or fewer sample cases.

5.41 Percentage of Self-Protective Measures Employed by Victims, by Type of Measure and Type of Crime, 1992

Self-Protective Measure	Crimes of Violence	Completed Violent Crimes	Attempted Violent Crimes	Rape	Robbery			Assault		
					Total	With Injury	Without Injury	Total	Aggravated	Simple
Total	100.0	100.0	100.0	100.0	100.0	100.0	100.0	100.0	100.0	100.0
Attacked offender with weapon	1.3	1.6	1.1	2.0*	1.3*	0.6*	1.8*	1.3	1.8*	1.0*
Attacked offender without weapon	11.1	17.1	7.4	6.9*	10.2	11.2	9.3	11.5	11.2	11.6
Threatened offender with weapon	1.0	0.5*	1.2	0.0*	0.3*	0.0*	0.6*	1.1	1.5*	0.9*
Threatened offender without weapon	1.6	1.7	1.5	2.7*	0.7*	1.5*	0.0*	1.7	2.0	1.5
Resisted or captured offender	19.0	26.8	14.2	20.2	25.2	34.9	16.5	17.7	16.1	18.7
Scared or warned offender	8.3	7.0	9.0	11.4*	9.1	7.6*	10.4	8.0	8.0	8.0
Persuaded or appeased offender	13.9	10.1	16.1	11.2*	17.1	8.7	24.5	13.4	8.7	16.1
Ran away or hid	19.6	14.4	22.8	18.0	18.0	15.8	20.0	20.0	24.2	17.5
Got help or gave alarm	11.3	9.3	12.5	7.3*	8.4	9.8	7.2	12.1	13.0	11.5
Screamed from pain or fear	2.5	5.1	0.9*	11.0*	2.8*	3.2*	2.5*	2.0	3.3	1.3
Took another method	10.6	6.4	13.1	9.4*	7.0	6.7*	7.2	11.3	10.1	12.0
Total number of self-protective measures	7,043,300	2,672,690	4,370,600	269,190	1,077,320	508,020	569,290	5,696,770	2,102,810	3,593,950

Source: National Crime Victimization Survey, 1992, from: Bureau of Justice Statistics. 1993. *Criminal victimization in the United States, 1992.* Washington, D.C., p. 85, Table 75. [See appendix entry 28]

Note: Detail may not add up to total shown because of rounding. Some respondents may have cited more than one self-protective measure employed. Percentages are calculated for columns. Table excludes series crimes. Series crime and other crime types are defined in the appendix. Aggravated assaults include all attacks (and attempted attacks) with weapons or, if no weapon was involved, those that result in serious injury. Simple assaults are attacked (and attempted attacks) without weapons resulting in minor or undetermined injuries requiring less than two days of hospitalization.

* Estimate is based on 50 or fewer sample cases.

5.42   Percentage of Self-Protective Measures Employed by Victims, by Selected Characteristics of Victims, 1992

Self-protective Measure	Gender			Race	
	Both Genders	Male	Female	White	Black
Total	100.0	100.0	100.0	100.0	100.0
Attacked offender with weapon	1.3	1.7	0.8*	1.1	1.6*
Attacked offender without weapon	11.1	13.8	7.8	11.1	11.2
Threatened offender with weapon	1.0	1.6	0.2*	1.1	0.3*
Threatened offender without weapon	1.6	2.3	0.7*	1.7	1.0*
Resisted or captured offender	19.0	21.9	15.4	18.8	19.5
Scared or warned offender	8.3	6.1	10.8	8.3	7.1
Persuaded or appeased offender	13.9	14.3	13.4	14.6	12.3
Ran away or hid	19.6	19.4	19.9	19.0	21.0
Got help or gave alarm	11.3	7.2	16.3	10.8	12.7
Screamed from pain or fear	2.5	0.7*	4.7	2.1	4.9
Took another method	10.6	11.0	10.0	11.4	8.2
Total number of self-protective measures	7,043,300	3,858,440	3,184,850	5,597,820	1,232,150

Source: National Crime Victimization Survey, 1992, from: Bureau of Justice Statistics. 1993. *Criminal victimization in the United States, 1992*. Washington, D.C., p. 86, Table 76. [See appendix entry 28]

Note: Detail may not add up to total shown because of rounding. Some respondents may have cited more than one self-protective measure employed. Table excludes series crimes. Series crimes are defined in appendix entry 28.

*   Estimate is based on 10 or fewer sample cases.

5.43   Percentage of Victimizations in Which Self-Protective Measures Were Employed, by Person Taking the Measure, Outcome of Action, and Type of Crime, 1992

Person Taking Action and Type of Crime	Helped Situation	Hurt Situation	Both Helped and Hurt Situation	Neither Helped Nor Hurt Situation	Don't Know	Not Available
Actions by victim						
Crimes of violence	59.8	7.7	6.6	10.6	8.5	6.7
Rape	58.2	3.1*	7.3*	12.8*	10.3*	8.3*
Robbery	55.3	9.4	10.0	10.4	7.8	7.2
Assault	60.7	7.6	6.0	10.6	8.5	6.6
Aggravated	64.9	6.3	5.8	7.2	9.5	6.3
Simple	58.6	8.2	6.1	12.4	8.0	6.7
Actions by others						
Crimes of violence	34.8	10.6	1.5	43.9	7.4	1.9
Rape	25.6*	0.0*	0.0*	50.7*	23.7*	0.0*
Robbery	29.1	11.8	2.1*	45.7	4.8*	6.4
Assault	35.9	10.5	1.4	43.5	7.6	1.1
Aggravated	36.8	9.5	0.8*	43.0	9.1	0.7*
Simple	35.5	11.0	1.7	43.7	6.8	1.3*

Source: National Crime Victimization Survey, 1992, from: Bureau of Justice Statistics. 1993. *Criminal victimization in the United States, 1992*. Washington, D.C., p. 86, Table 77. [See appendix entry 28]

Note: Detail may not add up to total shown because of rounding. Percentages are calculated within rows. Table excludes series crimes. Series crimes are defined in appendix entry 28. Aggravated assaults include all attacks (and attempted attacks) with weapons or, if no weapon was involved, those that result in serious injury. Simple assaults are attacked (and attempted attacks) without weapons resulting in minor or undetermined injuries requiring less than two days of hospitalization.

*   Estimate is based on 10 or fewer sample cases.

5.44   Self-Defensive Firearm Incidents, by Type of Crime, 1987–1990

Type of Crime	Number of Incidents 1987–1990	Mean Number of Incidents per Year
Rape*	7,552	1,888.00
Robbery	30,900	7,725.00
Assault	152,031	38,007.75
Personal larceny*	2,056	514.00
Burglary	34,259	8,564.75
Household larceny	28,139	7,034.75
Motor vehicle theft*	3,523	880.75
Total	258,460	64,615.00

Source: National Crime Victimization Survey, 1987–1990, from: McDowall, David, and Brian Wiersema. 1994. The incidence of defensive firearm use by crime victims, 1987 through 1990. *American Journal of Public Health* 84, no. 12 (December): p. 1983, Table 1. Used with permission. [See appendix entry 28]

Note: Table includes series crimes. Series crimes are defined in appendix entry 28.

*   Estimate is based on 10 or fewer sample cases.

5.45   Self-Defensive Firearm Incidents, by Victim-Offender Relationship, and by Use of Gun, 1987–1990

Type of Crime	Number of Incidents 1987-1990	Mean Number of Incidents per Year
Relationship between victim and offender		
Stranger	182,368	45,592.00
Casual acquaintance	23,003	5,750.75
Well known	24,955	6,238.75
Undetermined	28,134	7,033.50
Manner in which victim used firearm		
Discharged firearm	71,549	17,887.25
Used firearm only to threaten offender	186,911	46,727.75

Source: National Crime Victimization Survey, 1987–1990, from: McDowall, David, and Brian Wiersema. 1994. The incidence of defensive firearm use by crime victims, 1987 through 1990. *American Journal of Public Health* 84, no. 12 (December): p. 1983, Table 2. Used with permission. [See appendix entry 28]

Note: Table includes series crimes. Series crimes are defined in appendix entry 28.

5.46   Based on Gun Owners, Gun Use to Defend Self or Property, Percentages by Type of Gun Owned, 1993

	All Gun Owners	All Handgun Owners	Long-Gun Only Owners
"Not including military combat, have you ever used a gun to defend yourself, your home, your family, or your possessions, either by firing it or threatening to fire it?"			
Yes	15	20	7
No	85	80	93
No opinion	*	*	0
Based on those who have used a gun in self-defense, "Not including military combat, have you ever fired a gun to defend yourself, your home, your family, or your possessions?"			
Yes	47	48	32
No	52	51	68
No opinion	1	1	0

Source: McAnney, Leslie. 1993. The Gallup Poll on crime. *The Gallup Poll Monthly* 339 (December):56, Q. 54, and 55. Used with permission. [See appendix entry 13]

*   Less than 0.5 percent.

WHAT SHOULD COMMUNITIES OR GOVERNMENTS DO IN RESPONSE TO VIOLENCE?

5.47   "For each of the following, tell me if you favor or oppose it as a way of dealing with crime in the United States. First, do you strongly favor, favor, oppose, strongly oppose: Making it more difficult for those convicted of violent crimes like murder and rape to be paroled; making it more difficult for those accused of violent crimes like murder and rape to get out on bail while awaiting trial; enacting tougher gun control laws; prohibiting plea bargaining—where in exchange for pleading guilty, the defendant is charged with a lesser crime; making sentences more severe for all crimes; extending the death penalty for some serious crimes other than murder; limiting appeals to death sentences; putting more police on the streets, even if it requires higher taxes?" Percentages by Race, 1993

	Strongly Favor	Favor	Oppose	Strongly Oppose	No Opinion
Parole more difficult (total %)	66	16	8	9	1
Whites	68	16	7	8	1
Blacks	53	21	8	16	2
Restrict bail (total %)	59	16	11	13	1
Whites	61	17	10	11	1
Blacks	46	12	14	25	3
More severe sentences (total %)	48	31	14	4	3
Whites	48	30	15	4	3
Blacks	42	34	13	7	4
More police on street (total %)	43	37	15	4	1
Whites	43	37	14	4	2
Blacks	41	35	15	9	0
Tougher gun laws (total %)	40	24	20	13	3
Whites	38	25	21	13	3
Blacks	47	20	16	12	5
Limit appeals (total %)	37	23	21	14	5
Whites	38	24	21	13	4
Blacks	23	20	19	29	9
Extend death penalty offenses (total %)	24	27	30	15	4
Whites	25	28	30	14	3
Blacks	22	17	26	28	7
Ban plea bargaining (total %)	24	19	31	22	4
Whites	25	19	31	21	4
Blacks	19	12	30	31	8

Source: McAnney, Leslie. 1993. The Gallup Poll on crime. The Gallup Poll Monthly 339 (December): p. 31. Used with permission. [See appendix entry 13]

5.48 "Would you favor or oppose the following activities in high-crime areas in order to help reduce crime: Allow police to hold someone they suspect of committing a crime for 24 hours without bail; allow police to wiretap telephone lines of anyone they suspect; allow the police to stop and search anybody they suspect of having committed a crime; allow police to search a home without a warrant; make it illegal for anyone in the area to possess a handgun?" Percentages by Race, 1993

	Total	Whites	Blacks
Hold without bail			
Favor	74	77	54
Oppose	24	21	44
No opinion	2	2	2
Allow stop-searches			
Favor	60	62	37
Oppose	38	36	63
No opinion	2	2	0
Make handguns illegal			
Favor	38	38	38
Oppose	60	61	61
No opinion	2	1	1
Allow wiretaps			
Favor	36	37	24
Oppose	63	62	75
No opinion	1	1	1
Search homes without warrant			
Favor	18	19	4
Oppose	81	80	94
No opinion	1	1	2

Source: McAnney, Leslie. 1993. The Gallup Poll on crime. *The Gallup Poll Monthly* 339 (December): p. 32. Used with permission. [See appendix entry 13]

5.49   "In your view, should juveniles who commit violent crimes be treated the same as adults, or should they be given more lenient treatment in a juvenile court?" Percentages by Demographic Characteristics, 1993

Characteristic	Same as Adults	More Leniently	Tougher‡	Depends‡	No Opinion
Total	73	19	*	5	3
Gender					
Male	75	18	1	3	3
Female	71	20	*	6	3
Age (years)					
18-29	76	20	0	3	1
30-49	74	19	*	5	2
50-64	73	16	*	5	6
65 and older	68	19	1	8	4
Region					
East	71	20	1	6	2
Midwest	69	21	1	5	4
South	71	20	0	6	3
West	82	15	*	1	2
Community					
Urban	73	20	1	4	2
Suburban	74	18	*	5	3
Rural	70	20	*	6	4
Race					
White	74	18	*	5	3
Black†	67	27	0	4	2
Education					
College postgrad.	65	25	2	5	3
College graduate	67	24	1	5	3
College incomplete	74	18	0	4	4
No college	74	18	*	6	2
Politics					
Republican	75	17	0	6	2
Democrat	71	23	1	3	2
Independent	72	17	1	6	4
Ideology					
Liberal	72	18	1	6	3
Moderate	73	21	1	3	2
Conservative	74	19	*	5	2
Fear of crime					
Most fearful	78	12	*	6	4
All others	71	21	*	5	3
Income					
$50,000 and over	70	23	1	5	1
$30,000-$49,999	74	19	0	3	4
$20,000-$29,999	75	18	0	6	1
Under $20,000	73	19	1	4	3

Source: McAnney, Leslie. 1993. The Gallup Poll on crime. *The Gallup Poll Monthly* 339 (December): p. 36. Used with permission. [See appendix entry 13]

*   Less than one percent.

†   Includes oversample of 235 respondents.

‡   Response volunteered.

5.50   "How do you think society should deal with juveniles (those under age 18) who commit crimes: Should society place less emphasis on punishing juvenile offenders and more on trying to rehabilitate them, or should society give juvenile offenders the same punishment as adults?" Percentages, 1994

	Percentage
Rehabilitation	31
Same punishment	52
Other*	3
Depends on circumstances*	13
No opinion	1

Source: Moore, David W. 1994. Majority advocate death penalty for teenage killers. *The Gallup Poll Monthly* 348 (September): p. 3. Used with permission. [See appendix entry 17]
   *   Response volunteered.

5.51   "When a teenager commits a murder and is found guilty by a jury, do you think s/he should get the death penalty or should s/he be spared because of her/his youth?" Percentages by Demographic Characteristics, 1993

Characteristic	Favor	Oppose	No Opinion
Total	60	30	10
Gender			
Male	66	26	8
Female	56	33	11
Age (years)			
18-29	60	30	10
30-49	62	30	8
50-64	55	34	11
65 and older	63	25	12
Region			
East	57	32	11
Midwest	59	31	10
South	64	28	8
West	60	29	11
Community			
Urban	60	31	9
Suburban	61	30	9
Rural	60	28	12
Race			
White	60	30	10
Nonwhite	59	33	8
Education			
College postgrad.	52	39	9
College graduate	59	33	8
Some college	59	27	14
No college	63	29	8
Politics			
Republican	65	24	11
Democrat	56	37	7
Independent	61	28	11
Idealogy			
Liberal	53	35	12
Moderate	61	30	9
Conservative	63	28	9
Income			
$75,000 and over	68	28	4
$50,000-$74,999	62	30	8
$30,000-$49,999	60	31	9
$20,000-$29,999	66	22	12
Under $20,000	55	33	12

Source: Moore, David W. 1994. Majority advocate death penalty for teenage killers. *The Gallup Poll Monthly* 348 (September): p. 4. Used with permission. [See appendix entry 17]

5.52 "In your view, should the law require fines or prison sentences for the parents of juveniles convicted of major crimes, or not?" Percentages by Demographic Characteristics, 1993

Characteristic	Yes, Prison/Fines	Yes, Fines Only	No	No Opinion
Total	24	24	48	4
Gender				
Male	24	26	46	4
Female	25	22	49	4
Age (years)				
18-29	19	26	52	3
30-49	25	24	49	2
50-64	23	23	50	4
65 and older	29	23	38	10
Region				
East	23	24	48	5
Midwest	20	22	52	6
South	27	21	48	4
West	27	29	43	1
Community				
Urban	24	24	48	4
Suburban	24	27	46	3
Rural	26	20	49	5
Race				
White	24	24	48	4
Black*	24	18	52	6
Education				
College postgrad.	30	30	37	3
College graduate	30	26	40	4
College incomplete	26	27	44	3
No college	21	22	52	5
Politics				
Republican	25	27	44	4
Democrat	27	22	48	3
Independent	21	23	51	5
Idealogy				
Liberal	28	19	49	4
Moderate	22	25	50	3
Conservative	26	25	44	5
Fear of crime				
Most fearful	30	24	44	2
All others	22	24	49	5
Income				
$50,000 and over	26	25	45	4
$30,000-$49,999	26	24	46	4
$20,000-$29,999	20	22	54	4
Under $20,000	24	24	48	4

Source: McAnney, Leslie. 1993. The Gallup Poll on crime. *The Gallup Poll Monthly* 339 (December): p. 36. Used with permission. [See appendix entry 13]

* Includes oversample of 235 respondents.

5.53   "Which of the following measures do you think should be used for first-time juvenile offenders committing a major crime, but not murder—job training as an alternative to going to prison, disciplinary training in a special boot camp, or prison?" Percentages by Race, 1993

Reaction	Total	White	Black
Boot camp	66	68	56
Job Training	19	19	24
Prison	12	11	14
Mixed (volunteered)	1	1	3
None; other (volunteered)	1	*	2
No opinion	1	1	1

Source: The Gallup Organization. 1993. *The Gallup Poll public opinion, 1993*. Wilmington, Del.: Scholarly Resources, Inc., p. 213. Used with permission. [See appendix entry 14]
    *   Less than 1 percent.

5.54   "What is the best way to keep children in your community safe from violent crime?" Percentages, 1993

	Percentage
More after-school programs	34
More police and law enforcement	31
More restrictive gun laws	17
More drug and alcohol rehabilitation programs	9
Other	5
Don't know	4
Total	100

Source: Princeton Survey Research Associates. 1993. *Children's Defense Fund/Newsweek national poll of children and parents: Final top line questionnaire*, October 18–November 7, 1993, p. 6, Q. 11. Used with permission. [See appendix entry 9]

5.55 "How effective do you think each of the following measures would be in reducing violence in the public schools—very effective, somewhat effective, not very effective, or not at all effective?" Percentages, 1994

Measure	Very Effective	Somewhat Effective	Not Very Effective	Not at All Effective	Don't Know
Stronger penalties for possession of weapons by students	86	8	3	2	1
Training school staffs in how to deal with student violence	72	20	5	2	1
More vocational or job training courses in public schools	67	25	7	1	*
Drug and alcohol abuse programs for students	66	23	7	3	1
Values and ethics education for students	60	27	9	3	1
Education designed to reduce racial and ethnic tensions	57	27	10	4	2
Courses offered by the public schools in how to be a good parent	51	28	15	5	1
Conflict education for students	45	35	11	3	6

Source: Elam, Stanley M., Lowell C. Rose, and Alec M. Gallup. 1994. The 26th annual Phi Delta Kappa/Gallup poll of the public's attitudes toward the public schools. *Phi Delta Kappan*, (September): p. 44. Used with permission. [See appendix entry 58]
  * Less than one-half of 1 percent.

5.56 "Do you think the federal government should do more to regulate violence on television and in movies, should it do less, or is it doing about the right amount?" Percentages by Age, 1994

	Total	18-29	30-44	45-64	Over 64
Should do more	55	56	50	56	65
Should do less	9	9	10	10	3
Doing about the right amount	25	29	30	21	16
Don't know/no opinion	11	6	10	13	16

Source: CBS News. 1994. *CBS News/America Tonight poll: Too much TV and movie violence, but many say people ask for it*, July 26, 1994, p. 4, Q. 5. Used with permission. [See appendix entry 4]

5.57   "A judge in at least one state has ruled that public executions can be televised. Some people think that executions should be shown on television because it would be a deterrent to would-be killers. Others think executions should not be on television because such violence shouldn't be brought into people's living rooms. How do you feel—that executions should or should not be shown on television?" Percentages, 1977, 1991, and 1993.

	Roper 1977	Roper 1991	Times Mirror 1993
Should be shown	10	19	22
Should not be shown	85	77	74
Don't know/refused/other	4	4	4

Source: Times Mirror Center for the People and the Press. 1993. *TV violence: More objectionable in entertainment than in newscasts: News release*, March 24, 1993, p. 48, Q.33. Used with permission. [See appendix entry 57]

5.58 "Do you feel that public executions should or should not be shown on television?" Percentages by Demographic Characteristics, 1993

Characteristic	Should Be Shown	Should Not Be Shown	Don't Know/No Answer
Total	22.3	74.1	3.6
Gender			
Male	30.5	65.8	3.6
Female	14.9	81.6	3.5
Age (years)			
18-29	28.9	69.0	2.1
30-49	23.3	71.7	4.9
50-64	20.0	76.9	3.1
Region			
East	20.2	76.9	2.9
Midwest	22.0	74.8	3.2
South	24.1	70.6	5.3
West	21.9	76.3	1.8
Education			
College graduate	16.3	80.1	3.6
Some college	24.1	71.4	4.5
High school graduate	24.0	73.5	2.5
Less than high school graduate	23.7	72.1	4.2
Family income			
$50,000 and over	22.1	74.9	3.0
$30,000-$49,999	21.1	75.8	3.1
$20,000-$29,999	25.6	70.9	3.5
Under $20,000	24.3	71.6	4.1
Race			
White	21.1	75.5	3.5
Black	30.3	65.1	4.6
Other	31.9	66.2	1.8
Hispanic	27.3	68.6	4.0

Source: Times Mirror Center for the People and the Press data from: Maguire, Kathleen, and Ann L. Pastore, eds. 1994. *Sourcebook of criminal justice statistics, 1993.* Washington, D.C.: Bureau of Justice Statistics, p. 239, Table 2.109. Used with permission. [See appendix entry 37]

5.59 "What do you think should be the penalty for murder—the death penalty or life imprisonment with absolutely no possibility of parole?" Percentages by Demographic Characteristics, 1993

Characteristic	Death Penalty	Life, No Parole	Depends	Neither	No Opinion
Total	59	29	10	1	1
Gender					
Male	64	23	10	1	2
Female	55	34	9	*	2
Age (years)					
18-29	52	34	10	2	2
30-49	62	26	10	1	1
50-64	58	30	10	1	1
65 and older	63	28	7	0	2
Region					
East	60	27	10	1	2
Midwest	58	31	8	1	2
South	57	31	10	1	1
West	61	24	12	1	2
Community					
Urban	54	36	7	1	2
Suburban	65	22	10	1	2
Rural	58	28	12	1	1
Race					
White	62	26	10	1	1
Black†	38	45	12	1	4
Education					
College postgrad.	56	30	9	2	3
College graduate	60	29	8	1	2
College incomplete	58	29	10	1	2
No college	59	28	10	1	2
Politics					
Republican	68	23	8	*	1
Democrat	55	33	9	1	2
Independent	56	29	12	1	2
Ideology					
Liberal	48	35	12	2	3
Moderate	61	28	9	1	1
Conservative	63	27	8	1	1
Fear of crime					
Most fearful	58	31	9	1	1
All others	59	28	10	1	2
Income					
$50,000 and over	63	25	9	2	1
$30,000-$49,999	64	22	11	1	2
$20,000-$29,999	63	29	8	0	*
Under $20,000	52	37	9	1	1

Source: McAnney, Leslie. 1993. The Gallup Poll on crime. *The Gallup Poll Monthly* 339 (December): p. 35. Used with permission. [See appendix entry 13]

* Less than one percent.
† Includes oversample of 235 respondents.

5.60   Based on those who think the death penalty should be imposed for crimes other than murder (40 percent), "For what crimes besides murder should the death penalty be imposed?" Percentages, 1986

Crime	Percentage
Rape	54
Treason against the U.S. (traitors, espionage, etc.)	20
Drug dealing	14
Child molestation or abuse	35
Other	21
Don't know/no answer	5

Source: Associated Press/Media General. 1986. *The Associated Press/Media General Poll, November 7–14, 1986.* Used with permission. [See appendix entry 3]

5.61   "Do you favor or oppose the death penalty for persons convicted of murder?" Percentages by Race and Gender, 1994

	White		Black	
	Male	Female	Male	Female
Favor	82.8	74.9	56.7	47.5
Oppose	14.0	18.5	35.7	38.7
Don't know	3.3	6.6	7.6	13.8

Source: Davis, James A., and Tom W. Smith. 1994. *General social surveys, 1972–1994.* [Computer file]. NORC ed. Chicago, Ill.: National Opinion Research Center [producer]; Storrs, Conn.: Roper Center for Public Opinion Research [distributor]. [See appendix entry 18]

5.62   "Do you favor or oppose the death penalty for persons convicted of murder?" Percentages by Race, 1972–1994

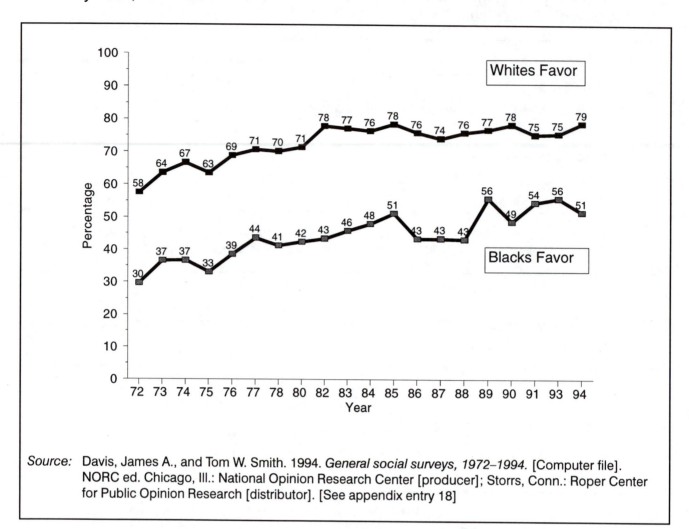

Source: Davis, James A., and Tom W. Smith. 1994. *General social surveys, 1972–1994.* [Computer file]. NORC ed. Chicago, Ill.: National Opinion Research Center [producer]; Storrs, Conn.: Roper Center for Public Opinion Research [distributor]. [See appendix entry 18]

5.63 "Do you favor or oppose the death penalty for persons convicted of murder?" Percentages by Gender, 1972–1994

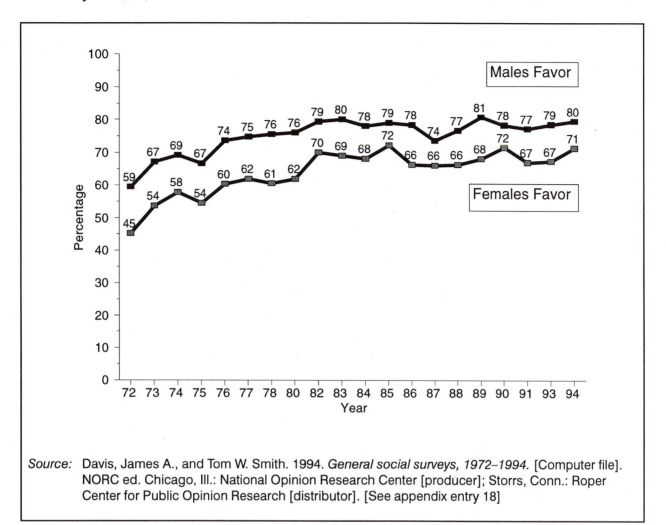

Source: Davis, James A., and Tom W. Smith. 1994. *General social surveys, 1972–1994.* [Computer file]. NORC ed. Chicago, Ill.: National Opinion Research Center [producer]; Storrs, Conn.: Roper Center for Public Opinion Research [distributor]. [See appendix entry 18]

5.64 "Do you favor the death penalty for people convicted of rape of an adult?" Percentages, 1991

	Percentage
Favor	24
Oppose	64
Depends*	7
Don't know	4
Refused	1

Source: Star Tribune. 1991. *Star Tribune national poll*, August 6–25, 1991, p. 3, Q. 10. Used with permission. [See appendix entry 43]
  * Response volunteered.

5.65   "Please tell me whether you strongly favor, favor, oppose, or strongly oppose a mandatory death penalty for major drug traffickers?" Percentages by Demographic Characteristics, 1990

Characteristic	Strongly Favor	Favor	Oppose	Strongly Oppose	Don't know
Total	42.3	30.4	18.3	5.5	3.2
Gender					
Male	44.1	30.1	17.5	5.8	2.3
Female	40.7	30.7	19.0	5.3	4.1
Race					
White	42.9	31.0	17.5	5.1	3.2
Nonwhite	9.2	27.2	22.4	7.7	3.5
Age (years)					
18-24	35.7	37.9	18.1	6.2	2.1
25-29	35.2	32.1	23.9	5.9	2.9
30-39	35.2	29.1	25.7	6.1	4.0
40-49	48.1	29.0	15.2	4.7	2.8
50-59	47.8	29.3	14.3	6.4	2.1
60 and older	50.2	27.9	12.6	4.6	4.2
Region					
East	41.4	32.1	20.6	4.8	1.1
Midwest	41.1	32.4	17.6	5.8	2.9
South	46.4	29.7	14.1	5.2	4.4
West	38.7	27.2	22.9	6.7	4.5
Education					
College graduate	32.5	28.7	26.1	10.6	2.1
Other college	42.6	34.9	15.4	5.5	1.6
High school graduate	44.3	31.2	17.4	2.7	4.2
Less than high school graduate	47.4	25.8	16.2	5.3	4.7
Politics					
Republican	50.4	31.3	14.0	2.6	1.4
Democrat	35.3	30.7	22.1	8.3	3.6
Independent	42.0	30.2	18.1	5.5	4.0
Income					
$50,000 and over	41.3	26.0	23.4	8.5	0.8
$40,000-$49,999	42.5	35.8	15.3	3.9	2.5
$30,000-$39,999	44.5	31.6	19.2	3.3	1.3
$20,000-$29,999	45.2	32.2	17.0	3.9	1.7
Under $20,000	41.6	29.1	18.3	6.3	4.6
Occupation					
Professional, business	37.6	30.2	22.0	8.2	1.9
Other white collar	43.9	32.1	15.3	4.7	3.9
Blue collar	43.1	30.1	18.8	5.1	2.8
Farmer	51.5	34.8	6.6	7.0	0.0
Non-labor force	44.9	31.1	16.4	3.2	4.3

Source: Princeton Research Associates data from: Maguire, Kathleen, Ann L. Pastore, and Timothy J. Flanagan, eds. 1993. *Sourcebook of criminal justice statistics, 1992*. Washington, D.C.: Bureau of Justice Statistics, p. 208, Table 2.56. Used with permission. [See appendix entry 37]

5.66 Public Support for Death Penalty for Specific Crimes, Percentages by Demographic Characteristics, 1988

Characteristic	Murder		Rape		Hijacking an Airplane		Attempting to Assassinate the President		Spying For a Foreign Nation in Peacetime		Drug Dealers Not Convicted of Murder	
	Favor	Oppose	Favor	Oppose	Favor	Oppose	Favor	Oppose	Favor	Oppose	Favor	Oppose
Total	79	16	51	42	49	45	63	33	42	50	38	55
Gender												
Men	83	13	55	39	58	38	66	30	50	43	40	55
Women	75	19	48	45	42	51	60	37	35	55	36	54
Age (years)												
18-29	83	15	59	39	47	50	66	31	45	50	31	66
30-49	80	16	49	45	46	48	62	36	38	55	35	59
50 and older	77	15	48	43	55	38	62	32	45	43	47	42
Region												
East	78	17	48	47	46	50	65	33	39	53	40	52
Midwest	79	16	49	43	44	50	62	34	39	50	34	57
South	79	13	54	39	53	41	61	35	47	45	39	55
West	81	16	54	41	56	37	65	31	43	52	40	55
Race												
White	82	14	53	41	51	43	66	31	43	49	39	54
Nonwhite	61	28	45	46	41	53	44	49	38	51	33	61
Black	57	31	40	50	40	55	42	52	38	51	28	67
Education												
College grad.	73	23	41	54	46	51	56	41	35	60	32	66
College incomplete	88	9	52	42	44	49	65	32	41	52	40	53
High school grad.	81	14	59	34	54	41	68	28	48	44	40	54
Not H.S. grad.	73	18	49	43	53	40	61	34	43	43	41	43
Politics												
Republican	90	6	59	36	54	41	74	23	50	44	43	52
Democrat	69	25	45	48	42	51	49	46	35	56	34	57
Independent	81	15	53	40	54	42	68	29	42	50	38	55
Household income												
$40,000 and over	84	13	51	46	56	42	67	31	40	54	38	60
$25,000-$39,999	77	18	49	43	41	52	61	36	39	54	37	57
$15,000-$24,999	84	13	60	36	49	46	62	36	46	48	39	57
Under $15,000	73	20	49	44	52	40	63	31	45	44	39	48

Source: The Gallup Organization. 1989. Public support for death penalty highest in Gallup annals. *The Gallup Report* 280 (January): pp. 28 and 29.   Used with permission. [See appendix entry 11]

Note: "Do you favor the death penalty for people convicted of ... murder, rape, hijacking of an airplane, attempting to assassinate the president, spying for a foreign nation during peacetime, drug dealers not convicted of murder?"

5.67   "In cases where death is caused from the use of drugs, would you favor the death penalty for the drug dealer who supplied the drugs?" Percentages, 1986

	Percentage
Favor	62
Oppose	32
Not sure	6

Source: NBC News and the Wall Street Journal. 1986. *Survey by NBC News and the Wall Street Journal, September 20–22, 1986.* Storrs, Conn.: The Roper Center, Q. R14. Used with permission. [See appendix entry 46]

5.68   "Which of the following murder cases, if any, would you consider justification for the death penalty . . . ?" Percentages, 1986

	Percentage
If murder is especially brutal	84
If murder is for hire	74
If victim was a child	79
If victim was a police officer	62
If victim was a prison guard	56
If convicted of killing more than one person	83
None of these	1
Don't know/No answer	4

Source: Associated Press/Media General. 1986. *The Associated Press/Media General Poll, November 7–14, 1986.* Used with permission. [See appendix entry 3]

Note: Asked of those who said that the death penalty should be allowed only in certain murder cases (56 percent). Adds to more than 100 percent due to multiple responses.

5.69 "Why do you favor the death penalty for those convicted of murder?" Percentages by Race, 1991

	Total	White	Black
Revenge; an "eye for an eye"	50	50	48
Acts as deterrent	13	13	16
Keeps them from killing again	19	18	23
Costly to keep them in prison	13	14	2
Judicial system is too lenient	3	3	2
Other	11	10	16
No opinion	2	2	2

Source: George Gallup Jr. 1991. *The Gallup Poll public opinion, 1991.* Wilmington, Del.: Scholarly Resources, Inc., p. 129. Used with permission. [See appendix entry 12]
Note: Asked of those who favor the death penalty.

5.70 "Why do you oppose the death penalty for those convicted of murder?" Percentages by Race, 1991

	Total	White	Black
Wrong to take a life	41	40	44
Punishment should be left to God	17	17	20
Persons may be wrongly convicted	11	10	16
Does not deter crime	7	8	7
Possibility of rehabilitation	6	6	4
Unfair application of penalty	6	5	5
Other	16	18	8
No opinion	6	6	7

Source: George Gallup Jr. 1991. *The Gallup Poll public opinion, 1991.* Wilmington, Del.: Scholarly Resources, Inc., p. 129. Used with permission. [See appendix entry 12]
Note: Asked of those who oppose the death penalty.

5.71   "Do you feel that the death penalty acts as a deterrent to the commitment of murder—that it lowers the murder rate, or not?" Percentages by Race, 1991

	Total	White	Black
Yes	51	53	38
No	41	40	53
No opinion	8	7	9

Source: George Gallup Jr. 1991. *The Gallup Poll public opinion, 1991.* Wilmington, Del.: Scholarly Resources, Inc., p. 130. Used with permission. [See appendix entry 12]

5.72   "To lower the crime rate in the United States, some people think additional money and effort should go to attacking the social and economic problems that lead to crime through better education and job training. Others feel more money and effort should go to deterring crime by improving law enforcement with more prisons, police, and judges. Which comes closer to your view?" Percentages by Race/Ethnicity, Community Size, and Victim Status, 1994

Characteristic	Spend Money on Social and Economic Problems	Spend Money on Police, Prisons, and Judges	Don't Know
Total	52	38	10
Race/ethnicity			
White	50	39	11
Black	56	35	9
Hispanic	56	36	8
Community size			
City	53	39	8
Suburb	56	33	11
Small town	49	39	12
Rural area	49	42	9
Victim of crime	46	43	11

Source: Los Angeles Times Poll data from: Maguire, Kathleen, and Ann L. Pastore, eds. 1994. *Sourcebook of criminal justice statistics, 1993.* Washington, D.C.: Bureau of Justice Statistics, p. 191, Table 2.43. Used with permission. [See appendix entry 24]

5.73 "Where does government need to make a greater effort these days: in trying to rehabilitate criminals who commit violent crimes, or in trying to punish and put away criminals who commit violent crimes?" Percentages by Race/Ethnicity, Community Size, and Victim Status, 1994

Characteristic	Rehabilitation	Punishment	Neither/Other*	Both Equally*	Don't Know
Total	32	49	2	8	9
Race/ethnicity					
White	31	50	2	8	9
Black	40	46	1	9	4
Hispanic	30	56	5	3	6
Community size					
City	32	47	3	8	10
Suburb	33	49	3	10	5
Small town	31	51	2	8	8
Rural area	34	52	1	5	8
Victim of crime	32	53	2	10	3

Source: Los Angeles Times Poll data from: Maguire, Kathleen, Ann L. Pastore, eds. 1994. *Sourcebook of criminal justice statistics, 1993*. Washington, D.C.: Bureau of Justice Statistics, p. 196, Table 2.48. Used with permission. [See appendix entry 24]

Note: Percentages may not add up to 100 because of rounding.
   *   Response volunteered.

WHAT CAUSES VIOLENCE?

5.74   Perceived Causes of Child Abuse, Percentages by Age, Race, and Gender, 1994

	Gender		Race			Age				
Contributes to child abuse	Male	Female	White	Black	Hispanic	18-24	25-34	35-54	55-64	65 and over
"Teachers hitting or spanking children in school"										
A great deal	14	23	18	20	27	29	23	16	12	15
Some effect	28	34	32	23	25	38	32	30	28	28
Not much	27	25	26	27	25	15	29	27	27	24
No effect	29	16	21	25	22	17	13	24	28	27
Not sure	3	2	2	5	1	1	2	2	5	6
"Parents spanking or hitting their children"										
A great deal	22	30	26	21	32	27	29	26	21	24
Some effect	44	46	46	45	42	52	45	45	44	41
Not much	20	16	17	16	15	14	16	18	19	21
No effect	11	6	7	15	9	6	7	8	11	12
Not sure	3	3	3	4	2	1	2	3	6	3
"Use of death penalty to punish murderers"										
A great deal	11	10	9	16	16	8	8	9	14	16
Some effect	14	20	16	21	24	16	16	18	16	15
Not much	15	18	17	16	11	20	21	15	11	15
No effect	55	46	52	43	44	55	50	53	49	41
Not sure	5	7	6	5	5	2	5	5	10	13
"Violence between husbands and wives"										
A great deal	67	75	71	69	67	73	74	72	70	66
Some effect	28	22	25	25	27	23	23	25	25	27
Not much	2	2	2	1	2	2	2	1	1	4
No effect	2	1	1	2	3	1	1	1	1	2
Not sure	1	1	*	2	-	1	*	*	2	1

See notes at end of table.

5.74 Perceived Causes of Child Abuse, Percentages by Age, Race, and Gender (continued)

Contributes to child abuse	Gender		Race			Age				
	Male	Female	White	Black	Hispanic	18-24	25-34	35-54	55-64	65 and over
"Violence on television"										
A great deal	34	50	42	42	42	25	32	42	57	62
Some effect	44	36	41	41	36	41	47	44	30	28
Not much	12	9	11	8	17	18	13	10	5	5
No effect	9	5	6	8	5	15	8	4	6	5
Not sure	1	*	*	1	-	-	-	*	2	-
"Heavy-metal rock music"										
A great deal	22	30	26	27	19	13	16	25	39	45
Some effect	31	35	33	31	42	25	35	35	31	34
Not much	20	16	19	15	11	26	24	18	8	9
No effect	23	14	18	18	24	36	21	18	9	5
Not sure	4	6	4	8	3	-	3	4	13	7
"Violence in movies"										
A great deal	35	48	40	50	38	25	32	43	49	61
Some effect	39	37	40	32	36	41	43	39	39	27
Not much	14	9	12	5	15	18	16	11	6	6
No effect	11	5	7	11	10	17	9	7	4	4
Not sure	1	*	1	2	1	-	-	1	3	2
"Toy guns and war toys, such as GI Joe"										
A great deal	14	19	15	27	19	12	15	15	17	25
Some effect	27	37	32	30	31	28	29	34	34	36
Not much	26	23	26	22	23	34	27	23	19	19
No effect	32	20	26	18	25	25	29	27	26	17
Not sure	2	2	1	3	2	1	-	1	4	3
"Racial discrimination and racism"										
A great deal	26	30	26	40	36	36	32	28	19	23
Some effect	43	42	45	31	42	37	39	46	47	39
Not much	13	13	14	11	10	12	13	12	16	17
No effect	15	12	13	15	11	15	13	13	12	15
Not sure	3	3	3	2	-	1	3	1	6	6

See notes at end of table.

5.74   Perceived Causes of Child Abuse, Percentages by Age, Race, and Gender *(continued)*

Contributes to child abuse	Gender		Race			Age				
	Male	Female	White	Black	Hispanic	18-24	25-34	35-54	55-64	65 and over
"Discrimination against people because of their sex"										
A great deal	15	16	14	22	22	19	17	13	10	22
Some effect	37	41	40	40	40	39	36	41	44	34
Not much	23	21	24	15	16	16	26	22	22	20
No effect	23	19	21	20	20	25	19	21	21	20
Not sure	2	3	2	4	2	1	2	2	4	4
"Poverty"										
A great deal	47	48	49	45	45	35	50	52	53	45
Some effect	41	39	40	38	45	50	42	38	39	33
Not much	5	5	4	7	3	7	3	4	2	10
No effect	6	6	5	8	5	7	4	6	6	9
Not sure	1	1	1	2	1	2	1	*	1	3
"Contact sports such as boxing, hockey, wrestling, and football"										
A great deal	4	3	3	6	9	5	1	3	4	7
Some effect	20	24	21	26	20	15	19	24	28	21
Not much	30	32	33	27	20	34	32	31	30	31
No effect	45	39	42	38	50	45	48	42	35	37
Not sure	2	1	1	3	-	1	*	1	3	4
"Drug abuse"										
A great deal	84	89	86	87	84	83	81	89	95	85
Some effect	14	9	12	13	15	15	17	10	1	12
Not much	1	1	1	-	-	1	1	*	1	1
No effect	1	1	1	-	1	1	1	*	1	1
Not sure	1	*	1	-	-	-	-	-	2	2

Source: National Child Abuse Survey as presented in: National Committee to Prevent Child Abuse, Chicago, Ill.   Used with permission. [See appendix entry 27]   Unpublished data, tables generated by National Committee to Prevent Child Abuse. 1994.

Note: "How much do you think this contributes to child abuse in this country: Teachers hitting or spanking children in school, parents hitting or spanking their children, use of the death penalty to punish murderers, violence between husbands and wives, violence on television, heavy-metal rock music, violence in movies, toy guns and war toys, such as GI Joe, racial discrimination and racism, discrimination against people because of their sex or poverty, contact sports, such as boxing, hockey, wrestling, and football, drug abuse?"   A dash indicates no cases in a particular category.

*   Less than 1 percent.

5.75 "What do you think is the single most important reason that the number of sexual assaults in your state in the past five years has increased?" Percentages, 1991

	Percentage
Legal system	8.8
Media	5.5
Drugs/alcohol	10.1
Moral/religious	5.1
Social issues	6.1
Blame women	2.6
Family	4.1
Blame rapists	3.8
Crime/population	2.5
More report it	1.9
Other	30.8
Don't know	18.7

Source: Star Tribune. 1991. *Star Tribune national poll*, Minneapolis, Minn., August 6–25, 1991, p. 1, Q. 4A. Used with permission. [See appendix entry 43]

Note: Asked of those who said the number of sexual assaults in the past five years has increased in their state (70 percent).

5.76 Percentages of Perceived Causes of Crime, 1993

	Critical	Very Important	Somewhat Important	Not At All Important	No Opinion
Influence of drugs	64	30	4	2	*
Lack of moral training	51	38	10	1	*
Availability of guns	45	26	18	10	1
Television violence	38	29	21	11	1
Absence of fathers	36	35	22	6	1
Poor quality of schools	34	39	19	7	1
Lack of jobs for young	32	38	22	7	1
Racism	31	30	27	10	2
Decline in influence of religion	29	31	25	13	2

Source: Newport, Frank, and Lydia Saad. 1993. Drugs seen as root cause of crime in the U.S. *The Gallup Poll Monthly* 337 (October): p. 33. Used with permission. [See appendix entry 13]

Note: "I'm going to read some reasons that have been given as the causes of crime in this country. While some people view all of these as important causes of crime, we'd like to know which factors you think are the most important. As I read each item, please tell me whether you think it is a critical factor, a very important factor, a somewhat important factor, or not an important factor."

* Less than 0.5 percent.

5.77 "What do you think is the most common reason some men commit the crime of rape? Is it because they are mentally ill, because they are influenced by pornography, because they are angry toward women, or is it because they are evil?" Percentages, 1991

	Percentage
Mentally ill	35
Angry toward women	25
Evil	16
Pornography	13
Other reason	6
Don't know	5

Source: Princeton Survey Research Association data from: Silver, Thomas H. 1991. Men, women, and rape. *The Polling Report* 7, no. 1 (January): p. 3. Used with permission. [See appendix entry 40]

5.78   "Do you think that coverage of news [on television about crime] encourages people to commit crime, or not?" Percentages by Demographic Characteristics, 1993

Characteristic	Yes	No
Total	43	54
Gender		
Male	43	53
Female	43	54
Age (years)		
18-29	35	63
30-49	41	57
50-64	42	56
65 and older	55	35
Region		
East	39	58
Midwest	39	56
South	48	49
West	44	54
Community		
Urban	40	56
Suburban	45	53
Rural	43	52
Race		
White	42	54
Black	43	55
Education		
College postgraduate	41	55
College graduate	39	57
College incomplete	43	54
No college	44	52
Politics		
Republican	46	51
Democrat	40	58
Independent	42	53
Ideology		
Liberal	39	57
Moderate	39	58
Conservative	47	50
Fear of crime		
Most fearful	50	48
All others	40	56
Income		
$50,000 and over	40	57
$30,000-$49,999	46	53
$20,000-$29,999	39	55
Under $20,000	45	53
Watch local news		
Daily	43	53
Several times/week	45	53
Occasionally/never	38	58

Source: McAnney, Leslie. 1993. The Gallup Poll on crime. *The Gallup Poll Monthly* 339 (December): p. 27. Used with permission. [See appendix entry 13]

Note: "No opinion" omitted. Percentages computed across rows.

5.79   "Do you think violence on television and in movies contributes to violence in our society, or doesn't it?" Percentages, 1994

	Total	18 - 29	30 - 44	45 - 64	Over 64
Contributes to violence	81	77	78	84	87
Does not contribute	15	19	20	13	6
Don't know/No answer	4	4	2	3	7

Source: CBS News. 1994. *CBS News/America Tonight poll: Too much TV and movie violence, but many say people ask for it*, July 26, 1994, p. 3, Q. 4.   Used with permission. [See appendix entry 4]

5.80   "As you probably know, there has been an increase in violence in the nation's public schools over the last decade. How important do you consider each of the following as a cause for this increased violence—very important, quite important, not very important, or not at all important?" Percentages, 1994

Cause	Very Important	Quite Important	Not Very Important	Not at All Important	Don't Know
Increased use of drugs and alcohol among school-age youth	78	17	3	2	*
Growth of youth gangs	72	19	4	3	2
Easy availability of weapon (guns, knives)	72	15	6	6	1
A breakdown in the American family (e.g., an increase in one-parent and dysfunctional families)	70	20	7	2	1
Schools do not have the authority to discipline	65	22	9	3	1
Increased portrayal of violence in the media (especially in movies and on TV)	60	20	14	5	1
Inability of school staff to resolve conflicts between students	59	26	11	3	1
Shortages in school personnel	52	26	15	5	2
Trying to deal with troubled or emotionally disturbed students in the regular classroom instead of in special classes or schools	51	27	16	4	2
A school curriculum that is out of touch with the needs of today's students	48	28	17	4	3
Cutbacks in many school support programs	45	27	18	6	4
Increased poverty among parents	44	29	20	6	1
Increased cultural, racial, and ethnic diversity among the public school student population	43	26	22	7	2

Source: Elam, Stanley M., Lowell C. Rose, and Alec M. Gallup. 1994. The 26th annual Phi Delta Kappa/Gallup poll of the public's attitudes toward the public schools. *Phi Delta Kappan* (September):43–44. Used with permission. [See appendix entry 58]
*   Less than one-half of 1 percent.

5.81 "What do you think is the most important cause of crime today? Is there another cause that is almost as important?" Percentages by Race/Ethnicity, Location of Residence, and Victimization, 1994

	All	White	Black	Hispanic	Victim	City	Suburb	Small-town	Rural
Social	88	86	99	89	93	91	89	86	85
Drugs/drug dealing	36	36	42	40	43	39	37	35	34
Economic/poverty/not enough jobs	35	33	42	41	33	37	38	32	34
Morality/values/decline of religion/breakdown of family/lack of parental supervision/ permissiveness	34	36	27	20	32	37	30	30	38
Poor education system	12	12	10	17	11	10	13	16	10
Children/teens joining gangs	5	4	11	4	8	8	5	4	2
Greed	3	3	1	1	4	3	4	2	5
Racial prejudice	3	2	5	1	1	2	4	3	2
Leniency	12	13	5	7	9	10	12	11	14
Sentences too light /too short/let criminals go free	6	8	3	2	5	5	8	6	7
Statutes/laws too lenient	4	4	2	2	3	5	3	3	4
Prisoners released too quickly/fast parole	2	2	-	2	1	2	1	1	4
Courts inefficient /overburdened	1	2	-	-	2	1	1	1	2
Too much plea bargaining	1	1	1	1	1	-	1	1	2
Prisons inadequate/lack facilities	-	-	-	-	-	-	-	1	-
Guns	7	7	9	8	5	5	7	10	5
Too many guns/gun control inadequate	7	7	9	8	5	5	7	9	5
Average citizens need more guns/ more gun access	-	-	-	-	-	-	-	1	-
Media/culture	5	4	4	4	7	4	6	4	4
The media/TV/violence on TV and in movies	4	4	3	4	7	4	6	2	4
Gangsta rap/rock music	1	1	1	-	-	1	-	1	-
Pornography	-	-	-	-	-	-	1	-	1
Police	1	-	4	3	2	2	-	2	1
Police do poor job	1	-	3	2	2	1	-	1	-
Too few police	1	-	-	1	-	-	-	1	-
Other	5	6	4	6	5	7	5	4	5
Don't know	3	4	-	7	-	1	3	4	6

Source: Los Angeles Times. 1994. *Los Angeles Times Poll-National Issues.* January 15–19, 1994, p. 3, Q. 41. Used with permission. [See appendix entry 24]

Note: A dash indicates no cases in a particular category.

Appendix:
Description of Data Sources

This appendix supplies information about the data sources used in the *Handbook*. Each data source is described in a structured abstract under the following topics:

Data Source Number

Target Population
  The group the study intends to describe.

Sample
  The procedures used to select a portion of the target population that is then used to make inferences about the target population.

Source of Information
  The method used to collect information from people about violent incidents.

Date of Collection
  The time interval during which the data were collected.

Reference Period
  The time interval described in the study.

Organization
  The agency or organization that collected the data. If the sponsoring organization is different, both the sponsoring organization and the collection organization are listed.

Additional Information
  Where appropriate, explanations of important data collection procedures and key concepts are provided.

Technical Reference
  One or more documents, relevant to the data in this volume, are cited to tell the reader where to find additional information about the methods used to collect the data.

Some technical terms used in this appendix are defined in a brief glossary at the end of the appendix.

Data Source 1

Age, Sex, Race, and Ethnic Origin of Persons Arrested (ASREO) (a part of the Uniform Crime Reporting Program of the Federal Bureau of Investigation)

Target Population: Persons arrested, cited, or summoned for specified criminal acts by state and local law enforcement agencies in the U.S.

Sample: Voluntary reports submitted by state and local law enforcement agencies. The number of cooperating agencies, consistency of reporting, and other measures of completeness varies.

Source of Information: Forms submitted by of state and local law enforcement agencies.

Date of Collection: Monthly.

Reference Period: Previous month.

Organization: Federal Bureau of Investigation.

Additional Information
The reports counted the number of persons arrested, not the number of charges. For adults, "arrest" was defined as detention with the intention of seeking charges against the person for a specific offense(s), and a record was made of the detention. Detentions of juveniles were counted as "arrests" when the circumstances were such that if the suspect were an adult, an arrest would be tallied. Federal offenses were included only when the arrest was for a federal crime which occurred in the agency's jurisdiction and the offense was also a crime under the state penal code. Where multiple charges re-

sulted from a single arrest, the arrest was classified according to the most serious charge.

A comprehensive analysis of coverage is not available. The FBI indicates, however, that these data did not cover the entire population of the United States at any time between 1960 and 1992. Rather, they estimate that these data covered between 65 and 94 percent of the U.S. population for age-specific rates and between 61 and 86 percent for race-specific rates (Federal Bureau of Investigation, 1993, pp. 205–207).

Technical Reference
Federal Bureau of Investigation. 1993. *Age-specific arrest rates and race-specific arrest rates for selected offenses 1965–1992*. Washington, D.C.: U.S. Government Printing Office.

Federal Bureau of Investigation. 1984. *Uniform crime reporting handbook*. Washington, D.C.: U.S. Government Printing Office.

Data Source 2

America Speaks Out: Citizens' Attitudes About Victims' Rights and Violence

Target Population: Adults living in households with telephones in the U.S.

Sample: Random digit dialing of geographic strata. Sample size = 1,000.

Source of Information: Telephone interviews.

Date of Collection: March 8–17, 1991.

Reference Period: Questions referred to time of interview.

Organization: Schulman, Ronca, and Bucuvalas, Inc., 145 East 32nd Street, Suite 500, New York, NY 10016. Conducted for the National Victim Center.

Technical Reference
National Victim Center. 1991. *America speaks out: Citizens' attitudes about victims' rights and violence: Executive summary*. Fort Worth, TX.

Maguire, Kathleen, Ann L. Pastore, and Timothy J. Flanagan, eds. 1993. *Sourcebook of criminal justice statistics, 1992*. Washington, D.C.: Bureau of Justice Statistics, p. 168, note to Table 2.8.

Data Source 3

The Associated Press/Media General Poll, November 7–14, 1986

Target Population: Adults living in households with telephones in the U.S.

Sample: Sample size = 1,251.

Source of Information: Telephone interviews.

Date of Collection: November 7–14 1986.

Reference Period: Questions referred to time of interview.

Organization: Associated Press, Media General.

Technical Reference
Associated Press/Media General. 1986. *The Associated Press/Media General Poll, November 7–14.*

Data Source 4

CBS News/America Tonight Poll: Too Much TV and Movie Violence, But Many Say People Ask For It

Target Population: Adults living in households with telephones in the U.S.

Sample: Sample size = 541.

Source of Information: Telephone interviews.

Date of Collection: July 26, 1994.

Reference Period: Questions referred to time of interview.

Organization: CBS Election and Survey Unit, 533 West 57th Street, New York, NY 10019.

Technical Reference
CBS News. 1994. *CBS News/America Tonight poll: Too much TV and movie violence, but many say people ask for it, July 26, 1994.*

Data Source 5

Census of Fatal Occupational Injuries, 1990

Target Population: All fatal work-related injuries of private wage and salary workers, public sector employees (both civilian and military), and the self-employed in all 50 states.

Sample: All work-related fatalities were included.

Source of Information: Death certificates, workers' compensation forms, and other reports provided by state and federal agencies.

Date of Collection: Continuous since 1992.

Reference Period: Previous year.

Organization: U.S. Bureau of Labor Statistics.

Additional Information
The study procedures required that fatalities designated as "work related" must be substantiated by two or more independent source documents or a source document and a follow-up questionnaire. The fatality was included in the census only if both the Bureau of Labor Statistics and the state agreed that there was enough evidence in the source document to determine that the fatality was work related.

Technical Reference
Toscano, Guy, and Janice Windau. 1993. Fatal work injuries: results from the 1992 national census. *Monthly Labor Review* 116, no. 10: 39–47.

Data Source 6

Census of State and Federal Correctional Facilities

Target Population: Inmates in state and federal correctional facilities in the U.S.

Sample: All state and federal correctional facilities and 67 private facilities under exclusive contract to house state prisoners. Data were collected from 1,287 facilities.

Source of Information: Questionnaires mailed to facility respondents; 2 mail follow-ups and final telephone follow-up. Response rate 100 percent.

Date of Collection: June 1990.

Reference Period: Previous year.

Organization: U.S. Bureau of the Census, for the U.S. Bureau of Justice Statistics.

Additional Information
Excluded from the sample were private facilities that did not hold exclusively state or federal prisoners, military facilities, Immigration and Naturalization Service facilities, Bureau of Indian Affairs facilities, facilities operated by local governments (jails), including those housing state prisoners, and public hospital wings and wards reserved for prisoners. Correctional facilities were not included if they were considered community-based facilities, meaning that 50 percent or more of the residents were permitted to leave the facilities unaccompanied for work or study.

Technical Reference
Stephan, James. *Census of state and federal correctional facilities, 1990*. Washington, D.C.: Bureau of Justice Statistics.

Data Source 7

Child Rape Victims, 1992

Target Population: Children (under the age of 18) in 15 states and the District of Columbia.

Sample: Fifteen states and the District of Columbia provided information on 26,527 rape victims under the age of 18. These were all of the states that collect information on the age of rape victims.

Source of Information: Telephone survey of state Statistical Analysis Centers and police officials of the District of Columbia, Nevada, and Wyoming.

Date of Collection: Information not provided.

Reference Period: 1992.

Organization: Bureau of Justice Statistics.

Additional Information
This study was done to supplement the National Crime Victimization Survey, which does not interview people under the age of 12, and the Uniform Crime Program, which does not provide information about the age of rape victims.

Technical Reference
Langan, Patrick A., and Caroline Wolf Harlow. 1994. *Child rape victims, 1992*. Washington, D.C.: Bureau of Justice Statistics.

Data Source 8

Children as Victims of Violence: A National Survey

Target Population: Children aged 10–16 and their caretakers in the U.S.

Sample: National sample was selected (using random digit dialing methods) and screened for presence of children age 10–16 in the household. The sample included 2,000 children (1,042 boys, 958 girls) and their caretakers (such as parents).

Source of Information: Telephone interview.

Date of Collection: December 1992, January 1993.

Reference Period: The previous year and lifetime occurrence of events.

Organization: Schulman, Ronca, Bucuvalas, Inc., 145 East 32nd Street, Suite 500, New York, NY 10016. Conducted for The Family Research Laboratory at the University of New Hampshire.

Technical Reference
Finkelhor, David, and Jennifer Dziuba-Leatherman. 1994. Children as victims of violence: A national survey. *Pediatrics* 94, no. 4: 413–420.

Data Source 9

Children's Defense Fund/Newsweek National Poll of Children and Parents

Target Population: Children aged 10–17 and their parents in the U.S.

Sample: Sample size = 758 parents.

Source of Information: Telephone interview.

Date of Collection: October 18–November 7, 1993.

Reference Period: Questions referred to time of interview.

Organization: Princeton Survey Research Associates, P.O. Box 1450, Princeton, NJ 08542.

Technical Reference
Princeton Survey Research Associates. 1993. *Children's Defense Fund/Newsweek national poll of children and parents: Final top-line questionnaire*, October 18-November 7, 1993.

Data Source 10

Drug Use Forecasting, 1990, 1991

Target Population: People arrested and booked by the police on drug charges in 23 cities for 1990 and 24 cities in 1991.

Sample: Sample size varied by city: minimum of 455, maximum of 2,157 in 1990; minimum of 681, maximum of 2,483 in 1991.

Source of Information: Interviews and urine test.

Date of Collection: Fourteen consecutive evenings, each quarter, 1990, 1991.

Reference Period: Time of arrest.

Organization: National Institute of Justice.

Additional Information
Drug Use Forecasting (DUF) data were collected at police booking facilities from people being arrested. Arrestees were interviewed and had urine samples collected on a voluntary and anonymous basis, with about 90 percent of those approached agreeing to the interview and 80 percent to the urine test. Data for adult male arrestees were collected at all sites; in some sites females and juveniles were also sampled.

The urine was tested for 10 drugs: cocaine, opiates, marijuana, PCP, methadone, benzodiazepines, methaqualone, propoxyphene, barbiturates, and amphetamines (National Institute of Justice, 1992, p. 2).

The 23 cities for 1990 were Atlanta, Birmingham, Chicago, Cleveland, Dallas, Denver, Detroit, Ft. Lauderdale, Houston, Indianapolis, Kansas City, Los Angeles, Manhattan, New Orleans, Omaha, Philadelphia, Phoenix, Portland, St. Louis, San Antonio, San Diego, San Jose, and Washington, D.C. Miami was added in 1991.

Technical Reference
National Institute of Justice. 1991. *Drugs and crime: 1990 annual report.* Washington, D.C.: U.S. Department of Justice.

National Institute of Justice. 1992. *Drug use forecasting: 1991 annual report.* Washington, D.C.: U.S. Department of Justice.

Data Source 11

Gallup Survey No. AI 875

Target Population: Adults (18 years and older) living in households in the U.S.

Sample: Geographically stratified random digit dialing. Sample size = 1,001.

Source of Information: Telephone interviews.

Date of Collection: September 25–October 1, 1988.

Reference Period: Questions referred to time of interview.

Organization: The Gallup Poll, P.O. Box 628, 47 Hulfish Street, Princeton, NJ 08542.

Technical Reference
The Gallup Poll. 1989. *Gallup Report* 280 (January): 35–36.

Data Source 12

Gallup Survey GO 222002

Target Population: Adults (18 years and older) living in households in the U.S.

Sample: Geographically stratified random digit dialing. Sample size = 1,010.

Source of Information: Telephone interviews.

Date of Collection: June 13–16, 1991.

Reference Period: Questions referred to time of interview.

Organization: The Gallup Poll, P.O. Box 628, 47 Hulfish Street, Princeton, NJ 08542.

Technical Reference
Gallup, George, Jr. *The Gallup Poll: Public opinion 1991.* 1991. Wilmington, Del.: Scholarly Resources, Inc., pp. vii–xi.

Data Source 13

Gallup Survey GO 422017

Target Population: Adults (18 years and older) living in households in the U.S.

Sample: Geographically stratified random digit dialing. The sample size was 1,244, including 870 whites and 314 blacks.

Source of Information: Telephone interviews.

Date of Collection: October 8–10, 13–18, 1993.

Reference Period: Questions referred to time of interview.

Organization: The Gallup Poll, P.O. Box 628, 47 Hulfish Street, Princeton, NJ 08542.

Additional Information
The design included an oversample of 235 black respondents. Results were weighted to obtain appropriate national estimates.

Technical Reference
The Gallup Poll. 1993. The Gallup Poll on crime. *The Gallup Poll Monthly* 339 (December): 38, 67–68.

Data Source 14

Gallup Sample GO 422025

Target Population: Adults (18 years and older) living in households in the U.S.

Sample: Geographically stratified random digit dialing. The sample size = 1,014.

Source of Information: Telephone interviews.

Date of Collection: December 17–19, 1993.

Reference Period: Questions referred to time of interview.

Organization: The Gallup Poll, P.O. Box 628, 47 Hulfish Street, Princeton, NJ 08542.

Additional Information
The design included an oversample of 750 adults who say there is a gun in their home or on their property. Results were weighted to obtain appropriate national estimates.

Technical Reference
The Gallup Poll. 1994. *The Gallup Poll Monthly*. 340 (January): 18–19, 59–60.

Data Source 15

Gallup Survey GO 422030

Target Population: Adults (18 years and older) living in households in the U.S.

Sample: Geographically stratified random digit dialing. The sample size = 693.

Source of Information: Telephone interviews.

Date of Collection: January 22–23, 1994.

Reference Period: Questions referred to time of interview.

Organization: The Gallup Poll, P.O. Box 628, 47 Hulfish Street, Princeton, NJ 08542.

Technical Reference
The Gallup Poll. 1994. *The Gallup Poll Monthly*. 340 (January): 59–60.

Data Source 16

Gallup Survey 422027

Target Population: Adults (18 years and older) living in households in the U.S.

Sample: Geographically stratified random digit dialing. The sample size = 1,023, but a half sample of 526 is used for the included items.

Source of Information: Telephone interviews.

Date of Collection: January 6–8, 1994.

Reference Period: Questions referred to time of interview.

Organization: The Gallup Poll, P.O. Box 628, 47 Hulfish Street, Princeton, NJ 08542.

Technical Reference
The Gallup Poll. 1994. *The Gallup Poll Monthly*. 341 (February): 2.

Data Source 17

Gallup Survey GO 22-00807-020

Target Population: Adults (18 years and older) living in households in the U.S.

Sample: Geographically stratified random digit dialing. The sample size = 1,022.

Source of Information: Telephone interviews.

Date of Collection: September 6–7, 1994.

Reference Period: Questions referred to time of interview.

Organization: The Gallup Poll, P.O. Box 628, 47 Hulfish Street, Princeton, NJ 08542.

Technical Reference
The Gallup Poll. 1994. *The Gallup Poll Monthly*. 348 (September): 46–47.

Data Source 18

General Social Survey

Target Population: Adults (18 and over) living in households in the U.S.

Sample: 1972–1974: modified probability sample using block quota. 1975–1976: half modified probability, half full probability. 1977–1994: full probability sample of the U.S. In 1994 the sample size was 2,992; since 1972, 32,380 have been interviewed.

Source of Information: Personal interview.

Date of Collection: Annual since 1972, February, March, and April, except for 1979, 1981, 1992 when no surveys were conducted.

Reference Period: Questions referred to time of interview.

Organization: National Opinion Research Center, University of Chicago, 1155 East 60th St., Chicago, IL 60637.

Additional Information
Blacks were oversampled in 1982 and 1987. One person per household was selected for the survey. Weights were used to adjust for the household size and the oversample of blacks, where appropriate.

Technical Reference
Davis, James A., and Tom W. Smith. 1994. *General social surveys, 1972–1994*. [Computer file]. NORC ed. Chicago, Ill.: National Opinion Research Center [producer]; Storrs, Conn.: Roper Center for Public Opinion Research [distributor].

Davis, James A., and Tom W. Smith. 1992. *The NORC general social survey: A users' guide*. Newbury Park, Calif.: Sage Publications.

Data Source 19

Hate Crime Statistics

Target Population: Residents of 11 states.

Sample: Only 11 states submit reports.

Source of Information: State submissions to the FBI.

Date of Collection: Annual since 1990.

Reference Period: Previous year.

Organization: U.S. Federal Bureau of Investigation.

Additional Information
These data were prepared in response to the Hate Crime Statistics Act of 1990 by the FBI and the Center for Applied Social Research at Northeastern University. "The 1990 Hate Crimes Statistics Act (Public Law 101–275) states, 'The Attorney General shall acquire data . . . about crimes that manifest evidence of prejudice based on race, religion, sexual orientation, or ethnicity . . .'" (FBI, 1992, p. 1). The report included the states that collected hate crime statistics and were willing to participate in 1990. Each state had independent laws and unique data collection strategies, so the data were not comparable (FBI, 1992, p. 1), and "*these limitations . . . make inappropriate any attempt to compare*

specific findings across states" (p. 5, italics in the original). There was no national collection under this system yet. These data included only those hate crimes reported to the police.

Technical Reference
Federal Bureau of Investigation. 1992. *Hate crime statistics, 1990: A resource book*. Washington, D.C.: U.S. Government Printing Office.

Data Source 20

Homicide as a Risk Factor for PTSD Among Surviving Family Members

Target Population: Noninstitutionalized, English-speaking adult residents of the U.S. who lost a friend or relative to criminal homicide or alcohol-related vehicular homicide.

Sample: Two-stage design. In Stage 1, random digit dialing tech-niques were used to screen a national sample of 12,500 noninstitutionalized adults to identify 206 respondents who were surviving family members and close friends of criminal homicide or alcohol-related vehicular homicide victims. In Stage 2, a sample of survivors and nonvictims identified during Stage 1 completed a 30-minute interview that assessed a variety of demographic and adjustment variables. The Stage 2 response rate was 84 percent.

Source of Information: Telephone interviews.

Date of Collection: July 1987–February 1988.

Reference Period: Lifetime.

Organization: Schulman, Ronca, and Bucuvalas, Inc., 145 East 32nd, Street, Suite 500, New York, NY 10016.

Additional Information
The post-traumatic stress disorder (PTSD) of homicide survivors (i.e., immediate family members, other relatives, and close friends) was assessed according to diagnostic criteria established in the DSM-III-R (American Psychiatric Association, 1987).

Lifetime PTSD was assigned to respondents who reported having experienced the symptoms meeting the criteria for a diagnosis of homicide-related PTSD at some point in their lifetime following the homicide. *Current PTSD* was defined as symptoms experienced within the six months prior to the interview.

Technical Reference
Amick-McMullan, Angelynne, Dean G. Kilpatrick, and Heidi S. Resnick. 1991. Homicide as a risk factor for PTSD among surviving family members. *Behavior Modification* 15, no. 4: 545–559.

American Psychiatric Association. 1987. *Diagnostic and statistical manual of mental disorders*. 3rd ed., rev. Washington, D.C.

Data Source 21

Inmates Under Sentence of Death

Target Population: Persons under sentence of death in state, federal, or military prisons in the U.S.

Sample: State, the District of Columbia, and federal prison systems.

Source of Information: Questionnaires completed by office of Attorney General in each jurisdiction.

Date of Collection: Annual.

Reference Period: Twelve months, January through December.

Organization: U.S. Bureau of the Census, for the U.S. Bureau of Justice Statistics.

Technical Reference
Snell, Tracy L. 1993. *Correctional populations in the United States, 1991*. Washington, D.C.: Bureau of Justice Statistics.

Data Source 22

Law Enforcement Officers Killed/Law Enforcement Officers Killed and Assaulted (LEOKA) (a part of the Uniform Crime Reporting Program of the Federal Bureau of Investigation)

Target Population: Federal, state, and local law enforcement officers who have full arrest powers.

Sample: All law enforcement agencies that reported to the FBI.

Source of Information: For homicide—there were three sources: (1) State and local law enforcement agencies participating in the UCR program provided preliminary reports of officers killed in the line of duty in their jurisdictions; (2) FBI field divisions and legal attache offices collected data and reported such incidents, within the

United States and its territories, or when an officer died in the line of duty when assigned to another country; and (3) the Bureau of Justice Assistance, administrator of the Public Safety Officers Benefit Program, supplied information on the survivors of police who received benefits. For assault—data were collected monthly from UCR contributing agencies. The reporting agencies offered services to 85 percent of the nation's population (FBI, 1993, p. 1).

Date of Collection: Continuous.

Reference Period: Previous month.

Organization: U.S. Federal Bureau of Investigation.

Additional Information
Data were for felonious or accidental death of police officers.

Technical Reference
Federal Bureau of Investigation. 1993. *Law enforcement officers killed and assaulted, 1992*. Washington, D.C.: U.S. Government Printing Office.

Data Source 23

Linked Birth/Infant Death Data Set

Target Population: Infants born in the U.S. during 1983, 1984, and 1985.

Sample: All linkable birth and death records for infants who were born in 1983, 1984, or 1985 and who died before reaching one year of age.

Source of Information: Birth and death certificates.

Date of Collection: Continuous.

Reference Period: 1983–1986.

Organization: National Center for Health Statistics.

Additional Comments
Infant homicides classified by mother's race and education were obtained from the national linked birth and infant death data sets distributed by the National Center for Health Statistics (NCHS). Birth records were located for 98 percent of the infant death records (98.4 percent in 1983, 97.8 percent in 1984, and 98.1 percent in 1985). Excluded were deaths that occurred outside the U.S. to U.S.-born infants; deaths that occurred in the U.S. to foreign-born infants; and births and deaths that occurred outside the U.S. to U.S. residents (NCHS 1990b).

Homicide was defined according to the International Classification of Diseases (9th revision) as external causes E960–E969. Of the 117,188 linked birth/death records, 581 were homicides (182 in 1983, 200 in 1984, and 199 in 1985). All 581 homicide victims could be classified by race, but only 417 could be classified by mother's educational attainment. Most of the missing data (141 cases) were accounted for by three states that did not record maternal education: California (66 cases), Texas (64 cases), and Washington (11 cases). The other 23 cases were scattered across the remaining states and the District of Columbia, with no more than 2 in any jurisdiction.

Births by race and mother's education were obtained from the Vital Statistics of the United States (NCHS 1987: 179; 1988a: 179; 1988b: 179).

Technical Reference
Loftin, Colin, David McDowall, and Brian Wiersema. 1992. Economic risk factors for infant homicide. In *Proceedings of the 1991 public health conference on records and statistics*. Hyattsville, Md.: National Center for Health Statistics, 273–275.

National Center for Health Statistics. 1987. *Vital statistics of the United States, 1983, volume I, natality*. DHHS Pub. No. (PHS) 87–1113. Public Health Service, Washington, D.C.: U.S. Government Printing Office.

National Center for Health Statistics. 1989a. *Linked birth/infant death data set: 1983 birth cohort*. [Computer file]. Hyattsville, Md.: National Center for Health Statistics [producer and distributor].

National Center for Health Statistics. 1989b. *Linked birth/infant death data set: 1984 birth cohort*. [Computer file]. Hyattsville, Md.: National Center for Health Statistics [producer and distributor].

National Center for Health Statistics. 1990a. *Linked birth/infant death data set: 1985 birth cohort*. [Computer file]. Hyattsville, Md.: National Center for Health Statistics [producer and distributor].

National Center for Health Statistics. 1990b. *Linked birth and infant death data set* [codebook and documentation]. Washington, D.C.: U.S. Government Printing Office.

Data Source 24

Los Angeles Times Poll Survey #328—National Issues-January, 1994

Target Population: Adults (over 18 years of age) living in households with telephones in the U.S.

Sample: Telephone numbers were generated from a computer list that includes all telephone exchanges in the nation. Random-digit dialing techniques were used to ensure that both listed and unlisted residences had an opportunity to be contacted. Results were adjusted to conform with census figures on characteristics such as sex, age, race, education, and household size. Interviewing was conducted in English and Spanish. Sample size = 1,516.

Source of Information: Telephone interviews.

Date of Collection: January 15–19, 1994.

Reference Period: Time of survey.

Organization: Los Angeles Times Poll, Los Angeles Times, Times Mirror Square, Los Angeles, CA 90053.

Technical Reference
Los Angeles Times. 1994. *Los Angeles Times poll: Survey #328-National issues* (January).

Maguire, Kathleen, Ann L. Pastore, and Timothy J. Flanagan, eds. 1994. *Sourcebook of criminal justice statistics, 1993*. Washington, D.C.: Bureau of Justice Statistics, p. 191, note to Table 2.43.

Data Source 25

Los Angeles Times Poll Survey #334—National Issues-April, 1994

Target Population: Adults living in households with telephones in the U.S.

Sample: Random digit dialing techniques were used (with numbers generated from a list that included all telephone exchanges in the nation). Interviewing was conducted in English and Spanish. Sample size = 1,682.

Source of Information: Telephone interviews.

Date of Collection: April 16–19, 1994.

Reference Period: Time of survey.

Organization: Los Angeles Times Poll, Los Angeles Times, Times Mirror Square, Los Angeles, CA 90053.

Additional Comments
Estimates were adjusted to conform to census figures on characteristics such as sex, race, age, and occupation.

Technical Reference
Los Angeles Times. 1994. *Los Angeles Times poll: Survey #334—National issues* (April).

Data Source 26

Monthly Return of Offenses Known to the Police (Return A) (a part of the Uniform Crime Reporting program of the Federal Bureau of Investigation)

Target Population: Crimes known to the police in the U.S.

Sample: Crimes recorded by police agencies that reported to the UCR program.

Source of Information: Reports submitted by local law enforcement agencies.

Date of Collection: Monthly.

Reference Period: Previous month.

Organization: Federal Bureau of Investigation.

Additional Information
The Uniform Crime Reporting (UCR) program of the Federal Bureau of Investigation (FBI) compiled information on crimes reported to, or discovered by, local and state police agencies in the U.S. It was an attempt to account, in a consistent manner, for crime known to police across the country despite jurisdictional variation in legal definitions and practices. In concept, all crimes that come to the attention of law enforcement, classifiable as UCR incidents, were reported through the UCR data collection system. The main data collection instrument in the UCR was a form called "Return A," a police agency's monthly summary of recorded murders, rapes, robberies, burglaries, larcenies, auto thefts, and arsons. Where there are multiple offenses within a single incident, only one offense, the most serious, is recorded. Order of seriousness (starting with the most serious offense) is as follows: 1. criminal homicide; 2. forcible rape; 3. robbery; 4. aggravated assault; 5. burglary; 6. larceny-theft (except motor vehicle theft); 7. motor vehicle theft; and 8. arson (FBI, 1984, pp. 33–34).

The number of reporting agencies varied from month to month. The FBI estimated that 95 percent of the total U.S. population was represented in 1993 by UCR data (97 percent in metropolitan areas and 86 percent in nonmetropolitan areas) (FBI, 1994, p. 1). Return A data reported in FBI publications includes estimates for agencies that reported incomplete data (pp. 375–377).

Definitions
Murder and non-negligent manslaughter were defined by the FBI as the willful (non-negligent) killing of one human being by another (p. 13).

Aggravated assault was defined as "an unlawful attack on one person by another for the purpose of inflicting severe or aggravated bodily injury. This type of assault is usually accompanied by the use of weapon or by means likely to produce death or great bodily harm. Attempts are included . . ." (p. 31).

Robbery was the "taking or attempting to take anything of value from the care, custody, or control of a person or persons by force or threat of force or violence and/or by putting the victim in fear" (p. 26).

Forcible rape was "the carnal knowledge of a female body forcibly and against her will. Assaults or attempts to commit rape by force or threat of force are also included; however, statutory rape (without force) and other sex offenses are excluded" (p. 23).

Index crimes include murder and non-negligent manslaughter, forcible rape, robbery, aggravated assault, burglary, larceny-theft (except motor vehicle theft), motor vehicle theft, and arson.

Population Groups
The FBI classifies law enforcement agencies into the set of population groups given below. As a general rule, sheriffs, county police, and state police report crimes committed within the limits of counties, but outside cities, while local police report crimes committed within the city limits.

Population Group	Agency Type	Population Range
I	City	250,000 and over
II	City	100,000 to 249,999
III	City	50,000 to 99,999
IV	City	25,000 to 49,999
V	City	10,000 to 24,999
VI	City[1]	Less than 10,000
VIII (Rural County)	County[2]	Outside of MSAs[3]
IX (Suburban County)	County[2]	Within MSAs[3]

[1] Includes universities and colleges to which no population is attributed.

[2] Includes those state police units to which no population is attributed.

[3] MSA = Metropolitan Statistical Area. An MSA is a county or a group of counties containing at least one central city (or twin cities), having a population of 50,000 or more, plus adjacent counties that are metropolitan in character and are economically and socially integrated with the central city. "Counties in an MSA are designated 'suburban' for UCR purposes" (FBI, 1994, p. 382).

4 Regions and 9 Divisions

Northeast

New England
Connecticut
Maine
Massachusetts
New Hampshire
Rhode Island
Vermont

Middle Atlantic
New Jersey
New York
Pennsylvania

Midwest

East North Central
Illinois
Indiana
Michigan
Ohio
Wisconsin
North Dakota
South Dakota

West North Central
Iowa
Kansas
Minnesota
Missouri
Nebraska

South

South Atlantic
Delaware
District of
  Columbia
Florida
Georgia
Maryland
North Carolina
South Carolina
Virginia
West Virginia

East South Central
Alabama
Kentucky
Mississippi
Tennessee

West South Central
Arkansas
Louisiana
Oklahoma
Texas

West

Mountain
Arizona
Colorado
Idaho
Montana
Nevada
New Mexico
Utah
Wyoming

Pacific
Alaska
California
Hawaii
Oregon
Washington

Technical Reference
Federal Bureau of Investigation. 1994. *Crime in the United States 1993*. Washington, D.C.: U.S. Government Printing Office.

Federal Bureau of Investigation. 1984. *Uniform crime reporting handbook*. Washington, D.C.: U.S. Government Printing Office.

Data Source 27

National Child Abuse Survey

Target Population: Persons aged 18 and older in the U.S.

Sample: Sample size = 1,250.

Source of Information: Telephone interviews.

Date of Collection: 1994.

Reference Period: Previous 12 months.

Organization: Schulman, Ronca, and Bucuvalas, 145 East 32nd Street, Suite 500, New York, NY 10016. Conducted for the National Committee to Prevent Child Abuse, 332 S. Michigan Ave., Suite 1600, Chicago, IL 60604.

Technical Reference
Daro, Deborah. 1994. *Public opinions and behaviors regarding child abuse prevention: The result of NCPCA's 1994 public opinion poll*. Chicago, Ill.: Center on Child Abuse Prevention Research.

Data Source 28

National Crime Victimization Survey (formerly the National Crime Survey)

Target Population: Non-institutionalized U.S. residents 12 years of age and older.

Sample: Stratified, multi-stage cluster sample of housing units surveyed every 6 months for a total of 7 interviews; before June 1984, 72,000 units were interviewed; from 1985 to 1993, 59,000 units were interviewed.

Source of Information: Mixed personal and telephone interviews.

Date of Collection: Continuous since 1972.

Reference Period: Previous six months.

Organization: U.S. Bureau of the Census, for the U.S. Bureau of Justice Statistics.

Additional Information
Occupants of sample housing units were interviewed seven times at six-month intervals over a three-and-a-half-year period in a rotating panel design. Placing incidents in a particular time of reference is emphasized. To assist respondents in placing incidents in a specific time frame, the first interview is not used to estimate victimization. Instead, the act of being interviewed helps define the specific reference period that respondents will be asked about in the second interview (e.g., the interviewer can say to the respondent, "Since we last talked together, has such and such occurred?"). The NCVS included victimizations that may not have been reported to the police (Bureau of Justice Statistics, 1994a). Crimes that respondents said occurred outside of the United States have been omitted from all tables and figures in this volume.

1993 Data
Data presented for 1993 are based on a redesigned questionnaire. This questionnaire employs a "short-cues" approach for stimulating respondent memory of victimization experiences and includes questions that directly ask about rape and sexual assault. These and other changes resulting from the redesigned survey instrument mean that the NCVS now detects victimizations not previously captured, and national estimates based on the new survey are substantially higher than those based on the previous survey (Bureau of Justice Statistics, 1994b, p. 1). Because the two survey designs differ so much, data for 1993 should not be compared to previous years of the NCVS (p. 2). At the time this volume was compiled, the final public-use version of the 1993 NCVS data tape had not yet been released. Data for 1993 in this *Handbook* are therefore preliminary and may vary slightly from the final figures.

Series Crimes
The NCVS is unique among victimization surveys in recognizing that some victimization experiences are not standard incidents that occur within a short span of time. These situations may have a repetitive, longer-term, or ongoing quality that makes it difficult or impossible for victims to distinguish details from one instance to another. An example of this might be a case of long-term spousal abuse in which the beatings are so frequent and/or similar that the victim cannot remember each occurrence. In the NCVS, such victimization experiences are called series crimes, and until the redesign (i.e., for 1973–

1992), they were defined as "three or more similar but separate crimes which the victim [was] unable to recall individually or describe in detail to an interviewer" (Bureau of Justice Statistics, 1994a, p. 143). When the redesigned survey was implemented (i.e., affecting the 1993 data), the threshold definition of series crimes was increased to six or more incidents that were similar, but indistinguishable from each other.

In general, the Bureau of Justice Statistics (BJS) omits series crimes from their national estimates of criminal victimization because victims were unable to recall details of each incident, including, sometimes, when the incidents occurred. Thus, in this *Handbook*, every table or figure presented that gives a citation to a published BJS report or document should imply to the reader that series crimes are excluded.

Not everyone agrees with the BJS policy, however. In 1992, series victimizations comprised approximately 8 percent, or about 600,000, of the 7.2 million violent victimizations reported in the NCVS (Bureau of Justice Statistics, 1994a, p. 143). The editors, in generating new tabulations from NCVS data files, chose to deviate from the BJS practice of excluding series crimes. Although respondents may be unable to recall details of every event in a series, respondents do provide details of the most recent event. Even if all previous incidents in a series are ignored, the most recent event can be counted as easily as any other stereotypical single-incident victimization. In our view, there is no reason to exclude these very real cases of victimization. Thus, every NCVS table in this volume that gives a citation to a computer-readable file should imply to the reader that series crimes have been included and that each series has been counted as a single incident. This includes all 1993 NCVS data appearing throughout the *Handbook*, as well as some special 1987–1990 tables in Chapter Four.

Definitions (1973–1992 data)
Aggravated assault was the "attack or attempted attack with a weapon, regardless of whether or not an injury occurred, and attack without a weapon when serious injury results. Serious injury includes broken bones, lost teeth, internal injuries, loss of consciousness, and any injury requiring two or more days of hospitalization" (Bureau of Justice Statistics, 1994a, p. 154).

Assault was "an unlawful physical attack or threat of attack. Assaults may be classified as aggravated or simple. Rape and attempted rape are excluded, as well as robbery and attempted robbery. The severity of assaults ranges from minor threat to incidents which are nearly fatal" (Bureau of Justice Statistics, 1994a, p. 154).

Carjacking was the theft or attempted theft of a motor vehicle by force or threat of force (Rand, 1994, p. 1).

Central city is defined as the largest city (or grouping of cities) in a Metropolitan Statistical Area (Bureau of Justice Statistics, 1994a, p. 154).

Hispanic is defined as "a person who describes himself or herself as Mexican American, Chicano, Mexican, Mexicano, Puerto Rican, Cuban, Central American, South American, or from some other Spanish culture or origin, regardless of race" (Bureau of Justice Statistics, 1994a, p. 155).

Non-Hispanic is defined as "persons who report their culture or origin as something other than 'Hispanic' as defined above. This distinction is made regardless of race" (Bureau of Justice Statistics, 1994a, p. 155).

Nonstranger is defined as "an offender who is either related to, well known to, or casually acquainted with the victim. For crimes with more than one offender, if any of the offenders are nonstrangers, then the group of offenders as a whole is classified as nonstranger" (Bureau of Justice Statistics, 1994a, p. 155).

Nonmetropolitan area is defined as "a place not located inside a Metropolitan Statistical Area. This includes a variety of localities, ranging from sparsely populated rural areas to cities with populations less than 50,000" (Bureau of Justice Statistics, 1994a, p. 155).

Rape was defined as "carnal knowledge through the use of force or the threat of force, including attempts. Statutory rape (without force) is excluded. Both heterosexual and homosexual rapes are included" (Bureau of Justice Statistics, 1994a, p. 156). Note, however, that until 1993 the NCVS did not directly ask victims if they were raped. "Rape" or "tried to rape" was recorded if the victim volunteered these responses to the questions, "How did the offender(s) attack you? Any other way?"

Robbery was defined as "completed or attempted theft, directly from a person, of property or cash by force or threat of force, with or without a weapon" (Bureau of Justice Statistics, 1994a, p. 156).

Robbery with injury was defined as "completed or attempted theft from a person, accompanied by an attack, either with or without a weapon, resulting in injury. An injury is classified as resulting from serious assault, irrespective of the extent of injury, if a weapon was used in committing the crime, or, if not, when the extent of injury was either serious (broken bones, loss of teeth, internal injuries, or loss of consciousness, for example) or undetermined but requiring two or more days of hospitalization. An injury is classified as resulting from a minor assault when the extent of injury was minor (for example, bruise, black eyes, cuts, scratches or swelling) or undetermined but requiring less than two days of hospitalization" (Bureau of Justice Statistics, 1994a, p. 156).

Robbery without injury was defined as theft or attempted theft from a person, accompanied by force or threat of force, either with or without a weapon, but not resulting in injury (Bureau of Justice Statistics, 1994a, p. 156).

Self-protective measures are defined as the following victim actions in response to attacks or threats: used physical force toward the offender, resisted or captured the offender, scared or warned the offender, persuaded or appeased the offender, escaped or got away, got help or gave alarm, reacted to pain or emotion or "other" (Bureau of Justice Statistics, 1994a, p. 128).

Simple assault was an "attack without a weapon resulting in either minor injury (for example, bruises, black eyes, cuts, scratches, or swelling) or an undetermined injury requiring less than 2 days of hospitalization. Also includes attempted assault without a weapon" [i.e., including attacks without injury or verbal threats of attack] (Bureau of Justice Statistics, 1994a, p. 156).

Stranger is defined as an offender the victim either said was a stranger, an offender the victim did not see or recognize, or an offender the victim only knew by sight. Crimes involving more than one offender are classified as involving nonstrangers if any of the offenders was a nonstranger (Bureau of Justice Statistics, 1994a, p. 156).

Suburban areas are defined as "a county or counties containing a central city, plus any contiguous counties that are linked socially and economically to the central city. On data tables, suburban areas are categorized as those portions of metropolitan areas situated 'outside central cities'" (Bureau of Justice Statistics, 1994a, p. 156).

Definitions (1993 redesign data):
Because the final 1993 data were not available at the time this volume was compiled, the definitions in this *Handbook* for the 1993 NCVS may vary somewhat from those that the Bureau of Justice Statistics chooses to use for these data. In general, definitions remain the same as above, but the redesigned survey allowed some modifications to a few crime classifications in the 1993 data. In particular, rapes were distinguished from other sexual assaults or unwanted sexual contact, and sexual assaults

other than rape were distinguished from nonsexual assaults. Also, verbal threats of rape, sexual assault, and nonsexual assault were distinguished from assaults that involved physical attacks or weapon threats. Specific changes from the 1973–1992 definitions follow:

Attempted rape was further defined as attempted forced or coerced sexual intercourse.

Completed rape was further defined as forced or coerced sexual intercourse.

Sexual attack other than rape with injury, a new crime classification, included incidents in which force or threat of force was used (either a weapon was present or other force was employed), and injuries were sustained during a sexual assault that did not include rape (defined above).

Sexual attack other than rape without injury, a new crime classification, was defined as a nonrape, sexual assault that did not result in physical injury, but involved the use of force (either a weapon was present or other force was employed).

Unwanted sexual contact without force, a new crime classification, was defined as nonrape, sexual contact against the victim's will, but did not involve the use or threat of force (e.g., no weapons present, no injury resulted). Although this classification may include acts that some would consider nonviolent, we include these incidents among other crimes of violence because unwanted grabbing, fondling, and other such contact: (1) is considered a crime in at least some states; and (2) was reported to interviewers in response to the question, "How did the offender try to attack you?" after victims had answered "Yes" to the question, "Did the offender THREATEN you with harm in any way?"

Simple assault is further defined as an assault without weapons (i.e., the victim was hit, slapped, knocked down, hit with a thrown object, grabbed, held, tripped, jumped, pushed, followed, surrounded, etc.) resulting in either minor injury or no injury. "Verbal-only" threats of assault are tabulated separately from other types of simple assault for the first time in the redesigned NCVS (see below).

Verbal threat of rape or sexual assault, a form of simple assault, was distinguished from other verbal threats against a person. No weapon was present, there was no injury, and no physical contact or action by an offender other than the verbal threat of rape or sexual assault was involved.

Verbal threat of assault, a form of simple assault, includes verbal threats to kill or otherwise attack, but does not include verbal threats of rape or sexual assault. No weapon was present, there was no injury, and no physical contact or action by an offender occurred other than the verbal threat to kill or attack.

Technical Reference

Bureau of Justice Statistics. 1994a. *Criminal victimization in the United States, 1992.* Washington, D.C.

Bureau of Justice Statistics. 1994b. *National crime victimization survey redesign.* Washington, D.C.

Rand, Michael R. 1994. *Carjacking.* Washington, D.C.: Bureau of Justice Statistics.

Data Source 29

National Electronic Injury Surveillance System (NEISS)

Target Population: Patients initially treated for gun-related injuries in hospital emergency rooms who were alive at the time of discharge from the emergency department.

Sample: Stratified probability sample of 91 hospitals in the U.S. and its territories that provided 24-hour service and had at least 6 beds.

Source of Information: Medical records.

Date of Collection: June 1, 1992–May 31, 1993.

Reference Period: Current incident.

Organization: U.S. Consumer Product Safety Commission (CPSC), for the Centers for Disease Control and Prevention (CDC).

Technical Reference

Annest, Joseph L., James A. Mercy, Delinda R. Gibson, and George W. Ryan. 1995. National estimates of nonfatal firearm-related injuries: beyond the tip of the iceberg. *Journal of the American Medical Association* 273, no. 22 (June 14): 1749–1754.

Data Source 30

National Health Interview Survey: 1992 Youth Risk Behavior Survey (YRBS)

Target Population: Non-institutionalized civilian population 12–21 year olds residing in the U.S.

Sample: Conducted as a follow-back survey to the National Health Interview Survey (NHIS). Persons aged 12–21 years were selected from households sampled in the 1991 (NHIS). The NHIS sample was a multi-stage, cluster-area probability sample. Questionnaires were completed by 10,645, or 77.2 percent of eligible respondents.

Source of Information: Respondents listened to a tape recording of the questionnaire and recorded their response on a standardized answer sheet. Answer sheets were returned in sealed envelope.

Date of Collection: April 1992–March 1993.

Reference Period: Lifetime, previous 12 months, and previous 30 days.

Organization: U.S. Bureau of the Census, for the National Center for Health Statistics.

Technical Reference
Center for Disease Control. 1994. Health-risk behaviors among persons aged 12–21 years—United States, 1992. *Mortality and Morbidity Weekly Report* 43, no. 13: (April 18): 231–235.

Data Source 31

The National Incidence Studies of Missing, Abducted, Runaway, and Thrownaway Children (NISMART)

Target Population: Children (under the age of 18) in the U.S. who have been abducted (by family or nonfamily members), runaway, abandoned, lost, injured, or otherwise missing.

Sample: Multi-frame study in seven parts, see below.
Source of Information: Varies with sample. See below.

Date of Collection: Varies with sample. Household survey conducted between July 26, 1988, and February 3, 1989.

Reference Period: Varies with sample.

Organization: Westat, Inc., 1650 Research Blvd., Rockville, MD 20850, and The Family Research Laboratory at the University of New Hampshire.

Additional Information
The National Incidence Studies of Missing, Abducted, Runaway, and Thrownaway Children (NISMART) collected data from six separate sources: a household survey, a survey of juvenile facilities, interviews with returned runaways, police records, FBI data, and a survey of community professionals (Finkelhor, Hotaling & Sedlak 1990). The focus of NISMART was on numbers of children and not on numbers of incidents, per se.

Sample: (There are seven samples)
Caretakers—Random digit dialing sample of 10,544 caretakers representing 20,505 children.

Juvenile Facilities—Household survey screened to locate children who lived at a facility. Follow-up survey sent questionnaire or interviewed staff members in 127 identified facilities.

Returned Runaways—Household survey screened to locate returned runaways. Follow-up survey interviewed 85 returned runaways.

Police Records—Stratified (by size) sample of 21 counties including 83 law enforcement agencies.

FBI Data—All records from the Supplementary Homicide Reports (for the 12-year period 1976–1987) of children where the circumstance code was rape, other sexual offense, other felony type, suspected felony type, or undetermined.

Community Professionals—Stratified (by urbanization) sample of 29 counties. In the selected counties, all child protection agencies, sheriff's offices, juvenile probation departments, and public health departments were included, along with a systematic sample of schools, daycare centers, hospitals, municipal police departments, mental health agencies, and social service agencies. A total of 735 agencies that had professional contact with children were selected.

Technical Reference
Finkelhor, David, Gerald Hotaling, and Andrea Sedlak. 1990. *Missing, abducted, runaway, and thrownaway children in America. First report: Numbers and characteristics, national incidence studies*. Washington, D.C.: Office of Juvenile Justice and Delinquency Prevention.

Finkelhor, David, Gerald Hotaling, and Andrea Sedlak. 1992. The abduction of children by strangers and nonfamily members: Estimating the incidence using multiple methods. *Journal of Interpersonal Violence 7*, no. 2: 226–243.

Data Source 32

National Survey of Children, Wave III, 1987

Target Population: Households in the contiguous U.S. containing at least one child (aged 7–11 in 1976).

Sample: Multi-stage stratified probability sample of households in the continental U.S. containing at least one child, in 1976. Included 1,081 parents, 1,147 children (2 were sampled from same family in 353 instances).

Source of Information: Personal interviews.

Date of Collection: 1987, the third wave of the study. The study started in 1976.

Reference Period: Respondent's lifetime and previous 12 months.

Organization: Child Trends, Inc., 4301 Connecticut Ave., Suite 100, Washington, DC 20008.

Additional Information
This was a national sample of children, who by this, the third wave of the study, were between 17 and 23 years old. The original sample (from 1976) was a multi-stage stratified probability sample of households in the continental United States containing at least one child aged 7 to 11. Black households were oversampled, and weights were developed to adjust for this. Between the first wave in 1976 and the third in 1987 there was considerable attrition. In the third wave, only 54 percent of those originally selected for interviews were interviewed, and 68 percent of those originally interviewed were interviewed in 1987. The attrition was not random, but occurred most frequently among blacks, those who lived in giant cities, those who used drugs or alcohol, and the poorer respondents. Weights were developed to adjust for these losses (Moore and Peterson, 1989, pp. 2–10).

Technical Reference
Moore, Kristin A., and James L. Peterson. 1989. *Wave 3 of the national survey of children: Description of data: The consequences of teenage pregnancy: Child Trends working paper no. 89-09.* Washington, D.C.: Child Trends.

Data Source 33

National Traumatic Occupational Fatalities Surveillance Systems (NTOF)

Target Population: Workers in the U.S. age 16 or older.

Sample: Individual death records from 52 vital statistics reporting units (50 states, New York City, and the District of Columbia) for workers 16 years of age or older who died as a result of work-related injury.

Source of Information: Death certificates.

Date of Collection: Continuous.

Reference Period: Previous year.

Organization: National Institute for Occupational Safety and Health (NIOSH).

Additional Information
Homicides were identified from the International Classification of Diseases (ninth revision) codes E960–E969. They were identified as work related when the official who prepared the death certificate marked the appropriate category for work related on the death certificate.

Technical Reference
National Institute for Occupational Safety and Health. 1993. *Fatal injuries to workers in the United States, 1980–1989: A decade of surveillance.* Morgantown, W.Va.: Center for Disease Control.

Data Source 34

National Vital Statistics System (NVSS)-Detailed Mortality Data

Target Population: Deaths occurring in the U.S.

Sample: All death certificates.

Source of Information: Death certificates compiled by local and state health departments.

Date of Collection: Continuous.

Reference Period: Not applicable; death certificates were forwarded to the National Center for Health Statistics annually.

Organization: Division of Vital Statistics of the National Center for Health Statistics.

Additional Information

These data came from the analyses of death certificates compiled by the Division of Vital Statistics of the National Center for Health Statistics (NCHS). Registration of births and deaths was a legal requirement in all states, and elements of the U.S. Standard Death Certificate, including such items indicating cause of death, were recorded and forwarded to NCHS through state vital statistics records offices. More than 99 percent of all deaths occurring in this country were believed to be registered in this system (U.S. Department of Health and Human Services, 1994, p. 18). Deaths were classified geographically by place of decedent's residence, unless otherwise noted. Fatal violence in this system was labeled as homicide and legal intervention. Homicide was defined as "injuries inflicted by another person with intent to injure or kill, by any means," (U.S. Department of Health and Human Services, 1989, p. 1042), and legal intervention was defined as "injuries inflicted by the police or other law-enforcing agents, including military on duty, in the course of arresting or attempting to arrest lawbreakers, suppressing disturbances, maintaining order, and other legal action" (this includes executions) (p. 1045). Because of their distinct definitions and reporting procedures, legal interventions and homicides can be separated in analysis. For homicides and legal interventions, all states were required to have the coroner or medical examiner investigate the death and certify the cause and manner of death. Cause of death codes were assigned according to definitions established by the International Classification of Diseases Ninth Revision, Clinical Modification (ICD-9-CM). Homicide and legal intervention was a medico-legal definition and is described in more detail below.

Definitions

Homicide and injury purposely inflicted by other persons (E960–E969) includes injuries inflicted by another person with intent to injure or kill, by any means. ICD-9-CM codes (adopted in 1968) are as follows:

E960 Fight, brawl, rape. Includes unarmed fights, brawls, beatings or fights with hands, fists, feet, and unarmed rapes.

E961 Assault by corrosive or caustic substance, except poisoning. Includes injury or death purposefully caused by corrosive or caustic substance, such as acid, vitriol, or other corrosive substance. Excludes burns from hot liquids or chemical burns from swallowing a corrosive substance.

E962 Assault by poisoning. Includes homicidal poisoning by any drug or medicinal substance, other solid and liquid substances, other gases and vapors, and all other specified poisoning.

E963 Assault by hanging and strangulation. Includes homicidal garrotting, ligature, hanging, strangulation, and suffocation.

E964 Assault by submersion [drowning].

E965 Assault by firearms and explosives. Includes fatal assaults by pistols, revolvers and other handguns, shotguns, hunting rifles, military firearms, other and specified firearms, antipersonnel bombs, gasoline bombs, letter bombs, and other and unspecified explosives.

E966 Assault by cutting and piercing instrument. Includes cuts, punctures, stabs by pointed or sharp-edged instruments such as knives, swords, daggers, axes, chisels, scissors, forks, ice picks, arrows, broken glass, hand and power tools (drills, rivet/staple guns, hedge clippers, saws) and the like.

E967 Child battering and other maltreatment. Includes acts by parents and other persons.

E968 Assault by other and unspecified means. Includes fire, arson, and other unspecified burns; pushing from a high place; striking by blunt or thrown objects; scalding by hot liquid; criminal neglect or abandonment of child, infant, or other helpless person with intent to injure or kill; bite of human being; and all otherwise unspecified means.

E969 Late effects of injury purposefully inflicted by other person. This category is used to indicate circumstances classifiable to E960–E968 as the cause of death or disability from late effects, which are themselves classifiable elsewhere. The "late effects" include conditions reported as such, or occurring as consequences one year or more after injury purposefully inflicted by another person.

Legal intervention (E970–E978) includes injuries inflicted by the police or other law-enforcing agents, including military on duty, in the course of arresting or attempting to arrest lawbreakers, suppressing disturbance, maintaining order, and other legal action. Legal execution is also included here. ICD-9-CM codes are as follows:

E970 Injury due to legal intervention by firearms. Includes gunshot wounds by revolver, pistol, machine gun, rifle, rubber bullets, shotgun, and otherwise unspecified firearms.

E971 Injury due to legal intervention by explosives. Includes injury by dynamite, grenade, mortar bomb, and other shells and explosives.

E972 Injury due to legal intervention by gas. Includes asphyxiation, poisoning, or other injury by tear gas or other gases.

E973 Injury due to legal intervention by blunt object. Includes hitting or striking injuries by batons, nightsticks, staves, or other blunt objects.

E974 Injury due to legal intervention by cutting and piercing instrument.

E975 Injury due to legal intervention by other specified means. Includes unarmed blows and manhandling.

E976 Injury due to legal intervention by unspecified means.

E977 Late effects of injuries due to legal intervention. This category is used to indicate circumstances classifiable to E970–E976 as the cause of death or disability from late effects, which are themselves classifiable elsewhere in ICD-9-CM. The "late effects" include conditions reported as such, or occurring as consequences one year or more after injury due to legal intervention.

E978 Legal execution. Includes all executions performed at the behest of the judiciary or ruling authority [whether permanent or temporary] as: asphyxiation by gas, hanging, poisoning, shooting, electrocution, decapitation, and other specified means.

Note that suicide and self-inflicted injury is classified under ICD-9-CM codes E950–E959. For deaths and injuries in which it was undermined whether the cause was accidental or purposeful, ICD-9-CM reserves another set of categories (E980–E989). Injuries that result from operations of war are classified into a distinct set of codes, as well (E990–E999). See U.S. Department of Heath and Human Services (1989) for details.

Technical Reference
U.S. Department of Health and Human Services. 1989. *International classification of diseases, ninth revision, clinical modification.* Washington, D.C.: U.S. Government Printing Office.

U.S. Department of Health and Human Services. 1994. *Vital statistics of the United States.* Hyattsville, Md.: Public Health Service.

Data Source 35

National Women's Study

Target Population: Women in the U.S aged 18–34 in 1989.

Sample: Random digit dialing; screen for eligible respondents; age and race weighted to match U.S. Census estimates. Response rate was 85.2 percent; 4,008 women were selected in 1989.

Source of Information: Telephone interviews.

Date of Collection: Wave 1, fall 1989; wave 2, fall 1990; wave 3, fall 1991.

Reference Period: Lifetime and previous year.

Organization: Schulman, Ronca, and Bucuvalas, Inc., 145 East 32nd Street, Suite 500, New York, NY 10016.

Technical Reference
Kilpatrick, Dean G., Christine N. Edmunds, and Anne Seymour. 1992. *Rape in America: A report to the nation.* Arlington, Va.: National Victim Center.

Kilpatrick, Dean G., Heidi S. Resnick, Benjamin E. Saunders, and Connie L. Best. 1994. *Survey research on violence against women: Measuring violent assaults against women.* Paper presented at the 46th annual meeting of the American Society of Criminology, November 11, Miami, Florida.

Resnick, Heidi S., Dean G. Kilpatrick, Bonnie S. Dansky, Benjamin E. Saunders, and Connie L. Best. 1993. Prevalence of civilian trauma and post-traumatic stress disorder in a representative national sample of women. *Journal of Consulting and Clinical Psychology* 61, no. 6: 987–988.

Data Source 36

National Youth Survey

Target Population: Persons aged 11–17 in 1976 in the U.S.

Sample: Area probability sampling of 1,725 youths in 1977 who were mentally and physically able to complete an interview in 1977.

Source of Information: Personal interviews.

Date of Collection: Interviewed initially in January–March of 1977, and subsequently in 1978, 1979, 1980, 1981, 1984, 1987, 1989, and 1993.

Reference Period: Previous 12 months.

Organization: Institute of Behavioral Science, University of Colorado, Boulder, CO 80309.

Additional Information
The National Youth Survey (NYS) was "a projected longitudinal study of a national probability sample of 1,725 youths aged 11–17 in 1976. Nine waves of data were available on this youth panel" (Elliott, 1994, p. 3). Only the first eight waves were used in this study. "Both self-reported and official record data were available for all respondents, and official record data were available for their parents or primary caretakers" (ibid.).

Definitions
Serious Violent Offenses (SVOs) included questions designed to reflect aggravated assault, robbery, and rape. The question for aggravated assault was ["Have] you attacked someone with the idea of seriously hurting or killing that person?"; for robbery, ". . . used force or strong-arm methods to get money or things from people?"; and for rape, ". . . had or tried to have sexual relations with someone against their will?" An analysis of these follow-up probes for SVOs revealed that in 50 percent of the events, a weapon was used. Two-thirds of these weapon events involved a gun or a knife. In 67 percent of reported events, some medical treatment was required.

Technical Reference
Elliott, Delbert S. 1994. 1993 Presidential Address: Serious violent offenders: Onset, developmental course, and treatment. *Criminology* 32, no. 1: 1–21.

Data Source 37

The People, the Press, and Politics 1990

Target Population: Adults in the U.S.

Sample: Multi-stage cluster sample, stratified by community size. Weights were used to adjust for "not-at-home" bias and to bring the sample into alignment with the demographic composition of the adult population of the contiguous U.S. population as enumerated in 1980. Sample size = 3,004 adults.

Source of Information: Personal interviews.

Date of Collection: May 1–31, 1990.

Reference Period: Time of survey.

Organization: Design and analysis by Response Analysis Corporation for the Princeton Survey Research Associates, Inc.; interviewing by Response Analysis Corporation. Study done for the Times Mirror Center for The People & The Press, 1875 Eye Street, N.W., Suite 1110, Washington, D.C. 20006.

Technical Reference
Times Mirror Center for The People and The Press. 1990. The people, the press & politics 1990. Washington, D.C., pp. 90–92.

Data Source 38

Physical Violence in American Families: A Resurvey (also called "National Family Violence Resurvey, 1985")

Target Population: Non-institutionalized adult population of the U.S. who were either (1) currently living as a male-female couple (married or otherwise), (2) separated or divorced within the last two years, or (3) a single parent with a child under age 18.

Sample: The sample design yielded independent estimates of four populations: (1) the nation, (2) black residents, (3) Hispanic residents estimates, and (4) residents of separate states. In addition to the main survey (sample size = 4,032), there were oversamples of blacks (sample size = 502), Hispanics (sample size = 185), 25 states (sample size = 958). Qualifying households were selected using random digit dialing techniques and a stratified area probability sampling frame. Seven sets of case weights were computed to adjust for disproportionate probabilities of selection and to permit the merging of any combination of the oversamples and the main sample.

Source of Information: Telephone interviews.

Date of Collection: June 10–September 15, 1985.

Reference Period: Previous 12 months.

Organization: Louis Harris and Associates for The Family Research Laboratory at the University of New Hampshire, Durham, NH 03824.

Additional Information

Conflict Tactics Scale (CTS). This scale measured the way people dealt with conflicts within the family, with responses ranging from talking about the problem to using a gun against the family member. One member of each household was interviewed and asked about whether they had responded to conflict with their spouse or a specific child using these items. They were also asked if their spouse used the tactics against them or the same child. A referent child also was selected randomly.

Definitions

Child abuse was defined as physical acts committed by the parents against the children that go beyond ordinary physical punishment. There were two measures for this, one that included items that were indubitably abusive, such as kicking and punching, and one that adds all items that could be considered abuse or punishment, such as hitting the child with an object such as a belt.

Spouse assault was defined as any violence occurring between spouses. Severe and minor spouse abuse were differentiated by risk of potential injury from the act.

Minor violence is a combination of items from the conflict tactics scale. The items for child abuse are: threw or smashed object; threw something at child; pushed, grabbed, or shoved; or slapped or spanked. For spousal abuse the items are: threw or smashed object; threw something at partner; pushed, grabbed, or shoved; or slapped.

Severe violence is also a combination of items from the conflict tactics scale, including for child abuse: kicked, bit, hit with fist; hit or tried to hit with an object; beat up; burned or scalded; threatened with knife or gun; or used knife or gun. For spouse abuse the items are: kicked, bit, hit with fist; hit or tried to hit with an object; beat up; choked; threatened with knife or gun; or used knife or gun.

Very severe violence is a subset of severe violence used to describe child abuse. It includes all of the items in the severe violence scale except for hit or tried to hit with object.

Occupational group: "Each respondent was classified as 'blue collar' or 'white collar' using the Bureau of Labor Statistics revised Occupational Classification System following a procedure developed by Rice, as given in Robinson, Athanasiou, and Head" (Straus and Gelles 1990: 138).

Technical Reference

Straus, Murray A., and Richard J. Gelles. 1990. *Physical violence in American families*. New Brunswick, N.J.: Transaction Publishers.

Louis Harris and Associates. 1985. Second national family violence survey: Survey methodology. *Physical violence in American families, 1985*. [Documentation for machine-readable files.] Ann Arbor, Mich.: Inter-university Consortium for Political and Social Research.

Data Source 39

The Police Foundation Law Enforcement Agency Survey

Target Population: Law enforcement agencies in the U.S.

Sample: Stratified sample of 1,111 agencies.

Source of Information: Mailed questionnaire.

Date of Collection: Mid-August 1992.

Reference Period: 1991.

Organization: The Police Foundation, 1001 22nd St., NW, Washington, D.C. 20037.

Additional Information

The sample was selected from an exhaustive list of law enforcement agencies provided by the Law Enforcement Sector of the 1990 Justice Agency List from the Governments Division of the U.S. Bureau of the Census. The sample was stratified by size. All state agencies, sheriff departments, and county police departments serving jurisdictions of 100,000 or more inhabitants and all agencies serving 50,000 or more inhabitants were included. Police agencies that served under 50,000 inhabitants were selected randomly from strata defined by population size.

Of the 1,697 agencies selected, 1,111 returned the mailed questionnaire; the overall response rate was 67.2 percent: 72.4 percent for municipal police departments, 88.9 percent for county police departments, 54.2 percent for sheriff's departments, and 90.0 percent of the state agencies.

Incidence rates were calculated by dividing the number of incidents reported by responding agencies by the size (number of sworn officers) of agency and multiplying the result by 1,000.

Technical Reference
Pate, Antony M., and Lorie A. Fridell. 1993. *Police use of force: Official reports, citizens complaints, and legal consequences*. Vol. 1. Washington D.C.: Police Foundation.

Data Source 40

Princeton Survey Associates for Troika Productions and Lifetime Television, January 4–6, 1991

Target Population: Adults living in households with telephones in the contiguous U.S.

Sample: Random digit dialing; sample size = 600.

Source of Information: Telephone interviews.

Date of Collection: January 4–6, 1990.

Reference Period: Time of survey.

Organization: Princeton Survey Research Associates, P.O. Box 1450, Princeton, NJ 08542. Conducted for Troika Productions and Lifetime Television.

Additional Information
Data were weighted to match Census data on age, gender, race, education, and region.

Technical Reference
Silver, Thomas H. 1991. Men, women, and rape. *The Polling Report* 7, no. 1: 3.

Data Source 41

Recidivism of Prisoners Released in 1983

Target Population: Prisoners released in 11 states in 1983.

Sample: From the 11 states (see below), samples of released prisoners were selected (method unspecified) separately for male and female prisoners that were representative by race, age, and type of offense. Sample size=18,374. "State and federal rap sheets were found for 16,355 of the 18,374 prisoners in the original sample" (p. 12). Weights were used to compensate for missing data.

Source of Information: The criminal history and demographic data on the released prisoners were obtained from the criminal identification bureaus of the 11 participating states and from the Federal Bureau of Investigation.

Date of Collection: Information not provided.

Reference Period: Prisoner releases in 1983 followed to the end of 1986.

Organization: U.S. Bureau of Justice Statistics.

Additional Information
These 11 states (California, Florida, Illinois, Michigan, Minnesota, New Jersey, New York, North Carolina, Ohio, Oregon, and Texas) released 108,580 prisoners in 1983, 57 percent of all state prisoners released that year (Beck and Shipley, 1989, p. 1).

The criminal history of the released prisoners were obtained from the criminal identification bureaus of the 11 participating states and from the Federal Bureau of Investigation. Only serious misdemeanors and felonies were included for this study.

Definitions
Recidivism was any arrest for a serious misdemeanor or felony reported to the FBI or state identification bureau.

Reconviction meant the person was convicted of at least one charge after their release from prison.

Reincarceration was any return to prison or admission to a local jail for a new offense.

Technical Reference
Beck, Allen J., and Bernard E. Shipley. 1989. *Recidivism of prisoners released in 1983*. Washington, D.C.: Bureau of Justice Statistics.

Data Source 42

The Roper Poll, 1992

Target Population: Non-institutionalized adults (18 years and older) living in households in the U.S.

Sample: Stratified multi-stage probability sample of housing units. Quotas were used achieve appropriate balances of various groups. Sample size=1,994.

Source of Information: Personal interviews.

Date of Collection: 1992.

Reference Period: Time of survey.

Organization: The Roper Organization. The Roper Center for Public Opinion Research, P.O. Box 440, Storrs, CT 06268–0440.

Technical Reference
Maguire, Kathleen, Ann L. Pastore, and Timothy J. Flanagan, eds. 1993. *Sourcebook of criminal justice statistics, 1992*. Washington, D.C.: Bureau of Justice Statistics, pp. 716–717.

Data Source 43

[Minneapolis] Star Tribune National Poll, August 6–25, 1991

Target Population: Adults living in households with telephones in the U.S.

Sample: Sample size=1,101.

Source of Information: Telephone interviews.

Date of Collection: August 6–25, 1991.

Reference Period: Previous five years.

Organization: The Star Tribune, News Research, 425 Portland Ave., South, Minneapolis, MN 55488.

Technical Reference
Star Tribune. 1991. *Star Tribune national poll, August 6–25, 1991*. Minneapolis, Minn.

Data Source 44

Study of National Incidence and Prevalence of Child Abuse and Neglect 1986 (NIS-2)

Target Population: Non-institutionalized children (under 18 years of age) referred to child protective services (CPS) and non-CPS agencies in the U.S.

Sample: Probability sample of 29 counties (reflecting 28 primary sampling units [PSUs]). Many agencies in each county were sampled (see below).

Source of Information: Questionnaire.

Date of Collection: September 7–December 6, 1986.

Reference Period: Previous 12 months.

Organization: Westat, Inc., 1650 Research Blvd., Rockville, MD 20850.

Additional Information
Data concerning cases of child maltreatment were collected from a national probability sample of 29 counties, where information was reported to "community professionals," including local Child Protective Services (CPS) and non-CPS agencies such as schools, hospitals, police departments, juvenile probation authorities, etc. (Sedlak, 1991, p. xi). In each county, the county CPS agency was included as well as 10 public schools per PSU, 5 daycare centers per PSU, 4 short-stay general and children's hospitals per PSU, 3 municipal police departments per PSU, 4 social services/mental health agencies per PSU, the county juvenile probation department in each PSU, the county sheriff or state police for each PSU, and the county public health department in each PSU—a total of 706 non-CPS agencies. Because the sample was of agencies and not of all child abuse incidents, this study may have represented only the most serious cases of child abuse (i.e., those most likely to come to the attention of a CPS agency).

Definitions
The annual prevalence estimates used the child as the unit of measurement, not episodes, families, or reports (pp. 2–15). If repeat incidents with the same child occurred, the child still was counted only once. Estimates were "unduplicated" and annualized from three months of data collected in the study.

Maltreatment included physical abuse, sexual abuse, emotional abuse, physical neglect, educational neglect, and emotional neglect, but excluded involuntary neglect, general neglect, and non-countable neglect (U.S. Department of Health and Human Services, no date, pp. 2–3, 2–4). "All types of maltreatment behavior must have been nonaccidental and avoidable. The study excluded problems or hazards which the parent/substitute lacked the financial means to prevent or alleviate and for which appropriate assistance was not available through public agencies. Also excluded was lack of care stemming from parent/substitute death, hospitalization, incarceration, or other circumstances which made it physically impossible to provide or arrange for adequate care" (Sedlak, 1991, p. 2–6).

Physical abuse included physical assault with and without implements (U.S. Department of Health and Human Services, no date, p. 2–3).

Sexual abuse included intrusion (i.e., evidence of actual penile penetration, whether oral, anal, or genital, homosexual or heterosexual), genital molestation (i.e., evidence of genital contact, but no specific indication of intrusion), and other or unknown sexual abuse (i.e., evidence of unspecified acts not known to have included intrusion or genital molestation—for example, fondling of breasts or buttocks or exposure—and/or allegations concerning inadequate or inappropriate supervision of a child's voluntary sexual activities) (Sedlak, 1991, p. 4–5).

Emotional abuse included close confinement (i.e., tying, binding, or other tortuous restriction of movement or confining to an enclosed area such as a closet as a means of punishment), verbal or emotional assault (i.e., habitual patterns of belittling, denigrating, scapegoating, or other nonphysical forms of overtly hostile or rejecting treatment, as well as threats of beating, sexual assault, abandonment, or other forms of maltreatment), and other or unknown abuse (i.e., overtly punitive, exploitative, or abusive treatment other than those specified under other forms of abuse or unspecified abusive treatment, including attempted or potential physical assault, such as throwing something at the child, potential sexual assault in which actual physical contact did not occur, deliberate witholding of food, shelter, sleep, or other necessities as a form of punishment, economic exploitation, and/or unspecified abusive actions) (p. 4–8).

Physical neglect included refusal of health care (i.e., failure to provide or allow needed care in accord with recommendations of a competent health care professional for a physical injury, illness, medical condition, or impairment), delay in health care (i.e., failure to seek timely and appropriate medical care for a serious health problem that any reasonable layman would have recognized as needing professional medical attention), abandonment (i.e., desertion of a child without arranging for reasonable care and supervision, including cases where children were not claimed for two days and where children were left by parents/substitutes who gave no or false information about their whereabouts), expulsion (i.e., other blatant refusals of custody such as permanent or indefinite expulsion of a child from home without adequate arrangement for care by others or refusal to accept custody of a returned runaway), other custody-related maltreatment (i.e., custody-related forms of inattention to the child's needs other than those covered by abandoment or expulsion; for example, repeated shuttling of a child from one household to another due to apparent unwillingness to maintain custody or chronically and repeatedly leaving a child with others for days/weeks at a time), inadequate supervision (i.e., child left unsupervised or inadequately supervised for extended periods of time or allowed to remain away from home overnight without the parent/substitute knowing or attempting to determine the child's wherabouts), and other physical neglect (i.e., conspicuous inattention to avoidable hazards in the home; inadequate nutrition, clothing, or hygiene; and other forms of reckless disregard of the child's safety and welfare such as driving with the child while intoxicated, leaving a young child unattended in a motor vehicle, and so forth) (pp. 4–11, 4–12).

Educational neglect included permitted chronic truancy (i.e., habitual truancy averaging at least five days a month if parent/guardian had been informed and had not attempted to intervene), failure to enroll a child of mandatory school age (i.e., failure to register or enroll a child of mandatory school age, causing the child to miss at least one month of school; or a pattern of keeping a school-age child home for nonlegitimate reasons—such as to work, to care for siblings, etc.—an average of at least three days a month), and inattention to special educational need (i.e., refusal to allow or failure to obtain recommended remedial educational services or neglect in obtaining or following through with treatment for a child's diagnosed learning disorder or other special education need without reasonable cause) (pp. 4–14, 4–15).

Emotional neglect included inadequate nurturance and affection (i.e., marked inattention to the child's needs for affection, emotional support, attention, or competence, including cases of nonorganic failure to thrive, passive emotional rejection of child, or apprent lack of concern for child's emotional well-being or development), chronic or extreme spouse abuse (i.e., chronic or extreme spouse abuse or other domestic violence in the child's presence), permitted drug or alcohol abuse (i.e., encouragement or permitting of drug or alcohol use by the child, including cases in which the parent/guardian had been informed of the problem and had not attempted to intervene), permitted other maladaptive behavior (i.e., encouragement or permitting of other maladaptive behavior such as severe assaultiveness or chronic delinquency under circumstances where the parent/guardian had reason to be aware of the existence and seriousness of the problem but did not attempt to intervene), refusal of psychological care (i.e., refusal to allow needed and available treatment for a child's emotional or behavioral impairment or problem in accord with competent professional recommendation), delay of psychological care (i.e., failure to seek or provide needed treatment for a child's emotional or behavioral impairment or problem which any reasonable layman would have recognized as needing professional psychological attention; for example, severe depression or suicide attempt), and other emotional neglect (i.e., other inattention to the child's developmental/emotional needs not classifiable under any of the above forms of emotional neglect; for example, markedly overprotective restrictions which foster immaturity or emotional overdependence, chronically applying expectations clearly inappropriate in relation to the child's age or level of development, etc.) (pp. 4–17, 4–18).

Technical Reference
Sedlak, Andrea J. 1991. *National incidence and prevalence of child abuse and neglect: 1988 (Revised Report).* Rockville, Md.: Westat, Inc.

U.S. Department of Health and Human Services. n.d. *Report on data processing and analysis: Study of national incidence and prevalence of child abuse and neglect: 1988.* Washington, D.C.

Data Source 45

The Supplementary Homicide Reports (SHR) (a part of the Uniform Crime Reporting Program of the Federal Bureau of Investigation)

Target Population: Homicides that occurred in the U.S.

Sample: All police agencies that submitted this form to a state UCR organization or the FBI.

Source of Information: Standard forms.

Date of Collection: Monthly.

Reference Period: Previous month.

Organization: U.S. Federal Bureau of Investigation.

Additional Information
The SHR reported characteristics of individual homicide incidents, such as the circumstances surrounding the incident, weapon, victim-offender relationship, and demographic characteristics of the victim and offender. No estimates were made for agencies that did not report. Most murders that occurred in federal jurisdictions, such as prisons, military bases, and Indian reservations, were not reported to the FBI (Rokaw, Mercy, and Smith, 1990). For example, the 1992 data file, distributed by the National Criminal Justice Data Archive, includes information on 22,716 murder and non-negligent manslaughter victims representing 95.6 percent of the total number (23,760) estimated by the FBI to have occurred (see data source 26 above). The SHR also includes records of justifiable homicides (i.e., police killings of felons, and citizens acting in self-defense) in addition to murders and non-negligent manslaughters (e.g., the 1992 data file includes information on 769 justifiable homicides).

Technical Reference
Federal Bureau of Investigation. 1994. *Crime in the United States 1993.* Washington, D.C.: U.S. Government Printing Office.

Federal Bureau of Investigation. 1984. *Uniform crime reporting handbook.* Washington, D.C.: U.S. Government Printing Office.

Rokaw, William M., James A. Mercy, and Jack C. Smith. 1990. Comparing death certificate data with FBI crime reporting statistics on U.S. homicides. *Public Health Reports* 105: 447–455.

Data Source 46

Survey by NBC News and the Wall Street Journal, September 20–22, 1986

Target Population: Adults living in households with telephones in the U.S.

Sample: Sample size=2,139.

Source of Information: Telephone interviews.

Date of Collection: September 20–22, 1986.

Reference Period: Time of survey.

Organization: The Roper Center for Public Opinion Research, P.O. Box 440, Storrs, CT 06268–0440.

Technical Reference
NBC News and the Wall Street Journal. 1986. *Survey by NBC News and the Wall Street Journal, September 20–22, 1986.* Storrs, CT: The Roper Center.

Data Source 47

A Survey of Experiences, Perceptions, and Apprehensions About Guns Among Young People in America (LH Research Inc., No. Study 930018)

Target Population: *Young People*: Students in the sixth through twelfth grades in public, private non-Catholic, and Catholic schools in the U.S. *Parents*: Adults living in households with telephones in the U.S. who have children under the age of 18.

Sample: *Young People*: A two-stage design was used. In the first stage, a random sample of 96 elementary, middle, and senior high (public, private non-Catholic, and Catholic) was selected. In the second stage questionnaires were distributed in classes in the selected schools. No other information is provided. Sample size = 2,508. *Parents*: Random digit dialing sample of U.S. households was screened for parents of children under the age of 18.

Source of Information: *Young People*: Anonymous questionnaires completed in class. *Parents*: Telephone interviews.

Date of Collection: April 19–May 21, 1993.

Reference Period: Questions referred to time of interview.

Organization: LH Research Inc., 1270 Avenue of the Americas, New York, NY 10020. Conducted for the Harvard School of Public Health.

Technical Reference
LH Research, Inc. 1993. *A survey of the American people on guns as a children's health issue.* (Unpublished). Prepared for the Harvard School of Public Health (June).

LH Research, Inc. 1993. *A survey of experiences, perceptions, and apprehensions about guns among young people in America.* (Unpublished). Prepared for the Harvard School of Public Health (June).

Data Source 48

Survey of Inmates in Federal Correctional Facilities, 1991

Target Population: Federal prison inmates.

Sample: Stratified two-stage design. In the first stage, prisons were selected from strata defined by security level; in the second, inmates within prisons were selected randomly. Sample size=6,572 prisoners.

Source of Information: Personal interviews.

Date of Collection: June, July, and August 1991.

Reference Period: Prior to current incarceration.

Organization: U.S. Bureau of the Census, for the U.S. Bureau of Prisons.

Additional Information
This sample of federal inmates represented 54,000 inmates. Information was collected on current offense, criminal history, family and employment background, drug and alcohol use, and activities in prison. Overall response rates were 93.4 percent (Harlow, 1994, p. 25).

Technical Reference
Harlow, Caroline Wolf. 1994. *Comparing federal and state prison inmates, 1991.* Washington, D.C.: Bureau of Justice Statistics.

Data Source 49

Survey of Inmates in State Correctional Facilities, 1991

Target Population: State prison inmates.

Sample: Stratified two-stage design. In the first stage, prisons were selected from strata defined by security level; in the second, inmates within prisons were selected randomly. Sample size=13,986 prisoners.

Source of Information: Personal interviews.

Date of Collection: June, July, and August 1991.

Reference Period: Prior to current offense.

Organization: U.S. Bureau of the Census, for the U.S. Bureau of Justice Statistics.

Additional Information
This survey of state prisoners sampled 13,986 prisoners, representing over 711,000 inmates. Information was collected on current offense, criminal history, family and employment background, drug and alcohol use, and activities in prison. Overall response rate was 93.7 percent (Harlow, 1994, p. 25).

Technical Reference
Bureau of Justice Statistics. 1993. *Survey of state prison inmates, 1991.* Washington, D.C.

Harlow, Caroline Wolf. 1994. *Comparing federal and state prison inmates, 1991.* Washington, D.C.: Bureau of Justice Statistics.

Data Source 50

Survey of Inmates of Local Jails, 1989

Target Population: Persons held in local jails.

Sample: Stratified two-stage design: in the first stage, jails were stratified into size by male and female populations; the second stage systematically sampled males and females within the jails. The sample consisted of 424 jails and 6,258 inmates, from which 5,675 inmates completed the interviews (7.7 percent noninterviews).

Source of Information: Personal interviews.

Date of Collection: July, August, and September 1989.

Reference Period: Prior to current incarceration.

Organization: U.S. Bureau of the Census, for the U.S. Bureau of Justice Statistics.

Technical Reference
Harlow, Caroline Wolf. 1991. *Drugs and jail inmates, 1989.* Washington, D.C.: Bureau of Justice Statistics.

Bureau of Justice Statistics. 1991. *Survey of inmates of local jails, 1989: United States.* [Computer file]. Ann Arbor, Mich.: Inter-university Consortium for Political and Social Research.

Data Source 51

Survey of Occupational Injuries and Illnesses, 1992

Target Population: Total private economy (except for mines and railroads). Private industries, excluding (1) the self-employed, (2) farms with fewer than 11 employees, (3) private households, and (4) employees with state, federal, and local government agencies.

Sample: 250,000 establishments. Data for mines and railroads were reported by the Mine Safety and Health Administration of the U.S. Department of Labor and the Federal Railroad Administration of the U.S. Department of Transportation.

Source of Information: Employer reports collected by state agencies for the BLS.

Date of Collection: Information not provided.

Reference Period: 1992.

Organization: U.S. Bureau of Labor Statistics.

Technical Reference
Bureau of Labor Statistics. 1994. *Survey of occupational injuries and illnesses, 1992.* Washington, D.C.: U.S. Department of Labor, p. 29.

Data Source 52

Survey of State Adult Protective Services and Aging Agencies on Elder Abuse in Domestic Settings for FY90 and FY91

Target Population: State adult protective services agencies in all 50 states, the District of Columbia, Guam, Puerto Rico, and the Virgin Islands.

Sample: For 1990, 29 states responded, and in 1991, 30 states responded.

Source of Information: Mailed questionnaires.

Date of Collection: December 20, 1991.

Reference Period: Fiscal year 1990, fiscal year 1991.

Organization: National Aging Resource Center on Elder Abuse, 810 First St., N.E., Suite 500, Washington, D.C. 20002–4205.

Additional Information
The National Aging Resource Center on Elder Abuse (NARCEA) sent questionnaires to state adult protective services (APS) inquiring about the total number of reports of domestic elder abuse, number of elderly persons involved in these reports, and the types of domestic elder abuse involved in these counts (Tatara, 1993, p. 5). NARCEA requested that states use the age of 60 as a minimum for the identification of elderly, but California, Oklahoma, and South Carolina used 65 as their lower limit (p. 11).

FY90 data came from these 29 states: Arizona, California, Delaware, District of Columbia, Florida, Hawaii, Idaho, Illinois, Iowa, Kentucky, Maryland, Massachusetts, Missouri, Montana, Nebraska, Nevada, New Hampshire, New Jersey, New York, Ohio, Pennsylvania, Rhode Island, South Carolina, South Dakota, Texas, Utah, Virginia, Wisconsin, and Wyoming.

FY91 data came from these 30 states: Arizona, Arkansas, California, Delaware, District of Columbia, Florida, Hawaii, Idaho, Illinois, Kentucky, Maryland, Massachusetts, Missouri, Montana, Nebraska, Nevada, New Hampshire, New Jersey, New Mexico, New York, Ohio, Pennsylvania, Puerto Rico, Rhode Island, South Carolina, South Dakota, Texas, Utah, and Virginia.

Definitions
Physical abuse was the non-accidental use of physical force that results in bodily injury, pain, or impairment (p. 8).

Sexual abuse was the non-consensual sexual contact of any kind (p. 8).

Emotional or psychological abuse was the willful infliction of mental or emotional anguish by threat, humiliation, intimidation, or other verbal or nonverbal abusive conduct (p. 8).

Other categories included neglect, financial or material exploitation, self-abuse/neglect, and all other types of maltreatment that didn't fit in these categories (p. 8).

Technical Reference
Tatara, Toshio. 1993. *Summaries of the statistical data on elder abuse in domestic settings for FY90 and FY91.* Washington, D.C.: National Aging Resource Center on Elder Abuse.

Data Source 53

Survey of Youth in Custody, 1987

Target Population: Juveniles and young adults in state-operated, long-term juvenile institutions.

Sample: The national sample design stratified by the size of the facility. Sample size=2,621 residents in 50 institutions in 26 states.

Source of Information: Personal interviews.

Date of Collection: Most interviews were completed by the end of 1987.

Reference Period: Lifetime, at time of offense.

Organization: U.S. Bureau of the Census, for the U.S. Bureau of Justice Statistics.

Additional Information
This was a national sample of juveniles and young adults in state-operated, long-term juvenile institutions. From a population of more than 25,000, 2,621 residents in 50 institutions in 26 states were interviewed. Because of California's Youth Authority facilities, a quarter of the sample were 18–21 years old (Beck, Kline, and Greenfeld, 1988, p. 1). Excluded from the survey were locally operated institutions, state facilities not designed for secure custody, and short-term or private institutions. The response rate was 89 percent (p. 9).

Technical Reference
Beck, Allen J., Susan A. Kline, and Lawrence A. Greenfeld. 1988. *Survey of youth in custody, 1987.* Washington, D.C.: Bureau of Justice Statistics.

Data Source 54

Time/CNN Poll of Gun Owners, December 15–22, 1989

Target Population: Firearm owners living in households with telephones in the U.S.

Sample: Sample size=605 firearm owners.

Source of Information: Telephone interviews.

Date of Collection: December 15–22, 1989.

Reference Period: Questions referred to time of interview.

Organization: Yankelovich, Clancy, Shulman, 3822 Campus Dr., Ste. 220, Newport Beach, CA 92660. Conducted for Time/CNN.

Technical Reference
Quinley, Harold E. 1990. *Time/CNN poll of gun owners.* Newport Beach, Calif: Yankelovich, Clancy, Shulman.

Data Source 55

Time/CNN Poll, April 30, 1992

Target Population: Adults living in households with telephones in the U.S.

Sample: Sample size = 1,102, including 798 white respondents and an oversample of 200 black respondents.

Source of Information: Telephone interviews.

Date of Collection: April 30, 1992 (the night after the Rodney King verdict was announced).

Reference Period: Questions referred to time of interview.

Organization: Yankelovich, Clancy, Shulman, 3822 Campus Dr., Ste. 220, Newport Beach, CA 92660. Conducted for Time/CNN.

Technical Reference
Quinley, Harold E. 1992. *Latest Time/CNN poll.* Newport Beach, Calif: Yankelovich, Clancy, Shulman.

Data Source 56

Time/CNN Poll, June 15–16, 1994

Target Population: Adults living in households with telephones in the U.S.

Sample: Sample size=800.

Source of Information: Telephone interviews.

Date of Collection: June 15–16, 1994.

Reference Period: Time of survey.

Organization: Yankelovich, Clancy, Shulman, 250 First St., Suite 320, Claremont, CA 91711. Conducted for Time/CNN.

Technical Reference
Quinley, Harold E. 1994. *Time/CNN poll.* Claremont, Calif: Yankelovich, Clancy, Shulman.

Data Source 57

TV Violence: More Objectionable In Entertainment Than in Newscasts

Target Population: Adults (18 years of age or older) living in households with telephones in the continental U.S.

Sample: Random digit dialing of telephone exchanges in the U.S., selected with probabilities proportionate to their size. Sample size=1,516.

Source of Information: Telephone interviews.

Date of Collection: February 20–23, 1993.

Reference Period: Time of survey.

Organization: Princeton Survey Research Associates, P.O. Box 1450, Princeton, NJ 08542.

Technical Reference
Times Mirror Center for the People and the Press. 1993. TV violence: More objectionable in entertainment than in newscasts. *Times Mirror Media Monitor* (March 24): 1–53.

Times Mirror Center for the People and the Press data, as presented in: Maguire, Kathleen, and Ann L. Pastore, eds. 1994. *Sourcebook of criminal justice statistics, 1993.* Washington, D.C.: Bureau of Justice Statistics, p. 237, note to Table 2.106.

Data Source 58

The 26th Annual Phi Delta Kappa/Gallup Poll of the Public's Attitudes Toward the Public Schools

Target Population: Adults (18 years of age and older) living in households with telephones in the U.S.

Sample: Unclustered, directory-assisted, random digit telephone sample, proportionally stratified (by 4 regions and 3 size-of-community categories). Weighted to match Census population estimates. Sample size=1,326.

Source of Information: Telephone interviews.

Date of Collection: May 10–June 8, 1994.

Reference Period: Time of survey.

Organization: The Gallup Organization, 47 Hulfish Street, Princeton, NJ 08542. Conducted for Phi Delta Kappa, P.O. Box 789, Bloomington, IN 47402.

Technical Reference
Elam, Stanley M., Lowell C. Rose, and Alec M. Gallup. 1994. The 26th annual Phi Delta Kappa/Gallup poll of the public's attitudes toward the public schools. *Phi Delta Kappan* (September): 41–56.

Data Source 59

World Health Statistics

Target Population: Residents of Member States of the World Health Organization (WHO).

Sample: Included are member states with a universal vital registration system that have reasonably complete certification of cause of death and the ability to report this data to the WHO in accordance with International Classification of Diseases (ICD).

Source of Information: National vital statistics registration systems.

Date of Collection: Annual.

Reference Period: Most recent year for which data were available.

Organization: World Health Organization (United Nations).

Additional Information
The ninth revision of the ICD was used in all countries, except Denmark and Switzerland, who use the eighth revision.

Technical Reference
World Health Organization. 1994. *World health statistics annual, 1993.* Geneva, Switzerland.

Glossary

Census
Collection of information from the whole target population.

Cluster sample
Sample design where groups of elements (clusters) are selected. A common example is the selection of several housing units from the same city block. Geographic clustering reduces the costs of field work because interviewers travel to one location to conduct several interviews.

Multi-stage sampling
A sample selected in steps or stages progressing from larger to smaller units. The units selected at each stage are subsets of the larger units selected at the previous stage. For example, counties, schools, classrooms, students might be selected in a four-stage sample.

Oversample
Selection of some groups (usually small groups that are of particular interest) with probabilities larger than those of other groups. This increases the number of sample cases from the small group that will be available for analysis.

Population
See "Target population."

Prevalence
In violence research, prevalence refers to the proportion of persons in a population who have experienced at least one violent event in a specified time interval. *Annual prevalence* is the proportion who experience one or more violent events in a 12-month interval. *Lifetime prevalence* is the proportion who have experienced the violent event at any point in their life prior to the point of data collection. This is different from the more common use of the term in epidemiology and medical research where it refers to the proportion of a population that have a disease at a point in time.

Probability sample
Selection of elements so that the probability of selection is known for all elements.

Random digit dialing
A sampling design that selects randomly from telephone numbers in order to obtain a sample. Designs vary in detail, but the most common procedures use telephone exchange or groups of exchanges as clusters and then randomly select from possible four-digit numbers within clusters.

Reference period
The period of time that is described by the study. For example, respondents in the National Crime Victimization Survey are asked about incidents during the six months prior to the month of the interview.

Sample
Subset of the target population selected in order to make inferences about the target population.

Sampling error
Differences between the target population value and the sample estimate that are due to the selection of a particular sample.

Sampling frame
The set of materials from which the sample is selected.

Screener
A question or series of questions in a survey designed to identify cases of interest. Further questions are then asked of the respondents who meet the screening criteria.

Stratified sample
The target population is partitioned into non-overlapping groups (strata)—such as geographic areas, gender groups, or community types—from which samples are drawn.

Target population
The group the study intends to describe.

Weighting
An adjustment to compensate for unequal probabilities of selection, nonresponse, or other considerations.

For example, if some parts of the population (such as black households or urban residents) are selected with probabilities higher than their representation in the population, then to make national estimates it is necessary to proportionately reduce the influence of the oversampled cases on the final estimate.

Index